Early praise fo

"There is a new activism emerging in   s
key leaders. In this excellent book, Wa   o
helped mold this new activism and the people who today walk by his side as
he strides toward justice."

—TONY CAMPOLO, *professor of sociology, Eastern College*

"This historic manifesto demonstrates Jim Wallis's fantastic ability to bring
together an unusually diverse range of people around a common vision. If
heeded, this important book will profoundly shape America, bringing desperately needed healing and justice. Wallis's best book."

—**Ron Sider**, *president, Evangelicals for Social Action*

"Armed with a preacher's parables, an activist's savvy, and a spiritually rooted vision of social justice, Jim Wallis exhorts us not to wet a finger to test the
wind, but to change that wind. This 'call to action' by one of the country's
most interesting religious leaders should capture the imagination of
Americans troubled about the condition of our society."

—**Robert D. Putnam**, *Kennedy School of Government*

"I have always known Jim Wallis to be a talented organizer, an eloquent
preacher, and a Christian visionary. With this book I see he is also a powerful and engaging writer. It's full of spellbinding stories that will lift anyone's
spirit, and it demonstrates convincingly that faith communities represent a
vast—and nearly untapped—resource for the renewal of our national life and
of the world."

—**Harvey Cox**, *Thomas Professor of Divinity, Harvard Divinity School*

"Jim Wallis is a preacher whose wisdom and prophetic vision can enlighten
people from all faiths and many who turned away from religion. *Faith Works*
paints a compelling picture of the way that social change in the twenty-first
century may be spearheaded by communities of faith. Wallis's life is an inspiration, and his strategic vision will light the path for all who wish to build a
more just and caring society. Responding to Wallis's call for renewal should
be our most immediate individual and societal priority."

—**Rabbi Michael Lerner**, *editor and author*

"Jim Wallis gives us true-life stories on how faith works. They will inspire! Wallis has spent his life putting faith into action. As the people in these stories will show, he is not the only one."

—**Tony Hall**, *U.S. Congressman, Ohio*

"Jim Wallis is, at one and the same time, bold and thoughtful, prophetic and practical. His voice is one of the nation's most important in our struggle to find the right relationship between religion and public life. *Faith Works* is important, timely, graceful, and inspiring."

—**E. J. Dionne, Jr.**, *syndicated columnist*

"In *Faith Works*, Jim Wallis has woven together a detailed road map for those interested in loosening the chains of social injustice. This book is a powerful resource for change!"

—**Millard Fuller**, *founder and president, Habitat for Humanity International*

"This book comes with a warning and a promise: its spiritual advice will not put you at ease, but if followed, it will surely bring you closer to maturity— and it will very likely bring you to the deep joy that only those who spend themselves for others can experience."

—**David Neff**, *executive editor,* Christianity Today

"At the end of a decade of the greatest growth in prosperity, how can it be that more people than ever are living below the poverty line? Jim Wallis challenges us all to examine this question and calls us to make a life-changing commitment to serve the poor in the name of Christ."

—**Richard E. Stearns**, *president, World Vision*

"Provocative, powerful, poignant, persistent, and practical writings from a committed man of faith. Thank you, Jim—for renewal of faith. The weary world rejoices!"

—**Sen. Alan K. Simpson**, *Kennedy School of Government*

"With the publication of *Faith Works*, Jim Wallis again demonstrates why his biblical vision and moral passion for social justice are national treasures. Thirty years before the now fashionable so-called faith factor entered our national policy and political discourse as a legitimate category, Jim Wallis was leading us to where we are today."

—**Rev. Eugene F. Rivers**, *National Ten-Point Leadership Foundation*

FAITH
WORKS

ALSO BY JIM WALLIS

Who Speaks for God?
The Soul of Politics
The Call to Conversion
Revive Us Again
Agenda for Biblical People

EDITED BY JIM WALLIS

Cloud of Witnesses
Crucible of Fire
Waging Peace
Peacemakers
The Rise of Christian Conscience

FAITH WORKS

How Faith-Based Organizations Are Changing Lives, Neighborhoods, and America

JIM WALLIS

PAGEMILL PRESS
A Division of Circulus Publishing Group, Inc.
Berkeley, California

Faith Works: How Faith-Based Organizations Are Changing Lives, Neighborhoods and America
Copyright © 2000, 2001 by Jim Wallis

Published by arrangement with Random House Trade Publishing, a division of Random House, Inc.

Cover photographs:
Weathervane ©Bettman/CORBIS
Blue Sky ©Richard Hamilton Smith/CORBIS
Rural Church in Autumn ©Buddy Mays/CORBIS

Printed in the United States of America

Library of Congress Cataloging-in-Publication Data

Wallis, Jim.
Faith works : lessons from the life of an activist preacher / Jim Wallis.—1st ed.
p.   cm.
Includes index.
ISBN 0-375-50176-2 (hc : alk. paper)
1. Voluntarism—Religious aspects—Christianity. 2. Church and social problems.   I. Title.
BR115.V64 W352000
261.8¢32 216dc21   99-040239

First Paperback Edition

Distributed to the trade by FaithWorks, a division of National Book Network
10 9 8 7 6 5 4 3 2 1   05 04 03 02 01

Contents

To my mother, Phyllis Ruth Wallis,
who showed me in her life and in her death
how faith works.

And to my wife, Joy Carroll Wallis,
who turns the walk of faith
into a dance of life.

Not Your Usual Book Tour

THE LAST CITY on my spring 2000 *Faith Works* book tour was Milwaukee. There I visited an "overflow shelter" run by the Red Cross and the Milwaukee Interfaith Conference, the sponsor of a Faith Works Forum. At about 1:30 P.M., the makeshift gymnasium was empty and quiet.

By 7 P.M. it would become a very noisy place, as fifty bunk beds would be filled with homeless women and their children. On many of those beds I saw little stuffed animals and toys marking the places of the kids who sleep there every night. They looked like my son Luke's favorite things. After three decades in the inner city, I should be used to poverty, but now I'm a dad and I felt like crying.

The Red Cross often runs shelters such as this after natural disasters like floods, tornadoes, and hurricanes. But what was the natural disaster in Milwaukee and the other sixteen cities I visited? Virtually every city had overflowing shelters, and food banks and soup kitchens were stretched beyond capacity. This disaster is called prosperity. It's a prosperity that has left far too many people behind, then made things worse for them—such as housing costs that have risen so steeply that even poor working families can't find a place to live. To put it in the plainest moral terms: this just isn't right. In a record-breaking economy, one out of six children in America are still poor; one in three are children of color. Something is terribly wrong with this picture.

But there's also good news—and that is the story of this book. The faith community is getting mobilized like never before in my lifetime. I saw evidence of that again and again in city after city across the country. Publishers like to send authors out to do media interviews and sign books in bookstores. But instead of bookstores, we decided to attend town meetings to launch this book. The nationwide tour demonstrated the message of the book: there is a movement in the making. In many cities, our Faith Works Forums were sponsored by churches and faith-based groups that are doing the work profiled in the book.

For example, the book tells the story of my visit several years ago to Sing Sing prison in upstate New York. (See chapter three.) We had an amazing night with the men in a New York Theological Seminary program inside Sing Sing that prepares prisoners for ministry. One man spoke movingly of a "train" that leaves poor neighborhoods like his. "You get on the train when you are nine or ten years old," he said, "and it ends here at Sing Sing." He vowed that when he got out, he would go back to his old neighborhood and help stop that train. At the first Faith Works Forum in New York City, two of the men I had met at Sing Sing were helping to lead the town meeting. They were home now, doing just what they had promised.

One of these men, Rev. Darren Ferguson, is now Youth Minister at Abyssinian Baptist Church and a consultant for the Exodus Transitional Community, a ministry for ex-offenders and at-risk youth. Darren is a gifted songwriter and musician, and his music has become an essential part of our annual Call to Renewal Summits—which bring together faith-based organizations from around the country. The other man, Julio Medina, is now director of the Exodus Community and has also blessed our Summits.

Also in the book and sponsoring the New York City forum was the People of Faith Network, led by Rev. Dave Dyson of Brooklyn's Lafayette Presbyterian Church. This middle-sized church has taken on the issue of sweatshops and built a network of eight thousand congregations. They won a code of conduct from the Gap when a Jewish rabbi threatened to tell his congregation of two thousand that shopping at the sweatshop-using Gap "violates Jewish law and ethics"! (See chapter 15.)

A forum at Harvard's Kennedy School of Government on "The Faith Factor in Politics" drew a capacity crowd of students and faculty who discussed how even presidential candidates were now debating the role of faith-based organizations in solving some of our most entrenched social problems. Sen. Alan Simpson, Rev. Jeffrey Brown, Father Robert Drinan, and columnist E.J. Dionne joined me in a discussion that would have been unthinkable just a few years ago.

Yet it has now become a national discussion. Early in the new administration of George W. Bush, he announced a "faith-based initiative" designed to stimulate new partnerships between faith-based organizations and the government. That partnership is now a controversial topic in the news, and a new chapter has been added to this edition of *Faith Works* to address it more fully. (See chapter 10.)

Our forum in Chicago drew a large and enthusiastic audience. Fifteen faith-based sponsoring ministries and projects demonstrated the political breadth of Call to Renewal, which brings them all together. Each group gave moving two-minute testimonies and ended with the same litany, "So join us in the Campaign to Overcome Poverty!" My spirits soared as we clapped with a gospel choir entirely composed of men who were former addicts and alcoholics and now sing of liberation.

Then came a Jubilee 2000 rally back home in D.C., after which several thousand people joined hands in a human chain around the U.S. Capitol. The Jubilee movement to cancel the debt of impoverished countries has caught the world's imagination and led to a significant victory in the U.S. Congress in the fall of 2000. (See chapter 15.)

Everywhere we went, the tour and book attracted media attention—most days were filled with radio talk shows, and the breadth and diversity of the audiences shows the great potential of this movement. For example, in Los Angeles I did interviews and talk shows on the NPR affiliate, the Pacifica station, the biggest conservative Christian radio outlet, a syndicated black radio program, and the mainstream local CBS station.

Perhaps the greatest surprise and satisfaction came in the interviews on Christian radio. The talk shows on National Public Radio stations, network affiliates, and various community radio outlets were more typical for me. But I was greatly encouraged by the interest from local and national Christian radio, and even more heartened by the response. What I found on conservative Christian radio shows was a deepening concern for people who are poor, on the part of both interviewers and callers. Most significant was the breaking out of old ideological categories. In an interview on the Salem Network (the largest chain of Christian radio stations in the country), the host said to me and to his audience, "You know, poverty is not a left-wing issue; it's a Christian issue, and it's time for us all to recognize that." Another show's host acknowledged, "You know, Jim, most of us wouldn't have had anything to do with you just a few years ago. We thought talking about poverty was left wing. But many of us are coming around and want to be with you now." Comment after comment and caller after caller expressed similar views.

It convinced me that the central message of this book is true— if poverty is to be overcome, it will take the insights and energies of both conservatives and liberals. As long as poverty fighting is seen as merely a left-wing issue, we will never succeed. And it's not just a matter of perception, it's also a question of content. *Faith Works* tries to lay out a new and balanced vision for how poverty might be overcome. The book does not just rehash old ideas, rather it speaks of a comprehensive plan for change, involving every sector of society—not just the government, nor just the "market," nor just churches and charities, as the various competing ideological options often suggest. The stories in *Faith Works* of the most successful and inspiring projects around the country are as new as the approach they suggest.

In the Pacific Northwest, the *Portland Oregonian* story about our event said: "Imagine attending a town meeting on ending poverty and coming away feeling hopeful instead of hopeless." In Portland, I also spoke to two thousand high school students holding a mock political convention at the Memorial Coliseum, and said that unless their generation helps create a new politics in this country, all our future political conventions were destined to be mock ones. The popular wisdom says that young people don't care about public life, but the popular wisdom is wrong! Breaking the death grip of money over politics and dealing with real issues like child poverty are things they care about deeply.

In Denver, my teacher and mentor, Dr. Vincent Harding, introduced the evening at Illiff Seminary. I also learned that in Denver, you have to work 97 hours per week at minimum wage in order to afford any sort of decent housing. It will take more than good personal motivation and responsibility to make enough affordable housing available to those working families who have no place to live; it will also take focused public action to ensure a sufficient stock of available housing. It may also take changed planning and zoning laws, which keep low and moderate income housing out of many wealthy areas.

In Milwaukee, a young evangelical pastor talked about relationships, as evangelical pastors often do. But that's why, this young minister said, he supports a living wage for anybody who's willing to work hard. "It's because I know Joyce," the minister said, "and how hard it is for her to support her kids." That's really it, I thought as I sat in that Milwaukee overflow shelter at the end of a long tour. If the faith community is really ready to get to know those kids who would be sleeping in the bunk beds that night, we won't just be providing them shelter. We'll start asking why the shelters are needed in the first place. Many similar stories are told in chapter two.

At the very end of the tour, I traveled to Ohio to do the baccalaureate address at Oberlin College. Being a long-time admirer of Charles W. Finney, the second president of Oberlin, I was especially eager for this first-time visit. This small Midwestern college was a hotbed of both revival and reform in nineteenth century America. Finney was the premier evangelist of his day and also a fervent abolitionist. Some say he was the first to pioneer the modern altar call, because he wanted to sign his converts up in the movement to abolish slavery!

I was full of questions as the campus chaplain showed me around before my speech. I asked to see portraits of the school's early leader and other mementos of this tumultuous period when evangelical Christians were also radical social reformers, not only on the issue of slavery, but also in fighting for women's suffrage and child labor laws (they waged the original anti-sweatshop campaigns!). Yet my campus host told me that revival and reform had been separated at Oberlin since the 1960s, and that while social reform was still a theme at the college, the spiritual roots had been mostly forgotten.

So, of course, I preached about Finney. I quoted him saying that true revival would always be "hindered" when the church took the wrong position on crucial issues of human rights. Finney had boldly called slavery "a sin," and I asked what he might say today about wretched poverty in a sea of prosperity. I also questioned whether "revival," or the power of faith, can really be separated from "reform," or the promise of real social change.

Can social transformation really ever occur without an accompanying spiritual transformation? Or can the impulse of reform last for very long without the motivation, sustenance, and hope that faith can bring? Does social reform without spiritual power just become political correctness? Those are questions Finney might also have asked.

They are also the questions of this book, and the tour taught me again that there are a growing number of answers around the country. More and more people are discovering that faith must be put into action, and that action is often sustained by faith. And the vital connection between the two is forging a new movement that is changing America. This is a new and revised edition of *Faith Works*. Events are now moving so quickly that the book needed significant updating! I invite you to read *Faith Works*, and I invite you to join the movement.

Foreword

JIM WALLIS BEGINS THIS BOOK with a birth and a death, polar realities of the life experience. The faith he espouses combines them into an ultimate triumph of resurrection, a spiritual transformation that reverses the natural cycle to produce birth from death and a life of sacrifice—"doing what is sacred." One dies to live, surrenders to gain. Our journey here is a mission of redemption and renewal.

Jim set out on his own mission when he began to question the comfort and isolation of his youth. His questions became a quest. To see where it's taken him, you need travel only a mile or so from the White House into a Washington rarely, if ever, frequented by the nation's movers and shakers. Here streets are littered, sidewalks stained, nights menaced. This is the Washington—the America—of the New Gilded Age. A few blocks from here champagne glasses tinkle, the powerful wheel and deal, and lobbyists count their takes as their accountants write off the larceny as a business expense. Here Jim Wallis has planted the little Sojourners community as if in a catacomb of Rome, so near to the heart of the Imperial City—and so far. Day by day a little healing happens here, a life gets mended, small miracles occur. It is even rumored that Jesus comes here, looking nothing like the poster on the Sunday-school wall, the figure with the sad spaniel eyes and luminous radiation encircling his head.

No, the Jesus who visits Sojourners more likely appears as a fresh-faced intern, a harried editorial assistant, a volunteer tutor, even a homeless man. All things are possible.

This is where Jim Wallis works, but from here he ventures forth on long, body-numbing tours to speak, organize, cajole, listen, inspire, negotiate. One week, you will find him with the cowboy-booted Presbyterian guardian angel of the dispossessed on the Arizona border; the next, arbitrating among rival gangs in Kansas

City; a few days later, orchestrating a meeting of North Carolina pastors and lay church leaders to make "welfare reform" work; and another week later, exchanging ideas in a theology class at Sing Sing prison, north of New York City.

His path takes him to Capitol Hill, too, but not to party with the good ol' boys whose hard eyes narrow as they divvy up their soft money. I have on my office wall a photograph of a Jim Wallis visit to Congress in 1995. Several men are shown handcuffed in the Capitol Rotunda. What's this? Have police finally arrested Gingrich, DeLay, Armey, and Archer in the act of selling off the government to favored pals? No. The culprits in the picture, manacled to protect the Republic, are evangelical Christians who have come to mount a quiet protest where it is unlawful to do so without an official approval. They are members of the Wallis-inspired coalition, Call to Renewal, whose mission is to ask America to remember the poor. They hoped to challenge legislators who were that very day rewriting the welfare laws without once having invited testimony from poor people. These Christians know the poor personally. They run health clinics, day-care centers, employment, housing, and loan programs in impoverished neighborhoods. They have come to ask Congress to give their people a hearing. Beneath statues of Washington, Jefferson, and Martin Luther King, the evangelicals knelt and prayed. The police did their duty and arrested them. As the Christians were led away they sang, "Lead me, O Lord, to Thee. Lead me, O Lord, to Thee." Watching in amazement as the handcuffed believers were rounded up, a class of eighth-grade children from a Catholic school, on a field trip from Virginia, broke into applause for their witness.

No politicians were present, however, as the singing and handcuffed Christians were marched from the Rotunda. Francis X. Clines, there for *The New York Times*, wrote: "The demonstrators barely made a ripple." There was no mention of the event on the nightly corporate news.

It is a strange time. The principalities and powers of the ruling order are waging a class war on the working poor. Corporate contributors are stacked in the Lincoln Bedroom like cordwood. The

GOP, reestablished as Guardians of Privilege, invites lawyers and lobbyists into committee rooms to write their tax breaks, subsidies, and loopholes directly into legislation. Public-opinion surveys report that the majority of citizens believe government is "run for the benefit of the few and the special interests, not the people"; that "business has gained too much power"; that corporations should share their profits more generously with "workers and communities"; that the government must help the most vulnerable "with employment, medical and child care."

Yet "the demonstrators barely made a ripple." It is a stony-hearted political class that occupies Washington today.

Against such obstinacy, deep in an era that exalts individual cunning in the pursuit of wealth and power while treating with contempt those who cannot compete, and facing political parties owned lock, stock, and barrel by moneyed elites, do Jim Wallis and his small community really think their actions matter? That economic justice is possible? That anyone's listening?

Most certainly they do. Faith sustains Wallis—faith in God and the belief that prophetic religion can still touch the nation's conscience. For twenty years the Religious Right has dominated the intersection where religion and politics meet. In the 1960s religious liberals spilled into the public square to call for racial justice and an end to the Vietnam War. The Right organized and roared back, taking control of the Republican party, turning conservative pews into political precincts and raising corporate and foundation money to create a vast propaganda machine. Conservatives changed the public debate to focus on other people's personal morality and their own private property. Their capture of the political agenda is one of the astonishing stories of the time.

But as you will read in these pages, Jim Wallis thinks they have run their course. Other voices are making their ways into the public arena, speaking prophetically of economic justice, spirituality, and politics. Their vision embraces faith-based justice and not just charity. Charity is commendable; everyone should be charitable. But justice aims to create a social order in which if individuals choose not to be charitable, people still don't go hungry,

unschooled, or sick without care. Charity depends on the vicissi-
tudes of whim and personal wealth; justice depends on commitment
instead of circumstance. Faith-based charity provides crumbs from
the table; faith-based justice offers a place at the table.

So Jim Wallis teaches newcomers to Sojourners that their personal choices are critically important, but he also teaches them
about the broader social and political forces that can dramatically
affect their lives. He nurtures family values, self-respect, tolerance
for others, and personal ethics. But he preaches social justice,
human rights, and corporate accountability. The man is hard to
put into a box and label. He gives conservatives their due, as
champions of values-based politics and critics of the bureaucratic
state. But he takes them to task for their awe of wealth, their tolerance of extremism, their militarism, and their malice toward
opponents. Liberals he praises for gender justice, environmental-
ism, and racial equality, but their cultural and moral relativism, he
says, have promoted bad choices among young people. "A new
political agenda may be in the making," he writes. Neither Left
nor Right, it will grow from "community-based citizen involvement around local issues" supported by prophetic religion. He
offers as an example the "living-wage campaign" in Los Angeles,
where low-income workers, labor unions, and religious groups
forged an alliance on behalf of better pay and conditions for the
working poor. The most dramatic moment came "with a holy
week procession in Beverly Hills, with Christian and Jewish religious leaders in their full clerical regalia alongside hotel workers in
windbreakers and jeans." Religious symbols aligned once again
with activists for justice.

What will come of it?

He does not predict. He will not even guess. He invokes
Thomas Merton: "Do not depend on the hope of results.... The
big results are not in your hands or mine, but suddenly happen, and
we can share them, but there is no point in building our lives on this
personal satisfaction, which may be denied us and which after all is
not that important."

Merton—and Nehemiah 2:18: *"Then they said, 'Let's start build-ing.' So they committed themselves to the common good."*

And off he bounds to the next town meeting, the waiting con-gregation, another hearing on the Hill (even as I write, he and sev-eral others are peacefully demonstrating against the corrupting influence of our campaign-financing system), a prayer service, a strategy session, that unfinished essay on the computer screen—and, oh yes, his bride, awaiting him at the altar. His mother will dance at their wedding, and the music and wine will flow as they did when Jesus danced to affirm faith and vows in an earlier reminder of resurrection and renewal.

Jim Wallis, dancing? What else would you expect from a man who marries Joy?

— *Bill Moyers*

Acknowledgments

MANY PEOPLE HELPED make this book possible. My longtime editor and old friend, Roy M. Carlisle, persuaded me it was time to write a book about how "faith works," and my wonderful agent and friend, Gail Ross, with her brilliant book sense, helped create the idea. Roy's tested wisdom and experience shaped the project all through the writing. I am also grateful for the enthusiasm shown about the book by Ann Godoff, the president of Random House, the publisher of the hard back edition. Susanna Porter of Random House proved to be one of the best editors I have ever worked with; she both believed in and improved the book enormously.

I was very pleased that PageMill Press, a new publishing venture led by Roy Carlisle, is releasing the paperback edition. Roy, Carol Brown, Patsy Barich, and the whole staff at PageMill sense the growing public recognition of the role for faith-based organizations in the fight to overcome poverty, and, hence, the timeliness of this revised and updated edition of *Faith Works*.

The Center for the Study of Values in Public Life at the Harvard Divinity School invited me to join them as a Fellow for the 1998–99 academic year, which became the perfect opportunity to write the book. At Harvard, my extraordinary research assistants, Emily Dossett and Michaela Bruzzese, were invaluable help with research, and Emily became a trusted editor as well. Duane Shank, my executive assistant back in Washington, also worked tirelessly with the necessary research, tracking down critical information, which he does like nobody else. Erin Card, my assistant, is working with her characteristic competence and grace to coordinate events around the release of this new edition of *Faith Works*.

So many friends and colleagues contributed by reading the manuscript, commenting on my ideas, serving as dialogue partners, telling me stories, and working on the same visions and projects together. That list includes: Nane Alejandrez, Tom Allio, Mary Jo Bane, David Batstone, David Beckmann, Larry Bellinger, Rose Berger, Peter Borgdorff, Jeff Brown, Marion Brown, Tony Campolo, John Carr, Rich Cizik, Brent Coffin, Chuck Collins, Yvonne Delk, Marie Dennis, John DiIulio, E. J. Dionne, Kathy Dudley, Carter Echols, Bob Edgar, Jamie Edgerton, Carol Fennelly, Max Finberg, Leah Gaskin Fitchue, Henry Freeman, Marshall Ganz, Wes Granberg-Michaelson, Tony Hall, Vincent Harding, Bryan Hehir, Bud Ipema, Scott Jackson, Tom Jones, Karen Lattea Kline, Michael Lerner, Skip Long, Michael Mata, Chuck Matthei, Ken Medema, George Mitrovitch, Calvin Morris, Ched Myers, Mary Nelson, Nancy Nienhuis, Richard Parker, Mark Publow, Cynthia Ranke, Roger Rath, Jim Rice, Mary Ann Richardson, Eugene Rivers, Richard Rohr, Joe Roos, Bob Sabath, Emory Searcy, Jr., Brian Sellers-Petersen, Ron Sider, Wallace Charles Smith, Ed Spivey, Jr., Glen Stassen, Rich Stearns, Jim and Barb Tamialis, Ron Thiemann, Beverly Vander Molen, Bill Weld-Wallis, Diana Jones Wilson, Bill Wylie-Kellermann, and all of my coworkers at Sojourners magazine and Call to Renewal.

I'm grateful for their feedback, counsel, ideas, and example. They have shaped my thinking and this book more than many of them know. But the responsibility for what the book says, and how it says it, is mine.

For the inspiration, sustenance, companionship, and editing suggestions that made the writing so much more possible, I thank my wife, Joy Carroll, and for constant delight throughout long book-writing days, I thank my son, Luke. For the faith that undergirds this book, I thank my mother, who died while it was being written, and my father, who continues mourning, but still believing.

A Personal Word

MY MOTHER DANCED at our wedding. Given the prohibitions on dancing in my evangelical upbringing, that was a pretty big deal. Joy and I took it that my parents were quite happy about our getting married. Mom could have passed for a woman fifteen years younger and looked positively vibrant as she whirled around the floor of the Anglican parish hall in South London. She and my father combined the marriage celebration in Britain with a much-anticipated monthlong holiday in Europe. They were very happy and healthy, and life was good—wonderful, really.

Almost a month later, my mother discovered that she had cancer of the stomach lining. Thus began a long battle, fighting the disease with a combination of conventional surgery and chemotherapy with alternative treatments of vitamins, serums, and an extremely healthy diet. At one point she was drinking so much organic carrot juice that she turned orange! My mom was so strong and determined that she survived a heart attack and heart surgery twice, and then the agony of shingles tested her even further—all seemingly consequences of the cancer and its treatment.

Learning that my wife, Joy, was pregnant, and that she would soon have a new grandson, my first child, seemed to give my mother added incentive to survive, and even to get better. After Luke arrived, she was absolutely thrilled to get to know our son and her thirteenth grandchild. I never saw her happier than when she held Luke in her lap, and he gave her all those generous smiles of his. Then my mom was excited to learn that her youngest daughter, Marcie, was expecting a new baby in May 1999, the day before her own seventy-fifth birthday. On she battled, looking more and more healthy after each setback.

But on April 30 I got a call from my brother, Bill, in Detroit. My mom had collapsed at home. She had an infection in her blood-stream. Four out of five cancer patients die from something other than cancer because the body has been weakened so much. However, the doctors and my dad seemed optimistic at first; she had always pulled through before. But three days later we got another call. My dad's voice sounded emotional and scared. "You'd better come." We flew from Boston just hours later. Now the doctors feared she might not live through the night. My sister Barb and I got to the Detroit airport at the same time from different parts of the country and hurried to my mother's bedside. When we got there, the first thing she said was to ask my dad whether he had got fresh milk for us back at the house and whether he had put clean sheets on the beds. Some things never change.

That very day, my sister Marcie made a bold move. Already in the early stages of labor, my youngest sibling decided to get in the car and drive three hours with her husband and three boys from western Michigan to Detroit, to be with her mother. Marcie had her medical records faxed to the hospital Mom was in and got there in time to visit her before checking into the maternity wing of the hospital, called, ironically, the Miracle of Life Center. The whole family was there now (five brothers and sisters and lots of grand-children) to hope and pray for a miracle...that Mom would live to see her new grandchild. Marcie told us the secret she had kept for months—it was a girl.

On the morning of Mom's seventy-fifth birthday, May 6, Marcie went into serious labor. They were two women on a mission: as my mother labored for her life with each breath, Marcie labored to bring forth new life. It seemed as if we almost lost my mom twice, but she was determined to hang on. Marcie had previously had dis-tressed deliveries with all of her boys, but this time her labor was smooth and quick. She knew what she had to do. The doctor who delivered Marcie's baby commented that he had never seen a woman more in touch with her body and more in control of her labor. There was not a sound in the delivery room during the whole ordeal.

At 1:35 P.M., Kaylee Ruth was born on the first floor while her grandmother Phyllis Ruth lay dying on the fifth. As soon as they could, the doctor and nursing staff wheeled Marcie and the baby into Mom's room, where we were all waiting so anxiously. The jubilation was overwhelming. The whole hospital had been following the drama, willing these two special people to meet and bending the rules for newborns. As my mother opened her eyes and held her new granddaughter, she smiled and said, "I'm very happy, I'm very happy." Those were her last words before she slipped into a coma. Both the doctor and nurse who helped Marcie deliver were in the room with us now, with tears in their eyes just like all the rest of us. The veteran obstetrician later remarked to the head of his unit that he had never been involved in so remarkable a birth story.

My mother's coma lasted another nine days. Now under hospice care in the hospital, she never came out of the coma, but was responsive the whole time, especially to my father, who never left her side. One morning he said with some alarm to the nurse, "Her hand is warm!" She replied, "Well, you've been holding it all night!" I stayed in the room round the clock for several nights until he seemed ready and eager to be alone with the woman he had been with since they were both sixteen. "We had some good long talks last night," he would say when I brought him clean clothes each morning. The long vigil was a challenge but proved to be a gift for my father, who later said that he needed that time to be able to let her go. The nursing staff treated my mother wonderfully during her last days. One of them said, "We all really care about her." They kept asking if there were any more babies coming or family holidays that were keeping her going! My mother was never afraid to die during her year and a half of sickness and never even complained about it; now she was showing how tough she really was. My theory is that she was still enjoying my dad's companionship too much to go quickly. And she always loved to have all her children and grandchildren around her. She was the center of our attention.

My mother passed away at 12:15 A.M. on May 15, 1999. My father, who was at her side, as he had been each day during this last two-week hospital vigil, said she went "calmly, peacefully, and beautifully." He called me, and I called my brothers and sisters, who were there in Detroit to be with her. We all went to the hospital to be with my mom and dad for an hour before we gathered up her things and brought my father home.

My mother's memorial service drew almost five hundred people, and the little church she and my father had helped to found had never been fuller. Women in the church from her generation always had to lead from behind the scenes. Even so, my mother was so widely known and loved that more people turned out for her memorial than for any other event in the church's fifty-year history. The tributes and testimonials went on for three hours, and would have gone much longer had my dad not finally said it was enough.

How did she find the time to do all those things for all those people, I wondered, and still make each one of her children and grandchildren feel so special? I realized it was simply the way she and my father treated people, and especially anybody in trouble or need, that had planted a strong social conscience in all her children. She taught us principles: if there is someone nobody is playing with, you play with them; if somebody is getting picked on, you defend them; never make fun of anyone for any reason, and don't ever be cruel to people. I didn't want my mother ever to catch me being mean to someone. Finally, she and my father always taught us to stand up for what we believed, no matter who disagreed. That last one would be tested when we kids would later apply the principles they taught us and make social and political commitments that were new and challenging to them. But even then, there was always support for their kids and, eventually, a good deal of agreement with them.

After a family burial service, out-of-town family headed home. Joy and Luke and I went back to Boston, where we had been living for a year as I was trying to finish this book. Now we'd all try to go back to our normal lives—with my mother's memory and legacy, but without her presence. My mother's obituary, printed in the Sunday *Detroit Free Press*, ended with these words: "She is remembered by her family, church, and friends around the world as a loving wife, devoted mother and grandmother, minister of hospitality, and exemplary woman of God."

Our family witnessed the grace of God over those two and a half weeks and the mystery of life and death, literally side by side. The grieving over my mother's passing and the joy over Kaylee Ruth's birth filled our hearts with tears of sorrow and joy. I have never experienced a more vivid illustration of death and resurrection bound together by the love of family and the love of God. It filled the hospital room so powerfully that many doctors and nurses commented on it. This hope of life in the midst of death is the very center of faith; in fact, it is what faith is all about.

Such times of great emotions and stress seem to focus many aspects of life and faith and test the meaning of both at very deep levels. They also bring back memories long forgotten but suddenly vivid. One for me was a simple prayer my mother taught me as a little boy, which I found myself praying with her as we kept a vigil with her night after night. It is a simple but strangely reassuring prayer.

Now I lay me down to sleep,
I pray the Lord my soul to keep.
If I should die before I wake,
I pray the Lord my soul to take.

Our prayer always went on to list all the people we prayed for each night and ended with a regular closing line that my mother must have found a necessary one, "And help Jamie [that's me] to be a good boy." I told her I would keep trying.

The vigil with my mother and the birth of Kaylee Ruth taught me important lessons about faith and how it works. I saw the primacy of love and the strength of fidelity. In the end, love is the measure of life. What happened with my family for two weeks in that hospital room, and what I saw between my mother and father, was simply a love story and a testimony to faith. In the testimonials to my mother from so many, I was reminded how teaching and living the most basic principles of kindness, compassion, and service are what finally draw people in to love and give authenticity to faith—it's what makes faith human. I was dramatically reminded of the risk taking, exemplified by my sister's courage, that always accompanies true faith. And I literally experienced how hope and life are always born anew, even in the midst of the deepest pain and grief. The mystery of faith is that life and death are always concurrent. Indeed, life comes out of death. That is the promise and power of faith.

My mother's death came in the midst of my final work on this book. Suddenly, the vigil with my mom and the book writing became deeply connected. In this book, I invite you to reflect with me on what faith means for our world today. The book will ask what it means to stand up for what you believe and how your beliefs can be put into action. So come with me on a journey.

The Difference That Faith Makes

Faith without works is dead. (James 2:26)

HOPE IS BELIEVING in spite of the evidence, then watching the evidence change. That's what I've learned after almost three decades of working for change as a person of faith. People often ask me, "Where have you found the strength to stay involved for so long?" or "How have you stuck with it and not burned out?" I've asked those questions myself. But more often I've asked myself how I can make the most difference in the world. For me, the answer to both questions is the difference that faith makes. What do I mean by faith? I like the definition used by the biblical writer of the Letter to the Hebrews: "Faith is the substance of things hoped for, the evidence of things not seen." Simply put, faith makes hope possible. And hope is the single most important ingredient for changing the world. It has continued to provide the energy and sustenance I've needed, not just to keep going but to be continually renewed.

Now you know and I know that religion has not always played a positive role in the world. I think sometimes God must get very embarrassed by some of the things we human beings say we do "in God's name." Tragically, religion has too often been a sectarian and terribly divisive force. In places like Northern Ireland and Bosnia, the battles are often disguised as religious, when underneath the conflicts are economic, cultural, ethnic, nationalistic, and always political. Religion is often used as a sword to divide, rather than as a balm to heal. And religious leaders and institutions can be guilty of the kind of power-politics tactics that tear people apart instead of bringing them together. Toward one another, the different religious communities sometimes behave no better than rival street gangs.

Any audience reading a book like this will be full of people who have had bad experiences with religion. Let's face it, most of us have. I felt virtually kicked out of the little church I was raised in when, as a teenager, I was made to feel very unwelcome. Lots of us know how it feels to be unwelcome in religious institutions. But that experience didn't cause me to lose my faith forever, and I hope others don't throw theirs away either.

I could be as skeptical as anyone about faith and religion. I probably know more about the sad side of the religious story than most. But I haven't stayed in that skeptical and cynical place, and here's why: I have also experienced the promise and power of faith. When slave masters put the Bible in the hands of their slaves, it was meant to control them, to turn their eyes toward heaven and away from doing anything about their plight on earth. But in that book the slaves found Moses and Jesus. Their faith became the foundation for their liberation, and its spiritual power enabled them to keep their eyes on the prize. I can say that too. I know the oppressive and divisive side of religion, but I've also found the transforming power of faith that can change lives, neighborhoods, and nations. I have a long history in the streets and in the places in this world where suffering is most intense. I've seen that suffering, but I've also seen the faith that can prevail in and through it.

In a public forum at Harvard's John F. Kennedy School of Government, I was challenged by a student who feared the danger of religion to human rights and couldn't see past the horrors of places like Bosnia. I didn't argue with her. I admitted that our history is full of such examples, and those on the inside of faith communities have the biggest obligation to be critical of religion gone bad. If we cannot acknowledge the reality of the darkness, we can give no credence to the power of the light. I gave my assent to her concerns, but then I told her it was my own identity as a Christian that most persuades me to care for the world. For me, my faith is what has consistently pressed me to search and work for the common good.

This book is full of stories about people who have acted on that positive vision of faith. Instead of divisive, they have found faith reconciling; instead of wounding they have found it healing; instead of debilitating, they have found it empowering; instead of creating more obstacles, they have found a faith that removes them. There is an enormous practical wisdom in these stories, and a compelling reason for faith.

The Test of Faith Is Action

Many people today are hungry for spirituality but have no appetite for religion. Still others, who are part of religious communities, are asking how their faith might be connected to the urgent problems of their world. But spiritual interest may no longer be enough. In today's world, the test of any authentic faith is action.

Much of life is a matter of faith, especially the parts that count the most. At the beginning of the new millennium, the spiritual is overshadowing the political as a preferred solution to social problems. The future promises to deepen the relationship between faith and politics. The biggest question is: Which will transform the other?

Perhaps the greatest heresy of twentieth-century American religion was to make faith into a purely personal matter and a private affair, which went neatly with the rise of the consumer society. With the advent of the television preachers, faith was turned into an occasion for conspicuous consumption and effective fund-raising. Faith became merely another commodity: "I have it, and you don't." Or worse: "Here's how you can get it too. Our operators are standing by!"

In the Bible, faith is not something you possess, but rather something you practice. You have to put it into action or it really doesn't mean anything. Faith changes things. It's the energy of transformation, both for individuals and for a society.

The Bible begins with the creation story—how God created the world and all its creatures, including us. From the beginning, the venue of faith is the world, what's happening in it, and how that squares with God's intentions. How these creatures are interacting with one another, the rest of Creation, and their Creator is the heart of the biblical drama. The place where we look to find the face of God is our life in the world. With God so interested in the world, it's a wonder that contemporary religion has often seemed so uninterested.

As recently as the eighteenth and nineteenth centuries, both England and the United States experienced revivalist faith as a catalyst for great social movements, such as the abolition of slavery, child labor reform, and women's suffrage. In this century, American black churches led the way in the civil rights movement by putting faith into action for freedom.

It took a lot of faith for those early civil rights activists to endure the hatred and violence of the system of racial discrimination. It also required a change in the nation's moral climate and values to end that system. Changing the entrenched pattern of racial segregation in the American South, ending apartheid in South Africa, or tearing down the Berlin Wall seemed virtually impossible before they happened. People had to really believe such things could be done before they *were* possible. That "believing" is the essence of faith and the beginning of any change. You must believe the change is possible before it ever will happen. Indeed, every important social change begins with some people believing it is possible. Hope always precedes change. Hope is the substance of faith and the only absolutely indispensable ingredient for individual and social transformation. I've learned that there is a spiritual chain of events in history: faith–hope–action–change.

It wasn't very long ago that few people held any real hope for change in South Africa. And it wasn't until I met with fourteen-year-olds in the black townships there that I became convinced of freedom's eventual victory. I saw that the children had decided something—that their country would be free. Change always begins with some people making decisions based on hope, and then staking their lives on those decisions. The difference between optimism and hope is that the former changes too easily; the latter is rooted in something much deeper. That something is faith. South African archbishop Desmond Tutu always said that people of faith are "prisoners of hope." The succeeding events in his country vindicated that faith.

Perhaps my favorite story of the power of hope comes from a memorable moment shared with Desmond Tutu in South Africa. I love to tell the story about the extraordinary drama I witnessed at St. George's Cathedral, in Cape Town, where the Nobel Peace Prize winner and Anglican cleric preached. A political rally had just been canceled by the white government, so Bishop Tutu called for a worship service instead, inside the beautiful cathedral. The power of apartheid was frighteningly evident in the numbers of riot police and armed soldiers massing outside the church. Inside, all along the cathedral walls, stood more police openly taping and writing down every comment made from the pulpit. When Tutu rose to speak, the atmosphere was tense indeed. He confidently proclaimed that the "evil" and "oppression" of the system of apartheid "cannot prevail." At that moment, the South African archbishop was probably one of the few people on the planet who actually believed that.

I had been clandestinely sneaked into the country to support the South African churches during a time of great crisis, and to report their story back in the United States. This was the first day of my six-week stay, and I had just arrived from the airport. Now I sat in the cathedral congregation and watched Archbishop Tutu point his finger right at the police who were recording his words. "You may be powerful, indeed very powerful, but you are not God!" And the God whom we serve, said Tutu, "cannot be mocked!" "You have already lost!" the diminutive preacher thundered. Then he came out from behind the pulpit and seemed to soften, flashing that signature Desmond Tutu smile. So—since they had already lost, as had just been made clear—South Africa's spiritual leader shouted with glee, "We are inviting you to come and join the winning side!" The whole place erupted, the police seemed to scurry out, and the congregation rose up in triumphal dancing. I had the blessing to be at Nelson Mandela's inauguration and to have some moments with Archbishop Tutu. He smiled when I reminded him of that day at St. George's. I said, "Bishop, today they've all joined the winning side!" They had indeed.

Perhaps we have reached so many personal and political impasses in America and the West because we have failed to recognize the moral and spiritual character of our problems. Yes, religion has too often been the occasion for dividing people into sectarian gangs and warring factions. But faith can also be the spiritual energy that enables the transformations for which our world so desperately hungers.

Many people today would like to find some way to practice their faith or spirituality, despite the excesses, corruption, or narrow regulations of religion that have turned them away. I believe the making of the modern Christian, Jew, or Muslim will be through action. When put into action, faith has the capacity to bring people together, to motivate, and to inspire, even across former dividing lines. We demonstrate our faith by putting it into practice and, conversely, if we don't keep the power of faith in the actions we undertake, our efforts can easily lead to burnout, bitterness, and despair. The call to action can preserve the authenticity of faith, while the power of faith can save the integrity of our actions. As the biblical apostle James put it many years ago, "Faith without works is dead." Indeed, faith shows itself in works—faith works.

An Unforgettable Encounter

I was preparing to leave for Seattle, to speak at the mayor's retreat for his cabinet and staff on the subject of "politics and values." Mayor Norm Rice had the political reputation of searching for practical answers to pressing social problems. So I was thinking about how to be most helpful in this retreat when I headed out of the house to get a few things for the trip. It was dark but not yet late. As I turned the corner onto the deserted street, my mind preoccupied, I wasn't "watching my back," as we say in our inner-city

Washington, D.C., neighborhood. By the time I heard the running feet behind me, it was too late.

I turned around, only to be hit by something sharp enough to open a gash over my left eye, and I immediately felt the blood running down my face. Several hands pushed me to the ground, and I heard a voice shout, "Keep him down! Get his wallet! Take his money!" Lying there on the cold pavement, I realized that after more than two decades of living and working in some of the toughest streets of America, I was being mugged, officially, for the first time. Believe me, it felt very official.

I popped up quickly to face my assailants, only to discover that they were all children: four young teenagers, not more than about fourteen. I had never seen them before, so we didn't know one another. They moved into a boxing stance and began to circle me. The youngest one (who couldn't have been more than twelve) clearly had watched a lot of television, because he began to flail away at me with earnest but ineffectual karate kicks. He was like a little mosquito buzzing around me.

Seeing that the kids weren't carrying weapons (which they often do in our neighborhood), I decided to confront them—not to hurt them, but just confront them with what they were doing. First, I scolded them: "Stop it! Just stop it! You guys got to quit terrorizing people like this." I watched as they dropped their hands. Then I looked right into their eyes and said, "I'm a pastor. You boys want to try to beat up a pastor and take his money? Come on ahead. Take your best shot. Let's see what you can do." Well, at that, they turned and fled down the street. But as they ran away, the little guy (my karate kicker) looked back at me with a sad face and in a sincere voice said, "Pastor, ask God for a blessing for me."

Well, there it is. The thing that everyone is most afraid of had happened to me. I'd heard the slogan "A conservative is a liberal who got mugged." Now I had been mugged; but instead of making me call for a police crackdown, it taught me something else. Even the kids running wild in the streets know they're in trouble and know they need a blessing. They know, as we all do down deep, that things need to change. I've heard people say that we're just going to have to write off a lot of kids, maybe a whole generation of them in inner cities. They're too tough, too hardened, too entrenched in destructive behavior. They're beyond our help, so the argument goes.

But here is where the element of faith comes in and the promise of hope begins. I don't romanticize poverty or fail to take seriously the violent threat that some urban youths pose. Now I've had several stitches to help me take it very seriously. But people of faith can't give up on those kids; it just isn't an option. They are children of God, made in the image of God, and must be treated that way—even if they don't behave that way themselves, maybe especially if they don't. If they've gotten lost somewhere along the way, that may say as much about the rest of us as it does about them. I'm neither surprised nor judgmental when schools, courts, and jails can't deal with some of our toughest street kids. Professionally speaking, they can indeed seem to be beyond our help. But that's why the people and programs that are rooted in faith often have success where others fail. They don't have the option to give up, they must treat each kid with his or her God-given dignity, they are motivated and sustained by things other than results, they can draw upon a hope that defies the odds, and they can offer a kid something far deeper than social services.

We can choose to cut kids off and lock them up, or we can make the commitment, often a faith commitment, to do what it takes to provide them with access to the nurture, discipline, and opportunity that all of our children need to live good and decent lives. If we can find a way to do that, we'll all benefit, or get the blessing, to use the words of the boy who asked for help.

National attention is being increasingly drawn to the success of faith-based efforts that are addressing many of the nation's most pressing social problems. We're beginning to see some solutions to the problems of youth violence and crime. Church-anchored programs are also showing real success in job readiness and welfare-to-work efforts. Overcoming addictions to substance abuse and combating family breakdown are other areas where the religious community has a good track record. Churches in local communities are addressing racial polarization, inadequate housing and education, and neighborhood disintegration. In many places, we're seeing some very hopeful signs. New models are being offered for after-school programs, youth mentoring, and community policing. Churches are deeply involved in helping to create low-income housing, provide child care, and promote community economic development. All over the country, congregations are becoming the primary support base for local and citywide community organizing.

Church-related programs are showing real and concrete progress, often where other efforts have failed. Anecdotal evidence of the accomplishments of faith-based programs is growing, and more systematic research is beginning to show significant patterns of positive results. Kid by kid, block by block, redemption programs are working. But they work even better with the support of surrounding community institutions, both public and private.

A New Kind of Activist

Today, I see a new kind of activist emerging. Not one who is angry or burned out, but one whose belief that things can be different goes deeper than a passing optimism and is rooted in spirituality. Bringing spiritual values to the difficult process of social change, these activists may be able to accomplish things that polarized political factions have failed to do.

Two of the most powerful forces in the world right now are *service* and *spirituality*. The growing influence of both is evident almost everywhere, and together they provide the most potent combination for changing our communities. Service and spirituality are growing streams of energy, which, as they begin to flow together, could create a mighty river of action. In hundreds of town meetings from Harlem, New York, to Orange County, California, I have felt the energy and witnessed the potential.

Students in record numbers are tutoring and mentoring inner-city children or devoting their spring breaks to building houses for low-income families. Grade-school kids are eagerly participating in recycling projects. People of all ages are trying to build community service into their vocations and lifestyles. Whole families are searching for ways of effective involvement. Moms and dads are taking their kids to community food banks and soup kitchens as well as soccer fields, because both service and recreation are crucial to youthful character formation.

Ask an audience of young people these days to give a year or two of their lives in community service, and you are likely to get a standing ovation. Our word "mission" comes from the Latin *missio*, which means "sending out." Today, more people are responding to the call. In a society increasingly bereft of meaning, a hunger exists for a mission that makes life worth living. When the only purpose the culture offers is endless consumption, service fills the void by providing a mission.

At the same time, religious and spiritual consciousness is on the rise all over the world. The secularist prophets of thirty years ago who predicted the demise of religion and spiritual values were simply wrong. Freudian therapists tried to tell us we would eventually get over the "illness" of religion, and *Time* magazine's April 8, 1966, cover asked, "Is God Dead?" But recent *Time* cover lines have included "Can We Still Believe in Miracles?," "The Search for Jesus," "Faith and Healing," "And God Said: The Genesis Revival," "Jesus Online: Finding God on the Web," and "Does Heaven Exist?" *Newsweek* says that their religion covers are now consistently their best sellers. Many churches and religious communities are experiencing tremendous growth, religious and spiritual publishing have achieved extraordinary heights, and popular movies and TV shows openly portray religious beliefs and spiritual values that would have been scoffed at in the entertainment industry just a few years ago. *Touched by an Angel*, which now relates religion to a variety of social issues, is one of the highest-rated shows on television.

Sociologist Andrew Greeley and many other observers suggest that the United States has the highest rates of volunteering in the world *because* it has the highest rates of religious participation and practice. The combination of service and spirituality is prompting solutions in local communities facing enormous crises. Faith-based communities have long provided the bulk of the nation's social volunteer force; now their successes are being studied by social policy analysts searching for new answers. Even the cynical media are paying attention. A *Newsweek* cover reads "God vs. Gangs," profiling the efforts of inner-city pastors to turn around youth violence; and the very secular *New Yorker* magazine features a lead article titled "In God They Trust," about some of the most promising church-based efforts aimed at combating urban poverty.

With hope on the rise and programs showing results, I believe we are seeing the beginning of a new movement for change in the aftermath of the Cold War, as the old solutions of both the Left and the Right fall away, and as we approach a new century and millennium. We've had plenty of very sophisticated analysis of what's wrong with the world, much of it quite helpful. But what's often been missing is more practical and accessible advice. What's been missing is a way to bring real solutions to the problems. What's been missing is the vision to help people connect the desire to change their lives with a commitment to change their communities. That vision will likely be rooted in moral and spiritual values.

My own background and commitment are in the churches, and most Americans are still members of churches. That's why many of the examples I use throughout this book are from churches. But many of the lessons are broadly applicable to other faith communities and to people with moral and spiritual concerns but no religious affiliation. Where I don't make all the broader applications, I leave it to the reader to do so.

Where We're Going

The lessons I've learned about faith and action over the last three decades are the basis for this book's step-by-step progression. They're lessons about how to make a difference with your life, and how to make a difference in your community. The lessons are also about the difference that faith can make in our lives, neighborhoods, and nations.

We start by engaging the world around us. Any new journey begins with questions, so "Trust Your Questions" is the first chapter. You will discover many people's stories in this book, and I thought it appropriate to begin with my own story. Trusting my questions started me on my life's journey. Because our questions lead us out of familiar territory, the second chapter is "Get out of the House More Often." When we do that, we begin to find out who we really are and what we can best contribute. And so my third chapter is "Use Your Gift." Do what you do best and apply it where it will do some good.

Once we're engaged, we begin to deepen our understanding of the world. In taking the creative and courageous steps of real involvement, we begin to discover that there is a real spirituality here. Chapter four is "Do the Work and You'll Find the Spirit." We eventually learn that there is more than one kind of poverty. And I call my fifth chapter "Recognize the Three Faces of Poverty." To begin to overcome these poverties, we have to learn the challenging sixth chapter, "Listen to Those Closest to the Problem."

As our understanding deepens, we learn the importance of having a strategy. We want to deal with the causes of problems, not just the symptoms; we're no longer satisfied with easy and surface responses, we want to find real solutions. So the seventh chapter is "Get to the Heart of the Matter." And as we search for real answers, we find that traditional political labels no longer suffice; we have to go deeper to the underlying values that make fundamental change possible. We begin to learn to "Throw Away Old Labels—It's Values that Count," the eighth chapter. Soon, we find that we can't accomplish much alone; we must reach out to build friendships and community and learn the ninth chapter, "Find New Allies and Search for Common Ground." All along, we've been learning that spirituality is an essential ingredient for social change and that communities of faith are playing a pivotal role in addressing our most pressing problems. Even government is becoming interested in new partnerships, and chapter ten reminds us to "Keep Your Eyes on the Prize." Now we look at the reasons why churches and congregations can make such a critical difference. Chapter eleven is "Tap the Power of Faith Communities."

There are crucial qualities and commitments that will guide the steps of the new spiritual activist we are envisioning. Chapter twelve, "Be a Peacemaker," shows how our violence-torn world will turn to those who have developed the skills to mediate and resolve conflicts, to build bridges, and to "learn the things that make for peace," to quote the words of Jesus. Chapter thirteen reminds us that there must always be inner work that can sustain the outer work. It's called "Be a Contemplative." Chapter fourteen is one of the most important. It's all too easy for us to get so caught up in our self-important, self-righteous, and self-deluding ideas that we forget that our faults and failures can sometimes teach us more than our strengths and successes. It's the lesson that must run throughout our work and our lives: "Keep It Human."

Finally, we learn to *think movement.* Chapter fifteen teaches us that nobody makes a difference who does not "Have a Dream," to quote Martin Luther King, Jr., and we lay out a possible agenda that could guide the spiritually based movement for social justice that this whole book calls for. Chapter sixteen is about how the real changes come, not just by lobbying for political power, but by changing the way a society thinks and feels about things. You can't just put up your finger in the air to see which way the wind is blowing; to make the significant changes, you have to "Change the Wind."

All through the book, I share my own life experiences and other stories from around the world that inform the chapters and give them a very human reality. But there is also a spirituality that runs throughout the book, and I've chosen a biblical text that expresses the heart of that spirituality. The text is from Chapter 58 of the biblical Book of Isaiah. Isaiah was a Hebrew prophet of the eighth century B.C. who laid out a vision for a good society. Still used extensively by both Jews and Christians today, Isaiah's wisdom reminds us that our own fulfillment in life is bound up with our neighbor's well-being. Only in reaching out to our brothers and sisters, especially those in most need, will we find our own best humanity. It is a spirituality in which everyone benefits and a new sense of community is the result. I believe it is a spirituality for our times. I hope that this insight we gain from Isaiah undergirds the whole book. So I would like to offer Isaiah's prophetic words here, at the beginning of the book, and invite the reader to use them as a meditation throughout the reading. Use the text as a touchstone, and Isaiah's wisdom will become more and more apparent as you move through the stories that shape the book. Don't just read, but hear the words of the prophet.

Is not this the fast that I choose: to loose the bonds of injustice, to undo the thongs of the yoke, to let the oppressed go free, and to break every yoke?

Is it not to share your bread with the hungry, and bring the homeless poor into your house; when you see the naked, to cover them, and not to hide yourself from your own kin?

Then your light shall break forth like the dawn, and your healing shall spring up quickly; your vindicator shall go before you, the glory of the Lord shall be your rear guard.

Then you shall call, and the Lord will answer; you shall cry for help, and he will say, Here I am. If you remove the yoke from among you, the pointing of the finger, the speaking of evil,

if you offer your food to the hungry and satisfy the needs of the afflicted, then your light shall rise in the darkness and your gloom be like the noonday.

The Lord will guide you continually, and satisfy your needs in parched places, and make your bones strong; and you shall be like a watered garden, like a spring of water, whose waters never fail.

Your ancient ruins shall be rebuilt; you shall raise up the foundations of many generations; you shall be called the repairer of the breach, the restorer of streets to live in. (Isaiah 58:6–12)

This is *not* a book to tell you one more thing you have to do. Instead, it offers a vision of how everyone in the community can become more healthy, healed, and whole. It makes the vital connection between service and spirituality, which is key to our future. From that connection flow all the "lessons" to change your world and heal your soul—here are practical lessons in what to do and how to do it. I hope readers will make another connection—between reading a book and joining a movement.

Engage
Your
World

CHAPTER ONE

Trust Your Questions

Who is my neighbor? (Luke 10:29)

EVERY NEW DIRECTION in one's life journey begins with some new questions, and so did mine.

I was just another white kid from everything that was "middle" about America. We were from Michigan. We were middle-class. We were Christians. We lived in a nice suburban Detroit neighborhood, and my brother and sisters and I all went to good schools. The world looked fine to us. My parents believed that we lived in the best city in the best state in the best country in the world.

My father graduated from the University of Michigan, was commissioned as a naval officer, and got married all on the same day in June of 1945. The government was anxious to get him and a fresh contingent of sailors off to the Pacific to help end the war. My mother had been strong enough to win his heart and win him over to her Christian faith. After the war, my parents settled their little family in a new three-bedroom house, in a neighborhood full of returning World War II veterans with families just like ours—all financed by the new Federal Housing Administration.

I grew up with an abundance of warm affirmations, constant kudos, and great expectations for success. The first of five children, I was "saved" at six and baptized at eight in the little evangelical church my dad and mom helped to establish.

I won't easily forget the night of my dramatic childhood conversion. A fiery evangelist had come to our church for a Sunday-night revival service, and all the kids were asked to sit in the very front rows. I felt as if the preacher was pointing his finger right at me when he said, "If Jesus came back tonight, your mommy and daddy would be taken to heaven, and you would be left *all by yourself*." Well that was sobering, especially when I realized that, as a six-year-old boy, I would have a five-year-old sister to support! That very night, I quickly asked my mother how I could be saved, being quite ready to repent of the sin and degradation of my first six years. But to her everlasting credit, she didn't talk to me about God's wrath but told me how much God loved me. That sounded great to me, so as best as I understood how, I gave my life to Jesus. Things went smoothly from then on. Good grades, sports, and youth group activities were my life's priorities. In fact, everything was going very well until some questions began to form in my head and heart as I became a teenager.

Questions of the Heart

I asked questions first in my own world of family, church, and school. In that world, everybody's dad had a job, dinner was on the table every evening, and only bad people that our family didn't know ever went to jail. We weren't rich (with five kids in the family, we spent most of our vacations camping at state parks in Michigan), but I had never met anyone whom I would call poor. But increasingly, I was hearing and seeing things that troubled me. On the news and in the papers, I was hearing more about inner-city Detroit, just a few short miles away. I read stories about unemployed fathers, hungry families, and overcrowded jails. Then there was this new civil rights movement in the South, and some minister named King.

Minister? The church where I grew up was literally the center of our lives. I wondered why the only black faces I'd ever seen in my church were on the missionary slides from Africa that we sometimes watched on Sunday nights. Weren't there black churches in Detroit? Why hadn't we ever visited one or invited their members to our church, as we did with lots of other white Christians? In Sunday school, I had been taught to sing:

> Jesus loves the little children,
> All the children of the world,
> Red and yellow, black and white,
> They are precious in His sight,
> Jesus loves the little children of the world.

I supposed that was true about Jesus, but I could see it wasn't true of the white Christians around me.

My high school government classes also taught me that in America, all people "are created equal." But as I listened to many of the white citizens of Detroit, I discovered that they didn't really believe that. Why was there such resistance among my classmates at our all-white high school when our young English teacher had us read a book about racism and talk about it?

My world was safe and secure, white and middle-class, and full of easy answers. But new questions were arising in the early sixties. I was just a teenager, but something didn't seem quite right. That's often the beginning of the process, the start of a journey—something doesn't seem quite right.

My questions were these: Why was life so different in "white Detroit" than it was in "black Detroit"? Why were so many people in the inner city without good jobs or decent houses? Why were there hungry families in the United States of America? Why were so many young black men in jail? While starting to look at the world around me, I also began to ask what our Christian faith said about the racial attitudes I was discovering. Why did we have no contact with the black churches? What did they think of us? Weren't we all supposed to be part of the "body of Christ"? After the questions began, things got difficult. When I raised my questions, I could feel the cool distance between me and many of the people around me, even those I had been close to since I was a little boy. Then the arguments came, in school, in church, and at home. The arguments were hard on all of us.

Some people told me I was too young to ask such things, and when I got older I would understand. Others admitted they didn't know why things were this way either, but it had always been like that. The only really honest answer I got was from a church elder who told me, "Son, if you keep asking these questions, you're going to get into a lot of trouble."

That turned out to be true. Probably the most important decision I made at that time was to keep asking my questions until I got some answers. I recommend that. Follow your heart, trust your questions, and pursue them until you find answers that satisfy you. How questions get put into our heads and our souls is a great mystery. I still don't know why these questions intruded into the mind and heart of a successful teenage kid mostly preoccupied with sports, grades, church youth groups, and, of course, girls. All I know is that the questions were there and wouldn't go away.

These questions of the heart, as I like to call them, are an entryway into our own spirituality. They beckon us to a deeper place and a more honest life; they are a call to conscience and, ultimately, an invitation to transformation. The religious would say that God puts those questions in our hearts; others might say they are a link to the spirit within us. The most important thing is that the questions be diligently followed; to turn away from them is to turn away from the voice of your own conscience and, perhaps, the voice of God.

Pilgrimage to Detroit

My pursuit of the questions took a teenage white kid from the suburbs into the inner city of Detroit. And there a whole new world opened up to me. As pilgrimages go, the one I made from the white suburbs to the inner city of my own town was a very short one—only a few miles. But it felt as if I was moving from one world to another, because I was. Was I scared? Sure, a little. But I also had to find out what was going on around me. I tried to find chances to connect to the city. After I got my driver's license, at sixteen, I would head downtown, find someplace to park, and just start walking around.

I found myself wandering the streets of downtown Detroit.

There I was, exploring a world very different from mine, strangely compelled by the "inner city," which everyone warned me to avoid. The homeless vagabonds, prostitutes, and young street kids were as intrigued by the sight of me as I was by them. I knew the people I grew up with would be terrified and horrified. Why was I there? I wasn't really sure. But the city drew me like a magnet. Life seemed more real there, more human, and more interesting than in the suburbs, which now felt artificial and isolating to me. The diversity also drew me. Where I lived and went to school and church, everyone was like us. In contrast, and in spite of all the differences, I felt somehow connected to the people in the city, felt that we were all related in some way that we just couldn't understand. I remember feeling that it was important to try to figure that out.

I also began reading, mostly books by black authors. One was a book titled *My Friend, The Enemy* by a young black Christian named Bill Pannell. He was from the same little denomination of churches that I was, the Plymouth Brethren, but from the group's black congregations. I had never known they existed. Bill's little book was about his very ambiguous relationship with his fellow white Christians. I found it fascinating, and since he lived in Detroit, I went to hear him speak. And what I heard him say made all the sense in the world. I knew that I was hearing the truth, and I was finally getting some answers to my questions.

Because of my church background, I started going to black churches. I really liked the sermons and loved the gospel choirs from the first time I ever heard one. People were always friendly and inviting, and I began to meet people who could answer my questions. It wasn't always direct; I didn't "interview" anyone, I just watched, listened, and asked people about their lives. I've always felt welcomed in the black churches and still do to this day. Maybe that's why the black church has always been a spiritual home for me. Of course, the answers to some of my earnest and eager questions were obvious, but I never felt patronized or dismissed. Listening to a good black preacher and a good gospel choir is always a very satisfying experience, one that I highly recommend. And you will always be welcome. What I found in the black churches was a lively faith, but one connected to a world very different from the Detroit in which I had grown up. And this different world was becoming clearer to me every day.

As I got ready to go to college, and then all during my university years, I took summer jobs in the city, putting me alongside young black men my age. From them I learned that we had grown up in two different countries, yet only a few miles apart. On factory assembly lines, where the temperature would regularly climb to over one hundred degrees, we had hot conversations about the world that would radically change my perceptions of it.

The Motor City was a racially divided town, a fact that became dramatically clear to the nation in the hot summer of 1967 when Detroit exploded into riots. I was there and felt my heart inflamed along with my city. The urban disorders that shook Detroit were blamed for polarizing the city. But in reality they simply revealed the deep racial polarization that was already there. Why were most of the white people around me so unwilling to look underneath the "riots" to find the reasons for them? I didn't understand everyone's defensiveness to all the questions that were growing in my head and heart. But I also recognized that some of the racial stereotypes I had learned as a white child were still inside me. I realized that I had a lot to learn, and to *unlearn*. So I made sure I got my own paperback copy of the famous Kerner Commission Report into the causes of the 1967 disorders and studied it diligently. I read the thick, well-documented report several times, until the pages became dog-eared. And through it, I learned how difficult it really was for America's black citizens to find "life, liberty, and the pursuit of happiness." I pored over the report's statistics on education, employment, housing, and police behavior, which revealed a nation, said the Kerner Report, "moving toward two societies, increasingly separate, and dramatically unequal."

The young men I was meeting were militant and angry, and as I listened to them I became angry too. During this same period, I first read *The Autobiography of Malcolm X*, written with Alex Haley, and I discovered that the young Malcolm had also spent some time in Detroit. Now I was beginning to see some of the life of inner-city

Detroit that had so shaped "Detroit Red," as Malcolm X was formerly known.

One person I've never forgotten is Butch, a black coworker in a downtown office building who taught me many lessons about life. We worked together as janitors, furniture movers, and substitute elevator operators. He was smart, and he always had a book sticking out of the back pocket of his khakis. But he wasn't going to university like me. Our paychecks had different destinations—mine to a college savings account, his to support his mother, brothers and sisters, and young wife.

On the days we ran the elevators, the company was legally required to give us extra breaks so our heads wouldn't start to spin. But on my breaks, I often rode up and down with Butch in his elevator, and on his breaks, he rode with me, so we could talk about politics. Our heads did begin to spin, but not just from the ride: rather, it was from what we were learning about each other's world—our families, neighborhoods, schools, hopes, dreams, and futures. I quickly learned that Butch knew much more about my world than I knew about his.

Meeting Butch's mother was an experience I'll never forget, and one I've come to realize was pivotal in my own pilgrimage. She wasn't especially political, and certainly not militant. But like my own mother, she loved her firstborn son and was afraid his radical ideas might get him into trouble. Because her husband had died young, she relied on Butch a great deal. During my visit, the youngest of Butch's brothers and sisters climbed right up into the lap of this strange white guy, with trusting smiles on their faces. The older ones held back, showing much more suspicion. It's a pattern I've often seen since. It doesn't take long for the experience of racism to erode childlike innocence and trust.

What I most remember from that first meeting, though, was a conversation in which Butch's mother related the experiences the men in her family had had with the Detroit Police Department. She told me the advice she gave all her children regarding the police: "If you ever can't find your way home and seem to be in a strange neighborhood, watch out for the police. If you see a policeman, quickly hide down a stairwell or behind a building. Just don't let him find you! After he passes by, it's safe to come out and find your way home." In Detroit, I had heard stories about the reputation of the white police for brutalizing young black people. But as Butch's mother spoke, my own mother's advice to me and my brother and sisters on the same topic rang in my ears: "If you're ever lost and can't find your way home, *look for* a policeman. He is your friend and will bring you home safely." Moments like that are truly converting experiences that stay with us for the rest of our lives.

It was my questions that led me to the inner city, to the black churches, to Butch's living room. Those questions eventually led me to the decision to become involved in the civil rights movement as a college student. Detroit was my early baptism of fire, teaching me how racism had betrayed the ideals I had been taught as a child. Another lesson I learned is that we are terribly diminished without our ideals, and the struggle to protect them is absolutely crucial to our integrity as persons and as a nation. That struggle always depends on asking the hard questions.

One Question Leads to Another

When I was a college student, the war in Vietnam was escalating, and so were the questions of a new generation. Vietnam became another classroom for a whole generation of Americans like me. My high school girlfriend's cousin Don and several other guys I knew were sent over there. Don had gotten into trouble, and the judge said he could choose between jail or the Marines. Back home, I got teargassed more times than I can count in peaceful demonstrations against the war, many of which I helped organize. One day, Don and I compared our experiences of Vietnam and realized we and our whole generation had all become veterans of the war, one way or another, some fighting in it and some fighting against it. The war shaped us all. Again we were criticized for raising questions, but it was the hard questions that finally shone a light on U.S. policies in Indochina and the logic of a war that degenerated into "destroying a village to save it."

As a young adult, I experienced the successes and failures of the student movements of the 1960s. During my college days, at Michigan State University, we learned how to put ten thousand people in the street in a few hours' time, but also how such a powerful movement could quickly collapse into moral confusion. I remember the first time antiwar protesters began trashing downtown store windows in East Lansing, Michigan, I wondered what was happening to us. I saw the dangers of hating your country (as some antiwar protesters came to do) instead of loving it enough to try to correct its mistakes. I questioned how a movement for peace could degenerate into bitterness, violence, and even hatred. I began to learn that it's easier to criticize your government's policy than to ask tough questions of yourself.

But I remember Martin Luther King, Jr., explaining his opposition to the war in Vietnam. "I oppose the war," he said, "because I love America. I speak out against it...with anxiety and sorrow in my heart, and above all with a passionate desire to see our beloved country stand as the moral example of the world. I speak out against this war because I am disappointed with America. There can be no great disappointment where there is no great love." King's opposition to the war was like the anguish of the biblical prophet Jeremiah, hurt by the sins of his people yet proclaiming the justice of God.

My experiences as a movement organizer were raising a number of deeper issues. Racism, poverty, and war had motivated my earlier questions. But what were the spiritual roots of social change? Was there a moral foundation upon which to build new political visions? Can political ideology alone answer the deepest longings of our hearts or resolve the problems of our public life?

My early disillusionment with the church had caused me to lose my childhood religion. But was I now finding my way back to faith? I began to look at Jesus again—or perhaps for the first time. I started reading the New Testament again, which I hadn't done in many years, just on my own. What I began to see in the first three Gospels was a Jesus who stood with the poor and marginalized and who taught his followers to be peacemakers, a Jesus I had never heard much about in church but was now rediscovering. I read Jesus's

Sermon on the Mount, which lays out the priorities of a new way of life in a new order that he called the kingdom of God. In this new order, the poor would be blessed, along with those who were moved by human suffering, who were merciful, who were gentle in spirit but hungry for justice, who were people with integrity, who were peacemakers, and who were persecuted for just causes. Somehow, I'd missed that in church.

But it was the twenty-fifth chapter of Matthew's Gospel that really caught my attention. In a scene of final judgment, Jesus asks the people who assume they are his followers how they have treated the hungry, the thirsty, the homeless strangers, the naked, the sick, and the prisoners. The question startles them, especially when he suggests that he has been all these things and they have not ministered to him. His would-be disciples are incredulous. "Lord, when was it that we saw you hungry or thirsty or a stranger or naked or sick or in prison, and did not take care of you?" Jesus's reply astounded me. "Truly, I tell you, just as you did not do it to one of the least of these, you did it not to me." Here Jesus was so identifying himself with the rejected and excluded of the world that to serve them was to serve him, and to ignore them was, indeed, to ignore him. I had never heard anything as radical as that, certainly not in all the revolutionary literature of the time that I was reading. It was humbling, too, for a self-confident student radical to realize that his life needed some changing. I knew more than ever, then, that I didn't have all the answers, but trusting my questions was still taking me to new places.

I decided to go to theological seminary in Chicago. There, I began to make the connection between faith and action that I mentioned earlier and that would become the foundation for my life and work. I began to learn that spiritual values could teach us much about the human condition while giving us new visions for social change. Hearts had to be changed as much as policies, and that was an even deeper challenge. I remembered that the civil rights movement, rooted in the black churches and a very powerful spirituality, was far more successful and morally centered than the youthful white student movements of the same period. Seminary was also where I began to learn the importance of community, about the problems and possibilities of living and working together with other people. Community was where we learned about ourselves and how much transformation each of us needed if the world was truly to be a better place.

In seminary, several of us began a little magazine, which I'm still involved with today. In each issue, *Sojourners* addressed the two topics you aren't supposed to discuss in polite conversation: religion and politics. And we committed the even greater offense of trying to put those topics *together*—today our masthead still reads, "*Sojourners*—Faith, Politics, and Culture." We thought that church and state should remain separate, but that moral values and public life ought to be connected.

Always, asking new questions led to wider involvements. During the 1980s, I learned how to mobilize churches around the country on a myriad of social issues. For example, the religious community became the animating core of a movement alerting the nation to the dangers of the nuclear arms race. We helped initiate the nuclear freeze campaign that brought in even wider constituencies. Our allies spanned the gamut from Carl Sagan to Billy Graham.

Questions about justice, peace, and faith can inevitably lead you beyond your own borders and to more questions. During the years of war in Central America, many of us made the pilgrimage south. I learned firsthand about the ravages of war on the northern frontiers of Nicaragua, where we took busloads of volunteers down dusty rutted roads with mortar shells shooting over our heads, seeking to create a new campaign called Witness for Peace amid cold war-inspired violence. We ultimately sent five thousand North Americans to Nicaragua to work for peace. Holding your pack over your head while crossing overflowing rivers in the Philippines, stumbling through rice paddies, sleeping in hammocks covered with mosquito netting, and celebrating the Eucharist on altars decorated with candles in Coke bottles will also raise many questions about your comfortable way of life back home. Having clandestine dialogues with Soviet dissidents in Moscow before Communism collapsed jumbled up the old Left-Right categories, made me rethink my political assumptions and deepened my commitment to genuine democracy. And meeting with aboriginal leaders in the Australian bush taught me new lessons about the arrogance of dominant cultures. Everywhere I went, I continued to learn the value and power of asking questions.

It's always the deeper spiritual questions that have such a capacity to change us. Keeping one step ahead of the security police in black townships, I got to know South African church leaders like Desmond Tutu, who deeply believed that one day their nation would be free. I experienced the power of hope as I never had before as black South Africans made believers of the rest of the world. I will never forget a day that transfixed the planet—May 10, 1994—when I stood with 150,000 cheering South Africans sharing tears of joy at Nelson Mandela's inauguration. It was one of those rare days when you can see and feel the world changing right before your eyes. Everyone spoke that day of "the miracle" that was occurring. Such a powerful event was humbling, reminding me that the really important changes surpass all of our individual efforts and tap a spiritual power that causes us all to be amazed by grace.

Failures also teach many lessons, as I learned in 1990, when a small group of American church leaders tried in vain to find a way to peace in Baghdad on the eve of the Gulf War. We seemed to persuade some members of the Iraqi cabinet that withdrawal from Kuwait would be far better than seeing the children of Baghdad bombed, but Saddam Hussein wanted war, as did George Bush. We felt we had failed. We came home and organized a service of more than eight thousand people praying for peace in Washington's National Cathedral on the night before the bombing began. Despite our best efforts, the war proceeded and most of the nation rallied around the CNN coverage of the quick U.S. victory. The peace movement was demoralized, and I became aware of how much my own ego had become invested in the quest for peace. A personal forty-seven-day fast, embarked on during the days of war that followed, probably taught me more about the deeper spiritual challenges to real peace than most of my organizing ever had. I saw more clearly than I had before that "peace" really does begin with me.

Spiritual Power

Today, we publish *Sojourners* magazine out of Washington, D.C., but it's not the Washington with which most people are familiar. In the "other Washington" people are not wealthy and powerful but poor and politically powerless. I live in Columbia Heights, about twenty blocks from the White House, where children who inhabit the inner city in the capital of the world's last remaining superpower sometimes go to bed to the sound of gunfire and experience violence, drugs, and despair as their daily norm. It's still a revealing question to ask why this is so. Our little Sojourners Neighborhood Center has for twenty years been a safe place and a beacon of hope for at-risk children and their parents, in what otherwise has often seemed like a war zone. Working with those kids, we try to practice what we preach, and through them we have learned close up the realities behind the problems that the city's media pundits ceaselessly debate from far above the fray. Living and working here has been an invaluable education for me, as well as a vital spiritual discipline. It continually raises new questions about how people, families, communities, and nations really do change—or don't.

My neighborhood has constantly given me a perspective that I would not otherwise have had. Once, I returned from a meeting at the White House about youth violence only to find the infamous police yellow tape on the sidewalk right across from my house, indicating where another young man had just been shot and killed. I remember reflecting that most people who attend such meetings don't come home to places like this.

Moving to inner-city Washington to work in the shadows of the nation's Capitol revealed a tale of two cities—a pattern I began to see internationally through increasing travel around the world. Everywhere, there was an upper city and a lower city, and the relationship between the two tells you much about a society. Asking questions about the lower city teaches you how things really are (especially for those at the bottom), rather than just what the people at the top say about their society. In most places I go, I try to be sure to visit both cities.

I'm on the road a great deal, so I get to know the most hopeful people and projects in America today and in many places around the world. Mostly, I try to help nurture and inspire what I think is the most important force for changing the world, or at least our own corner of it—namely, social movements with spiritual power.

Speaking from two hundred to three hundred times a year for more than two decades, and to audiences of all kinds, I've gotten to know America pretty well, and other parts of the world too. I've had the opportunity to travel to thousands of American cities, towns, and communities, and hundreds of places internationally—always speaking and listening, encouraging and being encouraged, mobilizing and seeing how people are organizing themselves. But it's always people's questions that interest me most. People often tell me that I'm at my best when responding to people's questions after my speeches. That's probably because I enjoy the questions so much and think they're so important.

Our questions are often shaped by where we're asking them from. Our vantage point is critical. My view of the world has always come from very diverse vantage points—from lovely hotel windows to dirty housing project balconies, from university lecture halls to homeless shelters, from the corridors of political power to the muddy roads of poor shantytowns, from the nation's great pulpits to the insides of assorted jail cells, where I've been sent probably twenty times by now for various vigils, marches, and peaceful actions of nonviolent civil disobedience. I've noticed how different the world looks from those different places.

The many examples of social change I've seen along the way have been a grounding for my visions of how the world might be different. I've had the blessed opportunity to be instructed and inspired by the very best efforts in the land and around the globe that are helping to turn our world in a better direction.

I've seen what really changes the world, what finally makes a difference. I've discovered that the world can be changed; we just have to learn how, and we have to begin close to home. And I would say the most important lessons I've learned have to do with the energy and power that come from bringing moral and spiritual values to public life. A spiritually rooted approach to social change not only offers good models for solving problems, but contributes what is perhaps the most valuable commodity in the struggle to genuinely transform our world: the presence and power of *hope*. It's often faith that makes hope possible, and when hope is present, new things begin to happen. So often, the most important question to ask is simply: Where can we find the hope here?

A New Table

Sometimes I've been able to help bring various efforts together or help people find common ground they didn't believe was possible. I've helped facilitate both gang peace summits and religious roundtables that brought warring factions to the table. The "table" has been a constant metaphor and tactic for me, a place to form new connections, ideas, and partnerships.

Always asking the question of how to put faith into action can land you in some unusual places and circumstances. In the early 1990s, for example, I became involved in supporting some of the gang truce movements that were emerging. One Sunday morning in 1993, I found myself sitting in a black Baptist church in Kansas City, Missouri, after a weekend Gang Peace Summit. In a congregation that included a couple of hundred former and current gang members from all over the country, I was reminded of how far I had traveled from the white suburbs of Detroit, Michigan. But on that morning, there was nowhere else in the world I would have wanted to be; I felt privileged to be there "at the table."

I'll never forget what happened that morning. Two young rival street warriors, who had been trying to kill each other all that past year, dramatically dropped their gang colors in the pulpit and resolved from then on to walk together on the road to peace. There wasn't a dry eye in the house. My tears were also for churches who couldn't or wouldn't come together for the sake of their communities, the way these young men and women were doing. It was that morning when the idea came to attempt a similar truce between the churches. If some Crips and Bloods can do this, why not the evangelicals and liberals, the Catholics and Protestants?

Just like the young gangsters, the churches would need a reason to come together, after years of acting like gangs themselves in their battles over turf, money, and power. Everyone knew the churches *ought* to have more unity, but as was the case with the street gangs, it would take a crisis to provoke a new coming together, one that people would feel deeply.

That crisis and opportunity came when Congress and the White House virtually ended the nation's sixty-year-old social welfare system in the fall of 1996. Most everyone agreed that the old welfare system wasn't working very well and certainly wasn't overcoming poverty. But the politicians ended it without first putting alternatives in place. That caused a shudder in the religious community, which, as a historic and major service provider, was now afraid that too much of the burden would fall on it. But at the same time the churches were sensing fresh responsibilities and even a new commitment.

Several colleagues and I decided to take a risk by calling together a summit of our own. Almost sixty church leaders gathered together at a new roundtable and for nine hours talked and prayed through the issues. After one of the most remarkable days any of us could remember, a new unity began to be forged. A vision of partnership began to emerge, first for the churches and then for other organizations and leaders in local communities. It was a unity for the sake of poor people who were facing a potential crisis greater than any in years. It seemed that the poor were bringing the churches together.

With the old welfare system gone, a whole new set of questions was now being asked. One was how to create the necessary alternatives before all the welfare cuts were put into place. That effort would take the involvement of the whole community—the churches, nonprofit organizations, businesses, unions, *and* government officials. Our guiding principle was that every group should do its part, and each would do what it does best. The solutions we needed now wouldn't conform to the old categories of liberal and conservative, Left and Right. Instead, we committed ourselves to forge a new kind of moral and community politics where *values* would be

more important than *ideology*. One of our central affirmations was
that the way to find common ground is to move to higher ground.
We named the new effort Call to Renewal to indicate that the task
would be as spiritual as it was political.

I agreed to be the convener of this new federation of faith-based
organizations—churches and religious groups with faith at their
center—who are trying to overcome poverty. We began to organize
town meetings and roundtables around the country, where new
questions and challenges were creating new partnerships. The two
hundred town meetings we did in the first two years convinced me
that a new era of multisector cooperation is indeed possible, with
pastors and nonprofit organizations coming together with elected
officials, police chiefs, and leaders in the business community and
labor to create strategies and to mobilize resources for community
change.

Call to Renewal holds the promise for a movement of faith in
action that brings together many constituencies from the religious
community and beyond. At a Washington press conference, evangelical leader Rich Cizik hopefully proclaimed, "The cold war
between religious groups over the poor is now over!" Again, new
questions were creating new possibilities.

What with *Sojourners* magazine and the home front, traveling
and speaking, teaching, and now Call to Renewal, life is busy. But I
have never felt more potential for significant change, precisely
because more people are recognizing the spiritual dimensions of
serious cultural and political transformation. Young former gang
leaders speak of the "spiritual power" necessary to overcome "the
madness" of urban violence. Religious leaders confess that their former divisions have hurt poor people. Elected officials are exploring
the benefit of partnering with faith communities, and a variety of
civic leaders are ready to build new alliances and find new answers
based on common values. Legions of students are having transforming experiences as they move out from their campuses to volunteer their time and energy as an expression of their spirituality.
Pastors and members of congregations are trying to find ways to
become better involved in their communities. People from all walks

of life are trying to find meaning and morality, not only in their personal and family lives but also in their work and vocations. Most important, ordinary people with jobs and kids are discovering that trying to make a difference in their own communities may be the best way to heal their own souls. People are trusting their questions and letting the questions lead them to new places.

Over the last three decades, I've experienced many large social movements and small local projects, neighborhood ministries and national coalitions, political campaigns and political protest, both victories and defeats, and with each one there have been lessons learned.

The journey begins by trusting your questions. Other lessons follow from that.

CHAPTER TWO

Get Out of the House
More Often

You are the salt of the earth....
You are the light of the world. (Matthew 5:13–14)

THERE IS A STORY about a young priest who was very nervous about his new responsibilities. He was especially worried about leading the Eucharistic liturgy. The priest has to say the right words in the right order—for instance, "The Lord be with you," to which the congregation duly responds, "And also with you." The new cleric was concerned that he might foul up his parts of the liturgy, causing the congregation to get their parts wrong too. The whole thing might fall apart, and he would feel like a failure. So you can imagine the young man's panic when he got up before the gathered parish that first Sunday morning, only to realize that his microphone had gone dead. Frantically, the rattled priest began to tap his finger hard on the silent microphone and exclaimed, "Something is wrong with this microphone." The congregation replied, "And also with you!"

I sometimes start with that story when I'm on the road speaking because it's always fun to begin with a good laugh. But the story also helps me introduce my next point. After the laughter dies down, I suggest that *something is wrong in our society*, and that most people feel it—all across the political spectrum. At that point, the heads begin to nod in agreement.

Despite the constant claims by politicians, Wall Street's elite, and the media pundits about what "good times" these are, most people sense that some things have gone wrong at the moral core of our society. Something about our values just doesn't seem right, and sometimes things really seem to be unraveling. But what is actually happening to us, and why, and what can we do about it? That we're not quite so sure about. To figure it out, we are going to have to understand our problems at a deeper level. Raising questions is a good start, but we soon have to decide how far we're going to pursue the answers. To go farther, we need to get some new perspectives. We learn that we can't just take this journey in our heads. We have to reach out to broaden our experience, to move beyond familiar places, and even to cross boundaries we never have before. So our second task is to "Get out of the house more often!"

The Journey Begins

To change our world, or our community, we first have to understand it. To understand it usually requires a change in our thinking. And for that to happen, we have to experience more of the world than we can know inside the comfortable confines of our lives. We have to cross the barriers that divide people and, indeed, that separate whole worlds from one another. Most of us are deeply programmed not to venture past those invisible but powerful signs that silently scream at us: No Trespassing! You shouldn't be here! You don't belong here! It's not safe! You won't be accepted! Stay where you are!

But I've found that those very powerful cultural messages are usually false, designed in part to keep us from seeing and experiencing people and parts of life that may change our perspective. It's not a big conspiracy; rather it's an ingrained cultural conditioning that keeps people in their own world and prevents them from experiencing another one.

Most of the people I've met who are deeply committed to social change will trace their own transformation to the time when they first went to a third world country, or even just across town to the inner city. There, in a world very different from their own, they had conversion experiences that would shape the rest of their lives. It wasn't so much reading a great book or hearing an inspiring lecture that changed them but rather their *experience* in a war zone, a refugee camp, a youth center, a women's shelter, or an urban church trying to hold a community together. Time studying at the university can, ultimately, be less educational for social change than time spent on a reservation, in a ghetto, in a barrio, or up a mountain holler.

When I talk to people about how change really happens, the first thing I try to impress upon them is that it is both *possible* and *worth it* to cross the normal boundaries of our lives, to escape our comfort zones and experience a different reality. That's always the first step. You can stay home and keep accepting the easy answers, or you can step out and make some new discoveries. If you don't get out, you'll never know what's really going on; if you do, a whole new world opens up.

And it's the more in-depth, longer-term experiences outside of your own world that can have the most lasting impact. My wife, Joy, is an example of that. At the age of eighteen, she spent a year working in the countryside of Haiti, the Western Hemisphere's poorest nation. Taking a year off before college, she plunged into a world very different from anything she had ever known. Joy had grown up in the working-class neighborhoods of South London, but she had never seen poverty like what she encountered in Haiti.

The actual work she did was for a project to bring clean and safe drinking water to people in a rural area. There is probably nothing more taken for granted in developed countries than clean water; yet the lack of safe water is a leading cause of disease and death all around the world. It is estimated that more than five million people, including two and a half million children, die each year from illnesses related to unsafe water and improper sanitation.

Living and working with some of the poorest people on earth for a year had a profound effect upon this English schoolgirl. Joy was forever sensitized to the plight of people at the bottom, those who are always shut out and left behind. Later, she became a priest in the Church of England. But she always stayed in the inner city and paid special attention to people who are poor, homeless, mentally and emotionally disabled, aged, immigrant, or outcast. Something got into her blood in Haiti, and it's never left her. Now she talks about starting a new church for the poor in Washington, D.C.

You also won't really know yourself if you stay inside the carefully constructed boxes of your life. Getting out of the house is actually the first step on a spiritual journey; take it and your life will begin to change. That is both the promise and the challenge. Only by the challenges encountered in stepping out do you learn what resources you have and what contribution you can make. What you gain is self-understanding as well as spiritual awareness. The path of self-discovery is critically linked to the process of social and political transformation. But the first step is to walk outside of the old, familiar places.

John Fife was a Presbyterian pastor in Tucson, Arizona. He was a preacher in cowboy boots, and his Southside Presbyterian Church was set in the beautiful landscape of the American Southwest. Pastors like John are expected to play it safe in regard to controversial social issues. But that expectation would soon change.

One day in the early 1980s, an immigration lawyer told John that a professional "coyote" (one who smuggled illegal immigrants across the border) had abandoned a group of Salvadorans in the desert. Half of them had died of dehydration, and the other half were picked up by the border patrol and hospitalized. As soon as they had recovered, the deportation process would begin.

The attorney said, "We've been talking to these people, and they're terrified of being sent back to El Salvador." At that time, most illegal immigrants from El Salvador were fleeing for their lives from their country's military government and death squads. Many of them were Christians, said the attorney. "The churches need to help us."

John Fife didn't really know where El Salvador was. "At that point I couldn't have put El Salvador on a map!" said the

Presbyterian pastor. When I later asked John why he had become involved with the refugees, he told me he had remembered the words of Jesus from the Gospel of Matthew: "I was a stranger and you took me in." So that's what John decided to do. What he didn't know at the time was how much that decision would change his life.

John and his church began a journey. First, they started a weekly prayer vigil for the people of Central America. Then they began to raise money to bail people out of detention and help relocate them. Many problems in our communities remain relatively hidden until we become involved in them. Then you can hardly understand why you never noticed such a big crisis before. The people in Southside Presbyterian Church began with the first group of refugees in trouble, but soon their relationships extended to many more. Members of the church got to know refugee families—sharing meals, stories, tears, and, yes, faith. Before long, John and his church members met others in Tucson who were befriending the new strangers in the community. Lots of ordinary people began to get involved—retired ranchers, teachers, nurses, students, nuns, priests, and homemakers. After about two years of this, they took the next step of helping to create an underground railroad for the fleeing refugees. The little church became deeply engaged in sheltering refugees from El Salvador and other countries in Central America that were caught up in terrible civil wars.

John and his parishioners got to know the U.S.-Mexican border quite well, assisting refugees on their difficult and dangerous journey to safety and settlement with sympathetic families. These citizens of Tucson not only took in the refugee families but became involved with their lives. People listened and learned from one another, and everyone was changed in the process.

Finally, the parishioners began to study the ancient tradition of churches providing sanctuary to those fleeing persecution from the authorities, and they decided that was what they needed to do. On March 24, 1982, Southside Presbyterian Church publicly received a family into the sanctuary of the church at worship and invited other congregations to do the same. These illegal aliens would now actually stay in the church, receiving its sanctuary and thus publicly defying the authorities. The INS (Immigration and Naturalization Service) and local police were reluctant to force their way into churches to arrest the refugees. Before long, a sanctuary movement had begun in the United States, and several hundred churches became involved. Two worlds met in those sanctuary churches across the country, and a process of transformation began.

Of course, it created great controversy, especially because the U.S. government had taken sides in the Central American wars and was politically allied with the government-sponsored military and paramilitary forces these refugees were fleeing. The refugees' stories of horrible violence occurring in their poor countries were more than embarrassing to the White House and Congress. Finally, sixteen people were indicted by the U.S. government for harboring illegal aliens and put on trial. In addition to John Fife, the defendants included a nurse, a housewife, a graduate student, three nuns, and a goat herder. All of a sudden, a local pastor in a sleepy Arizona town became a national figure. I had the privilege of speaking at the national conference on sanctuary called in Tucson to support those on trial. I met all the defendants, interviewed them for *Sojourners* magazine, covered the whole story, and was struck by how basic and "religious" their motivations were. John told me he was a longtime *Sojourners* subscriber and was astounded at now being interviewed in the magazine for simply offering the hospitality that "any Christian would" if he was aware of what was really going on with refugees like these.

John Fife's journey didn't start out political at all. These refugees he'd discovered were just people who were alone and needed help. For John and his congregation, reaching out to people in a particular situation of need had led to greater involvement, which led to greater understanding, prompting even more involvement. Soon these ordinary people, responding out of their compassion and faith, were put on trial as criminals. However, the integrity of the churches' actions and the power of those relationships was to prevail over the threats of governments, and the sanctuary workers were ultimately set free (in part because the government had collected evidence by sending in wired informants to infiltrate church prayer meetings!). The church defendants were at first convicted, but the charges were overturned on appeal. However, no one involved would ever be the same again.

John Fife went on to be elected for a term as the moderator of the national Presbyterian Church (the symbolic leader of the whole denomination), in a surprise vote that especially shocked him. Commitment can be a very attractive thing to people today. Now John is back at work in his little Tucson church, still wearing his cowboy boots, but operating with a much altered view of the world.

The journey begins in many ways. Today it often starts for young people when they decide to reach out in community service. All over the country, students are being offered the opportunity to step beyond the walls of their campuses by volunteering in the community. Those who decide to get involved often find it the most educational part of their college experience. Tutoring kids from an entirely different background from your own is guaranteed to change your perspective. Seeing the joy in the faces of a family moving into their first house—a house that you helped to build—is an experience most middle-class young people have never had before. Some students take the opportunity further by signing up for an overseas work project or otherwise spending time in another country. And it is changing the way those young people think.

Putting a Face on the Poor

My friend Joe Nangle, a Franciscan priest, often speaks of Olga, a poor woman he met while working in Peru. One day, Joe helped Olga bury her nine-year-old son in a paupers' graveyard; the boy had been killed by a hit-and-run driver and then denied dignity by a system that didn't care what happened to the children of poor families. "That day forever changed my relationship to Olga, and in some ways forever changed me," Joe says. "Perhaps for the first time I really saw what life is like for the poor—for that two-thirds of humanity who live as Olga lived, who bury their children as she did. From then on, and increasingly, Olga Valencia came to represent for me the literally billions of people, especially women, whose lives can hardly be called human. When I wanted to put a name and a face on 'the poor,' it was invariably Olga's name and Olga's face."

But priests aren't the only ones learning to see the poor. I met Dale Recinella in 1998 and soon learned about the extraordinary journey this middle-aged man and his family had been on. An international lawyer from Florida who made a high-six-figure income in the 1980s, Dale had decided to devote his energies and substantial skills to helping overcome poverty. Previously, he had arranged the financing on multimillion- and even billion-dollar deals for corporations, banks, and governments. He had helped to negotiate the contracts for Dolphin Stadium and the Port of Miami. Now he wanted to put together multisector partnerships to help move families out of poverty. But it all started with the awkward involvement of a high-priced attorney in a soup kitchen. Dale tells the story of how he began to change. Like many others, he saw some of the problems around him and decided to get involved. And like John Fife, he had no idea what he was getting into or how it would change him. Dale's recounting of his life-transforming experiences is compelling.

"Almost seven years ago, I started helping out at the noon meal of the Good News Soup Kitchen in Tallahassee. I showed up every day in my three-piece suit to help from eleven A.M. until one-thirty P.M. They assigned me 'door duty.' My job was to ensure that the street people lining up to eat waited in an orderly fashion. Every day, I stood at the door for an hour, chatting with the street people waiting to eat. Before I came to Good News, 'street people' was a meaningless term. It defined a group without defining anybody in particular. From the comfort of my car, my suburban home, and my downtown law office, street people were just 'those people out there somewhere.'

"Then one day an elderly woman named Helen came running to the Good News door. A man was chasing her and threatening to kill her if she didn't give him back his dollar. 'Tell him he can't hit me 'cuz it's church property!' she pleaded. In true lawyerly fashion, I explained that Good News is not a church but he still couldn't hit her. After twenty minutes of failed mediation, I bought peace by giving each of them a dollar.

"That evening, I happened to be standing on the corner of Park and Monroe. In the red twilight, I spied a lonely silhouette struggling in my direction from Tennessee Street. 'Poor street person,' I thought, as the figure inched closer. I was about to turn back to my own concerns when I detected something familiar in that shadowy figure. The red scarf. The clear plastic bag with white border. The unmatched shoes. 'My God,' I said in my thoughts, 'that's Helen.'

"My eyes froze on her as she limped by and turned up Park. No doubt she would crawl under a bush to spend the night. My mind had always dismissed the sight of a street person in seconds. But it could not expel the picture of Helen. That night as I lay on my fifteen-hundred-dollar deluxe temperature-controlled waterbed, I couldn't sleep. A voice in my soul kept asking, 'Where's Helen sleeping tonight?' No street person had ever interfered with my sleep. But the shadowy figure with the red scarf and plastic bag had followed me home. I had made a fatal mistake. I had learned her name."

That's what happens when you get involved. You learn people's names, and that makes all the difference. Poverty is no longer just a social or economic problem when you have a personal friend who is poor. Gang violence is not just a law-enforcement issue when you've spent time listening to a kid tell you why he has taken to the streets. "Welfare mother" is no longer a term of derision when you've gone over the budget of a woman who's trying to raise her kids on $410 a month. Personal involvement seems to defy the easy answers while at the same time it opens up the possibilities of real solutions.

It is just that sensitizing that the world so desperately needs. Joy Carroll, John Fife, Joe Nangle, Dale Recinella, and I were all raised in comfortable homes. None of us would have learned what we eventually did if we hadn't gotten out of the house. It has a way of changing your perspective, as Joe says…forever.

It's precisely that change in perspective that will make the most difference. And if you have in your mind the picture of a friend's face from the inner city of Detroit, a young child in Haiti, a refugee family from El Salvador, a grieving mother in Peru, or a homeless person on the streets of Tallahassee, it's easier to find the right perspective. I've learned many things about what really changes the world—and what makes a difference. Mostly I've learned that the world can be changed; we just have to begin by getting out of the house.

A Fair Test

The Jesuit Volunteer Corps, which sends young people into inner city and rural poverty areas for a year of service, has a wonderful motto: "Ruined for life!" Their simple idea is that once you've seen real poverty and gotten your feet wet by doing something about it, you won't ever be the same again. You'll be ruined for life. After that service, you may indeed go on to other things, but you will be a different kind of teacher, lawyer, doctor, social worker, journalist, business person, pastor, or whatever else you become. You'll also be a different kind of parent, church member, or community leader than you otherwise would have been. That year of hands-on involvement will change your perspective, they are convinced. And so am I.

My brother, Bill Weld-Wallis, coordinated the Jesuit Volunteer program in the Midwest for a decade and tells heartening stories of how most of his alumni have gone on to live lives of community service through their career, family, and personal choices. These were all ordinary people. They weren't activists or clergy or community leaders. They were just volunteers. What's most significant is what they became. Service is only the beginning; it's the transformation that comes from service that is the critical ingredient for personal and social change.

When I speak on college campuses, I often spend time with the students who are volunteering their time and energy in the community or around the world. I remember such an evening at a small college in central Texas. Before I gave the evening lecture, I had dinner with several of these young people who had decided to get out of the house. Some had just been to an international conference on peace in the Middle East and were planning on going back to work there for a year. Others had been to South Africa to serve in the efforts to build a new country free of apartheid. Still more had traveled to Central America to help with the shaky peace processes in those countries.

Virtually all of them had been extensively involved in volunteer projects throughout the United States. The conversation just crackled with energy and excitement. They had already learned so much, had so many more questions, and were hungry to keep going. Their experiences had already caused many of them to change their majors, and they were hoping it would change their lives. One could easily tell that these young people had come a very long way from the familiar worlds of suburban and rural Texas where most of them had grown up.

After my talk, we retreated back to the campus chaplain's house and continued the discussion. I challenged them. When I was their age, I told them, we could put ten thousand people in the street in two hours' time. In response to the civil rights movement and the Vietnam War, we became a generation forged in protest. Their generation had now also taken to the streets, not so much in protest as in volunteering. We marched in the streets for change; today's youth work in the community in order to make a difference.

The test of what my generation did, and what today's students are now doing, I suggested, is simply this: Will what you are doing change the direction of your life? My generation has often failed that test, and the test results for this generation are not yet in. If volunteer projects become merely the preoccupation of a few student years, to be forgotten when the larger life choices are made, little transformation will have occurred. But if this work changes the life trajectory of people, and shapes their most basic choices about faith, vocation, family, and money, especially in the most formative period of their lives, then real change will have begun. The students all thought that was a fair test, but a tough one.

One person who wants to change the lives of young people is Bart Campolo. He's the director of Mission Year, a rapidly growing youth volunteer program that is affiliated with Call to Renewal. Mission Year recruits college students to give a year of their time either before or after graduation. They move into an inner-city neighborhood to work with a local church. Their plan is simple and powerful. The young people go house to house, asking whether people would like them to pray for the needs of that home. Most of the people they call on say yes, many probably thinking "What could it hurt?" Sometimes the students pray right there on the doorstep or are invited into the house. But in the course of the prayer, the circumstances and needs of the people in that house are often made apparent. Aware of those needs, the students are then able to help people make connections to other sources of support or assistance. Maybe there's a need for a job, or some child care, or some household chores and repair work, or an educational opportunity, or after-school options for a kid getting into trouble, or an alcohol- or drug-rehabilitation program, or some support in a difficult domestic situation, or a health-care need, or maybe just a listening ear. The young people end up really praying for the people in the neighborhood where they are sent, and then helping to see that those prayers are answered.

My generation—the baby boomers—have become the biggest consumers in American history. Many of the old dreams and ideals have faded. Reality set in, and many compromises were made. Having once stepped out for change, many are now safely back within comfortable boundaries. Those who got more deeply involved in the organizing in the 1960s, and not just the marching, tended to feel the more lasting consequences. It is the depth of one's involvement that seems to make the most difference.

Now the members of my generation are stepping into positions of leadership throughout society. And many are remembering the formative influences of their student years and recalling commitments we once made. One hears more and more stories of people in successful careers deciding to do something they think more meaningful or important. I have increasing numbers of conversations with people in my generation who wish to somehow recapture the ideals they once professed but have gradually forgotten. Among my generation of now middle-aged professionals, a new spirit of community involvement may also be in the air. If a reawakening of conscience began to occur among a new generation of American leaders, in partnership with a younger generation hungry for service, exciting new possibilities for change could emerge.

Start by Doing Something

In America, we've gotten used to a pattern of public discourse that has become quite dysfunctional. A problem is stated, an argument erupts about its causes, the blaming begins, the rhetoric rises, the confrontation is joined and quickly becomes partisan—and nothing is ever done about the problem. There is another approach. A problem is stated. The various dimensions of it are described as best we can understand them. Then a strategy is conceived for *involvement* with the problem in the hope of finding the necessary solutions. Instead of rushing to theoretical debates, various community leaders and institutions begin to engage the situation, believing that a diverse set of people and resources will probably be necessary to solve the problem.

In the first process, the community or the nation gets further divided while no answers are found. In the second, the community is strengthened in a cooperative effort, and positive progress is more likely to be made.

In other words, the best way to begin solving a problem is to start by doing something. It's a simple notion, so simple it often escapes us. In the process of involvement, not only will likely solutions begin to emerge, but everybody involved may be changed by better understanding what is really going on. This more helpful process is starting to occur as more people choose to address problems in their communities by getting involved in them.

Integrity is also something that seems to be found in personal involvement, even if you're unsure how to proceed. I think the American people are more and more tired of people who profess to be experts on so many problems but have had little personal involvement in trying to solve them. Talk is cheap, as they say. Taking action doesn't provide panaceas, but at least it wins respect for actually trying to do something. Is it any wonder that Jimmy Carter is much more respected as former president than he ever was as president? When you ask people why, they don't speak of the impressive Carter Center in Atlanta; rather they conjure up the image of the former president pounding nails into a new house for a poor family on a Habitat for Humanity work project. And Mr. Carter is a serious builder, too, not a politician looking for a good photo op while painting over graffiti for thirty minutes in front of the network news cameras. I've been on one of the Habitat sites with Carter and seen how he doesn't tolerate idle conversation when there are houses to finish!

We have to dispel the myth that you really have to know what you're doing before you start doing it. Just accept the fact that you're going to make some mistakes. Everybody does. But that's the way we learn. The Sojourners Neighborhood Center didn't begin as a successful freedom school. We started, twenty-five years ago, by tutoring children who ended up on our front steps. We did it in our living rooms. None of us was an experienced tutor, but we'd all been to school. Training is vitally important, and we've done a lot of it over the years. But you've still got to start somewhere, and you'll never get the experience until you just begin.

We started *Sojourners* magazine much the same way. We were all seminary students who became powerfully moved by the idea that faith should show itself in action and that spirituality was vitally connected to politics. We had a message and needed a vehicle. Someone suggested that we start a magazine. None of us had ever done that before, but we were young and bold enough to think that we could learn. So without any journalistic experience, we launched a new publication. Our first mailing list came from a brainstorming session one night, and our first distribution strategy was one car heading east and one west with a new magazine hot off the press.

I've always likened publishing *Sojourners* to running a flag up a flagpole. Many other people at the time were also wanting to put their faith together with a commitment to social action. But they didn't know one another; they couldn't see one another on the ground. But when they saw that flag raised in the form of a new magazine, they headed to the flagpole, where they all met. That was the beginning of a constituency, a network, and a movement for faith in action that has grown until this day. And it all began with lifting a banner high enough for people to see it.

That's how change often happens, in a community or in a nation. Someone has to lift up a banner, and other people stream to it. Change often requires a catalyst, an occasion, an event, or a new initiative. Someone has to start something, and others will become involved. You may be the one to lift the banner, or you may be one of the crucial people to join in and help hold it up. At the beginning, you never feel ready, and you hardly ever know what you're doing. But you begin anyway, because change has to start somewhere.

Back Home

One night, my father was out at a church elders meeting when I called, so my mom and I had even longer to talk. She was reflecting on what a "good and exciting life" she and my father had been able to have. I asked her what were the most exciting parts. Of course, she lovingly named her children, their marriages, and her grandchildren. She was especially excited about the first child my wife and I were expecting. She spoke about the work of their church and all their friends. But what was most exciting to her was the mission work they had been able to do since they had retired. She ended up talking about that for at least the next hour.

During the years just before the fall of the Berlin Wall, my parents had volunteered with a missionary group that supported and assisted struggling Christians in several Eastern European countries. Communist regimes were very tough on religious believers, who faced isolation, discrimination, and even persecution for their faith. The group my parents joined worked to provide food, medicine, books, Bibles, information, communication, and Christian fellowship to the beleaguered Christians, often clandestinely.

As an older retired couple, looking like tourists in their minivan, my parents were the perfect ones to make the runs of contraband into tightly controlled East bloc countries. My parents! I could hardly contain my chuckles over the phone as my mother told me how she and my father would drive into a deserted Bulgarian forest to retrieve the illegal materials from the false panels of a minivan or the fake propane tank in the trunk of a car. My mom told me how my dad would sit in the driver's seat while she would lock herself inside the dark trunk and, with a flashlight, reach inside a fake propane gas tank to pull out dozens of books, papers, rations, and computer disks! "My arms are smaller than his," she explained. Then they would attempt to make contact (with passwords) with Christians they had never met in the massive gray apartment complexes of East European cities—bringing them critical and sustaining materials, hugs, and hope. "It was such a privilege to meet people who have sacrificed so much for their faith," she said. "Even though we didn't speak the same language, we always found ways to communicate." Though they had lived long, rich, and busy lives, my folks felt these were the most exciting times they ever had.

She knew I could easily understand that. My own pilgrimage had taken me from the inner city of Detroit to urban and rural terrains all across America, to Nicaraguan villages, Filipino barrios, South African townships, and Middle East refugee camps. My parents watched as their children, armed with the values they had taught us, ventured out of the house to places they never imagined we would go. Then, when they had the chance, they did it too, in their own way. We were blessed with a wonderful home, but all of us realized that sometimes you've got to get out of the house.

CHAPTER THREE

Use Your Gift

*There are varieties of gifts,
but the same Spirit. (I Corinthians 12:4)*

I'M AN OCCASIONAL LISTENER to a very popular National Public Radio show called *Car Talk*, with which I'm sure many readers are familiar. The call-in program is ostensibly about problems with your car, but it's the humor of the two brother mechanics who cohost the show that keeps most of us tuned in. When I'm home on a weekend, my Saturday-morning routine often has me in the shower with *Car Talk* turned up very loud.

On one such Saturday, I was showering, still half asleep, when I heard one of the *Click and Clack* brothers intone, "Never criticize a man until you have walked for a mile in his shoes." A long pause followed. Then he continued, "Because then, when you criticize him, you will be a mile away...and you'll have his shoes!" I remember laughing out loud under the shower spray. They had woken me up. I couldn't believe at first that he was actually repeating such an old tired slogan. But then he gave it a little twist, turned it into something funny, unexpected, and even provocative. They were being creative.

That's what we have to be—creative. When it comes to doing something about poverty, for example, we've got to move beyond the old tired slogans. We've got to stop talking about the underprivileged people who need some help from those of us who are better off. In the midst of busy lives and schedules, the more affluent are made to feel guilty enough to write a check or maybe even donate a little time. It's a small price to pay for a clear conscience. And all we're talking about is donating cans of food or helping a church or charity with a special Thanksgiving or Christmas dinner. The more serious ongoing work of dealing with poor people is left to the professionals, perhaps social workers or clergy. Worst of all, many people, while supporting cuts in public programs and taxes, still expect the government to "take care of" poor people.

All that needs to change and, thankfully, is beginning to. Consider this dramatic scene.

The Altar Call

The church hall was full of ordinary people from a middle-sized town in the Pacific Northwest. The subject was youth violence, which had become an increasing and frightening reality in the community. Some enterprising pastors and youth workers had assembled a wide collection of young people from the streets, representing gangs from virtually every race and ethnicity in the city, both male and female. The kids were quite a sight, sitting up in the front, being scrutinized by the respectable citizens of the community. Attired in backwards baseball caps, bandannas, and baggy pants, and with their body pierces and tattoos, they told their stories.

The young men and women were reluctant at first, but soon began to share their personal sagas of how they had fallen through the cracks and ended up on the street. The stories were very moving, and as is often the case, the personal and even intimate sharing began to break down the barriers of fear and distrust. The concerned but initially wary citizens began to understand how lost and lonely kids get lured into gangs and into trouble. Slowly they began to see these kids as "our children" and not just as "gang members."

But what happened next was truly remarkable. Somebody asked what they could do. One of the kids said, "I dunno, man, maybe you could figure out what you do best and just use it." Before long,

I was witnessing something akin to an old-fashioned altar call. A
college dean stood up and offered to take these young people on a
tour of his campus, and if they were willing to really work hard, he
would work on arranging the necessary scholarships. A downtown
pastor said he would open up his church after school and at night,
when the kids had said they had no safe places to go. A county
drug-enforcement officer asked if some of the kids might give him
advice about how to be most effective, and a cop said he would like
to get their help too. Several business leaders had jobs they wanted
to talk to the young people about. Even the media people who were
there said they would like to help get these kids' stories out to the
general public.

But my favorite was a middle-aged woman who stood up and
said, "I'm not the dean of any college, the pastor of a church, or
the president of a company, but I've got something to offer too.
I work at the McDonald's downtown and get a morning and afternoon break. Lots of you kids said you've got nobody to talk to.
Well, now you know where to find me, and I'll even buy you a cup
of coffee." I liked her offer the best because she understood an
especially important principle: Offering whatever you have and
whatever you are is enough. Too many people don't believe that,
so they don't get involved. Because we can't do what we think
would really make a big difference, we don't offer our own gift—
whatever that is.

Unlike many church and charitable organizations today, Jesus
taught his disciples not to value the biggest and most important
gifts, but rather those that are most sacrificial. One day while Jesus
was teaching in the Jewish temple, he sat down opposite the place
where people made their offerings and watched the crowd putting
money into the treasury. Many rich people put in large sums. Then
a poor widow came and put in two small copper coins, which were
worth about a penny. He called his disciples and said to them,
"Truly I tell you, this poor widow has put in more than all those
who are contributing to the treasury. For all of them have contributed out of their abundance; but she out of her poverty has put
in everything she had, all she had to live on" (Mark 12:43–44).

Be Creative

What I was seeing in the Pacific Northwest was not just concern, but *creativity* in action. Finding your own contribution takes creativity and, not surprisingly, your best contribution always comes out of what is most creative for you. Do what you do best, but do it in a way that makes a difference. How could your best gift be applied in new and creative ways to make real social change possible?

Creativity can be risky. Getting out of the house takes some courage, but getting involved will begin to test you. It may change your view of the world and your perceptions of who you are and what you can do. You'll learn to assess what you can offer, and even what you can handle. The important thing is just to start somewhere. Be creative and find someplace to make an investment of time and commitment, and the next steps will naturally follow. Even if it seems awkward at first, your creative personal involvement will help show you the way forward.

I talk to business people and bank presidents about helping former gang leaders start micro-enterprise businesses. I hear how busy professionals build time at a community food bank or homeless shelter into their family schedules. I listen to successful editors who look forward to their writing class each week with a group of urban youths. I've watched doctors set aside lucrative careers to set up clinics for at-risk kids. There's no substitute for personal involvement. No matter where you're starting, there is something you can do that will lead you to what might come next. People just like you are getting involved in mentoring, tutoring, or a myriad of volunteer efforts, and it is changing their lives.

Creativity must be applied in broad terms here. Whenever you really give of yourself, that's creativity in action. When you enjoy doing something so much you almost lose yourself in it—that's creativity and that's what will fulfill you. It's what you were made to be and do, and when you find it, nothing is more satisfying. It's not just ego to find your best gift; it's acting with creativity and integrity. Finally, it is acting in faith.

How do we harness that creativity to change our communities while at the same time fulfilling our souls? To be made in the image of God is to be creative. And to be fully human is to connect the image of God in you to that image in others—across all the dividing lines. Creativity might be more than volunteering in a soup kitchen, though that is always a good place to start. Stories of people from all walks of life who are finding their best contribution show the wide possibilities of creativity.

Some of My Friends

I want to give you examples from people around me—friends, coworkers, people in many walks of life—who have decided to be creative with the things that they do best.

My doctor is a woman named Janelle Goetcheus. Janelle was a successful doctor in the Midwest with a lucrative career. But something kept tugging at her soul. Janelle was feeling compelled to do something more important with her medical skills, something more consistent with her faith. In response to a clear sense of "call," as Janelle puts it, she and her whole family moved from Ohio to Washington, D.C., to join the Church of the Saviour, which, they heard, wanted to begin a medical ministry focused on poor and underserved people in the nation's capital. Dr. Goetcheus first opened the Columbia Road Health Services for recent immigrants from Central America, many of them without legal status in the United States. Soon the waiting room was filled with mothers and kids who couldn't speak English and had virtually nowhere else to go for medical care.

Shortly after that came Christ House, a medical facility for the homeless sick. Not allowed to stay in most hospitals but too sick to live on the streets, homeless men and women found a safe haven that was compassionate, personal, competent, and even cost effective (the cost for a person at Christ House is $47.00 per day, while the cost of the same services in the D.C. hospital system is almost $700.00). Janelle has helped to establish and staff several other clinics around the city and often can be found in the Health Care for the Homeless van that brings medical services to homeless people on the street who can't or won't go to a clinic. Other spinoffs followed, such as Joseph's House, a place to care for those living with AIDS.

Even beyond the countless numbers of poor people served by her clinics, Dr. Janelle Goetcheus has become the medical conscience of Washington, D.C. Public health officials, city council budget-cutters, and neglectful federal officials overseeing the District of Columbia have all felt the power of her soft-spoken but persistent advocacy of the health needs and rights of the poorest of the poor. Other doctors, all over the city, have lined up to offer their specializations to treat "Janelle's patients." And a new generation of young doctors has been inspired and trained by this woman who heard a call.

When my wife and I needed a doctor for our first pregnancy, Janelle suggested Dr. Mark Hathaway, a young man who had just finished his residency. We found him in our local neighborhood clinic, which treats very low-income people almost exclusively. When I asked this bright young doctor why he chose to work there instead of at a modern hospital, Dr. Hathaway replied, "I really like working with the people here, and I enjoy being a part of their lives." He also said he had been inspired by Dr. Janelle Goetcheus. She's one woman who has been able to make a real difference in health care for the poor throughout an entire city.

Henry Freeman is a fund-raiser, and a very good one. He raised millions of dollars for the University of Michigan as its vice president for development. But his Quaker social conscience prompted some changes, and soon he was raising millions of dollars for Earlham College, a small Quaker school in Indiana. Then what was happening in Central America began to trouble him. So he joined a group of people taking a trip to El Salvador to find out what was going on. I've described the impact of such journeys before. The trip changed Henry Freeman. More trips to El Salvador pricked his conscience as he met children in rural villages who would never have the chance to go to school. Henry decided to try to change that by doing what he does best—raising money. At last count, he had successfully put 150 Salvadoran children through school, and the first ones are already graduating from college. Many are now going back to their communities to help make a difference for their families and neighbors.

One day Henry got a package in the mail. In it was a large piece of paper with the fingerprints of many of the children he had put through school. It was their thank-you to this North American man who had made such a difference in their lives. The tears in the savvy fund-raiser's eyes indicated which part of his work was closest to his heart. It wasn't long before Henry was devoting all of his time to consulting on projects that he thought were making a real difference for social justice. *Sojourners* magazine was Henry's first consulting project, and he has really helped us. I've watched how effective a very skilled person can be when he applies his creative best to something he truly believes in.

And speaking of magazines, the story of our art director is another good one. Ed Spivey was surprised when a *Wall Street Journal* staff person told him that he had gotten the best job straight out of college among all 1971 journalism graduates. Starting as art director for the Chicago *Sun-Times* Sunday magazine was a big job for a kid from Vincennes, Indiana. I met Ed shortly after he moved to Chicago, when he began to attend events where I was speaking and came around to visit the little community we were starting on Chicago's North Side. When our fledgling publication finally needed a real art director, I invited Ed over for dinner, hoping to get some advice and maybe some volunteer time on evenings and weekends. But Ed surprised all of us when he said he was ready to quit his job and join us. I remember hearing that the *Sun-Times* managing editor took Ed out for lunch to try to dissuade him from "throwing away your career." But Ed persisted in his new calling, and he's been with *Sojourners* ever since, winning many awards for his designs and layouts.

So many innovative projects are underfunded, especially at first, and really depend on the commitments of people willing to offer their gifts and creativity to the enterprise at below market value. Ed's done work for scores of organizations and projects that he believes in, knowing that a message will get through much more effectively if it is well presented graphically and appeals to the senses as well as the sensibilities. Ed told me he would be embarrassed to be mentioned in the same chapter as people like Janelle

Goetcheus because he believes himself to be a very ordinary person who has just learned the skills of graphic design. But that's exactly why he does belong here. The world, or your part of it, will not be changed by a few highly talented professionals turning their successful careers in the direction of community service. Rather, our world will be transformed only when enough ordinary people decide to live by their best values and beliefs.

Dave Marsh is a carpenter who is also good at electrical and plumbing jobs. He and his father, Byron, did most of the renovation of the Sojourners Neighborhood Center, transforming an abandoned drug house into a beehive of activity and a beacon of hope for the children in one of Washington's most dangerous neighborhoods. They both seemed tireless in their efforts and were determined to finish the job, often on top of the other work they were doing. Dave and Byron were also wonderful to work with, showing great patience with our eager but not highly skilled volunteer workforce. We'd usually have to remind David and Byron to send us the bills for things, but oftentimes they would just sort of forget.

Dave has also often been my repairman, coming by after work to fix something that broke in the old row house where we live. Again, he often forgets to send the bill. When I press him on it, he tells me it's all a part of the ministry. On both his day job and his personal time, Dave Marsh has decided to put himself to work as a skilled craftsman committed to social justice.

Dave's day job is to supervise construction sites for Manna, a successful home-building project for low-income families in the District of Columbia. Manna exemplifies the best of the faith-based housing work going on across the country today. Manna has renovated or built more than five hundred units of housing for poor families in Washington, D.C., enabling many people to establish new beginnings for themselves and their children. Dave Marsh, John Swarr, Jim Dickerson, and all the others who make Manna possible have turned the practical skills of home building into a spiritual ministry. Millard Fuller, the founder of Habitat for Humanity, refers to such work as the "theology of the hammer." Through Habitat, one hundred thousand new units of housing have been constructed for low-income families in the United States and seventy-five countries around the world, providing more than five hundred thousand people with decent, affordable housing.

James Berge is my dentist. He and his wife have adopted several third world children. Once a year, Dr. Berge opens his office for Sojourners Dentist Day. For a pittance, all those who work at Sojourners Neighborhood Center or magazine get their teeth checked and cleaned. He also takes care of the teeth of any child who comes to the center for free. (Some of the kids say he reminds them of Mr. Rogers.) Dental care is something that many low-income children just don't get, so Dr. Berge's contributions are gratefully received. He says it's a privilege to help out. I think of Dr. Berge as a good example of the fact that we don't need everybody to help with our Thanksgiving community meal every year, but we do need Dr. Berge to be our dentist.

My favorite social policy analyst is John DiIulio. From an Italian working-class neighborhood in Philadelphia, John went to Harvard and graduated with a doctorate in political science. He was a tenured professor at Princeton at the age of twenty-eight. DiIulio has gone on to become a genuine public intellectual, directing major research centers, writing both popular and academic works on American government, crime, and social policy, and regularly contributing to scholarly journals, national magazines, and newspaper op-ed pages. But in the last few years, DiIulio's Catholic faith kicked in as his analysis of the real crisis facing urban kids deepened. He has given himself over to research, writing, and civic action on faith-based approaches to urban problems, "now my life's work," he says. DiIulio wasn't content with a successful career but rather chose to apply his particular gifts to a concrete social project: "Getting resources to people who are successfully working with the kids, and changing federal, state, and local government policies that will directly benefit those kids—that's my bottom line...that's it!"

DiIulio's support for urban black pastors in Boston, for example, was instrumental in gaining major national media coverage of their very hopeful efforts (including the lead feature in *The New Yorker* and the *Newsweek* cover story I mentioned earlier). Their successful efforts in dramatically reducing youth crime drew wide public attention to the promise of faith communities finding solutions to social problems all around the country. As an insider in the think-tank policy world, he has also used his influence with several foundations to secure major funding for efforts that would otherwise have struggled to get the resources they needed. John also volunteers at an inner-city school in Philadelphia, teaching street-level civics to urban kids. He's not only an intellectual but also a man who tries to practice what he preaches.

In January 2001, President George W. Bush appointed him director of a new White House Office on Faith-Based and Community Initiatives. John now has the opportunity to implement his belief in the promise of faith-based organizations.

You have to ask yourself what your goals really are. Do you just want to be successful, respected, and secure—perhaps prosperous or even famous—or do you also want to try to make a real difference? What do you most aspire to? Do you want to do something that will make a difference in the lives of people who need it most? "What are your best skills and gifts going to be used for in this world?" is another way of asking the question.

Those stories from my doctor, my fund-raiser, my art director, my repairman, my dentist, and my favorite policy analyst make the point. Discover what you do best, then do it in a way that makes a difference.

Sometimes taking the vocational skills you have developed and applying them to volunteer activities is a good way forward. Pulitzer Prize–winning *Washington Post* columnist Mary McGrory, for example, spends time each week teaching children how to read. Often, McGrory says, she just goes in and reads to children in school. All of us are busy, but few are busier than a successful national columnist and commentator. But at the national volunteer summit in Philadelphia, in April 1997, McGrory spoke movingly about the importance of her volunteer activity to the rest of her life and work. It is real, hands-on, practical, and personal. Sometimes you see the difference you are making; other times you learn how deep and complex the problems really are. But either way, you feel involved.

At our neighborhood center, we try to link every child or young person with adult mentors and role models who will help them find *their* creative gift. A group of young people will work with a poet on learning how to write poetry; the center has already published several wonderful volumes of poetry from the kids. If a young person thinks he or she might want to be an architect, we find an architect to serve as a mentor. Linda DeGraf, a local artist and teacher, helped the children to create their own mural, depicting the positive and hopeful things about our neighborhood. At first, the kids were convinced they couldn't do it—only real artists could do something like that. But she patiently showed them how to discover their potential. To their great surprise, the new young artists succeeded in producing a beautiful work of neighborhood art, a picture of which appeared on the front page of *The Washington Post's* District Weekly section.

Churches Can Be Creative Too

When the welfare bill passed in the fall of 1996, it sent everybody scrambling in states and communities around the country. The new law didn't really reform welfare; it just ended the old system—without any alternatives in place. Ever since, many people—from elected officials to service providers to local pastors—have been trying to figure out what to do. In the spring of 1997, I was invited to North Carolina to speak to pastors and lay church leaders on that subject. After relating the biblical imperatives to fight for poor families, I challenged the North Carolina churches to step forward. Be the leader here, I urged. Somebody has got to lead the way to make welfare reform really work. Someone has to show our society how to help families move out of poverty. The churches can't do it by themselves, I said, but they could play the leadership role as a catalyst, a convener, and a venue for finding some new solutions and building some new partnerships.

A year later, I was asked back. "We've been doing it," I was told by Diana Jones Wilson, the whirlwind of an organizer who invited me in the first place, "now it's time to talk about next steps." What I found in North Carolina was truly amazing. The churches had trained more than five thousand people to become involved in welfare-to-work efforts. Pastors were directly involved in the training, along with lay church members from all walks of life. Together they made plans for supporting people in the difficult journey from welfare and poverty to work and community. The churches were also taking a leading role in education and advocacy for state policy changes that would make a real difference to low-income people. In some counties, the church folks were now leading the state's welfare-to-work program. One day Diana called me. Her voice was calm, but I could tell she was excited about something. "I wanted to tell you what has happened as a result of the work we've done since you came two years ago," she said. She reported that the churches of North Carolina had just received a grant of $1.25 million from their state to support and expand their leadership in welfare reform.

In Raleigh, North Carolina, one of the most creative new programs has sprung up. The Jobs Partnership in Raleigh has organized one hundred churches to mentor former welfare recipients through a twelve-week training course that uses Bible study to teach workplace skills. In two years, three hundred program graduates have found jobs, and 95 percent still work for the first company that hired them. As program director Rev. Skip Long says, "All we've done is help them dream again."

In Holland, Michigan, a similar church-led program, the Samaritan Project, has established committees in local congregations to assist with transportation, child care, and job skills. With the churches in the lead, nearly every former welfare recipient in Ottawa County has found work. While Western Michigan has more and better jobs than some other parts of the country, the success of the effort is also due to the committed and creative leadership of many local congregations.

Riverside Church on New York City's Upper West Side has a long and distinguished history of social concern and action. For years it has implemented extensive social service programs out of its massive Gothic structure next to the Hudson River. But when the welfare bill of 1996 passed, the church mobilized as never before.

Under the leadership of its pastor, Dr. James Forbes, employers in the church began to provide jobs, volunteers helped prepare welfare recipients to get and keep work, groups organized to surround poor families with the support they needed to make the difficult transition, and many people got into the act of job training and preparedness. Jim Forbes's barber trained thirty welfare recipients to become barbers themselves! Almost any church, even those much smaller than Riverside, has lots of people with skills and creativity to share. It just has to be mobilized.

Rev. Kirbyjon Caldwell might have been a successful entrepreneur if he hadn't become a Methodist pastor. So he's combined both skills to create a powerful ministry of spiritual and economic development in Houston, Texas. Windsor Village St. John's United Methodist Church is providing an inspiring example of a church's ability to stimulate economic development in its community. Attendance in the church has grown from several hundred to ten thousand in less than a decade. Recently named as one of twenty-five national Congregational Resource Centers for the United Methodist Church's "Strengthening the Black Church for the Twenty-first Century" project, St. John's has been recognized for its vitality, growth, innovative worship style, and ministry focus. The church provides more than 120 ministry projects, including a community center, food pantry, drug- and substance-abuse counseling, support groups, a juvenile delinquency program, a housing initiative, and Patrice House, a twenty-four-hour nursery center. The church's efforts have also resulted in hundreds of jobs. And every time I see Kirbyjon, he has a new idea. He's become a prototype of the creative urban pastor.

People from almost every kind of work in the country are finding creative ways to shape their vocation in the direction of service and justice. It is possible. If nothing else, it is the children who cry out for our personal involvement. It's their vulnerability that calls us to start by doing something, not our own sense of readiness. Rabbi Hillel sums up our call to action well: "If I am not for myself, who will be? If I am only for myself, what am I? If not now, when?"

How to Slay a Giant

Community organizer Marshall Ganz tells a wonderful story from the biblical book of First Samuel, the story of David and Goliath. He uses this famous episode to illustrate the point I've been making about using your gift. Ganz recounts: "As you recall, Goliath comes forth from the Philistines to do battle with the Israelites. He is big, he is powerful, and he is a veteran of many wars. The Israelite soldiers are frightened. No one will volunteer to face him. At this point, David, a young shepherd, steps forth. 'I'll do it,' he says. The men laugh at him. He's but a shepherd, and a boy at that. But the spirit of the Lord has come into him. And pay attention to this. He doesn't know *how* he's going to do it before he volunteers to do it—no strategic plan for David.

"Well, he goes to see King Saul and King Saul laughs at him too. 'You're but a shepherd, but a boy.' 'Yes,' admits David, 'but I want to fight, I'm willing to fight, and no one else will do it anyway.' 'Well, all right,' agrees the king, 'but Goliath is an experienced warrior. Take my sword, my shield, and my helmet. Put these on. You'll need them to protect you.' Excited that he's been given the opportunity to fight, David puts them on, but as he gets them on he starts to feel uncomfortable. 'Wait a minute,' he thinks. 'I don't know how to use these things, I've "proved them not."' At that moment he glances at the small stream that is flowing by his feet and he sees five smooth stones there. And as he looks at the stones, he remembers, 'I'm not a warrior, but I am a shepherd. And as a shepherd I know how to protect my flock from the wolf and the lion—and it was with stones and a sling, not a sword and a shield. Maybe Goliath is just another wolf.' Well, you know the rest. He takes off the armor, picks up the stones, and, using his sling, defeats the mighty Goliath, surprised that a young shepherd boy should be the source of his undoing."

Ganz then reflects, "So what does this story teach us about strategy? Well, David comes up with a way in which resourcefulness makes up for what looked like a lack of resources. First of all, he doesn't have it all figured out before he acts. It's his commitment to act that puts him in a position where he really has to use his intelligence to figure out how to do it—he's motivated. What else? Where does he look for the answer? He considers using the tools of his powerful opponent to defeat him but thinks better of it. No, he reflects on his own experience, his own resources, and his own skills to find a means of defeating Goliath. And he finds the means when he recontextualizes the arena in which he finds himself—seeing it no longer as field of battle on which two soldiers will face each other, but as a pasture in which a shepherd confronts a wolf. He was an outsider to the battle. And as an outsider he saw resources others did not see, opportunities others did not see, and so devised a strategy which others did not devise—to Goliath's great surprise. Let us all learn to be David. Let us be faithful enough to trust our own spirit where others do not trust theirs, wise enough to draw on our own experience to see where others do not see, and courageous enough to act on what we do see where others cannot act."

David was a shepherd who knew how to protect sheep, and he defeated the feared Goliath by remembering who he was and using his own gifts. We are always tempted to defer to other people's experience and perspective instead of trusting our own. Instead, we need to find the courage to act upon what we see, not what others do.

Anyone Can Do This

One of the more interesting speaking requests I received recently was an invitation from inmates at the Sing Sing prison, just north of New York City. An innovative program at Sing Sing, run by the New York Theological Seminary, provides theological training behind the prison walls and is the only effort of its kind in the country. In a very rigorous course of study, the inmates examine theology, church history, and biblical studies in preparation for future ministry both inside and outside of prison. Many of these students also teach their fellow inmates in Sing Sing's college-equivalency program, there being no one else willing to do it after the federally sponsored college programs for prison inmates were cut, despite their enormously successful track record.

Students from both programs had studied my book *The Soul of Politics* and now were inviting the author to come and talk with them about it. When we asked about scheduling, they replied that they were a relatively "captive" audience and were "free" most nights of the week.

It was well worth the trip. Seventy men crowded into the room, and our discussion went on for three hours. Its intensity rivaled anything I had ever experienced at Harvard or other universities. More than three years after writing the book, they knew it better than I did. We scrutinized idea after idea, concept after concept, always asking how it might be applied on the street. Their clear motivation was to go back to the street, back to the community, with what they had learned. They were determined to influence young men to make different choices than they had. These inmates had, in fact, become experts in many of the social problems that plague our communities. They knew the realities firsthand and talked movingly about their lives and their experience.

Some knew they would never leave prison but had decided to dedicate themselves to ministering to fellow prisoners, helping their brothers turn their lives around. But others longed for the day when they would go home. Instead of escaping the realities from which they had come, most wanted to return to those places in order to change them. Most of the prisoners at Sing Sing, the inmates told me, have come from only about four New York City neighborhoods, in the poorest parts of the city. One man spoke movingly about "the train" that leaves from neighborhoods like his, loading on boys as young as nine or ten, and heading for the eventual destination of Sing Sing. How do we stop that train, he asked?

I was impressed. There were no doctors, bankers, or politicians here. These were almost entirely men who had started near the bottom of their society and ended up in prison, the very bottom. To succumb to bitterness, cynicism, or hopelessness here is very easy. Yet these men hadn't. Instead they had decided to take their gift— their experience—and use it to help change younger men's lives before it was too late. That's not only creative, it's courageous— two strengths our society desperately needs.

One of the Sing Sing theologians made a comment that stayed with me long after I left the prison yard. He was sharing his experiences of poverty, crime, and prison. He said he had clearly been on a downward spiral going to no place good. But then "a light came on," and he could see the trajectory of his life and where it was headed. That was when he decided to change his direction. Many of us are on a trajectory with our lives going nowhere good. We may not be headed to prison, except prisons of our own making. But we may also be missing a life direction that could result in accomplishments of lasting value or fulfill the deepest longings of our souls. We too need a light to come on.

We need many lights to come on if we are to overcome the poverty that grips our nation's soul. That will happen when all of us have the courage and the creativity to find our own best contribution. And as our brothers at Sing Sing remind us, it is never too late to find our gift.

Deepen Your Understanding

CHAPTER FOUR

Do the Work and You'll Find the Spirit

If you offer your food to the hungry and satisfy the needs of the afflicted, then your light shall rise in the darkness and your gloom be like the noonday. (Isaiah 58:10)

SPIRITUAL RENEWAL will supply the energy for justice. Faith and spirituality could become the most powerful forces for social justice in the beginning of a new millennium. That would seem, to many, a bold and even unbelievable statement, given the common perceptions of religion today and the inward preoccupation of so much contemporary spirituality. During much of the twentieth century, religion was regarded as a mostly private affair and, at its worst, was a reactionary influence. With the great exception of the black churches, religion in twentieth-century America has not been a great force for justice. Likewise, much of the resurgence of spirituality we've seen over the last several years has been successfully commercialized into mere self-help. Nonetheless, many factors now point to the probability that spirituality and faith will return to the dynamic social role they have often played before. The spiritual power of faith to change history is being rediscovered.

    I believe in the linkage of faith and justice in part because of my own story, which I told in chapter one. Now, as a new millennium is beginning, many religious people are being drawn into the struggle for social change, having seen and felt the limits of purely private religion. At the same time, many people outside of religion are hungry for the power and promise of spirituality.

Social movements need a combination of spirituality and practical goals. That's a lesson I've learned over many years. The civil rights movement evidenced a powerful spirituality. But it also held out the promise of freedom for black Americans, a tremendous motivating force. And it promised white allies the possibility of healing an uneasy conscience and fulfilling the ideals of the American dream. Dr. King used to say that he held his Bible in one hand and the American Constitution in the other. The most successful movements must offer people the chance to better their lives and fulfill their deepest moral convictions and aspirations.

Robert Putnam, in a much-discussed article titled "Bowling Alone," set off alarms about declining civic participation in American life. I participated in a three-year discussion, led by Putnam, which focused on how to rekindle civic engagement in America today. A very diverse group of scholars, journalists, elected officials, business people, artists, pastors, political analysts, and grassroots activists examined many areas of American life, searching for the things that create "social capital." One conclusion many of us drew from the Saguaro Seminar was that it takes more than activities to create positive social engagement; it requires a spirituality of social responsibility, by which I mean a reason for action that transcends ourselves. We can simply be critical of all the individualism and self-help energy in the Western world that focuses so much on ourselves, or we can try to link the desire for personal fulfillment with social responsibility by drawing on the ancient wisdom of Isaiah, which, as I'll explain, provides a powerful spirituality for social engagement.

Isaiah's wisdom suggests that it is really impossible to separate the desire for personal growth from the call for social responsibility. You may succeed in getting physically fit, but your 10 K run may take you past so many homeless people that you can't keep averting your eyes. If you achieve financial success, you'll discover that pollution, violence, and cultural decay don't stop at your carefully wired door alarms and security fences. Meditation may give you peace of mind, but it won't protect your family from unforeseen possibilities, like corporate downsizing. And your quality of life can be dramatically affected by social problems such as youth crime, racial hostility, economic dislocation, and the collapse of cultural values, or by overseas conflicts that don't get resolved by peaceful means.

No matter how much we try to love and guard our children, we can't ultimately shield them from what's going on all around them. If we are fortunate enough to raise our kids well, how will they react to kids who never had a "safe, fair, healthy, or moral start," to quote the priorities of Marian Wright Edelman's Children's Defense Fund? How do we explain to our children why people of different skin colors often don't live in the same neighborhoods or worship together in America? What if our kids ask us about the third world children whose exploited labor makes our family's clothes and prevents them from playing as our children do? And even if we manage to prepare for our children's education, foreign policy can send our young sons and daughters off to a dangerous war zone.

The health and well-being of our souls is of utmost importance. Can they ever be independent of the health of the world or the well-being of our neighbor? All our religious traditions say they cannot. Spiritual principles teach us that the best things we do for others are also the best things we do for ourselves, and that we are connected to one another whether we like it or not. Real security, faith reminds us, is found through widening and deepening our circle of community, rather than finding our own individual solutions.

Young people are discovering this wisdom. Frequently I speak on college campuses and find students signing up for service projects in unprecedented numbers. As I travel across the country, I find middle-class young people volunteering much more time than is needed to balance their résumés. Thousands of students are venturing beyond campus walls to spend hours each week with poor children, are giving up beer-drinking vacations in the sun to do work projects on their spring breaks, and are taking a year or two after college to plunge into tough urban neighborhoods and daunting overseas programs.

Isaiah's Wisdom: Connection and Meaning

I ask students why they are doing these things, frequently at genuine sacrifice and even real risk to themselves. It's sometimes hard for them to put their answers into words, but they always end up saying that the time they spend with an inner-city kid or working with a poor family on their new house makes *them* feel so much better—they feel better about their lives, their faith, their future, and their world. The most common words I hear are "connection" and "meaning." They talk about the connection they feel to people they hadn't felt connected to before. The connection brings healing and gives their life a sense of meaning and purpose.

The biblical prophet Isaiah understood this many centuries ago. In the Book of Isaiah, Chapter 58, the prophet describes what the Lord requires "to loose the bonds of injustice, to undo the thongs of the yoke, to let the oppressed go free, and to break every yoke." The prophet's call for direct personal involvement is as contemporary as if it were written yesterday: "Is it not to share your bread with the hungry, and to bring the homeless poor into your house, when you see the naked to cover them, and not to hide yourself from your own kin? Then your light shall break forth like the dawn, and *your* healing shall spring up speedily" (my italics). *Your* healing is at stake here, says Isaiah, not just *theirs*—the poor. Isaiah made a profound point that is often lost in self-help America today: the path to genuine healing and self-fulfillment is the journey that connects us to other people, and especially to poor and marginalized people.

Conventional wisdom expresses exactly the opposite. How often have you heard people say something like this: "I would like to get involved in some kind of service, but first I have to get my own life together." Isaiah is saying (and the college students are finding) that the best way to get your life together is to do something for somebody else—then will your light "break forth" and your own healing "spring up speedily." In fact, to focus only upon yourself and your own needs could prove to be a great obstacle to real satisfaction.

In other words, if you just work on getting your own life together you may never succeed in doing so. There are always enough things going on in our lives to absorb all of our attention and time. That may be the very trap that prevents us from really getting our lives in order. Contrary to what self-help logic implies, it is only the personal commitment to move beyond ourselves and the narrow confines of our own little worlds that can bring us the human fulfillment for which we hunger.

Isaiah's description of such human fulfillment is enough to excite the appetite of any self-help enthusiast: "If you offer your food to the hungry and satisfy the needs of the afflicted, then your light shall rise in the darkness and your gloom be like the noonday. The Lord will guide you continually, and satisfy your needs in parched places, and make your bones strong; and you shall be like a watered garden, like a spring of water, whose waters never fail. Your ancient ruins shall be rebuilt; you shall raise up the foundations of many generations; you shall be called the repairer of the breach, the restorer of streets to live in."

Isaiah's image of both personal and social healing is one of the most powerful in all spiritual literature. The connection between the two is crucial. Here is the bridge between self-help and social action so many in our society are looking to find. The link between personal growth and social responsibility is a spiritual one. How we long to be nurtured like a watered garden or to have our streets restored as good and safe places. And Isaiah was speaking to a people, not just to individuals. "If" you do these things, says Isaiah, "then" you will reap this harvest of healing. If you act in justice, you will know the healing that comes from reconnection. But you can't have one without the other.

It's inspiring to see what happens at our neighborhood center between an eight-year-old girl and a nineteen-year-old college sophomore from nearby Howard University who is helping her work on reading. The youngster thinks, "She's a black woman, just like I am going to be. She's smart and she's in college. She likes me, I can tell. And she thinks I'm smart, too. She thinks I could go to college. Maybe I will!" In the meantime, the Howard student is watching that child and thinking to herself, "This kid is changing my life. The best two hours of my week are the time I spend with her. That's when I feel like I'm making some difference in the world and my own life means something. We're making a connection here. I can't go back to my studies and career track to money and success as if nothing has happened to me. I want to do something with my life that makes a difference in the lives of kids like her!" That is what Isaiah is talking about.

It is not someone doing something "for" someone else. That's key. There's a relationship here that is changing *both* people. This crucial dynamic of transformation must be expanded to the broadest level if real social change is going to occur. But this isn't just limited to students and young people. The key is getting people of all ages and from all sectors of the society involved in offering their best gifts where they are most needed.

I remember one Sunday morning, preaching at Rising Hope Church, newly founded by Keary Kincannon, a former member of our Sojourners Community. He had become a Methodist pastor and had started a new congregation in Virginia, mostly for low-income people. They hold a wonderful service—friendly, warm, and open enough to attract poor people, among them several homeless people. I preached from the text of Isaiah 58, about how reaching out to others can help to heal your own soul. In the discussion time that always follows the sermon at Rising Hope, a member of the congregation shot his hand up and testified, "That's exactly what happened to me!"

His name was Chuck, and he proceeded to tell his story. "After my wife died, I got very depressed. I missed her so much, and life just didn't seem very good to me anymore. But I was coming to church, and that's when I met Wanda over there. She was homeless then and didn't have any place to live. I had space and decided I could take her in. Now I'm too busy to be depressed anymore! It's really working well."

All alone with no money or job, Wanda was living in shelters. But one day in church, a kindly older man said he had a spare room if she needed it. Chuck's house became a place to stay while Wanda got her life together. And that's exactly what she was now doing. "If you take the homeless into your house," said Chuck, paraphrasing

Isaiah, "then you'll get healed!" Isaiah was right, Chuck testified. "That's just what happened to me!"

Pursuing the common good *is* essential to our individual well-being. Healthy communities *are* critical to healthy families. The surrounding cultural values *do* have a major impact on the personal choices of our children. The quality of our political debate can serve or destroy the integrity of the public square, which affects our private lives in all kinds of ways. In all these things, the public and private are deeply connected. Breakdowns in families and communities will affect the larger body politic and, conversely, when the body politics is ill, the virus can infect us all. Human society is like a great piece of fabric; when the unraveling begins in one part of it, the tear threatens to undo the whole cloth.

Isaiah speaks to the point when he challenges those who simply engage in "the pointing of the finger, the speaking of evil." Rather, he says, "offer your food to the hungry, and satisfy the needs of the afflicted." In other words, stop all your blaming and posturing and instead do something concrete to make a difference and do some good. Isaiah directly enters the political arena when speaking of "repairing the breach" and "restoring of streets to dwell in." He directly poses the challenge of seeking the common good over partisan self-interest.

Are there not lessons to be learned in cooling youth violence, reducing teen pregnancy, overcoming addictions, ending homelessness, giving children a good start, helping welfare recipients succeed in work, or creating more equitable institutions? I think there are. But it all comes back to Isaiah's vital connection between personal well-being and social justice.

Islands of Hope

Those who say the world cannot be changed are mistaken. At a dinner I attended with several former members of Congress, governors, and mayors, a statement was made: "Nobody has answers anymore in America." I disagreed. I invited the politicians to name the social problems they were most concerned about, and then gave them the names of people and projects that are finding solutions to each one (sometimes naming efforts in their own states and cities). They were amazed to learn that answers to some of our most difficult problems are already out there.

I suggested these efforts were like islands in a vast and threatening sea. If you can swim to an island, you will probably be all right. But if you can't get there, or don't even know in which direction to swim, you will be in real trouble. Today, our islands are still too few and far between, but they are out there. Our task must be to connect the islands, create the resources to greatly expand their territory, and, finally, take what we can learn from the islands to forge new social policy. But first, we have to get the word out that changing our communities is *not* an impossible task.

How do we change the world, or at least our corner of it? That's the big question, isn't it? Sure, we can all improve ourselves; literally thousands of books have been written to help us succeed in changing our individual lives. But changing the world, by starting with where we live—now that's a different story.

I don't mean changing everything, especially all at once, or in a way that will last forever. No, we don't need any more utopian visions. Those have led to some of our worst problems. But we do need change, and most of us feel it. We need change in our neighborhoods, our schools, our congregations, our workplaces, our cities, our country, and, certainly, around our world. We don't need things to be perfect (they never will be); we do need a world that's more fair, more safe, more honest, and more just.

I'm appealing to the growing moral energy in the country for service, both in individuals and in families. And I'm especially hoping to engage a whole generation of young people, who are searching for meaning and connection.

The time is ripe to build a new spiritual movement for and with poor people. But such a movement must make the Isaiah connection between personal renewal and social change. If you do the work, you'll find the spirit.

CHAPTER FIVE

Recognize the Three Faces of Poverty

Blessed are you who are poor. (Luke 6:20)
One does not live by bread alone. (Matthew 4:4)
Then you will know the truth and the truth will make you free.
(John 8:32)

I'VE BEEN WORKING to overcome poverty for three decades now and have learned some things about it along the way. The first is that we still don't understand poverty very well. Many middle-class people seem to want to underestimate or minimize the problem of *material poverty*. Or we want to blame poor people themselves for their predicament. The systemic causes of poverty and the moral indifference of the affluent are not popular subjects in mainstream America. But at a deeper level, a materialistic society fails to recognize its own *spiritual poverty*. The fact that all our anxious striving has impoverished the soul of America is a spiritual reality that we are still not quite ready to face; yet, at some deep level, most of us know it is true. One of the ways I've changed is that I now take our spiritual poverty much more seriously than I used to. In battling to get the richest nation on earth to address its own widespread poverty and the appalling gaps between our lifestyle and that of much of the rest of the world, I often underestimated the spiritual consequences of the nervous and shallow existence so many people in the West find themselves trapped in. I've also begun to see how our political life suffers from a deep and growing spiritual and moral impoverishment. The widespread cynicism, the alarming levels of political withdrawal, the increasing control by moneyed elites, and the coarsening of our public debate can best be understood as a kind of *civic poverty*.

Isaiah's wisdom, which we have just discussed, actually addresses all three faces of poverty. In making the connection between personal and social healing, the prophet suggests that there is more to poverty than just economics. And there is a strategy here. Reach out to the members of your community who are poor or forgotten, and you will find satisfaction for your soul and health for your society.

Isaiah is not alone. All our religious and spiritual traditions focus on how we treat materially poor and excluded people, and suggest that the state of poor people is a moral test for the health of any society. And those traditions point us beyond mere charity as a response, calling us more prophetically to the deeper solutions of social and economic justice.

Yet those same traditions also draw our attention to spiritual poverty, which can be experienced among people of any economic status and in fact is often concentrated among the more affluent who have allowed their attachment to things to become a kind of worship in itself. The result is lives without a deep sense of meaning or purpose—lives that feel empty.

And I have come to believe that the breakdown in our public life can also be understood as a form of poverty—civic poverty. The rapid decline of genuine citizen participation and meaningful political discourse is not just a problem for politics, but a moral and spiritual threat to the very essence of democracy.

So we must recognize the three faces of poverty. Recognizing all three poverties and their relatedness is key to overcoming them.

A Climate of Denial

It has become fashionable today to ignore the existence of poverty—or even to deny it. The overgeneralized assumption that we are in the midst of good economic times is consistently used as an excuse to underestimate poverty. And despite the wisdom of Isaiah, our connection to poor people grows more distant. *The New York Times Magazine* cover proclaims "The New American Consensus: Government of, by, and for the Comfortable." The suburbanization of America has had a tremendous impact, and the flight includes almost everyone who can afford it. Only 66 out of 435 House districts are now urban and, after the next census, only 55 will be. With so many new gated communities, issues of poverty are just not on the nation's radar screen.

In 1962, *The Other America*, by Michael Harrington, woke up post-1950s America to the existence of widespread deprivation in the world's wealthiest nation and was credited with sparking President Lyndon Johnson's War on Poverty program. While real gains were made in those early years and the decades that followed, the war on poverty was never won. And as the effectiveness of government social programs has come under increasing scrutiny in more recent years, the need to find solutions to the nation's persistent poverty has fallen off the political agenda. Republicans offer a legislative plan of lowering taxes and expanding individual freedom, while Democrats offer a list of programs to enhance the quality of life for the middle-class, mostly suburban voters, who turn out on election day. Aiming either at the stockbrokers or the soccer moms, neither political party has talked about poor and left-out people for a very long time.

Instead of challenging old approaches and finding new strategies for overcoming poverty, many consider it intellectually and morally respectable to say "the other America" doesn't exist anymore. The problems of tens of millions of people below the poverty line are just explained away. They go on and off welfare; they get lots of other benefits; there are plenty of jobs out there for those who want them; people who are poor usually have other problems beside poverty; economic disadvantage is caused by failures in people's behavior, not in their society. We've all heard and perhaps even believed some of these sensible-sounding half-truths. This widespread social attitude claims, "Sure, there are some poor people, but nothing can be done about that, and it's probably their own fault anyway." But such half-truths are used to avoid facing the whole truth.

Even ten years ago, you could not have gotten away with denying poverty. The change in climate came in the mid-1990s with the rise of both political conservatism and a booming economy. Some conservative moralists have been trying hard to associate poverty with a lack of virtue as its primary cause, despite the fact that the Bible says the exact opposite—that in a society with widespread poverty, it is the virtue of the rich that is suspect. In the popular culture, individual liberty is in, while the common good is out. Self-help, not social concern, is what fills the magazines and bookstores, and a myriad of commercial offerings are supplied to improve our own quality of life.

The Biblical Argument

The biblical argument flies in the face of this climate of denial. My own moment of real awakening on the question of poor people came in theological seminary. Several of my fellow students and I made a study of every mention of the poor in the Bible. We found several thousand verses on the subject. In the Hebrew Scriptures, it was the second most prominent theme, idolatry being the first, and the two were often related. In the New Testament, one out of every sixteen verses had to do with wealth and poverty. In the first three Gospels, the subject is in one out of every ten verses; in the Gospel of Luke, it is in one out of seven verses. We were utterly amazed! We became even more incredulous as we discussed our findings and realized that none of us had ever heard a sermon at any of our churches on the danger of riches and God's concern for the poor! Yet the Scriptures were filled with this theme from beginning to end. Why the silence?

That seminary experience gave me one of my most tried and true sermon illustrations. One of my seminary colleagues had taken a pair of scissors to an old Bible, and he proceeded to cut out every single reference to riches or the poor. It took him a very long time. When he finally was finished, the Prophets were decimated, the Psalms destroyed, the Gospels ripped to shreds, and the Epistles turned to tattered rags. The Bible was full of holes. He still has that old torn-up Bible; he's kept it all these years. I used to take it out with me to preach. I'd hold it high above church congregations and say, "Brothers and sisters, this is our American Bible! It's full of holes!"

The clarity of the Bible on the subject of wealth and poverty seldom comes up in America. You can imagine my surprise when I opened up *The Washington Post* one day and found an op-ed piece titled "Woe to You Who Are Rich." Fascinated, I quickly read the opening paragraph, which began, "Assume that you had never read the New Testament and were given a quiz with the following question: 'During His ministry, Christ spoke out most often about (a) the evils of homosexuality, (b) the merits of democracy, (c) family-friendly tax cuts or (d) the danger of riches.' It turns out that Christ said nothing about the first three and a lot about the last one. But you'd never know it based on the rhetoric of many modern-day Christians—particularly politically active ones." The article was by Peter Wehner, the policy director of Empower America, a conservative Republican organization. Wehner pointed out that the Bible is very clear on the issues of wealth and poverty. The article went on to quote large portions of Scripture to show how spiritually dangerous wealth is, according to Jesus and all the biblical writers, and how insistent the Scriptures are in demanding compassion and justice for the poor and oppressed. The clear implication was that America's affluence puts the nation in great spiritual danger, and our lack of concern for the poor is a sign of our moral failing.

U.S. Congressman Tony Hall has counted over twenty-five hundred biblical verses of direct teaching on the subjects of hunger and poverty, a fact that he shared with us at a preach-in for the poor that Call to Renewal held in the U.S. Congress in the wake of the welfare cuts. Hall, a Democrat from Ohio, had just returned from the Sudan and was exhausted from his forty-one-hour journey but nonetheless wanted to tell us what he had just seen. The congressman spoke quietly and movingly about his time in the Sudan, where he saw hundreds of women and children starving to death. This soft-spoken Christian layman apologized for not being a great preacher like those gathered that day; he went on to say, "When I see a situation like that, there are a couple of Scriptures that really mean something to me."

He reached inside his suit-coat pocket, pulled out a small Bible, and quietly read from Proverbs 14:31: "He who oppresses the poor shows contempt for their Maker, but whoever is kind to the needy honors God." Congressman Hall went on, "We do something for God by being with the poor, preaching for the poor, legislating for the poor. The most important thing I do in Congress is to do the best I can for poor people." I had never heard so much powerful preaching in a single day before, but the most striking moment of the preach-in came when this sorrowful and tired congressman reported that people were dying needlessly because we didn't care and reminded us that God does.

In the present climate, we may well need to make that kind of religious or spiritual argument against poverty. The self-interest argument alone may not be enough. For years, liberals argued that an investment in the poor is in our own self-interest and good for the economy, at least in the long run. But the booming economy hardly needs those at the bottom anymore. And if we just build more prisons, privatize them, and make them profitable by turning the inmate population into a virtual slave-labor force to service the bottom rungs of the economy (to clean our schools and offices at night), we may finally have found a solution for what to do with poor people. It may sound chilling, but that's close to what's happening now. With prison construction and the security industry as two of our fastest-growing economic sectors, the affluent will be well buffered against any contact with poor people, and the current political ethic will make it easier and easier to ignore them.

Clearly we need a theology of solidarity that will bring us together, as Isaiah was calling for. Somehow, the well-being of the poor must be seen to be key to a society's health and welfare. Connecting with one another must be seen as essential for the sake of our own souls. It must never be a matter of guilt, because guilt is a motivation with little staying power. It must become a matter of our mutual well-being, and even our healing. For the poorest among us, the issues are those of survival. For the middle, it's the fear, alienation, and loss of human values in a market-driven culture. Many Americans today fear economic failure and at the same time find economic success increasingly meaningless. As for our society, we see a culture about to give up on finding solutions to any of these problems.

We have to start by understanding poverty better. I've said we have to recognize that poverty has at least three faces. Let's look at each one.

Material Poverty

The first great poverty is *material*. It's what we normally think of when we hear the word "poverty." But we still don't understand it very well.

Perhaps the worst thing about material poverty is the exclusion and isolation of those who experience it. There has been so much attention paid these days to what is happening at the top of the economic order that it's easy to forget there is still a very real bottom end. At the bottom, far too many of our fellow citizens are simply excluded from the mainstream of American life, almost untouched by the booming economy. Among those at the bottom are almost *one in six* of our children, who never chose to be born on the outside.

My sister and brother-in-law live right around the corner from me in the inner city of Washington, D.C. Barb and Jim Tamialis have a wonderful habit of adopting children who need a home. The latest addition to our family is my nephew Marquis, who was one of the district's countless street children. Marquis, whose mother was a crack addict and whose father was nowhere to be found, spent the first decade of his life living in nine different situations. When he became friends with my nine-year-old-niece Anika, his mother was in the D.C. jail. The two kids quickly became best neighborhood buddies, but when Marquis's seventy-five-year-old foster mother from across the street had a stroke, it looked as if he would have to move again. Anika got very sad, and when Anika gets sad, we get mobilized. Surveying Marquis's limited options, Barb and Jim decided to add him to their family, as they had earlier done with Anika. Everyone was thrilled, especially Marquis.

On one of the first days in his new home, Marquis was in the laundry room chatting with Julie Polter, who lives in the upstairs flat, while she did her wash. "How long are you going to be here?" Marquis asked. "Well, I suppose until I finish my laundry," Julie said, smiling. "How long are you going to be here?" she playfully replied. Beaming from ear to ear, the new ten-year-old household member asserted confidently, "I will be staying for ten thousand years!"

For millions of children like Marquis, the most basic provisions of safety, security, shelter, food, education, nurture, love, care, and, especially, any hope for the future simply cannot be assumed. In 1999, 32.3 million people—11.8 percent of the U.S. population—fell below the official poverty line. For a married couple with two children, the poverty level in 1999 was an income of $17,029. Many poor families have far less—in fact, 39 percent of all poor families have incomes *under* 50 percent of the poverty level. In other words, 4.6 percent of America's families are trying to survive on less than $8,515 a year. This is a striking contrast with the median American family income of $40,816. Even more dismaying, one-sixth of all our children—remember, that means twelve million of them—live in poverty.

Such poverty figures are related strongly to race and to changes in the economy. Although less than half of America's poor are black and Latino, poverty rates for minorities are triple those for whites: 23.6 percent of all blacks and 22.8 percent of all Latinos are poor, while only 7.7 percent of whites are poor. Racial minorities are also far more likely to move into or stay in high-poverty areas, where social problems are most intense, because they lack other options. Furthermore, the four recessions between 1970 and 1985 had a disproportionate impact upon blacks, regardless of family structure. The jobless rate tripled both in two-parent families and in single-parent black families. And even as the economy has improved, the jobless rate for blacks is still twice that for whites. While there has been some real improvement in middle-class black economic life, 33 percent of black children remain poor.

All poor children have been left out and left behind. And their numbers are growing. Urban demographers and criminologists predict that a critical mass of such children will reach their adolescent years with virtually no stake in their society. And some economists are now predicting that such children, on their present course, could cost the society as much as $8 to $10 trillion in social services, crime, and prisons.

These marginalized people of all ages are the most vulnerable of God's children. They are, indeed, the focus of religious concern in the Torah, the New Testament, and the Koran. It is always the treatment of "the other" that is the test of faith. But why is that? Why are our religious traditions so strong in commanding us to care for the widow, the orphan, the stranger, the forgotten, and the poor? The weak, vulnerable, and excluded become the standard for what the rest of society really means by "community." Who is part of the family and who is not? Who's in and who's out? Who is "us" and who is "them"? Who finally gets to be included in our circle of concern?

Let's put this question another way. Do we regard poor people as citizens or don't we? And if our poorest children are also citizens, what obligations do we have toward them? One thing is now clear: When people are excluded, there will be consequences—both practically and spiritually. The fundamental questions before us as a society are, simply: will we include the people in the bottom 25 percent, and, more profoundly, how can including them help to bring all of us closer together?

The Widening Gap

Increasingly, our economic system is producing a society of extremes. Despite a record-breaking economy, the gap continues to grow between the top and bottom of our society. Virtually no one disputes that anymore. Even *Wall Street Journal* articles now agree with the familiar adage "The rich get richer and the poor get poorer." The people at the top have received the lion's share of the economic windfall from the economic boom; the middle, far less; and the bottom, almost none at all.

As the stock market's Dow Jones average has climbed past the 10,000 mark, 42 percent of the benefits have gone to the top 1 percent of households and 86 percent of the benefits to the top 10 percent of households. Almost 90 percent of all stocks and mutual funds owned by households are held by the richest 10 percent.

In the past two decades, the lowest fifth of U.S. households have seen their after-tax income decrease 1 percent, while the top fifth have seen theirs increase by more than half. The income of the top 1 percent has increased by 157 percent.

Thirty years ago, the chief executive officers of most big companies made approximately thirty times what their average employees did. That 30 to one ratio still prevails today in places like Germany and Japan. But in the United States, thirty years later, the ratio of CEO earnings to average worker salaries in America's largest companies is now 531 to one, according to *BusinessWeek.*

Between 1945 and 1975, the great majority of Americans experienced real and measurable economic progress. The real income of average households doubled, and the percentage of Americans who are poor fell by 60 percent. During that period, inequality in income and wealth remained constant and even shrank a bit. Overall, the economy grew at rates better than we have experienced these last twenty years. The nation experienced prosperity, but it was much more shared than it is today. It used to be that a rising tide lifted all boats, but the current rising tide is lifting all yachts!

This growing discrepancy means a huge difference in financial security. In the United States, the top 5 percent of the population now control approximately 60 percent of the wealth, and the bottom 40 percent controls just 0.5 percent. And the top 1 percent of the population possess a whopping 40 percent of all American wealth. Since the mid-1970s, the top 1 percent of households have doubled their share of the national wealth. Never have we seen such a radical redistribution of wealth from the bottom and the middle of society to the top.

Globally, the picture is even starker. In the last five years the number of the world's very poorest people—those who live on less than one dollar per day—has grown 50 percent, from 1 billion to

1.5 billion. According to the 1998 United Nations Human Development Report, the three richest *people* in the world own assets that exceed the combined gross domestic products of the world's poorest forty-eight *countries*. Here are some other rather amazing facts from the same report: the world consumed more than $24 trillion in goods and services in 1997, six times the figure for 1995. Of the world's 6.8 billion people, 4.4 billion live in developing (i.e., poor) countries, the rest in transitional or rich industrial countries. Among the 4.4 billion people who live in the poorest countries, three-fifths have no access to basic sanitation, almost one-third are without safe drinking water, one-quarter lack adequate housing, one-fifth live beyond the reach of modern health services, one-fifth of the children do not get as far as grade five in school, and one-fifth are undernourished. The report estimates that basic education for all would cost $6 billion a year—while $8 billion is spent annually for cosmetics in the United States alone. Installation of water and basic sanitation for all would cost $9 billion—$11 billion is spent annually for ice cream in Europe. Basic health care and nutrition would cost $13 billion—$17 billion a year is spent on pet food in Europe and the United States. Thirty-five billion dollars is spent on business entertainment in Japan, $50 billion on cigarettes in Europe, $105 billion on alcoholic drinks in Europe, $400 billion on narcotic drugs around the world, and $780 billion on the world's militaries.

The 1997 United Nations Development Program Report claimed that poverty could be conquered worldwide in the next decade. The cost would be around $80 billion a year until the year 2007—which is less than one-half of 1 percent of global income and less than the combined net worth of the seven richest men in the world.

These are, of course, dangerous economic realities but, at a deeper level, they are profoundly moral and even religious issues. The biblical prophets consistently railed against such gross extremes.

When the biblical archeologists dig down into the ruins of ancient Israel, they find there were periods when the houses were more or less the same size, and the artifacts of life they unearthed show there was a relative equality among the people. During those periods, interestingly enough, the Hebrew prophets were quite silent; they had little to say. But the archeologists' diggings also uncover remnants of huge houses and little tiny hovels at other periods in the life of Israel, and other objects that show great economic disparities among the people. Not surprisingly, it's during those times when the prophets were most outspoken, denouncing the great gaps in wealth and the neglect of the poor. The Bible doesn't mind prosperity; it just insists that it be shared. Where are the prophets today?

Is Disney CEO Michael Eisner really worth $97,000 per hour, when his workers in Haiti make about 28 cents an hour? Should market calculations be sufficient to value anyone that much more than others? People seem shocked to hear media reports that Michael Jordan made more from Nike in one year than all the workers in all the Asian factories that make Nike shoes did. But will shock lead to public discussion about the morality of such global disparities? The lack of capacity for social shame in our modern society is a worrisome problem. Somebody should be embarrassed by how quickly and easily the upper slice of Americans are now making money, while millions of American children endure third world living conditions. These growing economic gaps have a spiritual aspect: Americans are growing further and further apart. Therefore, the economic movement of the country works directly against all our spiritual traditions that would seek to bring us closer together.

The affluent, successful, and attractive people who dominate television sitcoms and commercials are clearly not representative of society as a whole. Who is the target of an ad I saw recently in which a woman decides to buy a new refrigerator because she doesn't like the color of the old one anymore? It's a media illusion that almost everyone is enjoying the soaring market. For all the hype and hoopla about the economy, buying power seems to be more and more problematic for the majority. It seems to take more and more work from more and more people just to keep up.

In a society characterized both by extremes *and* a willingness to exclude significant numbers of people, all of us are in jeopardy. The old slogan "There but for the grace of God go I" is truer than ever in the rapidly changing global economy. Even CEOs are no longer safe from corporate downsizing, to say nothing of the many top-level executives who have seen their personal fortunes change almost overnight when a new merger occurs. The threat of downsizing is ever present now, whereas it was not in my middle-class parents' experience. Average workers are in a more insecure position than they have been at any time since before unionization, and wages have been fairly stagnant for a long time. Many Americans are just a paycheck or two away from poverty, stuck in the precarious bottom of the middle class. And most of us could easily fall onto hard times, with the loss of our job, health, or family stability.

Thus, while poor people are still bearing the heaviest burden, working-class and even middle-class people are also living increasingly insecure lives. Most families need two incomes to support a middle-class life, or even a lower standard. Education for our children is often bad or incredibly costly. The quality and dependability of health care is eroding, even for people lucky enough to have insurance. While the top end of our society is reaping incredible bonanzas, the majority feel as if they're not making much progress, while those at the bottom are completely off society's radar screen except when they commit crimes. The neat categories of rich and poor don't adequately describe our economy anymore; a new reality of middle- and working-class deprivation has entered the picture. Therefore, a society's commitment not to just leave people "outside the gate" is an important commitment for everyone. Harvard economist Richard Parker suggests we replace "anti-poverty" work with broad and fair social policies that would improve the lives of not just the poor but the middle class as well.

Spiritual Poverty

Many Americans are searching for meaning and connection in our materialistic society. This is a sign of our second great poverty, which is *spiritual*. I have learned that it's a mistake to be so focused on the material poverty of the people at the bottom that we neglect or underestimate the spiritual impoverishment of those in the middle and even at the top. The booming economy is putting enormous pressure on all of us. Most families today must have two parents working full-time. Opportunity, rather than coercion, is what the women's movement was aiming for, yet these days staying at home hardly seems a choice for most women. The result is a great scarcity of time.

Professor Regina Herzlinger of the Harvard Business School has written, "Today's workers with employed spouses and children have only 1.4 hours to care for themselves on any given weekday." Full-time workers spent 138 hours more a year working in 1989 than in 1969. With both mothers and fathers working so long and hard outside the home, there is less and less time for family, especially for the children, and for involvement in the community and institutions like the church and other voluntary associations.

The market also fuels a never ending and relentless cycle of consumption, which not only undermines our personal integrity but destroys our sense of *moral* balance. We spend far too much time and energy thinking and worrying about "things" and engaging in the constant activity of consumption. Whereas Descartes asserted, "I think, therefore I am," modern advertising wants us to believe "I shop, therefore I am." When the shopping mall becomes the center of American life, the societal result is a deep crisis of meaning. The obvious insight no one wants to say out loud is that shopping simply doesn't satisfy the deepest longings of the human heart. And if work's only real purpose is to allow for more shopping, we have a formula for meaninglessness and, ultimately, despair.

Jesus's first temptation, while fasting in the desert, was to turn stones into bread. Here was the temptation of the easy answer, the quick fix, the instant solution. Why deny yourself...anything? Television commercials have much the same message today. You can have all you ever wanted, and you can have it now! That was the tempter's promise, and it is the lure of today's consumer culture. But to more and more people in the modern corporate world, both work and consumption feel increasingly meaningless—but there's no time for anything but work and consumption. And that has consequences: anxiety, stress, alienation, and emptiness are some of the most common.

Probably nothing I preach on the road has as much impact as my recitation of Gandhi's "seven deadly sins." I've written and spoken about them extensively, and there is always a very powerful reaction. The seven maxims are indeed striking, but it is the response to them that I now find most instructive. After a talk in which I refer to them, there are always people standing in line to make sure they've gotten them all down on their scraps of notepaper. One Australian radio talk-show host almost jumped out of his seat when he first heard them. "That's us!" he exclaimed. "That's Australia; that's the Western way of life."

Gandhi used these warnings as a teaching tool, a primary instruction for students at his ashram in India. The seven deadly sins are these:

1. *Politics without principle*
2. *Wealth without work*
3. *Commerce without morality*
4. *Pleasure without conscience*
5. *Education without character*
6. *Science without humanity*
7. *Worship without sacrifice*

Gandhi's warnings go right to the heart of the values of the culture we live in. They have become our way of life. Gandhi's seven deadly sins are another way of describing our spiritual poverty.

The economy may be booming, but how happy is life in the gated communities? The poor aren't the only ones worried about their kids; the affluent are worried about their children's values or, worse, the consequences of their own values showing up in their kids. It is no longer just the children of inner-city poverty who are erupting in societal violence. Many of the shooting sprees in junior high and high schools that have shocked the nation were carried out by middle-class white kids from two-parent homes. Listening to them talk, you quickly discover that something has gone terribly wrong in their value system. Selfishness and violence go together, especially in a society whose popular culture regularly portrays violence as an easy solution to our problems. When delayed gratification, hard work, or long-term preparation are antiquated values, and when the popular culture glorifies the ethic of taking what you want by any means necessary, the consequences will show up first in the young.

Our kids get the idea quickly. Late one night, I watched a winsome six-year-old being interviewed about his role in a Nike commercial alongside Michael Jordan. *Tonight Show* host Jay Leno asked the bright-eyed little boy if he wanted to be an athlete "like Mike." "Oh, no," replied the child star. "I want to be an owner. I want the money without the sweat." He's already learning the cultural message.

Jesus responds to the economic temptation in the desert by asserting, "One does not live by bread alone." Bread is not bad; on the contrary, bread is good and we need it. But there are much more important things, and all of our spiritual traditions say that. All human beings need security, but too much can be as dangerous as too little. Jesus later advises his followers to resist the temptations of the easy life, to be more modest and patient, to simplify their lives rather than to complicate them further, and to replace anxious striving with prayerful trust.

What's Most Important?

At a retreat for pastors I was leading one weekend, our spiritual poverty became readily apparent. A young Presbyterian pastor began to bare his soul, confessing that his training had not prepared him for what he was encountering in his parish. Most of his parishioners were corporate executives, lawyers, or investment brokers who commuted every day from their suburban neighborhoods to high-powered jobs in New York or Philadelphia. The youthful cleric wasn't judgmental toward them but was deeply concerned, telling us, "They rise very early in the morning and are never back until late at night. Their credit cards are maxed out, they have no savings, and they must work constantly to maintain the lifestyles in which they're trapped. There is no time for family, community, church, or anything besides work and consumer activities. Marriages are on the rocks, kids are being neglected, alcoholism and other addictions are common, and spiritual life has long since died." Then he was silent for a moment before he spoke again. "I don't know how I can serve them!"

Across the room, a pastor on sabbatical from South Africa listened quietly. When no one else in the room responded to the young minister, the South African replied, "You know, we too have many people who must get up very early in the morning and don't return home until late into the night. The buses come at five A.M. to bring them to the work sites and don't return them to their homes until ten P.M. All they do is work, and there is little time left for family or anything else. Alcoholism and family breakdown are common. It causes great problems for the community and for the church. It seems like you have similar problems here in America. In South Africa, we call ours slave labor camps. It sounds like, in the United States, you have corporate labor camps." The two pastors immediately understood each other.

What's most important? It's a question that troubles more and more people today. At a leadership training institute I attended, we were invited to go around the room and answer the question, What are you doing with your life? One participant responded, "I sell salty snack foods." This very successful manager and, I would discover, very nice guy, seemed a little jolted by his own simple description of his life purpose. Answering that basic question of what we are doing with our lives can cause many a successful business, government, or civic leader to take stock.

Of course, the middle class isn't the only one buffeted by the pressures of a consumer society. As if material poverty were not enough, poor people often suffer spiritual poverty as well. The same materialistic values so characteristic of America's affluent suburbs can be found just as readily in poor communities. Here, too, the influence of advertising and the popular culture take their toll. Indeed, one could argue that the negative influence of excessive consumerism can be even more destructive in places where people have so little to start with. On a recent trip to a shopping mall, I was pleased to find a pair of khakis on sale for $19.95. But when I asked the young sales clerk how to wash and dry them, he didn't know—he always had his dry-cleaned! It doesn't take much arithmetic to figure out how many times over this kid pays for his pants—all just to maintain a certain crease and image somebody has convinced him is important.

John DiIulio, the social-policy analyst whom I spoke of earlier, describes a deep spiritual poverty among the most marginalized inner-city children. He describes it graphically as a kind of moral poverty. He points specifically to the large number of poor children who have almost no caring adults in their lives. Without any moral mentors or guiding influences, they are adrift in the middle of an ocean with no compass, surrounded by dangerous storms. "In sum, moral poverty is the poverty of being without loving, capable, responsible adults who teach the young right from wrong. It is the poverty of being without parents, guardians, relatives, friends, teachers, coaches, clergy, and others who habituate (to use a good Aristotelian word) children to feel joy at others' joy, pain at others' pain, satisfaction when you do right, remorse when you do wrong." DiIulio writes, "It is the poverty of growing up in the virtual absence of people who teach these lessons by their own everyday example, and who lovingly insist that you follow suit and behave accordingly. In the extreme, it is the poverty of growing up severely abused and neglected, of being surrounded and hounded by deviant, delinquent, and criminal adults and other older youth in a social setting defined by dysfunctional homes, disorderly schools, and dangerous streets. To grow up in abject moral poverty is to grow up believing that impulsive violence or reckless behavior is at least as right and rational as deferred gratification. It is to grow up feeling that cold-blooded exploitation is more natural than empathetic expression."

Yes there are other factors that turn well-loved teenagers into stone-cold killers. But, as DiIulio points out, "It is more typically a lack of decent parents and other responsible adults that puts otherwise normal children behaviorally at risk, giving them little chance of becoming a civil, sober, skilled, and self-sufficient adult, and a better than average chance of engaging in crime, succumbing to the blandishments of alcohol and illegal drugs, remaining unemployed, and bringing into this world more children whose main

patrimony is moral poverty." The moral poverty DiIulio describes
is a condition of the spiritual poverty we have been examining. It
can also occur when there is no economic disadvantage present,
and does so increasingly often as parenting and family life break
down across the economic spectrum.

The latchkey syndrome of many affluent homes can produce
similar moral poverty. The difference is this: The kids in the affluent suburbs of Virginia and Maryland, a few miles from where I live,
have more to buffer the bad decisions that arise from their own spiritual poverty. They or their parents have many more resources to
allow them second, third, or endless chances to redeem themselves
and turn their lives in a better direction after some initial bad choices. In effect, affluence often helps to mask moral and spiritual
poverty. In my neighborhood, in inner-city Washington, the bad
choices kids make can quickly become matters of life and death.
Sometimes there are no second chances for kids who are poor and
whose families have no resources to buffer them. The spiritual
poverty of poor people is often easier to see and harder to hide than
that of the more affluent.

But there is yet another kind of poverty that increasingly affects
us all.

Civic Poverty

The third great poverty is *civic* poverty—a decline in citizen participation in the political process, including voting, and an impoverishment of the political debate itself. During a lunch conversation
on Capitol Hill, a member of Congress made a sad admission to the
dozen of us seated around the table. "We really haven't done anything this session," he said. "Only ten seats going the other way
could change the party in control, and about forty seats are at play
in the fall elections. That's really the only thing anyone is talking
about up here. There's nothing else going on."

I was asked to say a few words to wrap up the event and could
respond only by reminding the group that a lot of other important
things were going on in the rest of the country (the millions of families, for example, trying to make the difficult transition from wel-

fare to work), and it was too bad that we weren't getting any help from Congress.

I know some dedicated elected officials who really would like to make a difference. But the system in which they operate has become so locked into rigidly polarized political debate that real answers to real problems can hardly be found. That fits the mood in most legislative bodies today, where politicians are looking not for solutions but just for people to blame. Winning elections and holding on to political power have clearly become ends unto themselves, with many lawmakers losing track of the reasons they are there. And winning requires an almost daily attention to fund-raising in order to meet the enormous costs of today's election campaigns.

Money so controls the political process that it is no longer hyperbole to say that the votes of Congress are for sale. While the legions of corporate lobbyists and their favorite members of Congress vehemently deny it, campaign contributions have become the quid pro quo of political benefits. Who of us will forget the refreshing honesty of oil mogul Roger Tamraz's 1997 testimony before a congressional committee? When asked if he would ever give so much money to the campaigns of politicians again (since his $300,000 contribution had not gotten him the lucrative contract he was hoping for), he candidly replied, "I think next time I'll give $600,000!" Under questioning from the Senate panel, Tamraz admitted that he was not even registered to vote and offered, "I think [money] is a bit more than a vote." Or as a senior citizen in a class I was teaching said insightfully, "Some of us have only one vote, and some others have literally thousands of votes."

What once were considered the most egregious examples of money's influence over politics have now become the pattern.

- ♦ The tobacco industry has contributed more than $13 million in soft money to the Republican party since 1995, and in 1998 Republicans killed any new tobacco bill to reduce teen smoking or reach a settlement of state lawsuits.
- ♦ Rich contributors to the Democratic party get now-famous sleepovers in the Lincoln Bedroom, and Asian business,

military, and government officials get endless appointments
in the White House before their contributions are discovered.

♦ The 192 members of the House of Representatives who
supported legislation to delay clean-air standards received
three times the political contributions from America's
biggest polluters as those who voted for clean air.

Clearly, these are good investments in politics for American corporations. During the 1950s, corporations provided 31 percent of all federal tax revenue. Now they provide only 15 percent, the difference being made up by U.S. taxpayers. With nearly 80 percent of all money that fuels election campaigns now coming from business contributors, it's not hard to understand how we got the corporate-friendly tax system that now rules the country. Indeed, just one-third of 1 percent of the population now virtually controls the funding of the nation's political process! Not surprisingly, almost all the budget cuts in entitlements made so far came from entitlements to the poor, while the subsidies and tax breaks to the rich and powerful have yet to be touched.

While these numbers aren't widely publicized, most Americans know they are realities and don't believe they are fair. Despite the steady diatribes between Republicans and Democrats, many people believe there is really only one political party in America: the party of the rich. PBS journalist Bill Moyers says, "Democracy depends upon the balance between organized money and organized people—those are the two ways to wield influence in our kind of society. There has never been a nirvana in American history when the elite didn't marshal their resources to protect their privileges. But what's different is the one-sidedness of it now, which is overwhelming the political process and leaving people angry and alienated.... Politics today has become an arms race, with money instead of missiles.... One side escalates, and the other follows suit. Faster and faster, the spiral has been growing. Today this arms race is undermining our system of self-government."

The great casualty has been the very soul of democracy, and one vital danger sign is the appalling low and dropping levels of voting and political participation in the United States. Only half of us bother to vote in presidential elections today, compared with 80 percent a century ago. In 1960, voter turnout for the presidential election was 63 percent; by 2000 it had dropped to 51 percent. Similarly, congressional midterm elections drew 47 percent in 1962, but only 38 percent in 1998. Also, voting rates are unevenly distributed by class. An *American Prospect* article, "The Big Tilt: Participatory Inequality in America," demonstrates that the lowest rates of participation are found among America's poorest citizens. In comparing people who are in the top tenth of the population in income (above $75,000) with those in the bottom fifth (below $15,000), the writers found that "the latter are about three-fifths as likely to vote, only half as likely to go to a protest or get in touch with a government official, only one-third as likely to engage in informal activity within the community—and only one-tenth as likely to make a campaign donation." Participatory inequality exists largely because political donations are replacing volunteering as the major means of political involvement, and money is more unequally distributed than time. Because of participatory inequality, the issues raised to public officials are skewed: the financial and social interests of the upper middle class are given much more attention than the questions affecting the disadvantaged.

A Debate of Extremes

Along with the widespread public perception that special interest groups now dominate politics, there is a growing public disgust at the nature of the debate itself, and the role of the media in particular. Extreme views virtually control the political debate, and more and more of the nation is just tired of listening. The talking heads of the TV news shows seem to have opinions on every subject every day and seem to think that just being on television gives them some credibility or moral authority. They must hope that no one ever asks the obvious question: "Just who are you people anyway, and what have you ever done that would make us want to hear what you have to say about this?"

Politics, like everything else, has become mere entertainment, and for that we need the clash of opposing opinions. But maybe some issues don't have just two opposing sides; maybe a variety of different angles and perspectives could help us find positive solutions. Instead, we see complex issues distorted in media-staged confrontations that virtually prevent the finding of any common ground.

I remember a request from one of the major networks to take part in such a staged battle. The National Religious Broadcasters Convention was in Washington, D.C., and most of the major figures from the religious right were in attendance. The network producer came to me with an idea. "I've heard there's somewhere in the Bible where Jesus gets mad at religious leaders and tips tables over in a church. Is that true?" Well, sort of, I replied. I filled in a few of the details for him—how Jesus once confronted the leaders of the Jewish temple for commercializing and corrupting the house of worship. "Great," he said. "That's what we have in mind. We'd like to film you walking into the convention center looking very angry. You probably shouldn't knock over any of their tables, but you could storm up to [he named one of the religious right's celebrities] and start an argument with him. We've already worked it all out with him, and he thinks it's a great idea!" That's really what he said. Instead, I suggested that they bring the conservative Christian leader over to my apartment in the inner city (only blocks away from the luxurious convention center) and film a conversation between us about the nature of Christian responsibility, especially to poor people. To their credit, that's exactly what they did, and the dialogue turned out to be quite constructive. The incident showed me again how addicted the media are to the two-sided confrontation, but also how a better dialogue can take place when that style of political discourse is challenged.

Listening to the rhetoric on both sides, you would think America is being forced to choose between the strategies of promoting family values or creating good jobs, between protecting the sacredness of life or defending the rights of women, between expanding economic opportunity or securing economic justice, between holding Hollywood accountable for its moral values or pressing large corporations to be responsible to their workers and communities, between upholding personal responsibility or working for racial equality. You would think, hearing the relentless conservative-liberal debate, that nobody could stand for all of the above, even though many Americans probably do.

Back to Marquis, my new nephew, adopted from the streets by my sister. He's a bit of a philosopher, so I asked him one day what he thought was meant by the now-famous African proverb "It takes a village to raise a child," which he was writing a report on for school. I could tell he was thinking about this one carefully because he took a few moments to respond. "Well," he said, "I guess it means that if I was outside playing and got all dirty and messed up and stuff, I could go to anyone's house to get cleaned up." Not bad, I thought. Not bad at all.

Some months later, Marquis was watching one of the national political conventions on television. A presidential candidate had made a statement about child rearing, and everybody was now arguing about it. The candidate exclaimed, "It doesn't take a village; it takes a family!" The great liberal-conservative debate quickly ensued: Village! Family! Village! Family! Marquis just shook his head as he left the room and said to his parents, "They just don't get the concept, do they?" No they don't, and because they don't, the public arena is dominated by a series of false choices that are killing our public discourse. This is civic poverty.

Just as was done during the era of the civil rights movement, a new generation could begin to apply our best moral or religious values to overcome the material and spiritual poverty that today shames and imprisons the soul of the wealthy countries. Together, we could also counter our civic poverty by searching for some real answers, instead of just finding more ways to argue over the questions. But that will require some soul-searching because the real issues are spiritual, not just political. And that realization is the beginning of both wisdom and transformation. In all that we do, we need to remember chapter five: Recognize the three faces of poverty.

CHAPTER SIX

Listen to Those
Closest to the Problem

*"What do you want me to do for you?" Jesus asked him.
The blind man said, "Rabbi, I want to see." (Mark 10:51)*

MY WIFE TELLS THE STORY of a young priest facing a tough assignment—his first attempt to teach a Sunday school class. Eager to be
accepted by the kids, he tried to portray himself as very casual and
accessible. He sat on the edge of a desk and asked a question of the
wide-eyed children. "Hey kids," he said, "what's gray, furry, gathers nuts, and runs up and down trees?" There was a long pause
while the kids looked at each other with puzzled faces. Finally, one
little boy ventured an answer. "Well, I know the answer should be
Jesus...but it sure sounds like a squirrel to me!"

The story reminds us that there is not always an easy religious
answer to every problem. Nevertheless, some of the most successful efforts in dealing with poverty and violence are emerging from
faith communities—meaning not only churches and congregations,
but a myriad of religiously and spiritually based nonprofit organizations. And many of those efforts teach us a clear lesson: Listen to
those closest to the problem.

Boston is the site of the much-publicized Ten Point Coalition,
sparked by Rev. Eugene Rivers. When Eugene Rivers's picture and

the Boston story were featured on the cover of *Newsweek* in the summer of 1998, the nation got a glimpse of new possibilities for faith-based solutions to the problems of urban poverty, youth violence, and crime. Eugene Rivers never expected such coverage by a national news magazine, and I remember the two A.M. phone call he made to tell me about it. But most stories don't begin on the cover of *Newsweek*, and this one didn't either.

Several years earlier, *Sojourners* began to report on *our* front cover what Gene and other black pastors were doing in Boston. Gene and I have carried on a twenty-five-year-long conversation as his pilgrimage has taken him from street hustling in Philadelphia, to idea hustling in the academic halls of Harvard, and finally to Boston's tough Dorchester neighborhoods, hustling to put his Pentecostal faith into practice. There, a heroin dealer gave some valuable advice to a handful of young black pastors who wanted desperately to do something to stop the violence on their streets and were willing to listen to anybody who might give them some ideas. The drug dealer said, "When the kids get out of school, we're there and you're not. When they're out on the streets, we're there and you're not. When momma sends Johnny out for a loaf of bread, we're there and you're not. All night long, we're there and you're not—so we win and you lose. It's as simple as that." The pastors knew that the bars and crack houses were open to kids at virtually any hour of the day, while their churches were closed and locked most of the time.

Some months later, a now-famous 1992 incident in a Boston church served as the catalyst for change. On the night of May 18, 1992, a wake was being conducted at Morning Star Baptist Church for a young man named Robert Odom, who had been shot in the head by an errant bullet during a drive-by shooting. All of a sudden, some gang members burst into the sanctuary, pursuing a rival gang member who was at the wake. They started shooting and chased him around the church, finally stabbing him, right up near the pulpit. It's hard to get more dramatic than that. Several meetings of clergy and community leaders followed.

At one such meeting, Rev. Jeff Brown of Union Baptist Church warned, "If the churches won't go into the streets, the streets will come into the churches." At a later meeting, Eugene Rivers issued a clarion call, saying it was time for the clergy to go out and walk the streets, dealing with troubled young people on a one-to-one basis. Several established clergy laughed at the suggestion, and one jokingly suggested that Rev. Rivers be appointed to lead the "street committee." "All right," said Gene, "I will." He then invited any pastor who was willing to join him to meet at his house the following Friday night, and they would start walking the streets together. Twelve showed up, and thereafter a small group of young pastors, in response to Rivers's invitation, started walking the streets at night, watching, listening, talking, and establishing a crucial relationship with street youth. That was the beginning of what would become the Ten Point Coalition and, eventually, a *Newsweek* cover story. The drug dealer's insight and the stabbing in the church led to the formation of one of the most effective church-based efforts in the country at combating youth violence and offering concrete hope to shattered neighborhoods in our urban communities.

Ten Point's approach is straightforward and simple—nothing will substitute for physical presence and unconditional but tough love. The churches make a very practical commitment to adopt gangs, local parks, particular blocks and street corners, and, most important, individual kids. The kids on the street have a sixth sense for consistency or lack thereof and are willing and eager to form natural kinships with anyone who seems to walk the walk and talk the talk. Committing to them is nothing less than a redemption strategy, block by block and kid by kid. In Boston and around the country, churches are beginning to divide up turf, just the way gangs do, to apply the love of God to the toughest neighborhoods in America. And the results are impressive.

I was involved with the Ten Point Coalition from its inception and can testify to its very practical and close-to-home approach. It's really an old approach, but one that has escaped us in our age of professionalism and bureaucracy, even in the churches. It used to be that all the adults in a community felt a responsibility for raising the kids in the neighborhood. You were as likely to be disciplined or looked after by somebody else's mom or dad as by your own. But as more and more families don't have both a mom and dad—especially a dad—and with role models disappearing in the communities where they are most needed, a lot of kids are just getting lost. Massive social welfare cutbacks, which have further abandoned many families to deeper poverty, have proven especially hard on at-risk youth. Add up all those factors and you have a recipe for disaster. Rivers cites studies claiming that by the year 2006, a large number of urban youth will reach the age at which criminal behavior normally occurs. His commitment is for the churches to reach them before all the negative social forces do.

The Ten Point Coalition has formed new partnerships and made new allies, first between churches and then with other agencies, both public and private. Of critical importance was a new cooperation between inner-city pastors and the criminal justice system, with the police in particular. In the past, the Boston police had antagonized the black community by making wide sweeps that seemed to indiscriminately target young black men. Now the police backed off and, in cooperation with black ministers trusted in the community, focused on a much smaller group of hard-core perpetrators. The ministers offered repeat offenders a real chance to turn their lives around, but if their violent criminal behavior continued, the ministers would assist the police in their arrest and incarceration. Jeff Brown, now one of the key urban leaders in Boston, says, "Our commitment is always to work with these kids, but sometimes you have to work with them in a prison ministry for a while. We had to come to the realization that some of these young people are so out of control that the only way they will listen to you is if they're behind bars for a period of time."

Obviously to play such a sensitive and difficult role, you have to know a community well—both the young people vulnerable to getting caught up in crime and their neighbors, who are the most frequent victims. You have to listen to those closest to the problem. And people have to trust you.

In 1990, there were 152 gun homicides in Boston and 1,100 gun shootings. But from the middle of 1995 to December of 1997, there was not one juvenile homicide in the city. When one did occur, the

whole community was activated by what should always be seen as a
rare and horrible occasion—a child being killed by a gun—instead
of a regular occurrence that many communities have come to
regard as normal. The murder rate in Boston for 1998 was the lowest since 1961. There is a track record of success that commends the
"Boston miracle." While many cities report drops in crime,
Boston's results are not only dramatic but instructive. Boston
reports a 77 percent decrease in violent crime since the early 1990s.
New York reduced crime by 70 percent during the same period. But
Boston took a community approach, while New York City became
a police state, sparking massive public protests against police policies and practices.

In Boston, where the police as well as the criminals are held
accountable for their actions, the complaints against indiscriminate
police harassment and abuse have gone way down. Boston has
proven that such real community-police cooperation can work. In
Boston today, the judges, cops, and politicians sing the praises of
the black pastors who lead Ten Point, and credit collaboration with
them for the city's significant reductions in youth crime and violence. Rev. Ray Hammond, the chair of Boston's Ten Point
Coalition, says, "We have demonstrated success in preventing the
violence that was devastating our communities. But now our focus
is on the development of real alternatives to violence and crime in
the lives of these young people." Ray and his wife, Gloria White
Hammond, are pastors of the Bethel African Methodist Episcopal
(AME) Church, where they are pioneering many very successful
programs, such as mentoring for young teenage girls to prevent
unwanted pregnancies. And the Ella Baker House, the impressive
ministry of Eugene Rivers's Azuza Christian Community in
Dorchester's Four Corners neighborhood, has become a model for
youth ministry around the country. Gene has now created the
National Ten Point Leadership Foundation, a network of black
church-based ministries in a dozen cities.

Jeff Brown was one of the original young pastors who first started walking the streets of Boston. He talks about the partnerships
that have been forged. "The Boston success story is not a solo act.

It is a choir, where police officers talk about jobs and economic parity, clergy talk about law enforcement, social workers talk about the importance of spiritual uplift, and the private sector talks about street-level intervention. It is a choir that harmonizes on the melody of community resurrection."

Essential to the success that the Boston pastors have found is listening to the right people, in particular to the kids on the street. Eugene Rivers's disdain for listening to the experts, the politicians, and even the leaders of the big-steeple churches, rather than the kids, has often gotten him into trouble. But while his strident criticism of others has sometimes been controversial, his commitment to listening to the kids on the street is right on target.

The Ten Point Coalition's success stems in part from its unapologetic spiritual basis. The poor urban youth are not just clients: they are the children of God, deserving of God's redemptive love. Street kids are not just participating in a program but rather are entering into relationships that are offering to help them change their lives. The pastors and youth workers who become involved are not in this for the money or their careers; they do it because they believe God has called them. Both the motivation of the workers and the possibility of spiritual transformation offer a much greater potential for success than more secular and bureaucratic social programs can normally provide. A spiritually based effort is more likely to listen to poor people themselves.

Whom Do You Trust?

Whom do we listen to and whom do we trust? *Trust* is essential to listening. Why do we continue to believe the myth that poor people don't know anything and can't be trusted? Where do you really find more truth about a society—at the top or at the bottom? Are the best solutions conceived in the corridors of power or in the neighborhoods? Do the poor really have no assets or resources, as most people think? Listening to the poor opens up whole new possibilities, ideas, and directions in overcoming poverty.

Why listen to the poor? Well, there are good biblical and ethical reasons. But there are also just plain practical reasons. Many youth-

and community-serving programs have found what Ten Point discovered: they couldn't get off the ground until they began to truly trust and engage and involve the people they were trying to serve. Many good and decent programs didn't become highly successful until the poor themselves were given a real hearing and became involved in their leadership. The presence of the poor in the discussion makes all the difference. I can testify to this fact. When young people are at the table for a discussion of youth violence and what to do about it, the conversation is very different from what it would be otherwise. Too often, the discussions we have about poverty involve only the people who are working to overcome it.

Rev. Sam Mann, a pastor and key figure in the Kansas City gang peace summit, wants to "raise the bar of inclusivity." He says those from the dominant social groups are going to have to learn to give up some of their control and their icons if we are really to have a new table around which everyone can meet. John DiIulio once told me his three principles for solving the country's worst societal problems: "One: Trust those closest to the problem. Two: Trust those closest to the problem. Three: Trust those closest to the problem."

Nearly every time I talk to Nane Alejandrez, he tells me he has "revised the business plan" and that he also has taken some more young people from the barrio up into the mountains for a sweat (a Native American prayer ceremony conducted around burning coals in a makeshift tent called a sweat lodge). Daniel "Nane" Alejandrez was once a drug addict, felon, and veteran of barrio warfare in California. He had seen scores of family members either die on the streets or end up in prison. But Nane had a spiritual conversion. He is now the director of Barrios Unidos, perhaps the most effective antiviolence youth organization working in Latino communities across the nation.

Barrios is involved in a myriad of youth activities and projects for community-based economic development. It is creating T-shirt and silk-screening businesses, computer centers, job-training projects, art shows, and alternative schooling. And it's working to steer street kids away from gangs and into positive community service. The young Barrios warriors are committed to a powerful combination of economic and spiritual development.

But because Nane was from the streets (and had the tattoos to prove it), no bank or credit union would give Barrios the initial investment capital it needed. Nane invited me to Santa Cruz, California, to see their activities and hear their exciting plans to expand. I was very impressed. "How much do you need to get this up and running?" I asked him. Nane wanted only thirty thousand dollars of loan capital but had no connections to get even that small amount. So I arranged a meeting with Gaylord Thomas, a savvy streetwise organizer himself, on the national staff of the Evangelical Lutheran Church in America. The Lutheran Church made a very important decision: they listened to Nane, took a chance on a grass-roots leader and program, and made Barrios a business loan with accompanying technical assistance. Barrios Unidos is now in more than twenty-four states across the country and is developing a whole new generation of Latino leadership. The city of Santa Cruz has helped Barrios to obtain almost a whole block in which to expand its successful operations. The Lutherans trusted the people closest to the problem, and never did they make a better investment.

In addressing problems like youth violence, addiction, family breakdown, and teenage pregnancy, face-to-face relationships engaging those closest to the problem have clearly worked far better than bureaucratic approaches. Even in the tough areas of housing, job creation, and environmental cleanup, smaller-scale and community-based programs are demonstrating results. And new community-policing efforts, in partnership with community-based groups, are helping to turn many neighborhoods around. But these close-to-home solutions work far better when they have the support of larger institutions in the wider community. Investing our time, energy, and money in such hopeful initiatives, started by those closest to the problem, is one of the best roads to social change.

Poor People, Not the Poor

Mary Nelson hates it when people refer to "the poor." She would rather speak of the new relationships through which all of us can participate in the exciting task of community development. In the West Side Chicago neighborhood of Garfield Park, the efforts of her Bethel New Life community organization powerfully demonstrate what low-income people can do if they mobilize their own resources. Mary Nelson is neither a black inner-city pastor nor a Latino community organizer but a white-haired Lutheran church lady with a powerful vision.

But that vision came out of listening to and forming relationships with the residents of an impoverished and forgotten local community. When Mary arrived in 1965 to support her brother David Nelson as the new pastor of Bethel Lutheran Church, things were very different.

"Three days after we got here, there were riots," she says. Two years later, the neighborhood had gone from 95 percent white to 90 percent black through the red-lining policies of banks and the block-busting tactics of Realtors who use race and fear to quickly change neighborhoods. When the turbulence subsided, the church had dwindled to thirty-five elderly members, the remnant of the ethnic German population who had fled Garfield Park with the arrival of African Americans. But the Nelsons stayed. Pastor Nelson knew that the only way to break into the rapidly changed parish was to literally go door-to-door and ask new residents, "How can we help?" The neighbors whom the Nelsons won over and the black youth who came to sing in the choir transformed Bethel into the church of six hundred members that it is today. "They call us a Lutheran-Baptist church," says Mary, smiling.

A housing crisis in the community gave Bethel its first mission. Mary recalls, "We looked around and said, 'Man, we better do something about housing or there won't be a neighborhood left to be a church in.' So with no money and no plan of action, we felt called by God to try and do housing." And they did. So far nine hundred units of housing have been constructed or rehabilitated through Bethel's efforts.

But what began as an effort to rebuild the community's housing stock soon became much more, as the need for long-term neighborhood sustainability became clear. Bethel New Life, with Mary

Nelson at the helm, transformed itself into an engine of comprehensive community development, creating new initiatives in education, employment, health care, senior and child care, transitional living for people who were homeless, and even an "incubation program" to assist budding entrepreneurs in getting new local businesses off the ground. Bethel has become one of the area's largest job providers, creating meaningful work for hundreds of people. A closed local hospital is currently being transformed into a new community center offering everything from preschool to the performing arts.

Mary draws lessons from the Bible about community organizing. At one of our Call to Renewal national roundtables, she led the morning devotions around a New Testament passage, Mark 2:1–12. Some men bring a sick friend to a house where Jesus is, so he can be healed. But the crowds are too large, and they cannot get near Jesus. So they cut a hole in the roof of the house and lower their sick friend, on his pallet, down into the room where Jesus is. Jesus speaks to him, and he is healed. She spoke of the need for teamwork and explained that every project requires an initiator (the visionary who came up with the idea of cutting a hole in the roof), implementers (the folks who made it happen by carrying the stretcher up to the roof and cutting the hole), intercessors (those who lead the way in prayer), and investors (those who supply the capital—someone had to buy the stretcher!).

Like Eugene Rivers and Nane Alejandrez, Mary Nelson organizes with a vibrant spirituality. She says that the "four G's" help keep Bethel New Life going. It's the "glue" of Christian community that keeps them all together, against anything that would tear them apart. It's the "gasoline" from the Sunday liturgy refueling stop, where community members are reminded that "despite setbacks, God is going to bring us through." It's the "guts" that helps in making tough but effective decisions (like mortgaging the church buildings to begin the first housing program). And it's the "grace" to remind them that while it takes hard skills to accomplish things, "it is faith that drives us." Like most good organizers, Mary Nelson has a well-developed theology of hope—you've got to when you face the threat of hopelessness every day. "You're always hovering between 'Boy, we're going to get this done,' and 'Boy, this is a terrible problem and there's nothing we can do about it,'" she says, "and a vociferous voice will lead you either way." But then the church lady turned streetwise organizer explains her bedrock faith: "The only way you can respond to that kind of thing is to say that the eyes of faith won't label anything as hopeless. God will make a way; God will help us find a way, and then you celebrate the victories and you mourn the losses and you move forward." Having worked with her on many a project, I can tell you that Mary Nelson is always moving forward, working side by side with the people of her neighborhood.

Poor people have resources, Mary insists, contrary to what most people think. Bethel's asset-based approach to organizing in a poor neighborhood has produced real results. The resources that poor communities have—time, energy, numbers, relationships, experience, talent, faith, and even some money—when pooled together, can become very significant. Bethel has successfully forged economic development in the kind of place where most people give up. Mary will tell you that we still have many misconceptions about the causes and consequences of material poverty. The idea that poor people have no assets is a myth; the problem is how to mobilize those assets. A whole network based around the concept of asset-based community development is taking hold around the country. The concept asserts that poor people and communities are rich sources of assets and gifts that must be recognized, developed, and mobilized. The goal is sufficiency, self-determination, and productivity for those who are now poor.

But listening to those closest to the problem means that you have to be close enough to hear. And doing that can sometimes be a little scary. Mary tells the story of a very bad period of horrific violence in their West Side Chicago community. Gangs, drugs, guns, and vicious turf battles were taking a deadly and mounting toll. Unsure of exactly what to do, several women from Bethel New Life decided to conduct a simple prayer vigil right on a corner where several young people had been shot. They chose to do it all night, right through the most dangerous hours. A small circle of women began their vigil one hot summer evening, carrying white crosses with the names of those who had died written on them. Fewer than a dozen women continued to stand alone on the street corner as the hour got later and later. Around midnight, with nobody else around, they spotted a group of young gang members headed their way. Swallowing hard, the Bethel women continued their prayer and singing. One of the young men walked right up to them and challenged, "Where's Cinque?" More than a little frightened, the women asked who Cinque was. He was a good friend who had been shot, the young man replied. "You forgot Cinque," he said. "Well, let's make a cross for Cinque, then," said Mary, and added, "perhaps you would like to join our vigil for a while." Amazingly enough, they did join the vigil that night, holding the cross with their friend's name on it. Standing there together in the middle of the night on that deserted street corner, the young men and the women began to talk. It was the beginning of a relationship that would see some of those young people become personally involved in the work of the Bethel community. But only those willing to stand close enough to listen will ever hear those closest to the problem.

Listening to those closest to the problem doesn't mean you don't use every resource from wherever you can get it to solve those problems. Mary and her coworkers have also learned how to work the system for some of the resources they need to complement their own community efforts. Both government and business recognize success when they see it, as evidenced by the $2.7 million welfare-to-work grant the U.S. Labor Department gave Bethel New Life to develop even more jobs. The results come when we realize that poor people should be defined not merely by what they need but by what they can do.

Overcoming poverty, not simply servicing it, is the vision to strive for. To do anything less not only is patronizing but creates dynamics of dependency and control. Effective organizing has as its goal the prophetic biblical vision of Isaiah for people who have been oppressed: "They shall build houses and inhabit them, they shall plant vineyards and eat their fruit. They shall not build and another inhabit, they shall not plant and another eat; for like the days of a tree shall my people be, and my chosen shall long enjoy the work of their hands. They shall not labor in vain, or bear children in calamity; for they shall be offspring blessed by the Lord." The prophet Micah, too, offers a compelling image for those who have been left behind: "They shall all sit down under their own vines and fig trees, and no one shall make them afraid."

When We Don't Listen

But we usually don't listen to the poor. On the contrary, it's easy to pick on poor people, to simply blame the poor for their poverty. We do it all the time in America. But living and working with those who are poor gives you a whole different perspective.

Thelma used to live next door. She and her family were there before we arrived in the neighborhood some twenty years ago. Thelma's husband had died, so the responsibility of keeping the family together fell to her. And she did it well. Three generations grew up in that house with, as far as we could see, good family values.

But because Thelma could never afford a down payment, she could never buy her house. One of our tenant organizers sat down with Thelma one day, and they figured out that she had paid for her place several times over in rent. Over the years, she was the most stable figure in the ever-changing history of a house that had had several owners during the period of her residence. The last owner was the D.C. government, which had done nothing to help Thelma own her own home. Instead, without fixing the plumbing or a leaking roof, they had raised the rent again. Thelma just couldn't afford it. One day, when I came home from a long trip, I was shocked to see that Thelma had moved out and her place had been boarded up. Ever since, we've had to fight to keep it from becoming a rat-infested crack house.

Thelma never got the equity from her housing investment that might have helped put her kids through college. She never received the home ownership mortgage tax deduction, a far bigger entitlement for the middle class than welfare is for the poor. And she never could get the parental help that many middle-class folks receive—a loan for the down payment on their first home. Listening to people like Thelma taught our community organizers more about the housing problem in America than attending meetings at the Department of Housing and Urban Development ever did.

There is a parable here. It's about class, race, and the economic system. It's not about Thelma's failures. Sure, poor people can make bad choices that entrench them in poverty. But there's more to it than that. In fact, as I said earlier, bad personal choices can have far more severe results for the poor than for the well-off. That's why we are very tough at Sojourners Neighborhood Center about young people making the right choices in life and not further compounding the poverty they started with.

But there are always social and structural reasons why some people are poor and others are not. For example, it would not be difficult for America to figure out a fair way for low-income families to buy their own homes, and that would make a great difference in the fight to overcome poverty. But we have *chosen* not to do it.

The Bible sees those societal choices as moral failures. Instead of ignoring the poor, it tells us, we should listen to them, pay attention to them, and even evaluate our success as a society by how we treat them. It's not that poor people are different from or better than anyone else. Not at all. Living and working in some of the poorest neighborhoods in this country for twenty-five years has taught me that those at the bottom have all the good and bad in them that people do anywhere else. But from a moral viewpoint, those at the bottom are the litmus test for the health of the whole society. That is both a religious insight and the beginning of political wisdom. If you want to really know the truth about a society, look to its bottom rungs. The perspective is clearer there and less subject to varnish and illusion. That's where you find out what is really going on and how best to change it. You are unlikely to learn it in any other place because, in part, the political and media centers that disseminate information about society don't want people to really know what is happening at the bottom. An honest view from the bottom is usually uncomfortable for those at the top.

Our traditional approach to the problems of poverty has been far too bureaucratic. We don't talk about the meaning of community, we just engage in endless arguments over resources and allocations. Now we've created a whole poverty industry, a professional social welfare bureaucracy that is rich in procedures and regulations but poor in genuine compassion and real connection to people. Unless we discover a new sense of family and community in America, we will never face our issues of poverty and racism. Where will we find the reconciling practices to bring the disparate parts of the American family together? How do we begin saying "we" instead of talking about "us" and "them"? Developing the big we will take a common vision and strategy "that will resonate around our kitchen table," as veteran antipoverty organizer Tom Jones puts it. He says, "Our great national initiatives in civil rights, women's rights, and the environment drew upon our collective social conscience, our sense of justice and fairness, and our confidence in creating opportunities. But it's been different with poverty."

Jones says candidly, after four decades of grassroots organizing and coalition building, "I think we have, in the end, attempted to resolve poverty with networks of professionals working in a well-meaning yet palliative social welfare industry, allocating an inadequate amount of resources to make life barely endurable for the poor. We didn't end poverty, we serviced it. Notwithstanding the billions of dollars and armies of workers and professionals (I include myself and most of my life's work), we must admit that after four decades, we are left with three significant facts: the quality of life for today's poor is as bad as, if not worse than, it has ever been; the separation and segregation of the poor from the rest of this nation is greater than ever; and more Americans than ever are either denying the degree and extent of poverty in America, or simply don't care." Jones calls for a commitment that moves beyond the provision of social services "to invigorate a sense of emotion, drama, and outrage around the issues of poverty and racism."

Mobilizing a New Alliance

That commitment will require a mobilization that touches every part of the community. It is a natural role for the religious community to transcend its own social-service mentality and remember its prophetic calling to seek justice. But it must go beyond the churches to engage the arts, media, academia, business and political leadership, and the hundreds of thousands of community and civic organizations—the civil society—that shape much of our social life. The task is simply to generate a new expression of compassion and resolution on behalf of poor people that connects them to the rest of us. It's about including people in the family and the body politic.

What will it ultimately take to overcome poverty? It simply won't happen until we see "the poor" as friends and neighbors, even brothers and sisters, who are not yet known to us. That will take relationship, partnership, and risk more than care, subsidy, and services. It will require our institutions to invest their assets, not just their surplus, and engage the gifts and talents of all their members, not just the leaders. It will require new ways of thinking and acting on the part of all of us. And it will take a reweaving of social relationships in our families and churches, as well as in our schools and workplaces. We must learn to perceive the poor not as a problem to be overcome but as precious resources that have been ignored—people who have gifts and talents that would extend and enrich the community once they were permitted to sit as friends and neighbors in the circles of our lives. Churches and other social institutions must learn to measure poverty by the numbers of children and families who are left outside their doors by a lack of welcome, as much as they are left outside the society by bad national policies. Ultimately, a social climate of shame should apply to those institutions and social bodies who will not come to terms with the "least" of our people, as Jesus would say.

Many of the successful social movements that have made a difference in history result from an alliance between middle-class people and poor people. Without the insight that comes from viewing a society from the bottom up and without the energy of the oppressed, middle-class advocates can't really understand what needs to be changed, nor do they have a constituency that demands it. And without the resources and access that the middle class brings, poor people often don't have the voice to finally make a difference. The abolitionist and civil rights movements in the United

States were good examples of alliances of the middle class and the poor, as are the myriad democratic movements in Latin America, Eastern Europe, and South Africa. Nothing is more satisfying than being part of a movement like that, one that anyone who wants to can join.

We know that government cannot alone solve the problem of poverty. Real solutions will need involvement from all of us. I've had the opportunity to be involved in several successful community-mobilizing efforts in every part of the country. One good example is Springfield, Ohio. We had several days of old-fashioned town meetings, bringing together very diverse churches and non-profit organizations, business leaders, the mayor and other government officials, and lots of ordinary people. One after another, good ideas and creative initiatives from around the country were discussed by the citizens of Springfield. Poor people were also heard, among them a former welfare recipient who lost her child care benefits when she got a raise from $8 to $8.50 per hour. She was trying to better herself, as the society says it wants her to do, yet working, she was poorer than she had been on welfare. This time, local political leaders were on hand to hear her problem. All agreed that some policy changes were in order. They had started to listen to those closest to the problem. A youth rally drew a racially mixed group of eight hundred mostly poor young people, attracted by good music, good food, one another, and Eugene Rivers's dynamic speaking. Sparked by Gary Percesepe, a local pastor with organizing energy, a local Call to Renewal roundtable came together, uniting people who hadn't worked together before.

One result is the Rocking Horse Clinic in Springfield—a new pediatric clinic for low-income children who otherwise have no health care. The new clinic was inspired by Jim Duffee, a soft-spoken Christian doctor, and funded by two hospitals that had never worked together before. It often takes a common project, like the Rocking Horse Clinic, to bring people together and excite a local community.

It isn't easy, but the people of Springfield are developing a common strategy for overcoming poverty, the only way welfare reform will truly work. It's difficult to get many different groups working together, but the principle of partnership is this—everybody does their share, and everyone does what they do best. Nobody gets to sit on the sidelines, and everyone brings some answers and some resources. It can work; I've seen it over and over again. Always, the key is listening to those closest to the problem.

Learn
Your
Strategy

CHAPTER SEVEN

Get to the Heart
of the Matter

For our struggle is not against enemies of blood and flesh, but against the rulers, against the authorities, against the cosmic powers of this present darkness, against the spiritual forces of evil in the heavenly places.
(Ephesians 6:12)

THE WORD "RADICAL" is widely misused and misunderstood. Its meaning goes back to "radix," or "root" (of the problem), but today it is merely a synonym for extremism. Too bad. Too many people are willing to address only the symptoms of problems and never get to the heart or root causes. We need to do more than pull people out of the river before they drown; someone needs to go upstream to see who or what is throwing them in. Asking why so many people are poor, why the affluent are so unhappy, or why the political process seems to be broken can get you into trouble, but also might lead to some real solutions.

I'll never forget a visit to our Sojourners Community from Archbishop Dom Helder Câmara of Brazil. The courageous cleric had become a champion for the poor in Latin America and throughout the world. Though in his mid-seventies, he wanted to walk the streets of our inner-city Washington, D.C., neighborhood and was full of questions about the life of its people. After listening intently to my description of housing patterns that were displacing poor people for the benefit of wealthy real estate speculators and affluent home buyers, Dom Helder shook his head knowingly. "It's the same way in Recife," the poor city in northeastern Brazil where he resided. I recalled a statement he had made years before: "When I feed the poor, they call me a saint. But when I ask why they are poor, they call me a communist." Communism is no longer the issue it once was, but the archbishop's question still generates great controversy. Asking "why" can lead you to the heart of the problem.

I also had the great blessing of meeting Dorothy Day several times. She was the founder of the Catholic Worker movement and became the conscience of the Catholic Church in her time. The Catholic Workers set up houses of hospitality, serving poor and homeless people across the country with works of mercy. More than one hundred Catholic Worker houses are still flourishing today, feeding the hungry and sheltering the homeless. It's easy to get caught up in the immediate when you are doing intense work with poor people because it's so difficult just to keep things going. But Dorothy always made sure the *Catholic Worker* newspaper spoke out against systems that made people poor, attitudes that divided them by race, and governments that turned them into cannon fodder in times of war.

Through their publication, public protest, and campaigns of nonviolent direct action, the Catholic Worker movement offered a prophetic witness alongside their works of mercy. In the opening scene from the movie about her life, *Entertaining Angels*, Dorothy is in jail for opposing H-bomb tests, and a poor and desperate woman is thrown into the cell with her. The picture of Dorothy Day cradling the frightened and crazed woman in her arms is a moving portrait of a moral leader who told the truth about political and economic power *and* took responsibility for the victims of that abusive power.

Dorothy was a mentor for me and taught me valuable lessons about the courage it takes to be prophetic, to speak to the deeper causes of things. She also showed me the importance of staying close to those who are victimized by power, instead of getting too cozy with the powers that be. Those in political power will often offer a kind of access to leaders of social movements, but it is often an access without content. The powerful may like to listen to your ideas and even read your books, but that may not lead to any meaningful changes. Talking to you makes them feel as if they're doing something, and they hope that might satisfy you, too. But it can't. I've learned that personal notes from politicians and presidents mean very little after your criticisms of their behavior appear in *The New York Times.*

The biblical prophets were not hesitant to challenge the rulers of their day. That task generally found them in the desert (the usual location for the biblical prophets) rather than in the corridors of power, where the king's false court prophets resided—the advisors who just told him what he wanted to hear. It's always safer for your soul to be arrested for protest outside the White House than to be invited in for breakfast. Having experienced both, I find the former perhaps less comfortable but much less dangerous. A little quote from Dorothy Day hangs on the wall of my study: "Most of our problems stem from our acceptance of this filthy, rotten system." Perhaps not very poetic, but the sentiment is a crucial reminder to anyone seeking social change.

No matter what our personal involvement is in the small and practical efforts to make change close to home, it is vitally important that we join with wider movements and campaigns to protest and challenge the larger forces that wreak such havoc in the lives of so many people, especially the poor. Such movements are always made up of ordinary people like us, and our involvement in them provides the broader context and credibility that our local efforts need.

To get to the heart of the matter, an activist sometimes needs to learn a little theology. William Stringfellow, a lawyer and Episcopal lay theologian, was a great teacher to a whole generation of activists looking for a deeper analysis of social and political problems. He explained theologically what I had learned in Sociology 101: that an institution is more than the sum of its parts and that it carries an ethos and spirit of its own. Stringfellow brought back to American religious and political conversation the biblical notion of "principalities and powers." He reminded us of the biblical theology that posits that institutional structures—governmental, corporate, and even religious—have a spiritual reality underneath their outward social and political manifestations. I recall many a conversation around Stringfellow's dining-room table when his theological analysis of political institutions shed great light on a political problem we were wrestling with.

Another of Bill's students was Bill Wylie-Kellermann, a Methodist pastor who lives in Detroit and is a close friend of mine. Bill is one of the best activist theologians in the country. He has a real gift for interpreting biblical passages, like the Ephesians text I refer to, and can probe the deeper spiritual and theological dimensions of social issues.

Bill says, "The struggle before us remains necessarily two-handed or two-edged, fusing social analysis and institutional reconstruction with discernment, prayer, and worship-based action." Here again, a faith-based activism brings new insights to the table. He continues, "One gift a church may bring, to any social struggle, is discernment. If the powers that be are realities both material and spiritual, described in the New Testament as being 'visible and invisible, heavenly and earthly,' then comprehending their workings would take an eye and a heart for the spirit." This biblical theology of "the powers" can be very helpfully applied to urban poverty, to nuclear weapons, to business and labor, to race, or even to professional sports, as Bill Wylie-Kellermann has done in his many writings on these subjects. Politics isn't the only problem; there is a spiritual warfare always going on as well, as the Bible suggests. Understanding those deeper spiritual realities is crucial. Let's look at some critical issues we face today, but let's try to get to what's underneath.

The Market and the Common Good

"Big mergers, soaring corporate profits, record salaries for CEOs and starting pitchers, but thousands of job layoffs for American workers. Happy holidays—here's your pink slip!" So began a column I wrote as Christmas 1998 approached, and a record year for

the American economy also became a record year for job layoffs.
What's wrong with this picture, I asked, and why was almost
nobody putting the two together? Why does Wall Street profit,
while workers and their families must take a hit?

From computer giants to the world's biggest oil companies,
merger has become the favorite sport of the world's corporate and
financial elites. Whether it's information-age giants like Netscape
and America Online or industrial-age behemoths like Exxon and
Mobil, those who run the economy agree on one thing—bigger is
better.

When Exxon purchased Mobil, creating the biggest and richest
company in the world, the historic antitrust victory of 1911 that
broke up the oil empire of John D. Rockefeller was reversed. But
Wall Street seems to be exempt from moral scrutiny. Costs must be
cut, said the new company's executives. What's the easiest way to
do that? Cut more jobs. An estimated ten thousand workers would
be sacrificed as a result of the Exxon-Mobil merger.

But those workers were not alone in facing the prospect of losing their livelihoods during that holiday season. For example,
Boeing was cutting forty-eight thousand jobs, owing to the Asian
financial crisis. But who precipitated that? It certainly wasn't the
workers who were losing their jobs; it was the financial investors
whose greed got a little ahead of their common sense. And didn't
American and other overseas investors encourage that lack of pru-
dence? The list of companies whose reorganizations and cost cutting were causing layoffs was long.

Throughout the nineties, the wave of layoff announcements
made grim holiday seasons for tens of thousands of workers. Company after company laid off longtime and loyal workers, all in the
name of being more profitable and competitive. Shareholder profits
seemed to be the only bottom line for these business corporations.

Let's take a look at some of the recurring facts of our economic
life today:

- Mergers are in, with new consolidations occurring every day.
- Costs are being slashed by the new supercompanies, with
  job layoffs as the favorite tactic.

♦ Almost every time jobs are cut, the companies' value goes up on Wall Street.
♦ And every time mergers happen and jobs are cut, the salaries of top executives go up.

Now consider the moral dimension of these economic realities. I know nobody does this—it involves the stock market, which is not supposed to be judged by any moral standards. The market is the great given; it's just what is. But do we really want to live that way? Few things impact our lives more than the economy—just ask all those folks who lost their jobs during the 1990s. So why do we continue to exempt economic behavior from moral scrutiny? Even the best business schools will now tell you that there are other stakeholders involved in business decisions—workers, customers, consumers, the community as a whole, the environment's well-being, and even future generations. But most of those other factors don't fare well with the increasing dominance of quarterly profit-and-loss statements.

Catholic social teaching has a useful concept known as the common good: Individual benefits are not enough to evaluate a society or its practices; rather, we need to be looking after the needs of the whole community, especially those who most easily are left behind. That's the common good.

But who was looking after the common good in the Exxon-Mobil merger? Can anybody seriously suggest that bigger, more powerful, and more profitable corporations will help to protect the interests of workers, consumers, the environment, local communities, and the forgotten poor? Is it right that the casino economy of Wall Street profits when the real economy of workers and their families suffers? Is it fair that the people who do the firing get a raise, while the people fired can only fear for the future of their families? But "right" and "fair" are not words that the market economy wants to bring into this conversation.

Several other little facts and media moments during the 1990s contrasted with the job layoffs.

The combined salaries offered to the top forty free-agent baseball players in the fall of 1998 amounted to $1.2 billion. How far would that have gone to rebuild the Central American countries devastated by Hurricane Mitch during the same period?

During the National Basketball Association's confrontation between players and owners, one player testified this fall that he needs $5,000 "walking around money" each week, and that the impasse with the league owners might force him to sell one of his nine cars. And the even greater wealth of the NBA owners got virtually no media scrutiny.

The disparity question isn't just about money: it's about a growing structure and culture of inequality that affects almost every aspect of our national life. It's also about democracy. Getting to the root of things here means refusing to see the issues as just economic, but seeing them as personal and moral also. That's the critical shift we need to make.

For some time now, I've been carrying on a private dialogue with a major leader of the religious right on many subjects, including economic justice. While we didn't agree on many things, he was remarkably sensitive to the issues of corporate downsizing and their effect on working-class families, even though he was the first to admit that his natural political allies in the corporate world didn't share that sensitivity. After several conversations, he shared with me that his working-class father had once lost his job, through no fault of his own. He remembered his dad crying at the kitchen table about it. It was still a personal issue for this conservative Christian leader, and it shaped his views of responsible and irresponsible corporate behavior. Don't ever let markets and politics exempt themselves from moral scrutiny. Raise the realities of what their behavior does to people's lives. Challenge the ethical foundations of their decision making. Get to the heart of the matter by raising the values questions.

The Nine-Hundred-Pound Gorilla

Whenever there's a conversation about politics, the subject of the great and growing gap between those at the top of American life and those at the bottom is like a nine-hundred-pound gorilla sitting in the room—it's just sitting there, but nobody mentions it. Well it's time we pointed it out. Moral integrity demands it. And the common good requires it.

I remember an excellent conference on renewing democracy held at the National Press Club. The room was full as a panel of eminent historians discussed the roles of the parties, the media, and presidential leadership as factors in democracy's success. Everyone shared alarm at the rapidly decreasing numbers of people voting and participating in politics today. The historians' conversation was both enlightening and fascinating. When it was opened up to questions, a young community college professor went to the floor micro-phone, rattled off a series of statistics about the growing economic disparities of American life, and asked what these realities might have to do with the declining health of democracy. The statistics he cited were stunning but not unfamiliar to the highly educated audi-ence gathered at the Press Club.

Wasn't the big gap in American economic life and the resulting disparity in political influence and involvement at the root of our stagnating political democracy? he asked. Historian James MacGregor Burns quickly responded, "That is the greatest moral issue of our era." I was struck by the clarity of the moment: "the greatest moral issue," he said. The other historians on the panel readily agreed, and went on to admit the many negative conse-quences for democracy caused by such wide economic cleavages. But the professors also agreed that the gap wasn't really a political question today, and nobody in either party was taking up the issue. Interestingly enough, the young academic's question galvanized the whole discussion as nothing else had up to that point. It was the only comment of the morning that got any applause from the audi-ence...sustained applause.

The conference's afternoon program featured a panel of "practi-tioners," of which I was a member. The first questions I asked were these: "If the big economic gap in American life is 'the greatest moral issue of our era,' why aren't we talking about it? If the great disparities are such an obstacle to democracy, why didn't the issue come up on the morning panel? Why was it left to one of the ques-tioners to raise it, and why isn't anyone taking it up as a serious political problem?" Again the audience was immediately engaged. People spoke of the ways the issue affects almost every other issue, from campaign finance, to corporate welfare, to the daily priorities of the U.S. Congress. We were finally discussing it.

Later, after arriving as a Fellow at Harvard in the fall of 1998, I saw the gap operating in the most dramatic ways. During that first year, the John F. Kennedy School of Government was having a weekly seminar on economic inequality. In the spring of 1999, a Kennedy School security guard wrote an editorial in the *Harvard Crimson* stating that in the last five years, he had only one fifteen-cent raise in his twelve-dollars-an-hour salary. The longtime employee also described how the university was now hiring contract labor security guards for even lower wages. During the year, Harvard students began a living-wage campaign at Harvard, and I spoke several times with some of the student leaders. To raise the issue of tremendous wage gaps at the nation's most prestigious university is to point your finger at the nine-hundred-pound-gorilla.

From a biblical point of view, the problem of poverty is, ultimately, a problem of wealth and how it is distributed. And the efforts to overcome poverty or revitalize democracy will, eventually, run up against the distribution problem. So why is it politically impossible to raise the issue in discussions about democracy or poverty? Why can't we discuss the many problems caused by such wide inequalities in our society?

I believe we can and we must. There are, indeed, tremendous political and economic interests that don't want the question to be raised. And those pressures usually succeed in keeping the issue off the table. After all, why would the people at the top of the economy, politics, and the media (who mostly control what questions do get discussed) want the issue to be the subject of a real public debate? You don't have to suggest a massive conspiracy to see that those who benefit most from the gap aren't the ones we can expect to raise the moral issues involved in the distribution of wealth and power.

But when the inequality issue is raised, it tends to provoke a lively public conversation. I get huge numbers of letters and e-mails in response to columns I write on the subject, from people all across the political spectrum. The same happens when I speak of it on the road or bring it up on a radio talk show. When the issue does come up in political campaigns, however rarely, it tends to generate lots of energy. When Pat Buchanan began to raise these topics in his presidential campaigns—corporate power, the "big boys," and the impact on working families—it set off a firestorm. But too often the issue is manipulated in demagogic ways by people like Buchanan, who look for people to blame rather than asking what we might do to build a more equitable American future "with liberty and justice for all." In economic matters, America has stressed liberty much more than justice.

The biblical prophets raised the issue of distribution again and again—and often in ways that were both creative and controversial. Prophetic speech and action were directed at the wealthy and powerful, while the dignity of the poor and oppressed were vigorously defended by those who spoke for God. Read through Isaiah, Jeremiah, Amos, and Micah to find a clear and courageous language for justice that is seldom heard in public discussions today. (For that matter, you seldom hear it in the churches, either.) Yet the economic disparities that provoked the biblical prophets would pale in significance compared with the great gaps we accept as normal in America today. We cannot talk about poverty without discussing the fundamental question of how wealth is distributed. And it's time we started talking about it honestly. That's not class warfare. It's just what the Bible teaches.

Race and Repentance

We cannot answer the question of whether we are getting to the root of our problems without also looking again at the persistent issue of race in America. Today, a shallow concept of "multiculturalism" may actually be hindering our progress. Just enjoying one another's music and restaurants is hardly enough. And the approach that "people of all colors are racists and need to repent" is neither good theology nor honest history. In the deepest and most honest sense, the real issue at stake in American racial history is the idolatry of white supremacy.

The persistence of white identity itself, with the accompanying assumption of white privilege, is still the major obstacle to real change in the racial climate. Italians, Swedes, Irish, and Germans, for example, were never a common ethnic group, but all became "white people" when they arrived in America. What does that mean? When I ask that question in audiences of white Americans, a new recognition often occurs. I make a joke about how Germans are pretty much like the Irish, and Italians can hardly be told apart from Swedes. "All the Europeans were pretty much the same, weren't they?" I ask. After the laughter subsides, I ask, "Why then, when you came to America, did you all become 'white people'?" There is no white history or culture or country. Race is not rooted in either biology or culture. It is a political construct, created for a social purpose.

Indeed, the "white race" was and is merely a political construction to supply an ideology, first for slavery and then for discrimination. That ideology must be dismantled if racial progress is to be made in America. And because the ideology of the white race is also an idolatry that challenges our true and common identity as the children of God, its exorcism is a spiritual and theological necessity.

More than thirty years after the death of Dr. Martin Luther King, Jr., America is still divided along racial lines. Why?

The facts: Two-thirds of black Americans have achieved middle-class status thirty years after the civil rights movement, but one-third remain in poverty—many seemingly trapped in the social pathologies of the urban underclass. At the same time, the increase in the number and profile of other racial minorities is dramatically changing the country's demographic landscape and enormously complicating America's increasingly colorful racial picture. And while many whites are still poor, poverty continues to be disproportionately the experience of people of color in America, especially among the millions of their children who have just been abandoned.

But racism is more than poverty. In 2001, middle-class African-American, Latino, Asian, and Native American parents are still able to tell personal stories of racial prejudice and discrimination directed at them or their children. Most white people, on the other hand, seem tired of talking about racism, are opposed to affirmative action, and want to believe that their country has now become a level playing field for all races. Few people of color believe that. Most significantly, the United States is still a very segregated society—from residential patterns to cultural associations to church attendance. The number of stable, racially integrated neighborhoods across the country is still pitifully small. And after school or work, people of different races in America spend precious little time together.

Have we made progress since the end of legal segregation? Undeniably. But have we come as far in the thirty years since the civil rights revolution as most of us expected we would? Obviously not. Most people today would probably agree that the hopes and dreams that followed the passage of the historic 1960s civil rights and voting rights legislation have yet to be fulfilled. As we enter a new century, America is still a racially divided society, where diversity is widely perceived as a cause for conflict more than for celebration. The question is why?

Clearly we underestimated the problem. Since the 1960s, we have learned that racism goes deeper than civil rights and, indeed, has survived the civil rights movement. Many social analysts and commentators have persuasively argued that racism goes deeper than mere prejudice and personal attitudes and is rooted in institutional patterns and structural injustices. At the end of his life, Dr. King was himself more focused on the issues of poverty, which, he believed, were the next front in the battle to overcome racism.

The depth of racism in the cultural and psychic history of the United States has seldom been fully comprehended. Especially underestimated has been the impact and enduring legacy of the institution of slavery in America. Perhaps we have yet to get to the heart of the problem because we have failed to perceive the fundamental spiritual and theological roots of racism in America.

In biblical terms, racism is an idol that enslaves people and nations in its deadly grip. An idol is simply a lie that people believe and worship. It's the idol of "whiteness" and the assumptions of white privilege and supremacy that have yet to be spiritually confronted in America, and even in the churches. White racism truly is

America's "original sin," to use an old theological concept bound up in the very founding of the nation. Building a nation on land stolen from indigenous people, with the use of slave labor from kidnapped black Africans, has left us with a legacy we have yet to fully deal with. The lack of true repentance for that sin still confounds our efforts to overcome it.

There is more to do than educating, organizing, advocating, changing consciousness, and changing policies. A more spiritual approach would suggest other kinds of action as well. In addition to the hard work of personal relationships, community building, and political and economic change, other responses may be required— like confession, prayer, conversion, and forgiveness. White privilege is hard to give up, and racial oppression is hard to forgive.

Today a deep conviction and growing passion about racial reconciliation is taking root in the very unexpected soil of the white, conservative Christian world. White evangelicalism was simply wrong for a long time on the issue of race. Indeed, conservative white Christians served as a bastion of racial segregation and a bulwark against efforts for racial justice for decades, in the South and throughout the country. All during the civil rights struggle, the vast majority of white evangelicals and their churches were on the wrong side—the wrong side of the truth, the Bible, and the gospel. I will never forget the words spoken to me as a white evangelical teenager by an elder in my home church when I began to ask questions about our city of Detroit's painfully obvious racism and its divided churches. Without apology he said, "Christianity has nothing to do with racism. That's a political issue."

For many years, when evangelical Christians gathered to draw up their lists of theological concerns, the sin of white racism was nowhere to be found. Recently, when conservative white Christians began to construct their political agendas, a recognition of racism's reality was absent from the list of issues: abortion, homosexuality, tax cuts for the middle class, and, yes, opposition to affirmative action.

But now some of that appears to be changing. One of the first signs was when the National Association of Evangelicals, the country's largest group of evangelical denominations and organizations, called together black and white evangelical leaders in 1997 and, in a dramatic moment, its leader confessed the sin of racism by white evangelicals, asked forgiveness, and committed the NAE to forge new multiracial relationships to change evangelical institutions. Even initially skeptical black evangelical leaders became convinced that the new direction was real. Similar declarations of repentance were made in the late 1990s by the Southern Baptist Convention and by white and black Pentecostals at a historic gathering that was dubbed the Memphis Miracle.

Perhaps the most visible white evangelical group now passionately invoking the language of racial reconciliation is the men's group Promise Keepers. In its large stadium rallies and in its list of "promises," a commitment to build relationships between white, black, and brown men has become more and more central to the Promise Keepers' mission. Black staff and board members of Promise Keepers testify to the sincerity of the efforts, but the real tests are still to come.

Clearly the pilgrimage to racial reconciliation must lead to concrete commitments to racial justice. Sitting around the campfire together singing "Kumbaya" and holding hands will not suffice. Outside the church meeting rooms and stadium rallies where white and black Christians are hugging one another is a nation where racial polarization is on the rise, where the legacy of discrimination is still present, and where the majority white population is signaling its tiredness with the "issue" of race by voting down long-standing affirmative action policies.

Will we move beyond the dialogues and presidential commissions that Bill Clinton held and commit ourselves to the personal relationships, institutional transformations, and social and political policies that would move us from soft multiculturalism to a racially pluralistic democracy? It's still difficult to get to the heart of any matter in America without probing the issues of race.

Volunteerism and Band-Aids

In a participatory democracy, citizens must make the crucial difference. For example, citizen action on a much broader scale will be crucial to overcoming the massive problems facing poor children and youth today. It is a noble call, which highlights the importance of citizen involvement for the health and vitality of a participatory democracy. But we should not believe that mere volunteerism is sufficient to resolve the nation's deep social crisis. Getting to the heart of the matter means we cannot let corporate and government leaders off the hook for their economic and political policies that helped create the problems in the first place. Citizen action is the crucial companion to, and not the private substitute for, vital government responsibilities.

Faith communities and the volunteers they motivate and organize are critical to delivery of resources that are lacking in the lives of the almost fourteen million young people most at risk in America today. And, in the era of welfare reform, churches and charities are being widely named as the heir apparent to the federal safety net.

But when you talk to any of the church-based service providers who work with poor people, you can hear the fear in their voices regarding budget cuts. Single adults looking for work (including many middle-aged women), and now many families, have lost their food stamps. Elderly and disabled immigrants losing their benefit checks are quietly telling Catholic Charities caseworkers that suicide might be their best solution. Families of disabled children who lose their extra support say they don't know where to turn. At our Sojourners Neighborhood Center, you can feel the panic among single welfare mothers with kids, who are beginning to realize that they will eventually be cut off, whether or not they find jobs. Those jobs, and the training, child care, and transportation necessary for the much-heralded transition from welfare to work that everyone wants, are not yet in place in the numbers needed.

America is engaged in a highly dangerous process of social engineering, risking poor people and their kids in the politics of untested state and local welfare schemes. Millions of people, many of them children, are in danger of falling through the cracks of a highly uneven patchwork system of welfare reform.

In this critical transition period, it is important that churches and charities not accept the role of merely cleaning up the mess from bad social policy. It is impossible for religious and other nonprofit organizations to take up the whole burden of social welfare. The numbers of people to be served and the dollars required would far outstrip church resources. To make up for government cuts in social services already enacted in the 1990s, each church in America would have to add $250,000 to its budget! Since most churches don't have budgets that high, it is clear that they alone cannot pick up the slack. Furthermore, a merely private charitable approach to social welfare would be an affront to the Bible, which also calls kings, rulers, judges, and employers to be accountable to the demands of justice.

Too often, advocates of volunteerism are suggesting that the system and culture are fine, we just need more volunteers to spend time with kids. When people encourage those who have done well in America to simply "reach down" to share their values and spare time with the less fortunate, some critical realities are forgotten.

Our cultural values and the priorities of the economic and political system are hardly friendly to children. We need volunteers not just to be with kids, but to begin to change the culture that is killing them. That is, in part, both a spiritual task and a prophetic task, and the role of faith communities. We should ask whether it bodes well for a nation's moral health when the corporate CEOs who come to "volunteer summits" make hundreds of times more than their employees do. Or let's ask the political leaders who show up whether it was just or fair for them to make most of their budget cuts in programs affecting poor people. And how about asking whether the same corporations involved in volunteer efforts "volunteer" to provide health care insurance to ten million uninsured children, many of whose parents are their own workers?

It is clear that both the government and the corporate sector see religious and other nonprofit organizations as crucial service providers. What is less clear is whether the perspectives of religious and grassroots nonprofits are welcome at the tables where real decisions are made in this society. Because neither the government nor the corporations have legs in local communities to actually reach the kids in most trouble, they need the nonprofit and neighborhood groups if anything is to be accomplished. But you can't have the work of the nonprofit sector without also inviting their ideas and values into the decision-making process. In a meeting between Colin Powell and religious leaders just after his 1997 Philadelphia Volunteer Summit, we suggested that the faith community could not, in good conscience, merely be a service provider to the poor, but must also take on a more prophetic social role if we're to be faithful to our biblical tradition. I told him we all knew he was a man of logistics and should therefore understand that his corporate and political sectors had few real connections into local communities. But if he wanted our "legs," in the "strategic partnership" with the religious community he had asked us for, he would also have to invite our voice at the table. And that voice would raise some of the harder questions mentioned above.

The religious community is making commitments every day to the poorest children in America and is eager to join together in new partnerships with both business and government. But if faith communities are to be strategic partners, the more prophetic voice of the pastors, nuns, and religious workers from poor neighborhoods must be heard. Corporate executives and White House officials might learn that Jesus did not suggest the answer to poverty was for the rich and powerful to volunteer some of their time to the poor and teach the values of success, but rather for rich and poor alike to undergo a change of heart and create a new community where everyone has a place at the table.

The Personal and the Political

When we talk about getting to the heart of the problem, a very big conflict always arises. There are those who believe the causes of our social problems are primarily personal, due to failures in the values and behavior of individuals. And there are those who see the causes as primarily structural, the consequence of unjust social and economic forces that powerfully define people's chances for success. I grew up with that first, more personal view, but found it to be very incomplete and over time came to adopt the more structural analysis. But having tried to combat poverty and violence for three decades now, I'm coming back to a more balanced view—one that recognizes that it is crucial to confront both personal and political realities if we are to make progress. Both personal responsibility and social justice are key to the solutions that we need.

We need to develop the capacity to look at both the personal and the political through a spiritual lens. One real advantage in the approach of faith-based organizations is the power of spiritual transformation and of real life changes that they offer the people they touch. This is especially true in areas like substance abuse and addiction. Here's where spiritually based programs have had their greatest success. Efforts like Teen Challenge, Victory Outreach, and countless lesser-known church-based programs have demonstrated remarkable results in turning people's lives around. Similar efforts in the Muslim community, especially with prison inmates, show the same achievements. These efforts aim to break the psychological and spiritual hold that addictions to drugs and alcohol have over people's lives, and they often lead former addicts to faith in God and real life transformations.

Poverty as a larger economic issue is related to many personal and relational factors: dysfunctional or abusive domestic relationships, chemical addiction, irresponsible and destructive sexual behavior, deficiencies in work habits or job experiences, emotional instability or depression, bad financial habits and choices, and a whole host of poor decisions that may lead to other problems. For example, many times homeless people have personal problems that go beyond being poor, and social efforts that offer a more holistic approach therefore have the best results. Even in the area of welfare to work, church-anchored programs that get underneath very real economic issues to other interpersonal, habitual, or motivational problems can make the most difference.

Helping people to turn their lives around, offering a supportive community, and providing practical personal guidance can be immensely helpful to persons who are struggling with the multiple burdens of poverty and a life that feels out of control. Those of not underestimate all of the other factors in people's personal lives that can cause poverty. Taking personal responsibility, making different moral choices, learning how to have healthy relationships, and developing good personal, work, and financial habits are all critical for people trying to get on the road to a better life.

At our neighborhood center, we don't just tell the kids that the system is stacked against them as low-income black young people. Mentors and role models teach them how important their decisions are to gaining freedom from oppressive circumstances. We impress upon them that their choices will make a critical difference in their lives.

On the other hand, addressing personal problems does not remove the need for social justice and sound public policies. For instance, without more low-income housing, many homeless people will stay homeless even if they are sober and working. Indeed, some homeless people are already sober and working, but they just can't make enough money to get a place to live. Similarly, many of the homeless suffer from psychological and mental illness; they require treatment programs and halfway community houses, and these simply don't exist in sufficient numbers. They were made homeless by shortsighted public policies that recycled them out of facilities for the mentally ill without adequate alternatives, and now they are left to wander the streets in their own confused worlds.

And I have known many people suffering from substance abuse who want to get clean and sober but cannot find or afford a treatment program. Most languish on waiting lists for months and months, and some are never able to connect to a detox or rehabilitation program that will accept them. Richer people with substance abuse problems can always find a good program; poorer people often cannot.

Likewise, a single mother now off the welfare rolls may get her life together, develop good work habits, and land a job, only to be poorer than before because she can't afford to pay for housing, child care, transportation, and health care for her kids. Without substantial education and training programs, many people simply will not have the skills to advance out of dead-end jobs. The fact is that minimum-wage jobs in the United States do not support a family. Many people work hard and full-time, yet remain poor. That's a social, and fundamentally moral, issue for society to face.

These are all structural problems, which can be remedied only by changes in social and economic policy.

It's often difficult to get people to think about the root causes of social problems, either personal or political. Even the brightest students in classes I've taught seem to find it easier to identify and go after one individual problem or another, rather than develop a strategy to address the big picture. But when people work to develop a more comprehensive and holistic approach, the results can be truly impressive.

The kids at our neighborhood center get it. They do indeed learn that their personal choices are critically important. But they also learn about the broader social and political forces that can dramatically affect their lives. When a very bad "juvenile justice" bill was before the Congress, our kids studied the issue thoroughly. They learned why such a bill would be so negative for young people like themselves and their friends (for example, the bill proposed incarcerating youthful offenders with older criminals in prison cells). After they had politically informed themselves, they marched up to Capitol Hill to lobby against the bill. Our own Congresswoman, Eleanor Holmes Norton, was so impressed that she decided she had to come visit a center that was producing such "active young citizens."

There are many good examples of how to address personal and political problems at the same time. While in Boston, I observed how the city's activists for the homeless are developing a comprehensive strategy, and seem to be getting a new kind of cooperation from many sectors of the community. First, the media have been engaged. I've never heard more radio shows designed to educate the public about the problem of homelessness. Engaging guests, such as a doctor who has devoted his life to serving the homeless or a street counselor who goes out from the shelters to find people on the streets, offer compelling and informative testimonies about the problem. Patiently, these activists answer callers' questions about the nature of homelessness and the homeless in ways that generate both compassion and understanding. They provide powerful examples of offering direct help and service to the myriad personal problems that homeless people face.

At the same time, the activists are also strong advocates for public policy change, challenging local and state officials with reliable statistics about the problem (e.g., how many people have died on the streets of Boston this winter because of the cold) and recommending concrete policy alternatives. They have even gotten the cooperation of the police, who are often very hostile and brutal to homeless people in many other cities. In Boston, the police are trying to become caring instead of cruel, to quote one homeless activist. The street counselors and homeless shelters are now coordinating with the police to find and offer concrete help and services to people without a place to live.

On one local radio show, the audience was enlisted to help find and serve homeless people by calling 911 whenever they saw someone who seemed to be living on the street. The callers were assured that the police would work with the street counselors to assist and care for the people they found. "You can help us find the people who need our community's help," listeners were told. I had never heard that before. They're working with the personal problems of homeless people, coordinating a public response, and advocating to change public policy—all to transform the lives of homeless people and families. Here is a community trying to work together to solve the problem of homelessness. All this is the result of leadership that insists on getting to the heart of the matter.

To get to the heart of the matter, we must deal with both the personal and the political. That's the picture of Dorothy Day in the prison cell, consoling a poor woman whom the system had just thrown away while she was protesting the system itself. An inspiring mentor, she never settled for easy answers but instead always asked hard questions. We should too—that is, if we hope to find some real solutions.

CHAPTER EIGHT

Throw Away Old Labels—It's Values That Count

Where there is no vision, the people perish.
(Proverbs 29:18)

THERE IS A VERY GOOD JOKE that I've heard around the country but never inside the Washington, D.C. beltway. It goes like this: A man is drowning in the Potomac. The Republicans hear about it and rush down to the river. He's slowly sinking about one hundred feet offshore and is crying for help. The Republicans throw him fifty feet of rope and tell the man, "The rest is up to you!" Then the Democrats hear about it. They too rush down to the Potomac. The poor man is now about to go under, still about one hundred feet offshore. The Democrats throw him two hundred feet of rope and then let go of their end!

Why is the joke so popular everywhere except inside the beltway? Perhaps because it touches a nerve. Perhaps because the public is reacting to the heartless conservatism and mindless liberalism that have dominated the political landscape for so many years.

At our 1993 gang peace summit in Kansas City, 164 present and former gang members from 26 cities continually broke out of these old categories. When the young people passionately spoke about the need for family values, respect, and personal morality, they sounded like a Young Republicans self-help convention. But when they prophetically called for an end to racism and police harassment and for a radical program of job creation and economic development, they seemed like radical populists. The point was that they looked to basic values and defied the old and dysfunctional political labels, and so must we if we are to change our communities. Throw away old labels; it's values that count.

The tired old political labels of liberal and conservative, Left and Right, don't mean much anymore. They just don't work on the street. It's true enough that the conservative ideals like personal responsibility, hard work, strong families, and moral values are absolutely essential for social change, as are the liberal ideals of social and racial justice, human rights, and economic fairness. But the old solutions posed by conservatives and liberals have created false choices between these ideals, false choices that have unnecessarily polarized us and become obstacles to real progress.

A conversation starting with shared moral and social values might begin to move us beyond the old entrenched positions. Why must we choose between good values or good jobs, between strong families or strong neighborhoods, between fighting cultural corrosion or battling racism? It's absolutely silly, and, worse, it's keeping us stuck in old ways of thinking. Those old labels are holding us back. Let go of them, and you'll be surprised by how much freer you will feel.

Neither Left nor Right

But it's hard to let go of old habits. Even though it's increasingly clear that the answers we need won't come from the Left or the Right alone, we continue to turn to one side or the other for solutions. The fact that even religious groups on both political sides tend to measure their success by marginal partisan political gains is especially disconcerting. Spiritually based social movements should measure their progress by concrete moral change and societal impact, not by adopting the false bottom lines of the pollsters and pundits. How can the election or defeat of a handful of members of Congress be viewed as a benchmark of victory either way, compared with monumental changes like the end of slavery or legal segregation led by religiously inspired abolitionist and civil rights movements of the past? Would the biblical prophets be satisfied with electoral body counts instead of the weightier matters of righteousness and justice?

Both the religious right and the religious left would do well to be more "religious" and less political. Unfortunately, some religious people are still lining up on one or the other side of our all-too-polarized political battlefield. Some conservative religious leaders succumbed to the temptation to play the role of power brokers on the inside of Republican party battles for power and influence. And some liberal religious leaders just clamored for photo opportunities at the Democratic White House.

Conservative religious activists have tried to take over the Republican party apparatus in local communities and turn out enough of their constituents to make them a real force in the party. They've certainly helped the Republican party win elections, but even some religious right leaders are now openly questioning whether that has really served to advance a moral agenda. Meanwhile, on the other side, liberal religious activists bemoan the state of American politics and claim that the American people have been confused and duped by a highly energized religious and political right wing that has outspent, outorganized, and outsmarted everybody else. They seem to assume that all the answers lie on the left side of the political spectrum, and they don't seem to question whether their dilemma is more than just tactical.

Isn't it about time to admit that neither liberal nor conservative solutions have been working very well, and that we need some new directions? That's what many people in this nation believe; I've heard it all across the country.

Conservatives have been right about many things: the importance of a values-based politics, personal responsibility, and strong families, and the dangers of bureaucracy to healthy citizenship. But conservatives have been wrong with respect to racism and their failure to defend the poor. Conservatives have been guilty of a double standard in attacking big government while uncritically championing both corporate power and militarism. And on the edges of conservatism, a legitimate pro-life commitment has been turned, by a zealous few, into an abusive and sometimes murderous crusade against the women and medical personnel at abortion clinics. Conservatives could learn much from the rich traditions of nonviolent movements in their efforts to change the nation's attitudes toward abortion. And some conservatives have also allowed their pro-family values to become obsessively focused on campaigns against the civil rights of homosexuals, who are irrationally and unfairly blamed for the very real breakdown of family life in America.

Liberals have been right in fighting for racial, economic, and gender justice, in protecting the environment, and in standing for peace. But the liberal left has too often failed to uphold critical personal and cultural values, such as strong family life, and has instead offered the nation a litany of moral relativism. For example, many now believe we must stop talking about giving fourteen-year-olds the information and tools to make their own decisions about whether to have sex. Instead, we are told we must create a moral environment around adolescents that persuades them that sexual activity at their age is a bad choice. Teaching young people both healthy sexual behavior and just racial behavior is essential to their learning positive values. Finally, liberalism has made a fundamental mistake in seeing a woman's right to choose as the only moral issue at stake in the abortion dilemma.

Both conservatives and liberals have often forgotten their best and original impulses while becoming tied to vested interests. Most conservatives can't seem to challenge the behavior of big corporations, even when they are trampling on the most sacred of traditional family and moral values. Similarly, many liberals never dare to challenge teachers' and public employees' unions or government bureaucracies, even when they protect only their own interest, rather than those of the people they are supposed to serve.

Conservatives have been too uncritical of Wall Street, and liberals have relied too much on state solutions to our social problems.

On the right, the market is the magical solution to every social problem. On the left, societal responsibilities have often been simply equated with governmental ones. What government can and must do, what the social responsibilities of corporations are, and what other civil institutions can best contribute are critical issues for both liberals and conservatives.

The new discussions we need require a values-based approach, instead of just taking sides. Making a moral impact upon a society usually requires subjecting politics to outside moral criteria, rather than merely playing the inside power games. Holding politics accountable is best accomplished by independent social movements with clear moral priorities. And that demands more than just seeking a place at the table of political power.

The Crisis and Opportunity of Welfare Reform

Political organizations—and especially politicians—resist the application of moral language to political decisions. Nonetheless, that is precisely what we must do. Once we have thrown away old labels, we begin the more difficult task of applying moral values to politics.

The 1996 welfare bill provides a good case study. Some fundamental values conflicts are at the center of it, its consequences will be with us for some time, and its aftermath affords new and important opportunities for moral political engagement.

Addressing Call to Renewal's 1999 National Summit on the Churches and Welfare Reform, Secretary of Housing and Urban Development Andrew Cuomo sadly reflected on what was going on inside the administration and the country at the time the bill was passed. "I was on the Welfare Reform Task Force for President Clinton. Believe me, it had nothing to do with any form of policy debate. Once the issue got to the United States Congress, it was a political debate. No one would say 'How do we really help people on welfare? Let's design an intelligent program to move people from welfare to work'—that wasn't the discussion. It was a political discussion, and we were demonizing the people on welfare. They were the enemy and this was a retaliation against the enemy."

Most Americans rightly favor a more decentralized, effective, and values-centered approach to alleviating poverty. But the bill dismantled a six-decade national commitment to provide a federal safety net for the poor and replaced it with block grants of federal money to the states, without any uniform national standards or accountability. The poor of Mississippi would now have to trust their fate to the social conscience of their state legislators and to a governor who cynically offered to buy each welfare recipient an alarm clock as his state's contribution to welfare reform.

The new system imposes a five-year lifetime limit on receiving benefits and requires most on welfare to find work within two years, without national commitments or funds to provide sufficient jobs and job training. Millions of mostly uneducated, untrained, and unskilled single mothers will now be forced to compete for the too few jobs that provide a living family wage.

It is right to help families to shift from welfare to work where that is at all possible, to move from federal bureaucracies to community-based programs, from dependency to self-sufficiency, from a system of permanent subsidy to one of transitional help. But it is another thing to slash and burn old systems and safety nets with no alternatives at hand. As one observer commented, "When they tear down a house, normally they get the people out first!" We now seemed quite ready to experiment radically with the lives of poor people and their children in ways we would never risk with our own kids.

Radical welfare reform was needed, but it should have been accomplished with a plan carefully designed, as much as possible, to protect the most vulnerable, especially children, from social abandonment. This bill did not do that. Before the bill passed, the Urban Institute predicted that a million more children would likely be thrown into poverty, and three to four million already in poverty could be plunged into even deeper jeopardy. We've already seen the statistics demonstrating that these predictions are coming true.

How did this happen? What were the political forces and moral choices that led to the passage of the 1996 welfare bill?

Bill Clinton's moral failure was to cooperate with this welfare reform process when he clearly knew better. But neither the

Republican Congress nor President Clinton were the only ones implicated in the decision. The welfare bill passed by Congress and signed by the president was the consequence of forces that have been growing for some time and which threaten to engulf the nation in even deeper social crisis.

The liberal moral failure was to block welfare reform for so long that it became too late to transform the system positively. The welfare system has been broken for some time. What was sincerely intended as support for our poorest and most vulnerable citizens often became a trap of poverty, despair, dependency, illegitimacy, and crime. While keeping some people from falling even further, the system came to foster rather than ameliorate social disintegration. Instead of providing emergency relief and transitional help, the welfare system was often helping to subsidize social pathology. Work, marriage, and home ownership are three pillars of American life (and antidotes to poverty); all of them were undermined by the nation's welfare and housing policies.

Too many Democrats ignored this growing disaster. Too many liberals cried "racism" when the system was criticized or warnings came about family and community breakdown. When the Democrats had the chance to fix the system, they failed even to try. Liberal politicians saw sympathetic voting blocs in bloated government bureaucracies that kept them in power while maintaining instead of transforming poverty.

Finally, welfare system failures could no longer be ignored, and public opinion turned not only against the system but, cruelly, against the beneficiaries of the system. Politicians exploited public frustration, and the clamor for change—any kind of change— became overwhelming before a responsible alternative could be developed to replace the broken system.

Again, Andrew Cuomo's words on the politics of welfare reform: "We wind up then blaming the victim. The government failures were not the problem of the recipient, but of the government that designed the programs in the first place. What the programs really did was dis-incentivize and penalize all the values and virtues that we espouse as American citizens. Look what the

programs did: dis-incentivized ownership...dis-incentivized marriage...disempowered the male...disempowered the wage earner.
And then we wound up penalizing and blaming the people who
participated in the program."

The conservative moral failure was to fan the flames of public
discontent with incendiary rhetoric that placed the principal burden
of poverty on the poor themselves. Who can forget Texas Senator
Phil Gramm's constant rebuke to the "people being pulled in the
wagon to finally get out and help push"? If liberals have bureaucra-
tized the poor, conservatives have demonized them.

Perhaps the worst moral failure (and a bipartisan one) was in the
choices made as to where to save money in the necessary attempt to
balance budgets and reduce deficits. Virtually all welfare experts,
such as former Senator Daniel Patrick Moynihan, have pointed out
in vain that welfare reform, in the short run, will cost more money,
not less, to effect the transition from welfare and dependency to
work and self-sufficiency. President Clinton's original welfare
reform plan also recognized that long-term success requires more
short-term investment in education, job training, and child care.

But the politicians decided to retaliate by taking money from the
people with the least political power. Neither Republicans nor
Democrats have been willing to save money where it could most
reasonably be cut—from unfair corporate welfare, unnecessary entitlements to the affluent, and still excessive military spending.
Though politicians hate the phrase, they have proven it true: Our
government is "balancing the budget on the backs of the poor."
During the debate, some legislators suggested that the savings from
food-stamp reductions could be used for a middle-class tax cut.
That is both immoral and outrageous. On the day the welfare bill
was passed into law, a biblical quotation from the book of Numbers
came to my mind: "Be sure your sin will find you out."

Welfare reform has become an excuse to stop worrying about
poor people. With politicians boasting about the number of people
being dropped from the welfare rolls, and with most Americans
having no contact with the people being dropped, poverty can finally just be forgotten. What happens to people that you don't know

and never hear about is a question that quickly fades from consciousness. And if you have some easy and comforting explanations for the poverty of the few poor people you do see on the street, your errands need not be interrupted by second thoughts.

There is good news and bad news about welfare reform. The bad news is that the politicians are asking the wrong question. The governors, the Congress, and the White House have all been busy congratulating themselves for rapidly falling welfare rolls. Indeed, they are the lowest in thirty years. But haven't we forgotten something here? The object wasn't just to get people off welfare. That's easy. You just cut families off, as states are now doing around the country. The goal was to move people from welfare to work and eventually out of poverty. Right? The National Governors' Association admits, "Reductions in caseloads are not the only measure of success for governors—states must also look at the number of recipients and former recipients who are working, the types of jobs they are getting, and whether their families are better off."

By this measure, welfare reform has not succeeded in addressing poverty; instead our policy has merely "turned the welfare poor into the working poor," says Mary Jo Bane of Harvard's Kennedy School of Government. And that's true only for the ones who are getting jobs. According to the National Governors' Association and the National Conference of State Legislators, only about 50 percent of welfare recipients who lose benefits are getting jobs, which means the other half are not. And of those getting work, most are stuck in very low-paying jobs that don't begin to provide a family income. Even though many are working more than forty hours per week, former welfare recipients who find jobs often earn between $8,000 and $10,000 annually—an income well below the poverty line for a family of three. So when these mostly single moms and their kids lose assistance, they're ending up poorer than they were on welfare.

For example, three out of four jobs that welfare recipients have landed don't have any health benefits, and after a year off welfare, people can lose their Medicaid. What kind of solution is that to poverty? The International Union of Gospel Missions reports that many of those coming to missions for shelter say they have lost government benefits. Homeless shelters in general report a shift in population, from men with substance-abuse problems to women with children; in fact, children now account for 38 percent of the homeless population, according to the U.S. Conference of Mayors. Hunger is on the rise as well; for example, a survey of former welfare recipients in Wisconsin discovered that "after leaving welfare, families were almost 50 percent more likely to say they had no way to buy groceries." The U.S. Conference of Mayors agrees: "Low-paying jobs that cannot support a household continue to be a very troublesome problem. Many cities report that welfare reform has had a negative impact on hunger and homelessness. Moreover, several cities expect a downturn in the economy, which will further increase the number of homeless and requests for food." The increasing need for health, housing, and food services shows that the welfare reform "solution" really isn't one yet. And if a recession were to occur at the same time that the really large cuts to single mothers and their children come into effect, we could see some very serious social dislocation.

Our current approach to welfare reform also ignores glaring contradictions. It is argued that social welfare is bad for the character of the poor, while the much more expensive corporate welfare that the government provides to the nation's biggest companies is seen to be good for the economy. A series of 1998 investigative articles in *Time* magazine pointed out the fallacy and fraud of enormous government subsidies and tax benefits to large corporations in return for the empty promise of jobs, which never materialized in city after city. Yet the vociferous critics of welfare to the poor were not seen jumping up and down to expose that scandal. Cutting payments to a single mother on welfare is viewed as sound fiscal policy, while continuing to subsidize McDonald's for advertising Chicken McNuggets in Europe is seen as healthy for business. I guess it pays to have good lobbyists. Perhaps the poor should hire some.

Our approach to balancing the budget also rests on inconsistencies. We're told to accept the fact that programs for low-income people have to be cut to make budgets balance, while more costly federal benefits for the middle class and senior citizens remain untouched. Logical means testing of government benefits is successfully blocked by powerful lobbies that the poor just don't have. The waste in social programs becomes another excuse for their elimination, while the even larger wastes of military spending, for example, are routinely accepted year after year. When fully 93 percent of all entitlement cuts have so far come from programs that benefit our lowest-income citizens, you have to ask whether the process of deficit reduction has been a fair one. One is left with the clear impression that some people have more clout than others when it comes to public policy decisions, and poor people don't really count at all.

I was as critical as anyone of the 1996 welfare bill, but that battle is past. And despite the larger political forces and their moral failings, there were people who were for the welfare bill and people who were against it out of the best of moral intentions. Some saw how ineffective and devastating to the poor the welfare state had become; others saw how devastating it would be to simply dismantle the old system without the necessary alternatives in place. Both those who believed that alternatives should have been created first and those who think they must be created now are coming together in new partnerships.

The good news about welfare reform is that the crisis facing our poorest mothers and their children has mobilized faith communities more than anything in a very long time. Mostly unnoticed by the mainstream media, faith-based organizations from across the political spectrum are becoming involved in the vital task of welfare reform and the deeper agenda of overcoming poverty. Since the welfare reform bill, more than sixty diverse church leaders have been meeting regularly at a Christian Roundtable on Poverty and Welfare Reform, sponsored by Call to Renewal. A new mobilization is definitely occurring, with conservative evangelicals working alongside Catholic, black, and mainline churches. People are again reading what the Bible says about God's concern for the poor, almost entirely missed in the rancorous debates of Christian politics these last two decades. Some of the very best work on the ground now is being done by churches, and new partnerships at the local level are beginning to make effective change a reality. Some are helping low-income families to succeed in work. Others are trying to reverse youth violence and teenage pregnancy. Many church-based organizations are helping to create jobs and housing, doing broad-based community organizing and linking with other institutions, including business and government.

In February 1999, nearly five hundred of those faith-based organizations from more than forty states gathered at Call to Renewal's National Summit, to pool resources, share best practices, and build a national network and voice on behalf of people who are poor in America. Among other things, they went to Capitol Hill to remind the politicians that the Bible says that lawmakers, too, will be judged by how they treat the poorest and most vulnerable in their midst. The churches won't let the politicians off the hook. They insist that this effort will take all of us. And it will. The job won't be done until families are not just off the welfare rolls but off the poverty rolls. Politically, it could be irresistible if religious liberals and conservatives came together around this agenda, and even that is beginning to happen. Around the country, we can already feel the beginnings of it. This is a wonderful example of throwing away old labels and concentrating on values instead.

Hungry for Values

These days, America is hungry for values. The old and outmoded questions are about liberal and conservative, Left and Right. But today the new questions are: What's right, and what works? What kind of nation do we want to be? What kind of people do we think we are? What are our responsibilities to one another? Who are our neighbors and how will we treat them? And what kind of world are we leaving for our children? Those are the really important political questions because they have to do with our basic values. It is increasingly clear that the future of American politics will be shaped by conversation about values.

My experience is that values-based efforts and projects around the country are the ones that are working the best. In every area of concern, you have to know what your values are if you are going to succeed. For example, if you believe that children's educational opportunities should not be governed by their parents' income or family's zip code, that value will shape your philosophy and strategy of education. If you believe that someone who is willing to work hard should be able to earn a living wage and support a family, that value will shape your view of economics. If you believe that those with money should not be able to buy extra political access and influence, that simple principle will shape your perception of politics. When they are based on such values, community efforts can bring diverse people together to fight for quality education, living wages, or campaign finance reform.

Instead of blaming other people for the problem, it's time for us all to ask ourselves, "Who is responsible for the people who are falling through the cracks in this community?" That's the question I ask over and over at town meetings around the country.

I asked it one day in Lancaster, Pennsylvania. Gathered together were many of the city's leading pastors and civic and business people. The mayor was there, along with the police chief and several members of the city council from both political parties. "Who's responsible?" I asked. "It's that Republican Congress," said some. "It's those failed liberal solutions," retorted others. Fine, I said, but you've just answered who's to blame. That's an old question and, indeed, there's plenty of blame to go around. I said that I thought both failed Democratic solutions and a draconian Republican Congress shared some of the blame for the situation in which the poorest residents of Lancaster County now found themselves. But I reminded the Lancaster civic leaders that I had asked a different question: "Who's responsible for the kids falling between the cracks, today, in Lancaster?" Finally they got to the right answer, as most people do. The answer is "We are." Communities are looking for fresh leadership today—not the old partisan kind, but a new bridge-building kind. Figuring out the right thing to do and a way to do it are the tasks that today's leaders should be addressing.

Therefore, our approach to social change must be values centered. Many people today want to use the language of "moral values," others prefer to speak in terms of "spiritual values," and lots of people still use the more traditional "religious values," but no matter how you phrase it, there is a growing consensus that the link between politics and values must be reestablished.

Even when you run into political disagreements, listen for what people's values are. You may find that underneath the ideological arguments there are some shared values that might form the basis for new conversation and cooperation. Don't get trapped in the endless political debate that seems to preoccupy the political and media elites. Take politics back from them and bring it into the community. Search for the deeper values and begin to build on them.

Town Meetings

At that meeting for community leaders in Lancaster, I asked a second question: "What is your strategy *together*, and how are you mobilizing the resources of this community, public and private, to do the job?" The civic leaders confessed that they really didn't have a common strategy or a plan to mobilize their resources. But they all agreed that that's why they had come. A rally had been arranged for that afternoon in the largest auditorium in town. Eight hundred people turned out, a big enough crowd in that town to attract significant media coverage. As I spoke to a very diverse cross section of the people and groups of Lancaster, I could feel the potential of a community becoming engaged in solving its problems as they built on common values.

During the 1996 presidential campaign, I embarked on a seven-week speaking tour that included sixty town meetings in thirty-four cities. I was campaigning not for any candidate or party but for the kind of values-based agenda that could revitalize American politics. In town meetings from Harlem, New York, to Orange County, California, I became even more convinced that many Americans are looking for a moral vision of politics beyond both the religious right and the liberal left.

A whirlwind tour during the election campaign provides quite a view of the country's landscape, including its political and spiritual terrain. The crowds were often two or three times what the organizers in each place had hoped for, indicating a widespread hunger for a moral vision of politics. I could feel the energy in the sanctuaries, auditoriums, and parish halls where people gathered. Despite their lack of enthusiasm for politics as usual (and for the choices available to them that year), there was clearly a hope for alternative possibilities.

"Tonight we are here to talk about politics!" declared Warren Braun in Milwaukee at the Catholic archdiocesan center. The overflow audience actually cheered in response. Even though the sandwiches had long since run out, they knew they were going to be fed by a discussion of "real politics" instead of the poll results and attack ads of that election year.

We talked about the meaning of *polis* (related to the word "politics"), as in the people, the public square, and the common good. It involves a discourse about values, right and wrong, and the ways of sustaining or restoring the healthy social and moral fabric of a society. It's about putting forth new ideas, solving problems, resolving conflicts, finding common ground, and making sure no one is left behind. (Of course, in the original Greek city-states from which the concept of "polis" comes, everyone except landholding males was left out of the discussion.) It requires an informed and involved citizenry who believe that what they think and do can make a difference, and that their real political involvement has to do with the time, energy, gifts, and resources they put into rebuilding their own local communities, not with just pulling a lever on the first Tuesday of November.

In city after city, we talked about that deeper meaning of politics and even the connection between spirituality and politics. We spoke of a politics that responds to the call of the biblical prophet Amos to "let justice roll down like waters," and also to the prophet Nehemiah's exhortation to "rebuild the city." Practical talk followed about how to restore the crumbling social and moral infrastructures of our communities with a combination of spiritual renewal and solutions that work.

In each place, there were lots of young people. The twenty-eight-year-old organizer in one city was thrilled, saying, "We have never got anyone out to peace-and-justice events who is under forty until now." In most places, elected officials eagerly jumped into the discussion about a new politics. The panels of respondents exemplified an extraordinary diversity—community organizers and local TV anchors, Jewish rabbis and evangelical ministers, state legislators and Orthodox priests, business executives and college professors, inner-city pastors and deans of Episcopal cathedrals. In every city, the audience was full of people from many walks of life. Even people from the Christian Coalition showed up, saying they were weary of "Christian" being so identified with just "Republican." And they met liberal Methodist clergy who were similarly eager to move beyond their assumed attachment to the Democratic party.

I've done literally hundreds of town meetings these last few years, in virtually every region of the country. And I have become convinced that a new value-based politics is begging to be born. Every one of these meetings became a kind of new table set in each community, where people sit down together for the first time. By the close of the evening, people find that they've enjoyed themselves, as at a good meal. Sustenance, relationship, new visions, and, most of all, real hope have been the result of such table fellowship. What we learn from such town meetings can significantly shape future community agendas.

Call-ins to the countless radio talk shows we do on the tours confirm what we hear each night at the town meetings—namely, that many people are vitally interested in the real issues at stake in our public life, that they are deeply disillusioned with both political parties and political choices in general.

What Are the Alternatives?

But what are the alternatives to the old political labels? And what does it mean to go beyond Right and Left? We certainly don't want to settle for a mushy middle. Searching for common ground is not the same thing as becoming a political centrist. Don't do the trendy thing of grabbing the political center; instead, search for the moral center of an issue or a public debate. Find common ground by seeking higher ground, and you'll discover a whole group of new and unexpected allies.

A new value-based politics could be moral without being sectarian. Most of us still probably think about predicting the future when we hear the word "prophetic," but its meaning in religious traditions has more to do with a social critique willing to raise the moral questions of justice that most ignore. Drawn from the more prophetic elements of our social, political, spiritual, and religious traditions, a new politics would identify common moral values on which to build. It would seek to articulate a moral vision of politics that is neither Left nor Right, but draws on the strengths of each side, learns from their mistakes, and transcends both with new solutions. A fresh discussion of values—both personal and social—is paramount in forging a new and prophetic vision that is morally rooted but not ideologically compartmentalized. A prophetic politics wouldn't hesitate to be courageous in its pronouncements and would seek to avoid being tied to predictable special interests. And it would insist on a strong standard of the common good to guide public policy. New political visions shouldn't be restricted to discussions of government policy but should also include conversations about the cultural and moral assumptions that are the unspoken underpinnings of our public discourse. For example, how does the influence of materialism fundamentally shape our political discussions? Rabbi Michael Lerner has critiqued the empty ethics of selfish individualism and offered instead a "politics of meaning." We might also ask how a more consistent regard for human rights, wherever they are violated, could challenge both ideological camps. A politics of values would raise the deeper questions that both the Right and the Left often leave out.

Rather than the old language of "the center" or "the middle," the challenge of building new common ground may be a better way to describe the quest for a value-based politics that is neither Left nor Right. In every region of the nation, the effort to build that common ground is being widely affirmed. All of these efforts are really ways of speaking about the need to rebuild our civil society, which has crumbled so badly. It is finally all about the politics of community, and that could become attractive to a whole range of people.

CHAPTER NINE

Find New Allies and Search for Common Ground

Then they said, "Let us start building." So they committed themselves to the common good. (Nehemiah 2:18)

YOU CAN'T DO IT ALONE. That's what the Jewish exiles discovered as they rebuilt their beloved Jerusalem. Together, they repaired the crumbling walls of the city—everyone with a job to do and all the work fitting together. Many urban pastors today, confronting the disarray around them, have preached from the prophet Nehemiah's description of how the city was rebuilt and renewed. It's become a text for our times as well as we find new allies and search for common ground.

All of the people in the parents group were poor. Their kids were enrolled in the after-school program at the Sojourners Neighborhood Center, and the parents were all glad for the extra help. While they were really concerned about the lives and futures of their children, they often felt a shortage of resources to offer their kids. Many were unemployed or underemployed, most had little education, and a majority were single parents with plenty of problems of their own.

When someone suggested at a parents' meeting that something needed to be done about the crack houses in the neighborhood, most were skeptical. Sure they wished the drug houses, which posed such threats to their kids, weren't on their blocks. They were protected, however, by drug dealers with money and guns. But what people can't do alone, they can accomplish together. That's the lesson the people of our Columbia Heights neighborhood learned through their campaigns to close several crack houses that threatened the life and peace of the neighborhood.

The effort was brought together by an unlikely organizer. Tammy Krause was a young Mennonite woman working out of the Sojourners Neighborhood Center. She, too, didn't seem to be a match for the drug dealers and the well-connected people who stood behind them. But Tammy was the kind of organizer who believed that ordinary people could solve their problems if they just pulled together. She believed in her neighbors, and after a while they began to believe in themselves. She developed the ability to walk and talk with people to gain their trust. And, of course, Tammy did a whole lot of walking and talking in the streets of the neighborhood. I remember many a conversation with Tammy on the front stoop of her house, next door to mine, when it looked as if the odds against us were just too high. There were certainly times when she was tempted to give up. But I saw in Tammy a combination of gritty determination and a real conviction that the people of the neighborhood had the potential to win this battle.

Those are the qualities that a successful organizer needs. She had confidence in the people she was working with and in their collective possibilities. One day when Tammy and I were walking down our street, one of the young prostitutes who worked the corner at night approached us and wanted to talk to her. As is often the case, drugs and prostitution had taken over this young woman's life. As Tammy took the young woman aside for a personal conversation; I could see that they had already developed a trusting relationship. The two women were about the same age, but their lives had been worlds apart. The understanding evident between them was a very hopeful sign.

Several months later there was a rally and press conference on Tammy's steps to celebrate a great community victory over drugs and violence. Reporters put microphones in my face to ask how we did it. I just smiled and pointed to all the happy neighbors in the front yard. Ask them, I said. "They're the ones who pulled this off."

The parents gained the courage to confront the surly drug dealers but also found the compassion to understand how people get caught up in drug trafficking. They learned how to trace the ownership of houses and property and how to track down slum landlords. They found effective ways to get the attention and cooperation from the police. And they learned about the kind of political corruption that provides cover for drug dealing and how to force politicians to go public for the sake of the neighborhood. Not only did they close down some of the worst crack houses, but they also arranged for the safe relocation of the women and children who were living in them. The drugs became the enemy, not the people who had become addicted to them.

A few years earlier in the neighborhood, poor renters in dilapidated inner-city apartment buildings formed the Southern Columbia Heights Tenant Union and eventually turned their housing into renovated tenant-owned cooperatives. People who weren't accustomed to even talking to their neighbors on the same floor became effective community organizers who regularly won battles for rent control at city hall. Living as a faith community in the neighborhood made it possible for Sojourners to help make many of these efforts possible. As the organizer of our tenant union, Jim Tamialis, like Tammy, learned to work behind the scenes, offering support to local neighborhood leaders. Unless they learned they had to do this themselves, it was never going to get done.

Social change is hard. We are often up against very powerful forces that resist any effort to change the way things are. Individuals can feel quite powerless against such forces. You quickly learn that joining with other people is the best way to make a difference. Not only is there strength in numbers, but there is also encouragement, inspiration, new ideas, new connections, and a mobilization of resources that wouldn't be possible if each of us was simply on his own. Sometimes the first step in getting involved is to find some people to get involved with.

The key word here is "community." It's not just that you can't do it alone but that you shouldn't. And you don't have to. People are nervous today about venturing out on their own. That comes, in part, from a lack of experience in community. The problem of self-definition today is connected to a lack of community definition. Both issues can be addressed when we talk about the power of a team, of collaboration, of support, and of the safety a group provides against the fear of failure. I can't put enough stress on the importance of building relationships in the struggle to change our communities and our world. Most everything comes out of relationships, and those who learn how to build them will have the most success.

Churches "Dropping Their Colors"

Common concerns are bringing former adversaries together in ways that reveal how outmoded our old political categories and divisions have become. Indeed, new configurations of issues and constituencies hold the real promise of some positive movement forward in a number of critical areas. Sometimes the most deadlocked people are the leaders of large institutions. The story of what some Christian leaders have done to come together around the issue of poverty has lessons for us all about how to find new allies and search for common ground.

On a sunny April day in 1997, sixty Christian leaders whose groups had been at odds with one another for years came together in a hotel conference room searching for some common ground on solutions to poverty. That Philadelphia Roundtable on the Churches and Welfare Reform has become a case study for me, a model of how diverse and formerly divided groups can join together for common purposes. As I've previously described, my own inspiration for calling the gathering together came from the experience of watching young street leaders from rival gangs drop their colors for the sake of peace.

Many of the participants, invited together by Call to Renewal, commented that they had never before met with such a broad and diverse cross section of church leaders and organizations. "This has been probably the most religiously diverse gathering of the Christian community to address the issue of poverty, certainly within this decade," said Wes Granberg-Michaelson, General Secretary of the Reformed Church in America. Too often, people just continue to talk to others in their own group about solving social and community problems, and we wonder why no progress gets made. New perspectives, new collaborations, and new resources can open up new possibilities.

Given the wide-ranging guest list, the amazing thing about the Roundtable is that it worked! There were several reasons why. To begin, the spirit of the day was humility. *Christianity Today* noted, "A confessional attitude also marked the meeting: recognition that as long as Christians are divided over how to respond to the plight of the poor, the church is part of the problem and not the solution." From religious right to religious left, church leaders confessed that their divisions had hurt poor people. Evangelical, Pentecostal, Catholic, Black, Latino, and mainline Protestant leaders and churches who had been at odds for years began to explore common directions. The crisis facing poor families in America was finally bringing the churches back together. At the beginning of our day, I suggested that when a hurricane is coming and you're passing a sandbag to the person next to you, you don't first ask if the person is a liberal or a conservative. You pass the sandbag and depend upon the help! We discovered that neither triumphalism nor defensiveness brings people together, while humility and willingness to learn from others do.

We also followed some ground rules. We stuck to the issue of poverty. We agreed to take others at their word, meaning challenges were in order but questioning others' motives was not. We pledged to listen to one another rather than make speeches, accepting that both liberals and conservatives had important things to contribute. Finally, we agreed to explore what our faith might be calling us to *do*—perhaps even do together.

We continued by asking three questions: Where do we have common ground? Where might we build common ground? And what are the biggest differences between us that need more conversation? Finding common ground is made more possible if the participants in the conversation can identify some common values, points of reference, and sources of authority. In this case, the religious leaders kept coming back to what the Bible said and Jesus taught, which helped enormously in establishing places of agreement from which to build.

To get at those questions, we followed a careful process built on three structured conversations, each connected to the next. First, we started with the *principles* we had in common. What beliefs, convictions, and commitments did we all share? Here's where the common reference points helped. We took out our Bibles and searched together to find what the Scriptures said about the topic of God's concern for the poor. Once we made our collective appeal to the Bible, there wasn't much disagreement about what it said. The church leaders came together, despite their differences in theological, social, and political views, because their shared Christian faith made it clear that Christ called his followers to serve "the least of these." And those most in need in this country were facing a real danger in the wake of the 1996 welfare bill. Beginning with principles is always best. This is where we usually have the most in common. Many people want a lot of the same things, even if they think they disagree on how to get there.

Second, we looked at some of the *practices* around the country that we could all support. Were there concrete social ministries that we all could agree were making the difference that we all believed to be critical? Several practitioners of successful programs were on hand to share their experience about what really works in overcoming poverty and violence. Again, it wasn't long before we agreed that such efforts deserved our support. Eugene Rivers of Boston's Ten Point Coalition and Mary Nelson of Bethel New Life in Chicago presented powerful examples of new and innovative faith-based practices emerging around the country. We discussed how such successful models can offer tools and resources for other communities if they are documented, evaluated, and shared. Taking action is very attractive to people, and doing things rather than just talking about problems has a real appeal. Build on that. There will always be more unity about concrete action than about theoretical debate.

Churches nationwide are opening their doors to create a safe place of refuge for children, families, and those most alienated in violence-torn neighborhoods. But *all* the doors should be opening, we agreed—suburban churches, too, partnering with urban congregations. We discussed the crucial importance of both the downstream ministries that rescue the people who are drowning in the river, and the upstream ministries that deal with whatever is throwing them in. That was a good transition to the next topic.

Third, we tried to see whether there were any public *policies* we might all be able to recommend. Certainly this was the most difficult, given the conflicts of politics; but even here, we made remarkable progress. There seemed to be a number of policy areas where some real convergence was possible. All agreed that personal responsibility is central to overcoming poverty, but so is combating the systemic economic and racial injustices that create or contribute to it. In smaller group settings, we began to explore how best to do that. Together we affirmed the critical importance of both strong families *and* good jobs that pay a living wage. For example, ending the marriage penalty in the tax code *and* expanding programs like the Earned Income Tax Credit, aimed at helping low-income working families, appeared to have broad support. Child tax credits, especially focused on families who need them most, had wide appeal, as did the principle that if people work full-time, they shouldn't be poor, but should make enough to support their families.

We all agreed that quality education should not be determined by how much money a child's parents make or where the family lives. Education for poor children has deteriorated so much that many of us were ready to experiment with new options, both public and private. Across the board, everyone affirmed the moral obligation of providing poor children with access to health care. Community policing, in conjunction with local church efforts, was lifted up as a real antidote to crime, and changing the policies of financial institutions to allow new capital formation for community-based economic development and micro-enterprise was cited as essential to turning poor neighborhoods around.

Churches must lead by example, we all concurred, but government does indeed have a responsibility to alleviate poverty and cannot abdicate that obligation to churches and charities. But rather than choosing between the government or the churches, most around the table were eager to explore new partnerships between them and with other sectors of society as well.

New alliances among government, business, and churches, everyone thought, are a vital step toward overcoming poverty. The need to hold corporations responsible to their workers and their communities as well as to their stockholders was also a crucial point of consensus. How government and business can effectively cooperate with faith-based organizations, which are often the most successful in addressing problems facing poor people, was perhaps the most challenging task to emerge from the Philadelphia Roundtable. Starting with the principles we shared and the practices we could all embrace seemed to make the discussion of policy more successful. There are important lessons here about the advantages of beginning with conversations about values and practical action before jumping into arguments about politics.

At the national Volunteer Summit, which followed our Roundtable, an even broader cross section of religious leaders was involved, along with many people who don't profess any religious faith. Christian, Jewish, Moslem, and Mormon religious leaders worked in cooperation with leaders from private and public sectors who were gathered together by the Philadelphia event. What brought us together was the crisis facing America's children, and their needs continually outweighed our differences.

Even some religious organizations who long opposed government welfare programs are now quite worried about what's going to happen to poor people and are calling for their constituents to respond in new ways. If they don't, the National Association of Evangelicals recently said, conservatives will rightly be judged as hypocrites. Recently, a very conservative evangelical leader said to me, "Christ calls us to serve the poor," and he's determined to press his business friends to hire welfare recipients. Conservative writers are calling on those who supported the welfare bill to take responsibility for the situation their political advocacy has helped create. The leader of one of the fastest-growing conservative Christian movements in the country confessed to me, "We need God to give us a heart for the poor."

At the second Roundtable in Washington, D.C., six months later in October 1997, the unity between the diverse churches and religious organizations had obviously grown much deeper. Now we could begin to move from common ground to common action, and the possibilities of a whole new movement to overcome poverty could clearly be felt.

The divisions haven't been just in the religious community. Other nonprofit organizations have also been disorganized and competitive with one another. Such internal strife, in the face of the hurricane of need we confront, is no longer tenable. Again, my discussions with social service providers around the country indicate a fresh hunger to come together and to join even more strategically with the religious communities who have often been their leading partners.

The process of starting with principles, moving on to practices, and then to policies has been tried in several local communities now and has met with real success. It seems to be a successful order of discussion. Try it yourself whenever you are trying to bring diverse people and groups together for a common purpose. It's a good way to find new allies and search for common ground.

The Shape of New Partnerships

I believe the future will see a myriad of new partnerships formed to solve many of our social problems. That's because the problems are simply too large for one sector of the society to be able to solve. It will take all of us, finding new allies and common ground. But for those new partnerships, we will need some new thinking. Bill Bradley has described American society as a three-legged stool, composed of the government, the market, and civil society. Each leg of the stool has a different "ethos," said the former senator, and when one leg is longer or shorter than the others, we lose our social balance. Practically, this means that you have to develop a strategy for the whole community, which includes the mayor and city council, the judges, the police, the churches, the schools, the nonprofit organizations, the business leaders, the union officials, our families, and even the media.

As to who should do what, there is a principle of Catholic social teaching that can help us here—it's called subsidiarity. "Subsidiarity" means responsibilities and decisions should be attended to as closely as possible to the level of individual initiative in local communities and institutions. Remember chapter six? Listen to those closest to the problem. Grassroots efforts, local organizations, families, churches, schools, local governments, small businesses, local unions, and so forth, are often the best venue for problem solving. "But," the same Catholic teaching says, "larger government structures do have a role when greater social coordination and regulation are necessary for the common good." Personally, I find the social teaching of the Catholic Church a rich resource in thinking through some of these complicated issues. Catholic social teaching is sometimes described as the best-kept secret in the Catholic Church! Nonetheless, I highly recommend it.

Perhaps the most helpful notion is the idea of the common good, which we have already discussed in relation to the epidemic of corporate mergers and layoffs in the late 1990s. The common good is a rich concept that can be applied to many areas of our social life and a unifying principle that can bring diverse people together. Listen to the wonderful definition of "common good" in Catholic social teaching: "the sum total of all those conditions of social living—economic, political, and cultural—which make it possible for women and men to readily and fully achieve the perfection of their humanity." Now who is going to want to argue with that?

The clear message we must get across is that overcoming poverty, for example, is not the job of one sector or sphere; it is a shared responsibility. And working out that shared strategy is the work we have to do together. Try to avoid a view that concentrates all social activity in the government or the perspective that privatizes poverty and leaves it to the market and the charities. Instead, stress the responsibilities of the whole community, with each sector or institution acting out of its own best vocation. In each of our local communities, and at the level of national politics, we must insist that there are public commitments, safeguards, standards, and allocations of resources that only government can accomplish or ensure. But at the same time, I believe that the vision and energy needed to overcome difficult social problems are frequently most available in what many have called the "mediating institutions" of civil society—including churches, family, schools, small businesses, unions, and a wide array of nonprofit organizations and voluntary associations. Why not use all our resources and institutions, and in the best possible combinations? That's the new partnership.

This pluralist approach to solving the problems of poverty could attract great support from concerned people across the political spectrum. Many now stress the importance of institutions that are intermediary between the individual and the state, while still affirming the crucial nature of government as a necessary countervailing force and protection against the otherwise unchecked power of large corporations in particular. These insights are not necessarily in conflict; they can work together. Neither a merely state-centered approach, nor a market-centered approach, nor a charity-centered approach is adequate to deal with the problem of poverty. A more promising direction is dynamic partnerships, linking the institutions of civil society, the government, and the economic sector of businesses and unions.

Getting Practical

I remember an occasion in Harrisburg, Pennsylvania, where a tragic event had just occurred. Two young teenagers had robbed a convenience store and killed the unarmed shopkeeper, even though he made no effort to resist them. Because the two boys were black and the store owner Asian, the fear of racial conflict quickly emerged. But the community mobilized rapidly and organized a service of healing. Leaders from both black and Asian communities spoke clearly and responsibly about the need to unite around the tragedy and focus on the crisis posed by children committing such senseless violence. I was asked to speak at the Sunday-afternoon meeting, and was greeted by the most diverse audience assembled for a very long time in that community. In the front row sat the family of the slain shopkeeper, sending a strong signal of courage and reconciliation. Community leaders from every racial and religious group in the city expressed their unity in focusing their collective energy on the youth in crisis. Such a coming-together depends almost entirely on the leadership that's offered. Someone needs to take the risk, reach out, build bridges, and establish trusting relationships. That's the only way it happens. Key people did that in Harrisburg, potential conflict was avoided, and needed reconciliation was the result.

It doesn't always take a crisis like that to bring people together. Sometimes it just takes somebody to articulate the crisis we are already in—especially our young people. Getting people to the table is key. And we are setting a new table. Today, new civic partnerships are emerging around the nation, where everyone—families, churches, schools, nonprofits, business, and government—can find a place at the table. It can happen in your community too. The future is in the formation of new multisector partnerships.

I remember discussing welfare reform on a panel with quite a cast of characters. The first speaker at one end of the table—and political spectrum—was conservative Christian leader Marvin Olasky, one of former House Speaker Newt Gingrich's philosophical advisors. Bruce Reed, President Clinton's domestic policy advisor, was also there. So were Republicans Richard Viguerie and Arianna Huffington, and Democratic Congressman Tony Hall. Rounding out the group were Millard Fuller of Habitat for Humanity and me. I was the last speaker. Marvin Olasky began by asking a question of the audience: "If you had a thousand dollars, would you contribute it to a faith-based organization or to the Department of Housing and Urban Development or the Department of Health and Human Services?" Most people answered that they would give it to a faith-based nonprofit, instead of HUD or HHS. Olasky thought he had made his point.

He concluded that faith-based nonprofits are just better than government, and everybody seemed, by their contribution choice, to
agree.

When my turn to speak came, I returned to Olasky's question. I
said, "Marvin, you didn't tell us something important—what is the
money for? If it's for after-school programs, youth violence or substance-abuse ministries, job-readiness training, family mentoring,
welfare-to-work programs, or even creating affordable housing...
terrific, our faith-based programs are pretty good at all those things.
But if the money is for building roads and bridges, faith-based
organizations are not really good at that, are they? If it's for providing supplemental income to senior citizens month after month,
most church budgets can't do that very well either, can they? If it's
for creating the seventy-five thousand jobs we're short in Detroit to
meet federal welfare-to-work requirements, churches can't do that
ourselves, can we? Nor can the churches in America provide health
care to all of our citizens, can we?" Olasky agreed. "So," I asked,
"aren't we all saying that we need new partnerships based on this
principle: Everyone does his share, and everybody does what he
does best." Everyone agreed with that, all across the political spectrum. It's a principle that will work.

Government Should Do the Right Thing

The outcome of welfare reform is still not clear. What federal,
state, and local governments decide could either reduce or expand
the ranks of the poor by millions. Many of the states today enjoy
budget surpluses and actually have more federal block-grant welfare
money available than expected. Resources put into job training,
child care, transportation, and health care for children could greatly ease the transitions from welfare to work, as could flexibility with
time limits and generous practices in areas like food-stamp eligibil-
ity. Ordinary citizens and local groups need to advocate for that. My
conversations with some of the state legislators charged with
responsibility for their state's welfare task forces indicate a real
moral wrestling with these issues, especially when the elected officials are also people of faith. Engage them, press them, and if you

are a part of a local community group, work to secure a place at the table where decisions are being made.

Thinking in new ways about the role of government in partnership with other institutions in the community is very important to success. In an article titled "Equal Partners: The Welfare Responsibility of Governments and Churches," Luis E. Lugo of the Pew Charitable Trusts sets forth some propositions that could help define the shape of new partnerships. Lugo says, "The *first* is that the duty of solidarity requires a commitment to the poor from all those in society who are in a position to help. The *second* is that government's specific calling to do justice involves an important distributive role. The *third* is that government shares responsibility in this area with other institutions of civil society and that its primary task is to cooperate with these institutions so as to enable them to be of service to the poor. The *fourth* is that true reform demands going beyond devolving power from the national government to the states to a real empowerment of the institutions of civil society. The *fifth*, and final, proposition is that such cooperation between government and faith-based charities can fully honor the spirit of religious liberty embodied in the First Amendment to the United States Constitution." No, government can not and should not try to solve all our social problems. Yes, government still has vital responsibilities to provide a just and compassionate framework for society. The catechism of the Catholic Church states that it is the responsibility of public authorities "to make accessible to each what is needed to lead a truly human life: food, clothing, health, work, education and culture, suitable information, the right to establish a family, and so on." It doesn't say that the government must provide all those things, but making sure they *are* provided is a duty of government.

I've come to know and appreciate Stephen Goldsmith, the former mayor of Indianapolis, Indiana. Steve was a young mayor who was not afraid to try new things, even when they conflicted with traditional political wisdom or party politics. He was a Republican and Jewish mayor who built alliances with black Baptist preachers and black Catholic priests in the solidly Democratic inner-city wards of Indianapolis. The new effort was called the Front Porch Alliance (a tip: it always helps to have a snappy name for your project). The Alliance fostered a new kind of public-private partnership between the city government and several local institutions, including the churches. For instance, several black pastors wanted to turn abandoned crack houses into drug rehabilitation centers but couldn't afford to purchase them because of the back taxes on the buildings. To expedite their efforts, the city forgave the taxes to help make the new drug treatment centers possible. Also, the best inner-city school in Indianapolis is a local Catholic high school that serves mostly low-income black families. But they didn't have a gym and couldn't afford one. So the city decided to make one of its nearby public recreational centers available to the school several times a week, thus again forging a new kind of partnership.

Republican party leaders wanted to know why Goldsmith was investing a disproportionate share of the city's infrastructure money for roads, sidewalks, sewers, and police protection in neighborhoods that have been Democratic strongholds. "They're never going to vote for you or us," party leaders warned him. "So why are you putting so much money and time there?" "Because that's where it's needed," replied Goldsmith. What a novel answer, and also a creative one. "My Republican perimeter isn't always happy with my focus on the inner city," Goldsmith told me. Creative solutions will often defy conventional wisdom and, as we've already said, cross party lines.

Good Business

Most of the social welfare debate has concerned government and the nonprofit sectors, with little attention given to companies who make a profit in a community but often take little responsibility for it. From a religious perspective, profits cannot be the only bottom line. A business must also be committed to the common good, the community's well-being. Indeed, businesses can be very helpful in finding real solutions to the persistent problems plaguing our communities.

My conversations with several bank presidents and entrepreneurs show that some of them are ready to pitch in. Practically, businesses must offer their time, expertise, and resources for community development. Businesses should be busy creating new jobs—as they always claim to be best at doing—where they are most needed, and which offer a living family wage (or at least lead to one). Entrepreneurs could also play a crucial support role in developing business plans and skills for new micro-enterprise efforts in poor communities. Changing restrictive financial policies and opening the door to capital formation for new people and constituencies are critical for the success of community-based economic development.

When Peter Pierce suggested to his bank board in Oklahoma City that they tithe a percentage of their profits back to the community, some members thought he was crazy. "This is a business, not a church or social welfare agency," they reminded him. But Oklahoma City had been racked by a terrorist bomb at the Murrah Federal Building, and the community needed some compassionate and courageous leadership. As president of the First National Bank of Bethany, Peter thought it was time for the business community to show some real civic commitment. He persuaded his board that the goodwill generated by such a signal from the bank would be good for everyone, including the bank. He won them over.

Peter invited me to speak at the annual banking lecture in Oklahoma City, held in honor of his father, who had pioneered community banking across the state. I described capital as being like "birds on a wire." Have you ever watched a big flock of birds perched on a telephone wire? They all sit there until, finally, one will venture to another wire. After a while, another one comes over, then another, and another. Eventually, they all fly over and perch on the new wire, after they've discovered that it's nice and safe. That's the way financial capital works too. When you're trying to secure investment in something new, the toughest thing is to get the first bird to fly. I told them the story of Nane Alejandrez and how the Lutheran Church decided to take a risk and invest in Barrios Unidos. They were like the first bird. After a while, other investors and backers came over to the Barrios "wire." Sometimes, we have to encourage a bank, or a business, or a church, to be the first bird to fly.

Similarly, Doug Price, president of the First Bank of Denver, Colorado, now has 30 percent of his loan capital going to people of color, a much higher percentage than is found at other citywide banks around the country. Both men decided that quarterly profit-and-loss statements are a far too narrow way of deciding a bank's policies. They are taking a long-term perspective, and they are asking questions about the vocation of a bank in a community. Just as Stephen Goldsmith asks what a mayor can do, Peter and Doug ask what a banker can creatively contribute. In all three cases, spiritual concerns are helping motivate their creative directions.

Churches can be critical partners in all these efforts, providing the link to poor communities and identifying the people, families, and projects most likely to succeed in new economic activities, from home ownership to business start-ups. Congregations working with the business community can be the cradles and crucibles for innovative economic development in low-income communities.

Churches must challenge local business people, including members of their own congregations, to uphold their social responsibilities: to fair and just labor practices, to racial and gender equality in the workplace, to environmental stewardship, and, yes, to an honest and fair relationship with the labor movement, whose rejuvenation and leadership role is essential to any real hope for economic justice. As a partner and a prophetic interrogator, the church could enter into a new, dynamic relationship with the business community that would be profitable for both, as well as for the larger community.

Churches can also prioritize jobs. Churches and religious non-profits can be highly successful with job-readiness programs, job linking (informal networks for sharing employment information), and job creation (helping develop micro-business plans and enterprises), as well as by providing quality, safe child care at affordable rates to single working moms.

Earlier we met Skip Long and the North Carolina–based Jobs Partnership, which has pioneered a new relationship between churches and companies. Skip and his business partner, Chris Mangum, lead an innovative church-business organization. A business is asked to provide a job, and a church promises to provide a ready-to-work, on-time, dependable employee, whom a congregation agrees to support for up to two years to ensure the employee's success in the job. The churches pledge to deal with all the other issues that make employment so difficult for people without much job history—transportation, child care, work habits, financial planning, and so forth. Where help is needed with substance-abuse problems or family issues, that is also made available. One hundred churches have already joined the Raleigh program. Their method is to adopt welfare families, much as churches had earlier adopted refugee families from Southeast Asia or Bosnia. A car mechanic or auto dealer in the church helps arrange transportation for the new workers, or they might ride in a car pool with other church members on their way to work. A church day-care center or other parents assist with child care. Where needed, help with family finances, job readiness, addiction problems, or personal counseling is made available. In the first two years, more than three hundred people, many who had been on welfare, have been successfully put to work and kept their jobs. With a proven track record, the Jobs Partnership idea is now spreading around the country.

Dani Barrett graduated in June 1996, a proud member of the Jobs Partnership's first class. Graduation marked the end of a long period of struggle and abuse for Dani, including living in a shelter with her children, abusing drugs and alcohol, and being diagnosed with bipolar disorder. As Dani says, "It was the worst of times, trying so desperately to regain our foothold on life while sinking further and further into the despairs of shelter life and family separation. Where was hope? Where was faith? Where was God? None of these things seemed to exist anymore." Dani first heard of the Jobs Partnership through John Bender, pastor of the Raleigh Mennonite Church, and another member of the church who was coordinating the program. The two men convinced her to give the program a try. Dani describes the transformation that took place during the Jobs Partnership classes: "I became aware of some forgotten truths in my life. The truth of my own self-worth; the truth of God's love and patience; the truth of God's expectations of me, his child." After twelve weeks of study, struggle, and prayer, Dani and several other women graduated, as "successful people in the eyes and love of God. We knew what was expected, knew how to fulfill that expectation, and would surely prosper and thrive. Well, at least be able to make a living!"

And make a living Dani does. She has had two different jobs since she graduated from the Partnership. The first was for a company that made fire engines; she was laid off last summer. Since then, however, she has worked with National Transportation Services as the CEO's webslinger—she designs web sites. As Dani says, "Nice gig, that!" On top of that, Dani is being transferred to the company branch in Mississippi, a mere fifty miles from where her parents live. Dani exclaims, "Too perfect!" In fact, she is now learning the patience and hope that come with faith, trusting that her "good luck" is part of God's plan for her. She states, "And so it goes. Boldly, expectantly, faithfully approaching God with every issue of every day. That's how I live my life now."

Just days after first meeting Skip and learning about his program, I was speaking to the Council of Churches in Fort Wayne, Indiana. They were enthusiastically telling me the wonderful idea they had for how local churches might surround a family with the support they need to make the difficult transition from poverty to work, dignity, and community. "God gave us this idea," they told me. "That's great," I responded. "And it's such a wonderful idea that God gave it to some other people too!" I gave them Skip's phone number and by 9:01 the next morning, they were on the phone together, and Skip Long was helping the churches of Indianapolis with a very good idea.

That kind of networking and community building is essential now. Churches and other nonprofit organizations are demonstrating success in communities across the country. But these innovative programs work best when they are fully supported by surrounding public and private institutions—government, schools, police, courts, and businesses. Public policy can do much to ensure that support.

A new *mobilization* will be required on a level we haven't seen before, combining the energy of the churches and nonprofits with both business and government. A new *strategy* will be required, based on empowering small-scale projects closest to the problems while tapping the moral strength of religious communities. A new *collection* of resources will be required, making a moral claim on public budgets, but also on the profits of corporations and the purses of philanthropic institutions. Finally, a new *accountability* will be required, holding us all responsible for the health of our communities.

Yes, when preparing for a coming hurricane, people don't ask one another about their political affiliations. When disaster hits, clean-up groups don't divide into task forces of liberals and conservatives. To "repair the breach," in the words we have previously quoted from Isaiah, will require a coming-together that we have not seen for many years. But it is time to come together, to find new allies, and to search for common ground.

CHAPTER TEN

Keep Your Eyes on the Prize

Come now, and let us reason together.
(Isaiah 1:18)

WHEN THE PHONE CALL came from Austin, Texas, I was surprised. Just two days after his election was secured in December 2000, President-elect Bush wanted a meeting with religious leaders to discuss faith-based initiatives in solving poverty. He was reaching beyond his base of conservative evangelicals. Would I come and suggest others who should be invited?

I was glad for the call because the subject was on my mind. While the American people and media had remained riveted to the presidential election, other news had fallen beneath the screen of national attention, including some alarming news about poor children and families.

The U.S. Conference of Mayors had just released its latest annual survey on hunger and homelessness in America's cities. In the past year, requests for emergency food had increased by 17 percent. Two-thirds of the people requesting assistance were members of families—children and their parents—and 32 percent of the adults requesting food were employed. Demand for emergency shelter had increased by 15 percent—the highest one-year increase of the decade—and of those, 36 percent were families with children. Thirteen percent of the requests for food and nearly one-quarter of the requests for housing went unmet due to lack of resources.

The leading causes of these increases? Low-paying jobs, the lack of affordable housing, unemployment or other employment-related issues, and poverty or lack of income led the list.

Just before the 2000 holidays, Catholic Charities had also released its annual report. It showed a "startling" 22 percent increase in the use of its emergency services of shelter, clothing, food, and medicine.

So it seemed appropriate, just a few days before Christmas, to be sitting in a Sunday School classroom in Austin's First Baptist Church with a diverse group of religious leaders having a conversation with George W. Bush. Mr. Bush listened and asked questions for over an hour, then stayed longer to mingle and talk to us individually. He said he believed in faith-based organizations and the important role they can play in solving social problems and wanted to make support for such efforts an important part of his administration.

George W. Bush asked us how to speak to the nation's soul. I suggested starting with our children, who embody our best hopes and reveal our worst failures as a society. We thanked him for being willing to include people in the meeting who hadn't supported his election and pledged to work with him *if* he chose to do something significant to reduce child poverty—fulfilling the promise made at the Republican National Convention to "leave no child behind."

We said that ideological warfare had allowed too many children to fall between the cracks of our faulty political discourse—liberal and conservative false choices about whether family values or living family incomes are more central to the causes and cures for poverty. I noted that churches across a broad spectrum are finding remarkable unity on these issues, and maybe it was time to try it on a political level. Evangelical and liberal, Catholic and Protestant, black and white church leaders have been convicted by prosperity's contradictions and united by the biblical imperatives of compassion and justice. Interfaith efforts have also greatly expanded. All around the country, faith-based initiatives to overcome poverty show remarkable progress. But presidential leadership is required, so the new President should send an early signal about poor children and families being high on his agenda.

Mr. Bush asked theological questions of the religious leaders, like "What is justice?" That is a key question, especially amid fears that an emphasis on faith-based initiatives will be used to substitute for crucial governmental responsibilities. We told him that in forging new partnerships to reduce poverty, the religious community will not only be service providers but also prophetic interrogators. Our vocation is to ask *why* people are poor, not just to care for the forgotten. Shelters and food banks aren't enough. We need solutions to the many problems of poverty, a pragmatic approach that produces results.

Could our divided political leaders come together around the moral cause of using our prosperity to finally address this nation's shamefully high poverty levels, especially among children? Could this divided nation find common ground if politicians would collaborate across old barriers as religious leaders have begun to do? Since neither party has succeeded in breaking the grip of persistent poverty, isn't a new bipartisan effort called for? Republicans preaching compassionate conservatism and family values, Democrats fighting for poor working families, and a religious community ready to lead by example and call the nation to its moral responsibilities could really do something significant about poverty.

Politicians Getting the Message

The emergence of the term "faith-based organization" in the political discussion, and its acronym, FBO, may signal one of the most significant new developments of American public life. During the 2000 presidential campaign, both major candidates raised the issue.

In an important May 1999 campaign speech, Vice President Al Gore proposed a "New Partnership" between the government and the pioneering efforts of faith communities, which are finding real solutions to the poverty and violence in many local communities around the country. The most important observation about Gore's speech was that he went beyond merely affirming the role of faith-based efforts as admirable or exemplary to speaking of their potentially strategic role. Gore offered faith-based organizations "a seat at the national table when decisions are made." He promised, "Today I give you this pledge: If you elect me President, the voices of faith-based organizations will be integral to the policies in my administration."

For his part, George W. Bush said in a July 1999 speech that he would "empower" faith-based organizations if he became president. He said he would "look first to faith-based organizations, charities, and community groups that have shown their ability to change lives." But after praising such organizations, Bush warned that it was not enough to "praise volunteerism." Most faith-based organizations struggle without the necessary resources to do their work, the Texas governor said. "Without more support and resources—both private and public—we are asking them to make bricks without straw." Like Gore, Bush called for new "partnership....We will recognize there are some things the government should be doing....Government cannot be replaced by charities—but it can welcome them as partners, not resent them as rivals."

All over the country, even where other efforts have failed, faith-based efforts are drawing national attention and making real progress on the most urgent social problems. Because of that, government officials are looking to partner with churches in new ways. The Call to Renewal's 1999 National Summit drew many state legislators and staff from nine state welfare agencies. We spent our final day together on Capitol Hill with Tony Hall and other members of Congress eager to move beyond partisan debate to a common-good focus on "what's right and what works." At our press briefing in the Rayburn House Office Building, we declared that poor people were a nonpartisan issue and overcoming poverty must become a bipartisan cause.

But if faith-based organizations are indeed invited to the table, our role should not simply be to make government more efficient, but to make America more just. It must not be just to "clean up the mess" created by bad social policy or to take the place of legitimate government responsibilities, but to be a morally prophetic voice for new policies.

In this partnership, our job will be to raise the common moral values on which our society must build and to insist on a strong standard of the common good to guide public policy. We should argue that the development of public policy must not be dictated merely by the clash of power and competing interests but also by fundamental questions of right and wrong; it must be shaped by asking what our moral vision is, what kind of people we want to be, and what kind of country we want to have. For example, the national silence on the rapidly growing social inequality in America is stunning. That is a profoundly moral issue to which the faith community must speak as a biblical issue of justice.

Today there is an incredibly vibrant citizen politics occurring in many local communities. Much of it is tied to nonprofit institutions, among them, many faith-based organizations. National politics must wake up to that and begin to connect with all the grassroots energy and innovation. Perhaps we are at the beginning of that recognition as more and more political leaders are showing interest in the FBOs. We must learn how to make the connections between spirituality and politics, while vigorously protecting the First Amendment. There is enormous potential here, not just a few exemplary programs, for a new vision of real social change.

Faith-Based and Community Initiatives

In his Inaugural speech, President George W. Bush spoke strongly and eloquently about poverty. "In the quiet of American conscience, we know that deep, persistent poverty is unworthy of the nation's promise," he said.

Nine days later, on January 29, President Bush announced the creation of a new White House Office of Faith-Based and Community Initiatives. "I want to raise the priority and profile of these issues within my own administration," he said. "I want to ensure that faith-based and community groups will always have a place at the table in our deliberations." He signed two executive orders creating the new office with a mandate to "clear away the bureaucratic barriers in several important agencies that make private groups hesitate to work with government" and named John DiIulio as its director.

I didn't vote for President Bush, but I welcomed the new White House office that will support "faith-based and community initiatives." As this book describes, denominations, congregations and faith-based organizations have provided services to their communities for years and have promoted linking the efforts of faith-based groups with government in ways that respect the first amendment and the pluralism of a democratic society. It's often those grassroots groups that are closest to a community's problems—and they are often the ones that can develop the most successful solutions. Why not forge partnerships with the most effective nonprofits, both religious and secular? And why discriminate against nonprofits because they are religious?

I believe that a vibrant civil society, with major participation from the religious community, forging new partnerships with government, is an essential ingredient in overcoming poverty. I also believe that the resources to solve the problem simply don't exist sufficiently in civil society alone. Government, at all levels, must be involved. The real question is how government can most effectively help mobilize new multisector partnerships and target its resources in the most strategic way.

In his announcement, President Bush said, "I approach this goal with some basic principles: Government has important responsibilities...government will never be replaced by charities and community groups." I agree: Government is an important part of overcoming poverty.

Bush also recognizes that faith-based organizations are only one part of a broader civil society. The inclusion of nonprofit community groups in the White House initiative is an important step toward revitalizing that sector.

And when he chose my friend John DiIulio to head the new office, I was pleased. I've known and worked with John for several years—in fact, he has been on the board of Call to Renewal and

served as cochair of our policy team. John is one of the most knowl-
edgeable and committed people in the country on finding effective
community-based solutions to poverty and violence. Like me, John
didn't vote for George W. Bush. He is a Catholic Democrat who is
especially trusted by clergy in the black churches.

The new White House Office is clearly focusing on inner-city
churches directly serving their communities. Those churches and
their pastors operate on the ground, in the neighborhoods, and get
results, according to DiIulio. His primary connections and confi-
dences are not in white suburban evangelical churches, but in black
and Latino faith-based urban programs. For him, that's where the
real action is.

In a speech to the National Association of Evangelicals, DiIulio
admonished "predominantly white, ex-urban evangelical" leaders
for their lack of involvement in solving urban problems. He went
on to say that their objections to the new faith-based initiative
would "rankle less if they were backed by real human and financial
help" in overcoming poverty. DiIulio doesn't claim to be an expert
on evangelical affairs. But as an evangelical myself, I know the
rebuke rings painfully true—the white suburban evangelical churches' record on urban poverty is not one of which to be proud.
Indeed, that's why evangelical groups like the NAE and World
Vision are trying to change the stereotype.

The White House office promotes "funding results, not religion." In his NAE speech, DiIulio made it clear that the government will not fund proselytizing, but will support social service programs that can be separated from a specifically religious message.

He concluded his speech to the NAE by saying: "To me, the
essential Christian social teaching is that there are no 'strangers,' only
brothers and sisters we have yet to meet, greet, get to know, and
come to love. I pray daily that I may honor that teaching in word and
deed.... Together, let's hold each other and all God's children, especially our poor and needy...in our hearts. If we do, then yesterday's
disagreements and today's misunderstandings will be eclipsed
tomorrow by faith-based and community initiatives so self-emptying
in their obedience and love that they move the very heart of God."

President Bush's decision to expand partnerships between religious organizations and federally financed social services has sparked a raging political controversy about the separation of church and state. The potential of government partnerships with faith-based organizations in helping to reduce poverty is in danger of being destroyed by the bitter polarities of Left-Right politics—like so many other things in American public life. A recent study conducted by the Pew Forum on Religion and Public Life and the Pew Research Center for People and the Press shows that 75 percent of the American people support the concept. But that strong majority might well be confused by the stridency of the arguments from liberals and conservatives. We have been bombarded with polemics when what we need is a healthy debate about how new civic partnerships could play an important role in helping our poorest citizens find some hope.

Liberals offer alarming predictions that the wall of separation between church and state is about to be torn down, and conservatives predict massive secular conspiracies to discriminate against religion. Religious right leaders say churches will have to deny their faith to receive public funds, while secular leftists claim overzealous evangelical groups will use public funding to proselytize homeless people. We're either about to become a theocracy, if you listen to critics on the left, or have a government that refuses to let church groups help the needy because of "Christophobia," if you heed the charges from the right.

In all the controversy, we're losing sight of the poorest and most vulnerable, especially children, who desperately need new solutions. And we are trying to resolve every concern at either the theoretical level or, in the worst-case scenarios, instead of joining together to work out honest and sometimes difficult issues on the ground—in relation to the actual programs that are already serving people in critical ways.

There are three important questions that should be kept at the center of this debate.

Church and State

The first question is about *church and state*. The First Amendment ensures that government can neither establish nor interfere with religion, but its purpose is not to discriminate against faith-based groups in their service to the common good. It is a mistake to exclude faith-based organizations from partnerships that include public support simply because they are religious.

Here's a funny story about the cooperation between government and the church. Many people are familiar with the Catholic social service centers named after Saint Vincent de Paul. Because these centers provide basic and needed social services, they sometimes receive some public funds, often channeled through Catholic Charities, the large religious service organization that has used government funding for many years. One day, a Catholic monsignor was taking a visiting federal Housing and Urban Development department official on a tour of Catholic social services in a major city. After seeing the impressive work done at the city's Saint Vincent de Paul Center, the government official reminded the Catholic leader that they received HUD money for some of those programs. When the Catholic monsignor acknowledged that fact, the HUD official told him they would have to change their name to the Mr. Vincent de Paul Center! The story highlights the importance of distinguishing between what Harvard Divinity School's Father Bryan Hehir calls "sensible vs. silly rules" in fashioning good partnerships between church and state.

The 1996 welfare reform legislation contained a provision that has come to be known as "charitable choice." It was designed to allow faith-based organizations to compete for government funding of social service programs, while protecting their religious identity, and to encourage middle-sized and smaller FBOs to compete without discrimination. With the Bush administration's support, the significance of charitable choice has increased. Sooner or later, every local community will have to come to terms with the opportunities and questions it raises. In my view, it is an opportunity that should be explored while the complex and controversial questions are resolved. It is clearly an issue we need to better understand.

Most Americans agree that faith-based organizations providing social services—soup kitchens, homeless shelters, after-school programs, day-care centers, job training—can receive government funding for those services. But other types of programs—drug and alcohol rehabilitation ministries, for example—are often grounded in changing a person's behavior through conversion. These programs based explicitly on evangelism should not be directly funded by the government. Some have suggested other possibilities—for example, a voucher program that empowers the recipient to choose a program, like we've often done with educational grants that can be used at religious colleges.

The idea of public-private partnerships including faith-based organizations is not new. Billions of federal dollars have gone into overseas relief and development efforts through faith-based organizations such as Catholic Relief Services and World Vision. Here at home, significant public funding has supported the work of Catholic Charities and Lutheran Social Services, among others. The first federal office on faith-based and community partnerships was in President Clinton's Department of Housing and Urban Development under Andrew Cuomo. HUD's effective partnering with black churches, Catholic sisters, and Jewish community groups to increase low-income home ownership and affordable housing for low-income families bears emulating in the new administration.

The most important thing here is that public funding be for public purposes, that only the social services of faith-based organizations be supported by tax dollars, and not their religious or proselytizing efforts. It's not impossible to separate social services from religious activity. But it's both unnecessary and counterproductive to strip away the religious character of faith-based organizations in order for them to receive any public support. Charitable choice is designed to prevent such government discrimination against FBOs while protecting their essential religious character.

Most religious groups, including mainstream evangelical organizations like the NAE, understand that church-state separation means funding only their social services. The Constitution clearly forbids directly funding the religious activities of faith-based organizations or government deciding which groups are really religious. And we must not let political leaders divide and conquer us. No one wants a governor or mayor, for example, to pick his favorite faith-based organization, put his state's or city's money there, and leave out other groups.

We must also protect new church-state partnerships against self-serving and sectarian agendas from any side. Piling public money on church altars is not a good idea. The creation of nonprofit corporations for faith-based ministries, separate from congregations, is a very prudent step to take.

Legislation to expand charitable choice was introduced in Congress in March 2001. The vitally important debate on the question should take up critical issues like hiring and requirements for setting up separate nonprofit organizations and, hopefully, lead to broadly acceptable ways of effectively utilizing faith-based organizations while protecting the First Amendment.

I believe it is entirely possible for faith-based groups to work with government in ways that respect the First Amendment and the pluralism of a democratic society. The guidelines for how best to do that will inevitably be the subject of public discussion and even legal battles. But the separation of church and state need not require the removal of faith from public life.

In fact, focusing primarily on church-state controversies is a distraction from the real issue. For decades, liberals and conservatives debated the welfare system while millions of children remained trapped in misery. We must not get sidetracked again into a debate that leaves our poorest children behind.

Instead, we should keep our eyes on the prize, as the old civil rights anthem says, and focus our energies on the most effective models for overcoming the poverty that imprisons our youngest and most vulnerable citizens. The president says that "compassion is the work of a nation, not just a government." But justice, not just compassion, is necessary to overcome poverty, and that is also the work of a nation.

The Role of Government

The second question concerns the *role of government*. President Bush has said that faith-based organizations cannot "replace" the role of government, which still has the responsibility for the large questions of Medicaid for poor children, health care for the uninsured, education, and housing policy to name a few. With or without faith, grassroots efforts that save kids or rebuild neighborhoods can't provide a social safety net for our whole society.

Whether the administration will keep that pledge will become evident in how its policies impact people in poverty. It will become clear in who most benefits from tax cuts, in the details of the federal budget, and in whether the crucial supports that low-income families need are included in the 2002 welfare reform reauthorization funding.

In the spring of 2001, I spoke at a large interfaith conference in England. The British Labor government, led by Prime Minister Tony Blair, wanted to make a major new effort to partner with faith-based organizations. Blair delivered an excellent speech, taking clear government responsibility for budget and funding priorities that aim at overcoming poverty. But he also talked about the unique contribution faith-based organizations can make and invited them to be partners with the government.

Blair affirmed that, "Community action has always been a central mission of the churches and other faith groups....And in carrying out this mission you have developed some of the most effective voluntary and community organizations in the country."

He continued: "It is misguided and outdated to suggest that there is a straight choice between voluntary activity and state activity. The two should go together. And where the two do go together—the government fully realizing its obligations, looking to the voluntary sector as partner not substitute—the impact is far greater than government acting on its own." He went on to take responsibility for the government funding priorities that aim at overcoming poverty.

I also visited a faith-based organization called PECAN, located in a poor community in London. They participate in a government-funded job-training program, ironically called the New Deal, aimed at unemployed young adults. The government agencies that run the New Deal program are often just offices where bureaucrats sit waiting for people to come in. When they do, they are handed one hundred forms (that's right) to fill out. PECAN, on the other hand, sends their workers into the community, often knocking on doors in housing projects to find the people that need the job-training program. They then help the young people fill out the confusing forms. And before the people come each day for their job training, the staff gathers to pray for each of them (on time not funded by the government). What the people get at PECAN is not proselytizing, but job training. Guess which program works the best?

Britain is a very secular country, and talking about faith-based partnerships won't gain any politician many votes. They are talking about it because it works and actually helps people to escape poverty. Nobody in Britain wants government to fund religion—just results.

During my visit, I met with many government ministers, Members of Parliament, and lots of faith leaders from many different communities. Perhaps the best meeting I had was with Gordon Brown, the Chancellor of the Exchequer, who, as minister of the Treasury, is the second-most powerful politician in Britain. Brown is the one who pushed the Jubilee 2000 campaign for debt reduction through the British government. His understanding of how faith-based partnerships could work for everybody's benefit made me want to move to England or, at least, send all our government leaders (from both parties) to London for some needed education.

There is a progressive, democratic, and pluralistic way to create faith-based partnerships that will really help to overcome poverty, as Mr. Blair proposed. Liberals in this country are making a foolish mistake by equating faith-based initiatives with right-wing politics and the Bush administration. And conservatives are make a hypocritical mistake in hoping faith-based initiatives might fulfill their dream of getting government out of social welfare programs.

The potential of the faith-based initiative need not remain trapped in pro-Bush or anti-Bush politics. Many liberals so distrust

President Bush and the Republican party's commitment to reducing poverty that they see the faith-based initiative as merely a deceptive way to shift the burdens of social welfare without the resources to carry it. And some conservatives support the faith-based initiative because they do see it as an alternative to significant public spending to reduce poverty and as a cover for tax cuts, while others are looking to support their favorite religious ministries.

We must also be unswerving about the role and responsibility of government policies in providing the necessary resources to allow these programs to realize their potential. Cutting spending on domestic programs while expanding the role of faith-based service providers clearly will not work. But faith-inspired programs and movements are becoming more and more crucial to social change worldwide. Such partnerships will be undertaken with governments across the political spectrum, and faith-based organizations must keep the pressure on all of them to put poor people on their political agenda.

The Conscience of the State

My third, and most important question, concerns the faith community's *prophetic voice.* Will partnership with the government mute or magnify the religious community's advocacy for social justice? My deepest concern is the prophetic integrity of religious groups who might appropriately receive some government funding. Why? Because those in power often prefer the service programs of religious groups to their prophetic voice for social justice.

I know from experience. In the early days of the Clinton administration, the president expressed support for the work many of us in the religious community were doing to solve social problems. I remember personal notes from the White House and talk about "working partnerships." But in 1996, President Clinton signed a welfare reform bill that lacked crucial supports needed for single mothers and their children to move out of poverty. Police arrested fifty-five inner-city pastors in the Capitol Rotunda as we read the words of the biblical prophet Isaiah, "Woe to the legislators of infamous laws who cheat the poor among my people."

The personal notes from the White House stopped and discussions of partnerships suddenly ended. Dialogue with the president apparently didn't include criticism. But in the biblical tradition of prophets like Isaiah, the religious community is called to speak truth to power. Having had breakfast in the White House and been arrested for protesting its policies, I've learned the former is more dangerous to the prophetic vocation.

How can religious groups safeguard their prophetic integrity as they partner with government? That's far more important than the legal controversies. The biblical prophets held rulers, judges, and employers accountable to the demands of justice. We should too. Faith communities must never become mere service providers; we are also called to be prophetic interrogators. Why do so many people remain poor in the midst of such amazing prosperity?

Dynamic new partnerships between faith-based groups and government are vitally needed, but they must not mute our prophetic voice. Faith-based groups that provide a social service must also be moral interrogators of the economic and political systems that make that service necessary in the first place. To prophetically challenge unjust structures and policies is part of our religious vocation, and we must not let potential government funding undermine it. Funding partnerships with government must not become a way for political leaders to buy off and silence religious leaders.

Rev. Martin Luther King, Jr., once said, "The church must be reminded that it is not the master or the servant of the state, but rather the conscience of the state." Practically, that means evaluating all government policies by how they impact poverty. Will people of faith challenge excessive tax cuts and budget priorities that benefit the wealthy and leave few resources to invest in effective antipoverty strategies? Will we push for a health care policy that includes the ten million children who are without coverage? Will we advocate for poor working families who need livable incomes and affordable housing? When it comes time to reauthorize welfare reform, will we make sure to fund the critical elements that families need to move out of poverty's deadly cycle?

If words don't turn into deeds, then legislators, mayors, governors, and presidents must hear the prophetic voice of faith-based organizations paraphrasing the prophet Amos: "Take away from me your empty words, but let justice roll down like waters, and righteousness like an ever-flowing stream."

A dramatic example of this prophetic voice occurred behind the scenes as Congress debated the tax cut bill in the spring of 2001. Several faith-based organizations did something very important—they helped make sure that America's poorest families were included in the benefits of the new tax cut. Religious leaders joined to support the valiant efforts of child advocates and low-income people's organizations who were able to insert a refundable child tax credit into the legislation, one aimed at helping the nation's poorest children who had been completely left behind by the original White House tax cut proposal.

Not making enough to even pay income taxes, many poor *working* families would have received nothing from the big tax cut, even though they pay payroll and other taxes. It's clear that they need more support than the top 1 percent of America's income earners and taxpayers—the ones who benefited the most from this tax cut. The tax cut increases the child tax credit from $500 to $1,000 over several years—a good pro-family initiative. But a single working mother with two kids making $24,000 per year would have received absolutely no help in the White House plan. By making the child tax credit partially refundable—like a tax rebate—now she does.

The refundable child tax credit will reach nearly seventeen million low-income children, and help five hundred thousand children in poverty, according to the Children's Defense Fund, who helped lead the fight for it. But it really was a fight.

Conservative Republicans tried to kill the "kid credit," as the refundable child tax credit came to be called, arguing, incredibly, that the $20 billion it will cost would leave less to reward wealthier tax payers. The battle became a child tax credit for the nation's poorest families versus further lowering tax rates for those at the top. Those policy choices were enough to prompt significant involvement in the debate by the religious community. We argued that if wealthy and middle-class families should get child tax credits, so should poor families.

Call to Renewal organized a delegation of faith-based organizations—including the U.S. Catholic Conference, World Vision, the Congress of National Black Churches, the Christian Community Development Association, Evangelicals for Social Action, and the Mennonite Central Committee—to visit key Republican leaders in the House and Senate. *The New York Times* reported: "Some of the religious groups among the strongest supporters of the president's [faith-based] initiative went to Capitol Hill this week to tell Republican lawmakers that continued support would be linked to tax breaks for the working poor." We told the Republican leadership what I told the *Times:* "If this tax cut is passed without help for the poor, then it will be very difficult for us to support them on faith-based issues."

Members of our delegation and other religious leaders also spoke to officials at the White House Office of Faith-Based and Community Initiatives, urging them to push the administration to support the refundable credit. Other high-level appeals were made directly to the White House. "The credibility of the supporters of the faith-based initiative might suffer if the administration is seen offering strong words on confronting poverty but then allows the only provision of the tax bill which directly helps poor families to be removed," wrote Bishop Joseph A. Fiorenza, president of the National Conference of Catholic Bishops, in a letter to President Bush.

The broad effort for a refundable tax credit was led by the Children's Defense Fund and a network of low-income groups called the National Campaign for Jobs and Income Support, and they deserve the credit for this important victory. Their forces effectively urged many Democrats and moderate Republicans to put a refundable child tax credit into the Senate version of the tax cut bill—it had been missing in the House bill. But key Republicans threatened to kill the provision in the conference committee, and the White House wasn't supporting it.

During the heat of the congressional debate on whether the final version of the tax cut bill would retain a refundable child tax credit, the religious voices were coming from every direction. Action alerts were sent to tens of thousands of faith-based activists.

The *Boston Globe* reported, "Pressure came from an unexpected quarter yesterday as House and Senate conferees struggled to craft a final version of President Bush's tax package: Religious leaders, who demanded that any bill expand aid to working poor families with children. A religious coalition headed by the group Call to Renewal directly linked the tax plan to the group's continued support for another key element of Bush's agenda, his faith-based initiative...." The *Globe* also reported that even opponents of the credit, such as then-Majority Whip Sen. Don Nickles, said the efforts of the religious organizations had been a factor.

A key supporter was moderate Republican Sen. Olympia Snowe, who vowed to vote against the final bill if it excluded the refundable child tax credit and pushed other colleagues to do the same. Snowe courageously insisted, against a great deal of pressure, "It's a working-family issue. They pay other forms of taxes, and they otherwise would not benefit from [the tax bill]."

Two significant things were accomplished. First, poor families and children got significant help—one of the more important measures in years, according to Marian Wright Edelman of the Children's Defense Fund. Refundability itself is an important principle to strengthen, and the Catholic Bishops have been working on a refundable child tax credit for ten years. Second, some *terms of engagement* were established between faith-based organizations and the Bush administration. We took the important step of linking our support for faith-based initiatives to the administration's support for important policy matters that impact the poor. In doing so, we clearly said we cannot support the faith-based initiative without White House leadership on other key issues that affect the poor. The faith-based initiative alone is obviously not enough to overcome poverty. New policies and new resources are required, and faith-based initiatives can only work in partnership with good government policy.

Many of us opposed the size and priorities of the administration's tax cut, but gaining the child credit for those at the bottom was still a significant victory. The prophetic voice of the faith communities was exercised in the debate, critically supplementing our role as service provider. Now that the terms of engagement are clearer, a working relationship with this administration could have both more effectiveness and deeper integrity. Important issues loom on the horizon, like the crucial reauthorization of welfare reform.

In summary, I have no idea whether President Bush's faith-based initiative will ultimately turn out to be substantial or merely symbolic. But whether people trust the president or not, the faith-based initiative can be supported and used to raise the most important issues of biblical justice to the very administration that has proposed the initiative.

First, we should support faith-based and other community initiatives at the grassroots level precisely because they have such great potential to help children and families escape poverty.

Second, we should do it only in ways that keep social services and religious activities separate.

Third, we should insist on partnership between religious organizations and government, rather than replacement of one by the other, and not allow anybody to abdicate their responsibility. The role of government, especially in its budget priorities, is crucial.

Fourth, we should seize the moment as a prophetic opportunity, rather than just a danger. With all the attention on faith-based organizations, it may be the best time to speak the biblical language of both compassion and justice. While doing the work of compassion in neighborhoods across the country, we can and must also make the demands of justice known to those in power.

That approach would begin to move us beyond Left and Right and, most important, would focus us all on the real goals of overcoming poverty for our poorest children. Let's discuss the real questions, but let's not allow our poorest children to left behind in the wake of ideological arguments.

CHAPTER ELEVEN

Tap the Power of Faith Communities

Do not be conformed to this world, but be transformed by the renewing of your minds. (Romans 12:2)

THE UNITED STATES is a very religious country. We have always been so and continue to be, despite the alleged secularization of American society. The Pulitzer Prize–winning historian Garry Wills says, "Every time religiosity catches the attention of intellectuals, it is as if a shooting star has appeared in the sky. One could hardly guess, from this, that nothing has been more stable in our history, nothing less budgeable, than religious belief and practice. Religion does not shift or waver; the attention of the observers does.... Technology, urbanization, social mobility, universal education, high living standards—all were supposed to eat away at religion, in a wash of overlapping acids. But each has crested over America, proving itself a solvent or a catalyst in other areas, but showing little power to erode religion. The figures are staggering. Poll after poll confirms them."

Perhaps the most famous evidence of American religiosity is the polling that George Gallup has done over many years. According to Gallup, 95 percent of Americans say they believe in the existence of God (only 30 percent of Western Europeans say they do). Fully

85 percent call themselves Christians, 65 percent say they are currently members of a church or synagogue, and 45 percent report they attend a religious service weekly (60 percent say they have attended within the previous month). Ninety percent of Americans say they pray at some time in the week. A third say they read the Bible weekly or more often, and a fifth of the American population participate in a Bible study group. Religion is "very important" to 55 percent of the American people, "fairly important" to 30 percent, and "not very important" to only 15 percent. Those figures were almost twenty points higher in the 1950s and '60s but have remained steady for the last two decades. Even if we account for a little fudging in people's answers to polling questions, the degree of religious conviction in the United States is still amazingly strong.

The breakdown of denominations in round numbers goes like this: 60 percent of Americans call themselves Protestant, about half in mainline churches and half evangelical or fundamentalist; 25 percent are Catholic; 2 percent each are Jewish, Orthodox Christian, Mormon, and other (including growing numbers of Muslims, Buddhists, and Hindus). Only 10 percent of the American people list their faith preference as "none."

In addition, churches and organized religion consistently rank at the top of America's "most trusted institutions," far outdistancing the military and the Supreme Court, and thirty to forty percentage points ahead of the Congress, the press, organized labor, and big business. Religious leaders, especially Billy Graham, have ranked consistently high in most-respected people polls for decades. Yet, interestingly, groups like the Moral Majority and the Christian Coalition, along with leaders like Jerry Falwell and Pat Robertson, are viewed favorably by only 25 percent of the public and unfavorably by 45 percent; the rest have no opinion or knowledge of them.

The perennial issue of the separation of church and state, while critically important, is widely misunderstood. The nation's founders did a highly original and farsighted thing when they decided there would be no state-sponsored religion in America. But contrary to some conventional wisdom, that decision to separate the state from any religious establishment was made not to weaken the role of religion in the new republic but to strengthen the independent values of religion in order to better undergird democracy. Again, Garry Wills explains: "Neither Jefferson nor Madison thought the separation would lessen the impact of religion on our nation. Quite the opposite. Churches freed from the compromises of establishment would have greater moral force, they argued—and in this they proved prophets. The first nation to disestablish religion has been a marvel of religiosity, for good or ill. Religion has been at the center of our major political crises, which are always moral crises—the supporting and opposing of wars, of slavery, of corporate power, of civil rights, of sexual codes, of 'the West,' of American separatism and claims to empire. If we neglect the religious element in all these struggles, we cannot understand our own corporate past; we cannot even talk meaningfully to each other about things that will affect us all (and not only the 'religious nuts' among us)." Wills simply documents what most of us know from experience—the role of religion in American public life is a well-established tradition, a deep influence in our culture and history.

Shifting Away from the Religious Right

Clearly, the religious right has dominated the media's coverage on religion and politics in the last two decades. But that is changing. Perhaps the media have focused so much on the religious right because of its emphasis on electoral politics and gaining power within the Republican party. The media's notoriously short attention span is more suited to the wins and losses of elections than to long-term efforts to turn neighborhoods around. And power is more interesting to the press than works of mercy and compassion.

The religious right beat the left to the punch in making the critical link between politics and moral values. But their agenda was too extreme and alarming to many, and they long ignored central biblical themes such as racial reconciliation and compassion for the poor. In the end, their too-close involvement in Republican party power politics denied them the moral high ground that any movement toward a more spiritual politics needs.

But religious conservatives have done a much better job of focusing their message, engaging the media, and building a national movement with local efforts than most of us doing faith-based on-the-ground social justice work have done. A cover story in *The Boston Globe Magazine* was titled "One Nation Under God: How the Religious Right Changed the American Conversation." And, indeed, it has. Even though I don't share many of their political conclusions, I am not one of those people who think that the religious right has been an entirely negative force in American politics. The need for more value-centered politics, more support for families, more concern about the moral degradation of the popular culture, and more emphasis on the value and dignity of human life are all positive concerns. The *Globe* article pointed out that even if one doesn't share their entire political agenda, one must admit that the religious right has changed the conversation. Now, everyone is talking about their issues.

But the conversation about religion and public life appears to be changing again. Today, new findings point to the potential for renewing religion's role in seeking social justice. First, a recent survey shows that 86 percent of the American people (religious or not) believe that "churches and religious organizations should spend more time helping the poor." When churches show little concern for the poor, this is perceived as a big gap in their integrity, say more and more people. The general public consistently views Jesus as being on the side of the poor and oppressed, and the hunger for making that connection back to Jesus and restoring the churches' social justice leadership is now evident in many places.

Second, it used to be that grassroots community organizing around the country was led by political parties, clubs, and labor unions committed to economic justice. But the nature of community organizing has fundamentally changed, and today most of it is being done through the churches. It takes several forms, but most of the nation's largest community-organizing networks—such as the Industrial Areas Foundation (IAF), the Gamaliel Foundation, Direct Action and Research Training Center (DART), and the Pacific Institute for Community Organization (PICO)—have now chosen the churches and local congregations as their primary organizing base and constituency. Several other community- and economic-development networks are explicitly Christian. Then there are all the other social ministries carried out by the churches and congregations in every community across the country.

I decided to calculate roughly how many people are involved in faith-based community organizing, community development, or social ministries—just by totaling their numbers in various national, regional, and local networks, and in the myriad church ministries that survey results report. The results were startling. The number of religious people involved in grassroots organizing, community development, and social justice ministry is greater today than the numbers claimed by the major organizations of the religious right. According to my rough calculation, the number of people involved in efforts to promote social and economic justice in their communities exceeds three million, with an estimated twenty thousand groups or congregations involved. In addition, surveys show that over 90 percent of local church congregations have some sort of social ministry. Indeed, many churches associated with the religious right are among those involved in social service ministries.

Another discussion is making its way into the public arena through the religious community. It's the moral conversation about poverty, racism, and the growing economic inequality in America. New religious voices are beginning to be heard and are attracting public attention, and it is possible to see how the religious community might now impact the national debate on these issues of social justice. As Fred Clark, a young organizer from Evangelicals for Social Action, said at a Call to Renewal town meeting, "We must look forward to the day when the politicians feel they have to 'pacify' the churches on the issue of poor people, just like they have tried to do on other issues." When *The New Yorker*, *George*, *The New York Times*, and even *Worth* magazine all focus on the connection between spirituality and politics and faith-based solutions to social problems, something new is in the air. In addition, a whole series of essays in scholarly and social policy journals have appeared, showing the positive results of faith-based initiatives. The articles have been very interesting indeed, with reporters who normally deal with secular issues struggling to understand something that they recognize has growing social and political significance. It's the first time in several years that media coverage of religion's role has not even mentioned the religious right. They are not part of this story.

Joe Klein, in a *New Yorker* article called "In God They Trust," described the dramatic reduction in youth crime in Boston we've already discussed, and how "unconditional love" is an effective program to save kids from the ravages of drugs, violence, and poverty. Naomi Wolf, writing in *George*, said that the "blend of compassionate political action and spiritual rhetoric" is the right combination to mobilize people in a new political direction. She said, "This newly energized movement…may well be the winning center of American politics of the near future."

John DiIulio is convinced that a "God-centered and problem-centered approach" will provide the most successful strategy. He believes that the right-wing political agenda of groups such as the Christian Coalition won't ultimately speak to the place where most Christians and most other Americans really are now. Rather, a new agenda that is neither Left nor Right, which combines personal responsibility and moral values with a frontal assault on racism and poverty, will be increasingly successful.

America today is a pluralistic society, one composed of many faiths and spiritual interests. Any new social agenda must work within this increasingly diverse culture. Ron Thiemann, a Lutheran theologian at the Harvard Divinity School, insightfully points out that religious pluralism, not secularism, is the greater challenge ahead in American life. A growing interest in spirituality has disproved and confounded the advocates of secularism. But that interest takes many shapes today. There is much going on in American religion beyond the churches. An increasingly lively Jewish Renewal movement is evidencing both an inviting spirituality and social commitment, which attracts many who have been repelled by organized religion. There are 4.1 million Muslims in America today, more than the number of either Presbyterians or Episcopalians and, soon, more than the number of Jews. There are also 2.4 million Buddhists and one million Hindus, and both religions are growing.

To navigate such diversity, both absolutism and relativism are inadequate, says Thiemann. The best way forward may be a "pilgrim discipleship," and by this he means being committed to the truths of one's own belief but open to the fresh insights of others. He names four characteristics of a pilgrim discipleship: God is a transcendent mystery; out of death comes life; true religion shows itself in ministry to outcasts; and be prepared for the unexpected. Finding God in unexpected places, while maintaining a strong commitment to one's own faith, opens one up to others and leaves no room for arrogance, only humility.

Many people today are more comfortable with "spiritual" rather than "religious" values. But religious or spiritual experience reveals what the spiritual dimension has the power to do and why it must be at the center of any efforts to change our communities.

Radical Religion

I walked through the historic Holy Trinity church on Clapham Common, in South London. This Anglican parish was the home church to William Wilberforce, the abolitionist English Parliamentarian who wrote Britain's antislave trade legislation. Wilberforce, and a group of Christian laymen called the Clapham Sect, were behind much of the social reform that swept England in the late eighteenth and early nineteenth centuries. The current vicar was very proud to show me around. On the wall were pictures of these typically English-looking gentlemen who helped to turn their country upside down. Other such memorabilia abound in the beautiful old church, now perched on the edge of the rich green expanse of urban park that the English call a common.

The vicar specifically pointed to an old, well-worn table. "This is the table upon which William Wilberforce wrote the antislavery act," he said proudly. "We now use this table every Sunday for communion." I was struck—here, in dramatic liturgical symbol, the secular and the sacred are brought together with powerful historical force. How did we ever separate them? What became of religion that believed its duty was to change its society on behalf of justice?

William Wilberforce was a convert of the religious revivals that transformed eighteenth-century England. His life and his vocation as a member of Parliament profoundly changed by his newfound faith, Wilberforce became a force for moral politics. His mentor, John Newton, had helped sail a slave ship before he was converted, then turned against slavery and became well known for writing the beloved hymn "Amazing Grace." Newton's immortal words, "Amazing Grace, how sweet the sound, that saved a wretch like me," spoke not merely of private guilt and piety, but of having turned from being a slave trader who trafficked in human flesh to being a religious leader who helped lead the battle against slavery. His conversion produced a social and political transformation as well as a personal one.

The same became true of Wilberforce, who first heard Newton speak when he was young but regarded his real conversion as resulting from a conversation with his mentor in 1786. Two years later Wilberforce introduced his first antislave trade motion into Parliament. It was defeated, and would be defeated nine more times until it passed in 1807. It was a historic and moral victory, but Wilberforce wouldn't be satisfied until slavery was abolished altogether. He tirelessly worked toward that goal, year after year. Finally, in 1833, Parliament passed a bill abolishing slavery, and Wilberforce died three days later, his work finally done. Wilberforce's life is a testament to the power of conversion and the persistence of faith.

Similarly, in nineteenth-century America, religious revivalism was linked directly with the abolition of slavery and movements of social reform. Christians helped lead the abolitionist struggle, efforts to end child labor, projects to aid working people and establish unions, and even the battle to obtain voting rights for women. Here were evangelical Christians fighting for social causes, an activity that evangelicals are hardly associated with today. Nineteenth-century evangelist Charles Finney, the Billy Graham of his day, didn't shy away from identifying the gospel with the antislavery cause.

He was a revivalist and also an abolitionist. For him, the two went together. Finney is said to have invented the "altar call," well known to us today in gatherings like the Billy Graham crusades, where people are invited to get up out of their seats and come down to the front of the pulpit to profess their new faith. Finney invited people down the aisle too, but his motivations are reported to have been very pragmatic also. He wanted the names of his converts in order to sign them up for the abolitionist cause. He was an organizer as well as an evangelist. And he had an agenda.

The Big Split

So what happened to Christianity in this century? Put simply, there was a big split. American Protestantism split into two camps in the early 1900s. The schism went deep and remained a permanent divide throughout the rest of the twentieth century. The fundamentalists took the conservative road of personal piety and correct doctrine, while the modernists chose the liberal path of the social gospel. And the two choices were conceived by most as mutually exclusive. One group would come to be called evangelical and the other liberal.

Both fundamentalist and liberal Protestants questioned whether the large numbers of Catholic immigrants arriving in America in the twentieth century were really Christians—their Catholic religion would not be accepted. And most white churches of all denominations wished to keep segregated from their black Christian brothers and sisters, who started their own churches.

Thus four basic constituencies of American Christianity remained apart through most of the twentieth century: evangelical, mainline Protestant, Catholic, and the historic black churches. Each developed its own Christian culture and world, complete with schools, other institutions, language, traditions, networks of relationships, agendas, priorities, and, of course, opinions about the other groups.

I was raised in the evangelical world ("evangelical" generally replaced "fundamentalist" after World War II). Our small Plymouth Brethren Assembly in Detroit, Michigan, saw itself as a direct descendant of biblical Christianity and the early church. We looked upon other evangelical churches favorably, as long as they "preached the gospel." The Baptists and independent Bible churches were closest to us. But most of the mainline liberal Protestant denominations were deeply suspect theologically, and all Catholics were targets of our evangelism because we thought they worshiped Mary and the pope rather than God. Nobody ever talked about the black churches; it was as if they didn't exist.

Later I discovered that Catholics learned similar prejudices about us Protestants as they were growing up, and that liberal Protestants regarded most evangelicals as unsophisticated, uneducated, and unpleasant. No matter where they lived, evangelicals were seen as Bible-thumping street preachers who might corner you and ask, probably in a Southern accent, if you were saved. Interestingly, black Christians didn't perceive great differences among the warring white church factions, at least so far as racism toward them was concerned, which seemed to be the one thing most white Christians had in common.

Twentieth-Century Ecumenism

If we are to successfully tap the power of faith communities, we have to understand them. A little history of the churches' divisions may help those working for social change—whether they themselves are religious or not—who want to collaborate with the churches. "Ecumenism," or the effort on the part of churches to get together in the twentieth century, never broke down the divisions I've described above. In fact, the modern ecumenical movement has occurred almost solely among mainstream Protestant churches. The formation of the Federal Council of the Churches of Christ in America and various church councils in Europe at the beginning of the twentieth century launched the collaboration of the leading Protestant denominations. Later, consolidations into the National Council of Churches (NCC) in 1950 and the World Council of Churches (WCC) in 1948 completed the task. But again, many churches and groups were left out. It is significant to note that the principal reasons for coming together had to do with missions and service. "Doctrine divides but service unites" became an early motto whose spirit was key to future, wider, ecumenical realities.

With the formation of these councils, Presbyterians and Methodists, Episcopalians and Congregationalists, Lutherans and some Baptists, among others, came together for at least some common goals. And some of the results were, indeed, impressive—for instance, the leadership the National Council of Churches offered in the American civil rights movement and the role of the World Council of Churches in helping to end apartheid in South Africa. However, efforts to agree on theological issues and matters of church order and polity were usually much more problematic than joint efforts on common social agendas.

Evangelical Christians were rarely at the ecumenical table—both by choice and by exclusion. In fact, the ecumenical table has belonged to liberal Protestants, who have been adamant gatekeepers. Consequently, evangelicals formed their own networks, such as the National Association of Evangelicals, founded in 1942; established a myriad of para-church organizations for mission; spawned great student movements such as Inter-Varsity Christian Fellowship and Campus Crusade for Christ; and conducted joint evangelistic efforts, most notably the Billy Graham crusades, which even made common cause with mainline Protestant and Catholic churches.

Within the two Protestant camps, scores of organizations and associations were produced. Both liberal and evangelical groups founded their own colleges, institutions, and publications. Evangelical pastors read *Christianity Today*, founded by Billy Graham, while their liberal Protestant counterparts read *The Christian Century* or *Christianity & Crisis*, the latter founded by eminent theologian Reinhold Niebuhr.

All along, Catholics have pursued their own course, evolving from a marginalized church, full of many new immigrants, to a major cultural and political force by the end of the twentieth century. They, too, generally, have not been at the ecumenical table of liberal Protestants and, like the evangelicals, developed a whole network of schools and other institutions that made a deep impact in local communities around the country. Catholics actually have become a bridge constituency in American church life, espousing much of the cultural conservatism embraced by evangelicals as well as the social conscience shared by liberal Protestants, particularly in relationship to the poor. Catholic bishops could find themselves outside the White House protesting partial-birth abortions one day and the signing of a draconian welfare bill the next.

The black churches in America have defied the polarization between white liberals and conservatives by consistently prioritizing both spiritual conversion and social justice. In spite of having their own divisions, the biblical balance of personal piety and public prophecy for justice has remained strong in most black congregations of all denominations, while their white counterparts created a century of false choices. The black churches in the South and around the country led and became the moral infrastructure of the civil rights movement—the greatest ecumenical moment of the twentieth century. Nevertheless, black Christians were still not given a real place and voice at ecumenical tables controlled by white Christians for most of this century. As we enter the twenty-first century, that finally has begun to change.

Beyond the evangelicals, mainline Protestants, Catholics, and black churches, perhaps the greatest uncharted religious movement of the century was the Pentecostal and charismatic revivals, which emphasized direct personal experience of the Holy Spirit and very lively expressions of worship. Though treated with suspicion by all the other church groups, Pentecostals are the fastest-growing sector in the worldwide church at the beginning of the twenty-first century. While their appeal crosses all denominational, racial, and even class lines, twentieth-century Pentecostals and charismatics became another group unto themselves, often distrusting those who didn't share their litmus tests of what it means to be "filled by the Holy Spirit."

The other constituency that doesn't fit neatly within the boundaries of the four groups is the Orthodox churches. These are the congregations from the Eastern Christian world, whose blend of deep worship, powerful liturgy, and personal piety offers a different perspective in Western ecumenical debates.

The Twenty-First Century Church

But the prospects for churches coming together and playing a more helpful social leadership role are much brighter now. Understanding the changes now going on will help anyone who wants to work with the churches.

The church of the twenty-first century will look quite different from the church today. Yes there will be a church, despite the dire predictions of many who keep pointing to declining church rolls and influence among the mainline Protestants. There may even be more churches and more people going to them than we see today. But the churches themselves will be different, and the relationships among them will consequently be changing.

The best way to describe how the churches have been operating is likening them to *vertical* silos—tall, narrow structures into which ideas and leadership are dropped from the top, in the hope that they will reach down to the grassroots level. But the vertical style of organization and leadership that has characterized most churches is already changing. In the future, *horizontal* patterns of relationship between congregations will be the normative style, and those ecclesial interconnections will go beyond denominations to cross the lines that have divided us for a century.

These new connections are profoundly local and focused on cooperation around specific and practical issues facing communities and neighborhoods. Three factors are producing the new horizontal configuration: a cultural crisis of values, a deep spiritual hunger that transcends old ideological and religious categories, and a more recognized social role for churches. Together, these forces will call forth a new ecumenical reality. The vertical constituencies of the twentieth-century American churches will come together horizontally for twenty-first-century projects and endeavors. Indeed, it is already happening.

In the final quarter of the twentieth century, the rigid patterns of American church life began to change. The civil rights movement and the war in Vietnam impacted a new generation of evangelicals. They discovered the forgotten evangelical movements of the nineteenth century, whose strong social conscience focused on abolitionism, concern for the poor, and the equality of women. They began to meet children of mainline Protestantism who were also hungry for a more personal spirituality and a deeper grounding in biblical faith. Catholics, taking permission from Vatican II, also rediscovered the Bible and embarked on a spiritual pilgrimage of personal and parish renewal, but with a social conscience that twentieth-century evangelicalism lacked. Black congregations grew within the predominantly white denominations, soon to be followed by their Latino and Asian brothers and sisters. Pentecostal pastors in storefront churches began to look outward.

The real ecumenism of the last twenty-five years has taken place in soup kitchens and homeless shelters more than at tables of theologians trying to find unity on the meaning of the Eucharist. Instead, Methodists, Baptists, Mennonites, and Catholics have been sharing bread together at nuclear test sites, outside the White House or the South African embassy, and in the jail cells to which they were taken after their spiritual protests.

I remember the May 1985 events that Sojourners sponsored around the Christian holiday of Pentecost in Washington, D.C. Christians from around the country conducted nonviolent civil disobedience at symbolic sites around the city to register their moral conscience regarding many issues that cut across traditional political lines: budget cuts against the poor, the superpowers' deployment of first-strike nuclear weapons, the American wars in Central America, the Soviet invasion of Afghanistan, and the nation's acceptance of 1.5 million abortions every year.

We soon had the D.C. jail full of Christians—hundreds of them singing and praying through most of the night. The jail acoustics seemed favorable and we sounded pretty good. By the end of the night, the jailhouse choir was taking requests from the guards to sing their favorite hymns! Baptist and Benedictine choir directors, evangelical pastors and Franciscan priests, Presbyterian theologians and Maryknoll sisters, and lay people from virtually every denomination spent the night in jail, not only singing, but talking with one another.

"The whole church is here," exclaimed an exuberant clergyman. "I must be in heaven," smiled a Catholic sister as she woke up to the strains of "Amazing Grace," coming from the men's side of the jail. And one seminarian, who had slept all night on the concrete floor, said he would have paid money to be there for the best theological education he'd had so far.

Spiritual Formation

It's not only social action that is bringing people together, but also their spiritual hunger. Catholic spiritual programs that focus on personal and parish renewal have grown around the country. Evangelical Bible studies have proliferated across the nation, involving people of every and no denomination. And prayer circles of support can be found now in virtually every workplace, including the halls of Congress. When Christians pray and study the Bible together, they also talk and come to know and support one another across all the former dividing lines.

As our culture's values continue to disintegrate, centers of positive values and activities will draw more and more people. Instead of just complaining and blaming others, church congregations could become the places where moral reconstruction begins, if they are ready to rise to the challenge. Within the nurturing bonds that churches provide, broken families can be supported and many put back together again; children can find role models and moral guidance to navigate dangerous cultural waters; employers can be motivated to serve the common good, not just the bottom line; and young people can learn the deeper rewards of service compared with the numbing drive of materialism.

Churches, not just New Age seminars, could respond directly to the obvious spiritual hunger across the land and be less afraid of its excesses. Congregations can become the much-needed places of spiritual formation that our society desperately lacks, stressing character over success, spirituality over consumption, fidelity over gratification, honesty over expediency, leadership over celebrity, and integrity over everything else. Limitless technology, endless consumption, and never-ending work have clearly not answered the longings of the human heart. The spiritual hunger at the end of the twentieth century is even greater than at its beginning, and the churches still have the best opportunity to respond.

In order to respond to that spiritual hunger, the churches need to turn their present divisions into resources for renewal. Virtually every denomination began with an impulse for reform, an insight that was unique, or a truth that helped define it. Each therefore has, within its own history, a tradition of renewal. Yet most of those renewing impulses have long since been forgotten, and the traditions have simply turned into divisions.

The transforming power of the early church is still embedded in the traditions of every congregation today. The renewing power of every Catholic religious order or Protestant denomination is available to be appropriated anew. Indeed, the Catholic orders are all learning that the road to renewal begins with a return to the earliest "charisms"—the founding ideas or purposes that created the community—and then with the application of those charisms to the contemporary world.

Increasingly, American Protestants choose their churches with little reference to denomination. Other factors are more important: neighborhood location, Sunday school and youth activities, stimulating preaching and worship, and community service. Some might call that a reflection of the wider society's consumer mentality, but it also reflects a desire to relate church in more meaningful ways to families and local communities. In fact, many families are turning to independent community churches, which are now the fastest-growing segment in the country. Most Catholics still select a parish for Mass but are more and more involved with Protestants in everything from social ministry to Bible study and prayer. And younger evangelicals are far less fearful than their parents were of mixing with both Catholics and other Protestants. Black Christians still understand the central role of the black church in their communities but now can be found partnering with white congregations for the sake of inner-city ministry and racial reconciliation.

Drinking from Other Wells

The denominational ties and loyalties that Christians feel today are weaker than ever. And never before have Christians been more interested in traditions other than their own. Many people find themselves drinking from wells of spirituality far afield from where they began. Catholic retreat centers are overflowing with Protestants. Lively evangelical services draw crowds of hungry worshipers from every denomination. And few can fire the souls of American Christians, regardless of their racial and cultural identity, more than a black preacher or choir. When church-led efforts to meet the social needs of the community have opened up in urban churches, they have drawn volunteers from every kind of church and others from no church at all.

We can see the possibilities of churches and denominations turning their divisions into the spiritual wells of tradition from which we all drink. Important theology can be found in virtually every church tradition, and it should not simply be amalgamated into a new ecumenism. In other words, ecumenism for the twenty-first century should not be viewed as a bland, common-denominator Christianity. Rather, it should emerge from the exciting rediscovery of the strength of each of our traditions, which are seen as gifts to be offered instead of walls to divide.

That could produce wonderful results. We all could recover the wonderful Catholic sense of God's presence in all of life and the world, and regain a commitment on the part of every church to take spiritual responsibility for the life of the parish in which it finds itself. The depth and quality of Catholic social teaching also offer much to Protestants who are looking to move beyond the old categories of Left and Right, and the spiritual formation available from Catholic religious communities could be a powerful resource for the whole of the church.

The evangelical invitation of a personal relationship with Jesus could bring people back to the churches, where membership has been steadily declining. The spiritual energy and passion of evangelical churches are desperately needed today in churches where both are in short supply. If Bible study and prayer again become mainstays of Christian life, small groups doing both would draw spiritually hungry people who are not inclined to venture into a more formal church service.

Mainline Protestant churches could rediscover the best of their own social gospel tradition, which refused to separate personal piety from social action. Instead of backing off from strong social commitments because of declining numbers, the major denominational churches could strengthen their prophetic social witness by renewing their call to evangelism. And the exemplary commitments of many mainline Protestant denominational churches to the gifts and leadership of women could offer much to many Catholic, evangelical, and black churches whose patterns are still quite patriarchal.

Both evangelical and mainline Protestant churches could recover their historical roots in the revival traditions and in the reformed traditions from which they come. The revivalist movements swept across nineteenth-century America, making converts and challenging the social evils of the day. The Reformed tradition refused to divide life into sacred and secular, private and public, and insisted that everything must be brought under the Lordship of Jesus Christ.

The Anabaptist tradition, which created the Historic Peace Churches of Mennonites, Brethren, and Quakers, could teach the contemporary world about the limits of military force in resolving conflicts. Their strong witness for nonviolence, peacemaking, and simple living could speak to a great hunger today from both the religious and the nonreligious.

White Christians could finally look to their black brothers and sisters for instruction in how to feed hungry souls and bodies. The spiritual power and social courage of the black churches have provided the best single contribution of American Christianity to the worldwide church. It is time for that contribution to be fully accepted at home.

The great influx of Latino and Asian Christians to the United States is further transforming the churches, and the emergence of Native American congregations offers to diversify the face of American Christianity even more. All of these should be allowed to express their own indigenous spiritualities.

As the traditions that divide become the resources that renew, we will see the emergence of a new ecumenical table in every community. Old ecumenical structures must give way to new ecumenical networks. The mainline Protestants who controlled the old table are vitally needed at the new one, but it is no longer their table; in fact, no one needs to control it.

The Protestant denominations of the World Council of Churches and the National Council of Churches seem to be recognizing this new reality and are making attempts to reach out to other families of churches. Catholics and evangelicals are finding they have more and more in common as well, and both seem willing to sit down with their mainline Protestant neighbors. Some white Christians finally understand how much they need their black and brown brothers and sisters, especially in a society desperate for models of racial repentance and reconciliation.

This new table of Christian unity is possible only as we seek to find the common ground that has been hidden by our divisions. If we don't, a new period of division awaits us, perhaps not along denominational and constituency lines but along social and cultural cleavages. Instead of helping to resolve society's deepest conflicts, the church would likely ratify them. How tragic if the future church were simply defined by pro-gay and anti-gay congregations, pro-choice and pro-life partisans, and conservative and liberal voting blocs. It's a future we can avoid, but only if we let our theological vision and spiritual clarity—rather than political positions—define our public witness.

Every large-scale Christian project and endeavor must strive to bring all the church families together. On many community issues, we must learn to sit down with brothers and sisters from other faith traditions. We have yet to determine the shape of a new interfaith collaboration that moves beyond highly unsatisfying lowest-common-denominator worship services to real partnership, where everyone is free to be and bring who they are. But that is already beginning too. I've seen it all around the country.

Instead of a church made up of divided kingdoms and warring factions, the church of the twenty-first century could well become a rich mosaic of interconnected faith communities. Nothing would be better news for a society looking for social leadership, cultural healing, and spiritual grounding.

The "Body of Christ"

That twenty-first-century church can already be found. I was teaching week-long courses in western Canada and in the American Southwest. Both were titled "Who Speaks for God?" and both included clergy and lay leaders from across the whole theological and denominational spectrum. We had twenty-seven-year-olds and eighty-seven-year-olds, pastors, professors, doctors, nurses, lawyers, union members, community organizers, business people, economists, directors of homeless shelters, computer programmers, schoolteachers, retired people, students, mothers and fathers, longtime activists, and new explorers.

A recurring theme in both classes was the hunger for new "dialogue," for "bridge building," and for new relationships across former dividing lines. Once again I saw how weary people have become of the old liberal/conservative debates that have turned the churches against each other. Class members came from all of the old sides, but shared a community of sorts for the week in residential settings and discovered that they really did have more in common as Christians than their various churches had been able to find.

Growing unity on the problem of poverty was evident throughout the week, and the prospect of forming new partnerships back home in their local communities was particularly exciting to many. But we didn't shy away from the hot topics either. We also talked about abortion, family values, and homosexuality. After a whole morning session on abortion in Canada (where the issue is also very divisive and controversial), one of the clergy in the class remarked, "I've never been in a better conversation on abortion. Nobody walked out, and people didn't even start yelling at each other. We all listened for a change. It was really amazing."

Both the sanctity of human life and the rights of women were affirmed. Through discussion, people on different sides of issues found it possible to agree on the importance of traditional two-parent families for raising children without scapegoating single mothers or blaming homosexuals for the breakdown of heterosexual families. And both the Right and the Left got criticized for trying to divide the church over issues such as these. People were tired of the extremes controlling the debate on many issues, and were looking for some common ground without compromising their convictions.

But in addition to finding common ground, there was a real enjoyment of the diversity of the faith community. When we can stop fighting for a moment, we begin to realize the richness of the many traditions and experiences that are the church. Young Christians were clearly marveling at the wisdom and faith of those much older. Pastors across denominational lines began openly sharing their joys and their struggles and praying for one another. We both laughed and cried together, rejoicing together over new marriages and babies and sorrowing together over circumstances of sickness, loneliness, and loss. Several people began to talk about "the body of Christ," a traditional term for the church, and the oldest member of the New Mexico course exclaimed on the last day of class, "We should get together next year. I think we're a great group!" Addresses, phone numbers, and e-mails were eagerly exchanged, and many expressed the extra support they will now feel just knowing that "you all are out there." Some suggested we were parting like teenagers leaving friends behind after summer camp. Not only was it a lot of fun, but it again proved to me that our divisions can be overcome.

Perhaps it is easier in a beautiful summer setting for a week with normal responsibilities left behind. But I wondered how church people could begin to experience some of that same depth of sharing and community across the normal boundaries of our lives. Christian unity does not come easily, and it must never come at the expense of gospel truth. But all too often, in the name of our truths, we have just been attacking one another in the churches, and a disbelieving world sees no reason to join us. Remember how Jesus said the world will know we are Christians? "That you have love one for another" was not a commandment to be easily set aside because of

honest disagreements among Christians. It was that love which
Jesus called us to, and two groups of Christians got to experience
it, in the lush forests of British Columbia and in the spectacular
desert of northern New Mexico. It was enough to make you fall in
love with the church again and gave me a very exciting glimpse of
the twenty-first-century church.

A New Social Role: Why Faith Communities Will Lead

As well as responding to the crisis of values and society's spiritual hunger, faith-based groups have an advantage over many other
institutions when it comes to the kind of community organizing
and development most needed today. It finally comes down to the
question of social leadership—who is best situated to offer critical
components like vision, direction, credibility, longevity, trust, and,
of course, organizable constituencies. Faith communities may be in
the best position to lead efforts for social renewal because of their
inherent characteristics and commitments, enabling them to be
community conveners in broad-based efforts involving many different kinds of organizations. There are three sets of essential ingredi-
ents that are at the heart of why it is so critical to tap the power of
faith communities.

Message and Motivation

In a society where market values increasingly predominate, faith
communities can offer a sense of meaning, purpose, and moral value
that is increasingly missing in the society. When people feel reduced
to mere consumers and life is reduced to shopping, faith communities can speak directly to the deep spiritual hunger that so many
people experience. In the community of faith, persons are more
than marketing data for advertisers or polling data for politicians;
they are the children of God with immense and sacred value, created in the very image of God.

Faith communities are also best situated to speak to society's
moral and spiritual impoverishment, which others seem to accept as
inevitable. They can help to reestablish a sense of ethics and values.
The faith community makes it possible to do more than look out

for number one. Faith communities offer people practical opportunities to love their neighbor, serve their community, contribute to a larger purpose, and sacrifice for something worth believing in. In the faith community, the values of compassion, community, and solidarity have a theological foundation, not merely a sentimental one. Hope is more than an optimistic feeling; it is a firm conclusion drawn from trusting the promises of God.

The values you need for organizing are rooted in the very essence of the faith community. Eugene Rivers, pastor of the Azuza Christian Community in Boston, says that "only the church has the moral authority and the vocabulary to introduce transcendent concepts of personal worth and the sacredness of life that will both inspire responsibility on a personal level and introduce purpose and definition to the role of civil government on a societal level." Thus, faith can be used to undergird, legitimize, and inspire social action.

Counterculture and Prophetic Voice

Faith communities are intended to be distinct communities, with ethics distinct from those of the surrounding society. The apostle Paul writing to the Romans says, "Do not be conformed to this world, but be transformed by the renewing of your minds." Alternative visions arise from alternative communities. Such communities can become support bases for nurturing and training, networking and mobilizing. The symbols and rituals of the faith community can become powerful educators and mobilizers for committed and even risky action. For example, black churches in the South constituted a coherent subculture in the midst of a white-dominated society. As such they reminded their members who they really were and what they could really do. Churches became the practical place to organize car pools to sustain a bus boycott and the spiritual place to prepare oneself for nonviolent confrontation with police clubs and dogs.

A countercultural community can have a prophetic public voice. Here is where the authority and trust that religious communities often enjoy in our society can be utilized for the common good. Who will tell the truth, or even try to find it, when falsehoods prevail? Who

will stand up for those who are being left out and behind, or whose
human rights are being violated? Who will question the easy and
hedonistic assumptions of the popular culture? Who will challenge
the government's authority when it becomes violent and abusive?
Why did the government of El Salvador assassinate Archbishop
Oscar Romero? They were afraid of his authority in challenging
their political repression. And as a slain martyr, Romero gained even
more authority. The faith community has the moral authority to
make justice a priority.

Institution and Constituency

The most common institutions in local communities are the
churches and the schools—and the churches are in much better
shape than the schools. Churches have budgets, buildings, several
kinds of meeting spaces, kitchens, nurseries, bathrooms, and parking
lots—all of which are fundamental assets you need for organizing.
They also have staffs, a cadre of professionally trained leaders, ties to
larger denominational structures with greater resources, and a widely trusted historical tradition to build upon. Churches are the institution most commonly found in every kind of neighborhood, across
all geographic, racial, cultural, and class boundaries. In some poor
communities, churches are virtually the last standing institution. In
those situations, it's often only the churches that have the moral
authority and institutional presence to lead efforts for civic reconstruction. With proximity to the problems, churches can work from
the bottom up, redeeming kids one by one, claiming whole blocks
and neighborhoods for transformation, calling for moral, civic, and
political renewal in the broader community, city, and nation.

And, of course, the churches have a constituency. They actually
have members—another prerequisite for organizing—who can be
mobilized and brought together. The very nature of a universal
membership in the faith community can be instrumental in helping
to overcome the divisions between people that are the greatest
obstacle to organizing. And members of faith communities can be
motivated to act not just in their own self-interest, but rather on the
basis of the deeply held spiritual and moral values that undergird

their faith. That faith can provide the staying power so critically needed for long-term campaigns. Religious institutions also have enduring power, as opposed to some other community institutions that are often here today and gone tomorrow. Most churches plan to be a part of their communities for a very long time, and therefore have a vested interest in their well-being.

Additionally, because churches are built on relationships, they can provide a strong base for the kind of relational organizing style that is proving to be so effective around the country. Community organizer and sociologist Marshall Ganz speaks of this as a "covenantal" organizing style. He contrasts it with "issue-based organizing," which is more "contractual": "It has a limited, short-term, outcome-based focus; it often brings people into coalitions that dissolve immediately after the objective is attained, or isn't." Ganz prefers "interest-based organizing," which is "covenantal." It has a longer-term focus of "identifying and developing those common interests which are affected by a variety of issues that come and go," he says. "Interest-based organizing places a greater emphasis on building relationships as a way both to discern interests as well as to construct new interests which only emerge in the context of new relationship."

What Would Jesus Do?

Finally, faith communities also have the enormous advantage of being able to raise the fundamental religious questions that can radically reshape the political conversation. I found myself speaking at Point Loma College, a conservative Christian school in San Diego, California, which, that very night, would be the host city for the 1996 election campaign's second and final presidential debate. The whole town was buzzing about the great event and wondering how one might get into the hall to participate.

I asked the students two simple questions. First, I asked what they would ask Bill Clinton and Bob Dole if they were in the room for the debate. Quickly the hands shot up—the favorite questions were about abortion, lowering taxes ("I'd ask why are my dad's taxes so high"), and the president's alleged extramarital affairs. All the first group of questions were more or less what one would expect from the children of affluent suburban Republican and conservative evangelical families in Southern California. Fair questions to be sure, but hardly representing a comprehensive moral agenda. My second question to the students was different. I asked them, "What would Jesus ask if he were in that hall tonight?"

Now the room was quiet and you could almost feel the students thinking. Very slowly the first hand was raised. "Jesus would ask them how they were treating the poor." Then another hand. "He would probably ask them to treat each other better too." And a white student said, "Jesus would certainly have something to say about racism." These were the same students who just a moment before had acted like anyone else of their race, class, and political party. But when the "Jesus question" was raised, it changed the outcome of the whole discussion.

My mother used to tell us kids that that was always a good question—"What would Jesus do?" But our own church never asked the question when it came to racism. After years of organizing in the civil rights and antiwar movements, I came back to faith through the same Jesus question. Despite the church's misrepresentations over many years, most people (religious or not) know that Jesus stood for compassion, caring, and justice. Somehow, Jesus has survived the churches and all of us. To invoke the name of Jesus still raises the right questions in relation to social policy, even when religion is not really a part of the conversation. The name of Jesus still has the authority to interrogate our social priorities.

Somehow, the world understands that Jesus stands for "the least of these" even when the churches don't. That is the great spiritual gap of the twentieth-century church. At the beginning of a new century and millennium, we have to signal something new. And it's already beginning to happen. There is a very popular bracelet worn by millions of young people today that simply displays the letters WWJD, standing for What Would Jesus Do. My mother was right. And it's a question that could bring many people together, even far beyond the churches. If you can find a way to ask such a religious, spiritual, or moral question you'll open a much wider world of possible answers.

Guide
Your
Steps

CHAPTER TWELVE

Be a Peacemaker

Blessed are the peacemakers, for they will be called children of God. (Matthew 5:9)

TRYING TO HELP MAKE PEACE, resolve conflicts, and end senseless violence has been a pretty constant theme for me over these last thirty years. I've become convinced that peacemaking is a very practical thing. The great philosophical and theological debates become less important when you are confronted by violence that needs to be stopped. I've learned that lesson on battlefields both far away and very close to home.

After a Labor Day 1996 Sojourners community picnic, I was driving home in my pickup truck. It was only four in the afternoon, on a beautiful end-of-summer day. Most everyone in D.C. had the day off, and people were out on the street with their kids. The day was full of sunshine and smiles. All of a sudden, four young men burst into the intersection I was passing through, just a block from our Sojourners office. Three of them were chasing a fourth, waving the biggest machetes I had ever seen. It appeared that they had already caught him, because he was cut and bleeding badly. And now they were moving in to finish him off.

I struggled to know what to do. First, I honked my horn, hoping that might distract or scare them away. It didn't. So I positioned my truck between the three attackers and the boy being pursued.

The kid thought quickly and literally jumped into the back of my pickup truck. Seeing the opportunity, I quickly sped away, driving him to safety. After our mad rush, I stopped at a gas station just a few blocks away and got out of the truck to see how the boy was. He was so frightened he wouldn't even let me take him to a doctor. After a few words, he disappeared back into the streets, and all that was left for me to do was to mop up his blood from the back of my truck.

An experience like that makes you think. The next weekend, I headed up to New York City to preach in the historic Riverside Church. In my sermon, I reflected on my fresh encounter with the violence of the street. When our children are taking after each other with guns and knives, I told the congregation, we don't have a youth crisis, we have a societal crisis in which young people are bearing the brunt of our values crisis. It's not that the kids on the street or in the suburbs haven't gotten our values; but rather that they have, and that's the problem. Where do they learn to compete violently for territory and control, to kill one another over a pair of sneakers, or to seek immediate gratification over integrity and fidelity?

It won't be enough to merely make changes in public policies; we have to change the culture—its assumptions, values, ethos, and "habits of the heart," as cultural critic Robert Bellah would say. I'll never forget what a young Crip gang member told me in the Watts district of Los Angeles right after the 1992 riots there. A small group of Crips and Bloods were explaining the new and fragile gang truce they were trying to build when a young man said, "We've got some habits that only God can cure." As he spoke, I realized he was speaking not just for himself but for all of us. We've got some habits that must be cured if change is ever to be possible.

Conflict and Violence

Conflict has always been a part of human society and history. Both my experience and my theology suggest to me that violence arises directly out of the human heart and our pursuit of power. Differences arise in families, neighborhoods, communities, races and tribes, institutions (including churches), and, of course, nations. And those differences easily lead to conflict. The critical question is how to deal with that conflict. Violence is what happens when conflict is not resolved in peaceful ways.

But violence is also inherent in the very structures of society. I've learned that the extent of violence depends on at least three factors. First, personal and cultural values can either increase or reduce violence. Second, social policies and structures that are just will decrease the levels of violence in a society; conversely, unjust social structures clearly produce more violence. The third crucial factor is simply our response to violence. When we accept it, or are intimidated into acquiescence in the face of it, the power and even the reign of violence will increase. But when ordinary people are empowered to stand up to it, and even to intervene in the midst of it with *nonviolent action*, then its power recedes.

Today we see a growing interest in nonviolent conflict resolution. According to the Institute for Conflict Analysis and Resolution at Virginia's George Mason University, nearly one-third of all students in American public schools have had some exposure to conflict-resolution skills. There are hundreds of community-based dispute-resolution centers through which thousands of mediators have been trained to help individuals and organizations resolve their problems. Conflict-resolution skills are a core element in the curriculum at our Sojourners Neighborhood Center. Our kids live in a world where making the right decisions about real or potential conflicts can literally save their lives. For them, peacemaking is not an esoteric or abstract political issue.

Most of us who live in cities have seen the "orange hat patrols," people in neighborhoods taking back the streets by patrolling in pairs in the evenings. Ordinary people have been very successful in cities around the country in reducing street crime through their simple presence on the streets. New groups are emerging all the time, such as Families Against Violence Advocacy Network, a broad-based network of organizations, families, and individuals committed to violence prevention and the promotion of alternatives to violence in our families, schools, and communities. They promote the

"Family Pledge of Nonviolence," which says, "Making peace must start with ourselves and in our family. Each of us commits ourselves as best we can to become nonviolent and peaceable people: to respect self and others, to communicate better, to listen, to forgive, to respect nature, to play creatively, to be courageous." The pledge has been adapted for schools and is available in eight languages.

In a world filled with violence, the peacemaker is probably our most-needed figure. We often desperately need those who are able to bring warring parties to the negotiating table. Jimmy Carter has gained far more respect for his peacemaking work out of office than he ever did as president, but wouldn't it be even better if heads of state were committed to peacemaking while they had the political power? However, what Carter and some others have shown is the powerful potential to resolve terrible conflicts in peaceful ways through direct *intervention* in those conflicts. Most of the world's conflicts are actually resolved in peaceful ways. Both internationally and domestically, disputes over a whole host of policy issues are resolved daily without recourse to violence. Peacemaking is simply the attempt to expand the number of conflicts resolved by nonviolent means.

But today we face what many have called a culture of violence. It's in our families, our streets, our media, our gender patterns, our racial divides, our domestic politics, our global economy, and our military policies. Personal violence arises from many factors. It comes from too much pressure and stress, too much anger, too much hateful talk, too many unresolved conflicts, and destructive patterns in relationships. Violence is exacerbated by too little communication, too little support, too little respect, too few resources, too little education, too many guns, too prevalent drugs and alcohol, and too many images of violence in our heads from our movies, music, and television. The social and political factors that inspire violence are also many: great gaps between rich and poor, far-flung economic interests, civil wars rooted in ethnic and tribal conflict, big military budgets, the booming business of international arms sales, competitive arms races, the acceptance of the morality of weapons of mass destruction, the rise of terrorism in response to real or imagined grievances, and various political and religious ideologies that justify wars, holy and otherwise. And the surreal video-game character of modern wars, displayed nightly on CNN, serves to distance us from the faces of the real casualties. It's precisely that distancing of victims that allows violence to grow.

Modern warfare prides itself on weapons technologies that allow political and military leaders to speak of wars without casualties. But what they really mean is wars without military casualties. It used to be that soldiers were killed in war, and civilians were for the most part protected. But that has radically changed since World War II. Increasingly, soldiers are protected and it's the civilians who are the principal casualties of war. Now we bomb from high in the sky, insulated from the human face and the consequences of war.

Our Response

Merely arguing over the causes of violence produces new conflicts and dead ends. Intellectual battles will do little to calm our streets and resolve our international conflicts. The real issue is our response to violence. The violence is there: it is destructive and generally doesn't resolve conflicts, but it often complicates and exacerbates them. We don't need more arguments; we need strategies that stop, reverse, and ultimately heal our violence.

Violence has its root causes, as we have already seen. And anything we do that addresses those root causes is a nonviolent strategy. Whenever the presence and power of violence is accepted, its control or dominion becomes stronger. Before very long, the rule of violence seems almost total, and everyone cowers in fear and compliance. We've seen that happen over and over again. Families, whole neighborhoods, and even entire countries can become caught up in the grip of violence, and its control over people's lives can seem absolute. It is only when that control is challenged, and the violence morally exposed, that the rule of violence begins to diminish. The issues are often as spiritual as they are political.

I remember going to Northern Ireland several times, invited by both Catholics and Protestants seeking to challenge the power of violence in their country. At the Corrymeela community, on Northern Ireland's rugged coast, Catholics and Protestants committed to reconciliation tried to change the direction of their country. I once led a week of reflection there for a thousand people on Jesus's Sermon on the Mount. The first session was striking—a whole line of women in the first row held hands and shed tears as I spoke. Afterward I learned they were the mothers of children, both Catholic and Protestant, who had been killed in the Northern Ireland conflict. Now they had joined together to end the madness. Mothers like these marched in the street through the militant strongholds of both sides, defying the power of the violence that had stolen their sons and daughters from them. I thought of those women when, in 1998, Northern Irish leaders John Hume and David Trimble were awarded the Nobel Peace Prize in honor of the peace settlement that had finally come to their war-weary land. Both were careful to say that they accepted the honor in the names of all those people, including the mothers, who had fought to end the rule of violence in their beloved country.

It's often been the mothers who lead the way, always regarding the losses by violence more personally than politically. In Argentina and many other Latin American countries the "mothers of the disappeared" refused to go away or to back down in the face of threats from military dictatorships that had kidnapped and killed their husbands, sons, or daughters. I've met such mothers in Central America, whose courage in confronting violence confers a compelling authority upon them in the community and creates a real dilemma for those who depend upon the reign of terror.

In my hometown of Detroit, I met Clementine Barfield of SOSAD, Save Our Sons and Daughters. She had lost her own child to drug-related street violence and had organized other mothers who shared her tragic experience. Again, that initiative created authority and leadership, and SOSAD's voice was a powerful one calling for the love of mothers, fathers, and neighbors to take back the streets. Clementine Barfield proudly gave me a SOSAD T-shirt and button after I spoke at a rally in Detroit. "We are making a difference," she said.

And the mothers do. Both dictators and drug dealers have backed off from the kind of direct citizen action exemplified by ordinary people from Northern Ireland, to Latin America, to the inner cities of the United States. I remember another experience with pastors from the Ten Point Coalition in Boston. I was speaking to another rally, this time in a park that had been notorious for drugs and violence. But that night, the whole community had turned out with families, children, and sleeping bags! They intended to sleep all night in the park with their children, demonstrating how safe it was now that the community had taken back this public space from the rule of violence. Pastor Bruce Wall and other ministers had led the way in forging relationships with the young men who had dealt the drugs and turned the park into a war zone. Instead of pushing them out, Pastor Wall told me, they had invited them in—into relationship with the churches and the community. Some had accepted the invitation, but even those who didn't knew that the community had now reclaimed the park. The neighbors were ecstatic that violence had lost and community had finally won.

Such victories over violence always begin with somebody deciding to *do something* about it and taking direct action, getting involved and not just watching and lamenting the violence from the sidelines. When young people from gangs around the country decided to try to "end the madness" by holding a gang peace summit, most observers were skeptical. I've already discussed how I became involved when invited by these young men to be an "adviser" to the summit's process.

For days, I watched the young people wrestle with the causes of violence in themselves and in their society. They decided to be the ones who would take personal direct action to end the street warfare. Marion Stamps, a community organizer from Chicago who has since passed away, described it: "The summit signified reunification of the black and brown poor and oppressed communities, and it came from the bottom up instead of top down. If we are to unite our communities and stop the violence, it has to take place from the bottom up."

Relationships, which have endured for me, came out of that experience. I have watched many of these young people literally risk their lives for the sake of peace. These are the true peacemakers, the ones who are making a real difference. As one participant at the peace summit said, "The hope of the gang summit will spread—kid by kid, gang by gang, city by city. It will grow by patience, perseverance, exhausting work, and undeniable love. It won't be effectively spread through the media, but through hundreds of grassroots efforts and organizations that now need our support."

That support needs to come from many sources. One place is the church. Rev. Jerry McAfee, a pastor in one of Minneapolis's poorest neighborhoods, was at the peace summit and spoke bluntly about the church's role. "It has nothing to do with coming into a building. We've become so comfortable that we don't move outside of our buildings. That's insane. Our church is located right in the heat of things. I stake that ground, that's my corner. I run that turf. The brothers, they know me, I know them. They eat at the church. They don't attend the church all the time, but they know the door is open. They come in with their hats on and their pants sagging because I've given them an invitation: You come through that door when you're ready."

There are definitely tools and resources that can be brought to bear in peacemaking. Right after the peace summit, I spoke to about two thousand conflict-resolution practitioners gathered for their annual national conference in Portland, Oregon. Here were some of the most experienced people in the country. I had just come from the raw street environment of the summit, where young people who had been offered very few resources were engaged in a struggle to overcome a deeply embedded violence that daily threatens to overwhelm their lives and neighborhoods. Now I looked out over the vast crowd of experts in the field, most of whom were white and middle-class. What if we brought these skills to bear in a new partnership with urban youth leaders who were really trying to make a difference? I asked. Building new networks and sharing resources across many boundaries could be key to the success of peacemaking. Though this was a secular conference, the preacher in me couldn't help but issue an altar call. And they responded.

A Change of Heart

My father was scheduled to be part of the invasion force of Japan at the end of World War II. I grew up believing that the atomic bombing of Hiroshima and Nagasaki probably saved my father's life and enabled him and my mother to start our family. But as I grew older, I had a change of heart about nuclear weapons. While the role and necessity of the first atomic bombs in bringing about the surrender of Japan will be forever debated, it was finally faith that turned me, and ultimately my father, against nuclear weapons. To threaten such ultimate weapons of mass destruction against hundreds of millions of God's children and, indeed, creation itself, became morally unacceptable to more and more religious people in the 1970s and '80s. In fact, the churches became the animating core of the movement in America, that attempted to halt and reverse the nuclear arms race.

The early protest of prophets like Daniel and Philip Berrigan, Elizabeth McAlister, Jim and Shelley Douglass, and a host of others willing to engage in nonviolent civil disobedience gradually became a mainstream movement in the churches, involving both clergy and lay people in every denomination. *Sojourners* played an active role in that movement from the earliest days, analyzing nuclear weapons both technically and theologically, producing study guides for the churches, organizing statements to be signed by key church leaders, and hosting national events and actions where large numbers of Christians expressed their spiritual and political opposition to the nuclear arms race. Our Peace Pentecost action in 1983 resulted in the largest mass arrest in Washington since the rallies against the war in Vietnam, with 242 Christians handcuffed for praying for peace in the Rotunda of the U.S. Capitol.

A documentary film, *Be Not Afraid*, was produced from that event, and it demonstrated the breadth and depth of the growing religious peace movement. It also showed how the movement was rooted in worship and prayer more than political ideology. There was no sympathy for the Communist government in the Soviet Union among these Christians, but there was solidarity with its people and all those who were similarly targeted by nuclear missiles. It was the nature of these weapons themselves and the theological imperative for resistance that drove the protests.

We kept seeing changes of heart on nuclear weapons, often from unexpected quarters. I remember a letter I received from a pastor in Germany, with a clipping from a newspaper there that quoted Billy Graham on his first visit to Auschwitz. Graham was reported as saying, "The present insanity of the global arms race, if continued, will lead inevitably to a conflagration so great that Auschwitz will seem like a minor dress rehearsal." Until that time, Graham, like many Americans, was assumed to be generally supportive of his government's nuclear policies. I wrote to him to see if the quote was accurate and whether it reflected a change in his attitude toward the nuclear arms race. He replied saying that the quote was indeed accurate and he was in the process of changing his views on nuclear weapons. I knew that Billy Graham had been preaching throughout Eastern Europe and the Soviet Union. Like any good preacher, he fell in love with his congregations, and he began to imagine them as the targets of U.S. nuclear weapons. When I asked whether he would like to do an interview to express his changing perspective, he readily agreed. *Sojourners* published the cover story as "A Change of Heart." There was great pressure on Billy Graham not to do that interview, I later learned, but he did it anyway.

In that interview, Graham said: "I guess I would have to admit that the older I get the more aware I am of the kind of world my generation has helped shape, and the more concerned I am about doing what I can to give the next generation at least some hope for peace....I have gone back to the Bible to restudy what it says about the responsibilities we have as peacemakers. I have seen that we must seek the good of the whole human race, and not just the good of any one nation or race....We live in a different world than we did a hundred years ago, or even a generation ago. We cannot afford to neglect our duties as global citizens. Like it or not, the world is a very small place, and what one nation does affects all others...."

"Christ calls us to love, and that is the critical test of discipleship. Love is not a vague feeling or an abstract idea. When I love someone, I seek what is best for them. If I begin to take the love of Christ seriously, then I will work toward what is best for my neighbor. I will seek to bind up the wounds and bring about healing, no matter what the cost may be. Therefore, I believe that the Christian especially has a responsibility to work for peace in our world."

For many of us, peacemaking required a change of heart. *Sojourners* helped to initiate the nuclear freeze campaign in the United States, and it developed great momentum and popular support. But it didn't succeed in stopping the arms race. President Ronald Reagan's huge military buildup during the 1980s did help to bring down a Soviet Union already collapsing under the weight of its own internal failures and corruption. Communism virtually disappeared, but nuclear weapons did not. In fact, nuclear proliferation in Israel, India, Pakistan, North Korea, and elsewhere brought new dangers. And the very real threat that massive amounts of nuclear material, now inadequately protected by a weak, broke, and unstable Russian state, could fall into the hands of terrorist groups or rogue states like Iran and Iraq poses frightening possibilities. So far, the end of the cold war has not led the world's political leaders to take the historic opportunity to abolish nuclear weapons, many of which still remain on a hair trigger.

Today many former military leaders and heads of state are also having a change of heart about nuclear weapons. Somehow, time away from their former responsibilities has given them the space to reflect. One of the most dramatic conversions has occurred in someone who knew nuclear weapons very well. General Lee Butler spent his career in the nuclear arena with the U.S. Air Force, ending as commander of the nation's nuclear forces. In a *Sojourners* interview, Butler said: "During [my] last years of active military service, it became clear to me that we had lost all sense of proportion regarding the theory and practice of nuclear deterrence. Ultimately what mattered was how I chose to respond to my dismay. Finally, I simply answered the voice of my conscience.... today I strive to understand how we came to normalize the process of shearing away an entire society, to accept as a routine price of deterrence slaughtering populations wholesale. We not only treated these policies and practices as normal, but invented sophisticated theoretical schemes and strategic underpinnings to structure this normalcy. In many respects, we elevated it to theology....

"As I have learned about the efforts of people who've been involved in the cause of nuclear abolition going back decades, I must say that my admiration for them has deepened. I can now see more clearly their alarm and their moral outrage, their indignation at the almost cavalier manner at which nuclear weapons were added to our arsenal and their numbers increased beyond any reason."

Now, instead of enjoying a quiet retirement, Butler has dedicated himself to the cause of abolishing nuclear weapons. "I find that my conscience and my sense of social responsibility require more. I am experiencing something of the earlier calling to the ministry. The voice is clear and insistent: You know too much and you have abiding concerns that make it irresponsible for you to sit on the sidelines while others grapple with this matter of such overriding importance."

A Better Way

The end of the cold war against Communism left the United States without a single overarching "enemy." But it has not resulted in peace. All of a sudden we are at war again, with an enemy that few of us understand. The U.S. government is telling us we have entered a new "war against terrorism," one that may last for years or even decades. If that is so, we are beginning with the wrong strategy. Let's be clear: There is never any justification, or even explanation, for the kind of terrorism we now witness around the world. The world is full of grievances, real and imagined. But the taking of innocent life in response to those grievances is never morally acceptable. Never.

The question is how to deal with terrorism. The United States has decided upon a unilateral military strategy to counter terrorism and, indeed, to go on the offensive. That is a moral and political mistake.

Military means have not been effective in combating terrorism. The full force of the Soviet army, like the British army before them, was unable to defeat the guerrillas bunkered down in the mountains of Afghanistan. Why do we think the United States can be successful in defeating the same people who have now become anti-American terrorists? Where has a purely military strategy worked? Can we afford to build a cruise missile for every terrorist? On the contrary, U.S. military strikes make terrorist leaders international household words and confer upon them a status they might never achieve otherwise.

Terrorism could become the new enemy that we have lacked since the fall of Communism, bringing the needed excuses for more military buildups and weapons systems, more simplifying of complicated realities, more means justify the ends thinking and acting, and more violent conflict. That conflict would likely continue to escalate, one strike countering another, each one putting more and more people, especially civilians, at greater risk. More strikes against U.S. citizens will cause public clamor for counterstrikes, and with more U.S. counterstrikes, the hunger for retaliation from the aggrieved parties will increase. When casualties on both sides grow, the perpetrators of the violence will both be accused of terrorism. And the prospect of the introduction of weapons of mass destruction is too terrible to contemplate. But we must.

There is a better way. The best way to counter terrorism is to isolate the perpetrators and decrease their public support by taking the wind out of their sails and the energy out of their cause. A genuine commitment to democratic reforms (for example, in the Middle East), an increased respect for human rights across the board (not just for our friends), and a willingness to seek genuinely international solutions to long-standing grievances can blunt the cycle of violence. The United States, for example, must stop applying double standards in places like the Middle East, honoring some UN resolutions and ignoring others. Such solutions would be politically costly but are preferable to endless rounds of futile and costly violence. And such political courage would go a long way toward undermining the causes, grievances, and support base of terrorists favoring extreme solutions.

Because much of today's terrorism is more theological than ideological, it poses the real danger of a perceived confrontation between the Christian West and Islamic fundamentalism. There is profound misunderstanding between Christians and Muslims, which underlines the potential for conflict, even though the mainstream of each religion does not want it. Therefore a new effort, perhaps led by the American churches, must be undertaken to increase understanding and respect between Christians and Muslims. Religious leaders could undertake conflict resolution across political lines, learning to trust and respect each other. The American public must learn not to equate "Muslim" and "Arab" with terrorism.

We must not begin a new war against terrorism. Instead we must commit ourselves to a new strategy. Both religious teaching and political wisdom suggest a different course than the one now embarked upon by the U.S. government. It is not too late to reexamine that course.

And there are even deeper questions. As I said earlier, warfare itself has now fundamentally changed. It used to be that, in war, civilians were protected and soldiers died. Now that has been reversed. Today, nations protect their military forces and sacrifice the enemy's civilian populations. None of our religious traditions will support that. Even the "just war" tradition does not allow the deliberate targeting of civilians and their societal infrastructures to protect soldiers' lives. When planes fly high enough to avoid being shot down, there is less accuracy in bombing and more civilian loss of life.

Unlike earlier generations, shaped by the terrible human cost of both World War II and the Vietnam War, kids growing up today can believe that video-game wars match the real thing.

Ethnic, religious, nationalistic, and economic clashes have replaced the ideological battles of the cold war. But individual nations, especially the most powerful ones, have too many vested interests in those conflicts. Only collective international action can prove effective and trustworthy. We must either strengthen existing international institutions or create new ones to deal with the conflicts that will inevitably arise around the globe.

The dangers posed by terrorists and dictators should not go unopposed. It is a mistake to underestimate the threats they present to world peace, threats that must be resisted. And resisting them requires a commitment to real multilateral action—an effective international court of justice, perhaps the development and funding of sizable multinational peacekeeping forces prepared to intervene to protect human rights, a broad-based commitment to selective but consistent economic sanctions, and a strong preference for genuinely international solutions. This will not be easy. It will mean strengthening the international institutions and rule of law that the United States often resists, perhaps in an effort to preserve its superpower position. It also means a commitment to explore alternatives other than war to resolve international conflicts.

Specifically, the creation of a much stronger international court could be central to resolving many of these conflicts. War criminals could be indicted for their crimes and international warrants issued for their arrest. Bringing the full weight of international opinion to bear against criminal behavior would be much more effective if there were legal and institutional mechanisms to do so. The international community could then be called upon to isolate the perpetrators and undermine their power without attacking their people.

To back up such judgments with more than symbolism, it would be necessary to create an international police force with adequate backing, sufficient funding, and extensive training in conflict resolution. Such a force should be genuinely international, using personnel from the regions where conflicts occur as well as those from other countries. Lightly armed—or unarmed, as Gandhi suggested—this force would bring the physical presence that the resolution of conflict usually requires, but without the military provocation that can easily escalate a crisis. If the full and legal weight of world opinion were behind such a force, petty dictators would have to think twice about attacking it.

A lesson we must learn is that the international community must respond to the gross violation of human rights much more quickly and effectively. We were late in the Balkans, as we have been in Africa and so many other places around the world. Economic sanctions, used effectively in situations like South Africa, were applied only halfheartedly and inconsistently in the Kosovo conflict. Strong, sensible, selective, and strategic international economic sanctions and incentives can and do work.

Theologian Hans Küng points out that governments and military forces are not always the best agents to resolve complicated international conflicts, like those in the former Yugoslavia. Churches and religious leaders, he suggests, could play a potentially effective role in bringing warring factions together across national and ethnic battle lines. What if religious leaders and large numbers of carefully trained peacemakers were to intervene directly in the world's worst situations of conflict, in numbers that could make a real difference? Gandhi, a master tactician, spoke of the possibilities of a "nonviolent army" deployed to be an alternative to war. But that would entail a serious commitment to embracing the risks of peacemaking.

Just Peacemaking

It isn't mere utopian dreaming to say that many of our conflicts might be resolved in ways that don't require violence. History can teach us many lessons here. A recent project of twenty-three scholars and ethicists, convened by Professor Glen Stassen of Pasadena's Fuller Theological Seminary, has published *Just Peacemaking: Ten Practices for Abolishing War*—practices that could begin to resolve international conflicts in more effective and less destructive ways. These practices are being tried in conflicts around the world and in many cases are producing results. They are indeed very practical, and can serve as lessons for peacemaking. As you read them, ask how each principle could be applied close to home, as well as around the world. The "Just Peacemaking" practices include:

1. *Support nonviolent direct action.* Simply put, taking nonviolent direct action is the best way to peace. Nonviolent movements are spreading widely and producing results: ending dictatorship in the Philippines; bringing about nonviolent revolutions in Poland,

East Germany, and Central Europe; transforming injustice into democratic change through human rights movements in Guatemala, Argentina, and elsewhere in Latin America; and ending apartheid in South Africa, without the civil war many feared. We should encourage and support these movements.

2. *Take independent initiatives to reduce threats.* If you are deadlocked, show some initiative. Independent initiatives, from either side in a conflict, go beyond the slow process of negotiation to decrease distrust between adversaries. Verifiable actions with a clearly announced purpose can invite reciprocation.

3. *Use cooperative conflict resolution.* Bring in a third party to help resolve the problem. This method can encourage adversaries to listen to each other and seek long-term solutions, which can help prevent future conflicts.

4. *Acknowledge responsibility for conflict and injustice and seek repentance and forgiveness.* Accepting our own responsibilities for our part in a conflict will often open up the possibilities of others doing the same thing. In countries around the world emerging from years of dictatorship, the search for truth and the acknowledgment of responsibility for past practices can lead to a more peaceful future. For instance, the South African Truth and Reconciliation Commission and similar efforts in several Latin American countries have prevented long-standing bitterness from erupting into the violence of revenge.

5. *Advance democracy, human rights, and religious liberty.* Extending freedom seems to lead to peace. There is extensive evidence that the spreading of democracy and respect for human rights, including religious liberty, is widening areas of peace. During the entire twentieth century, democracies have fought no wars against one another and have had fewer civil wars. They also generally devote lower shares of their national products to military expenditures, thus decreasing threats to other countries. The most important development in international relationships is the shift from an emphasis on national sovereignty to a focus on human rights.

6. *Foster just and sustainable economic development.* I have a little framed placard on my desk that says "If You Want Peace, Work

for Justice." And it's true. "Sustainable development" means meeting the needs of today without threatening the needs of tomorrow. It occurs when those who lack adequate material and economic resources gain access, and those who have the resources learn to control them and prevent environmental degradation. Unjust social economic policies and structures can lead to violence. Democratic economic development greatly reduces it.

7. *Work with emerging cooperative forces in the international system.* In other words, don't be afraid to work with others who are building the conditions of peace. Recent trends have altered the conditions and practices of international relations to make it possible for countries to form voluntary associations for peace and other common purposes. These changes include: the decline in the utility of war, the priority of trade over war, the strength of international exchanges and communications, and the gradual ascendancy of liberal representative democracy and mixed economies. These trends, and the international associations they make possible, should be encouraged and strengthened.

8. *Strengthen the United Nations and international efforts for cooperation and human rights.* Peace normally comes through collective action. Such collective action by nations is increasingly necessary to resolve the problems of an interdependent world. The United Nations organization, regional organizations, and multilateral efforts in peacemaking, peacekeeping, and peacebuilding are increasingly effective. Countries working together to meet human needs for food, hygiene, medicine, education, and economic cooperation are less likely to go to war against one another.

9. *Reduce offensive weapons and weapons trade.* Putting down our weapons is essential to peace, on the street and around the planet. Modern weapons have become so destructive that war is not worth its cost. This growing understanding is a key factor in the decrease in war between nations. Further efforts to reduce offensive weapons and shift toward defensive capabilities strengthens this trend. Recent international treaties to ban chemical and biological weapons, stop the spread of nuclear weapons, and reduce strategic nuclear weapons are important steps.

10. *Encourage grassroots peacemaking groups and voluntary associations.* Empower people; it's a good way to peace. We're seeing the creation of an international civil society of people's movements, and as the peoples of the world come together to solve human problems cooperatively across borders, they increasingly press their governments to do likewise. Governments should foster this growing civil society, protect such associations by law, and work with them toward common goals.

New developments in each of these practices are encouraging; individually and together they could lead to significant change. In other words, these things work. They are not simply ideals, but are visibly happening around the world and are effectively reducing levels of conflict.

In my experience, many of the same principles that are effective in resolving international conflicts also work in overcoming domestic street violence, conflicts between groups, and even family disputes. Take direct action; if you are deadlocked, one side should show some initiative; use a third party; accept your responsibility for your part in the conflict; extend freedom; encourage justice; don't be afraid to cooperate with others and use collective action; drop your weapons; and empower people. These are all good principles to make peace on many levels. I've seen all of it work.

Who's Responsible?

The problem of violence always raises the question "Who's responsible?" Today the violence isn't just in the inner-city scenes like the one I described at the beginning of this chapter. White suburban kids with intact two-parent families are nonetheless deciding to open fire on their fellow students at academically successful schools around the country. It seemed that the last slain student had hardly been buried in Littleton, Colorado, when six more students were shot in Conyers, Georgia. It's time we probed the issues of responsibility.

When an unidentified parent faced the camera at a televised town meeting in the wake of the Littleton shootings, she spoke with the pain, anger, and authority of someone who had suffered a very

great loss. Her eleven-year-old daughter had been in the line of fire
when two young boys had donned military fatigues in Jonesboro,
Arkansas, the previous year and turned automatic weapons on their
schoolmates.

Now she was standing to speak to the nation from a Jonesboro
church, linked electronically to a group of traumatized parents, students, and other citizens in a Colorado living room: "There's never
been anybody we could hold responsible. We couldn't hold the
boys responsible because they were just children. The parents
weren't responsible because who wants to blame parents? And, you
know, you can't blame the media because the media says 'It's not
our fault.' And the gun culture, it's not their fault, so I want the
world to tell me whose fault is it we got fifteen kids dead along with
five last year? You know? What is wrong?"

With a moral authority no one seemed to question, the
Jonesboro mother had pressed to the heart of the dilemma: How
do we assess responsibility? Then she answered her own question:
"I hold a gun-toting nation responsible. I hold a nation that will
allow a child to watch many hours of violence on television, but the
parents have a problem with these same children going to a funeral. That makes no sense to me. If they're going to watch violence
then let 'em go to the funeral, let 'em see what happens when somebody's shot....I hold parents responsible because parents are
responsible. Know what your child's doing....I mean this here is
my child. I find out what she's into. And it's my responsibility to
society to know what she's into." The audience burst into sustained
applause.

In a culture that is nonjudgmental, fearful to lay blame, and anxious to be tolerant and ultimately politically correct, we often hesitate to deal directly and honestly with the causes of such tragedies.
It's time to look at the big picture behind all the places in America
where children are killing one another and other people. What must
we do?

Hold parents responsible. It's just bad parenting for mothers
and fathers not to know that their children are ingesting the worst
poisons of popular culture and obtaining guns and making bombs

in their own homes. To know these things and not intervene is inexcusable. If we don't spend enough time talking with our children to know what they're doing, listening to, watching, playing with, and even thinking, we're just not doing our jobs as parents.

That job includes intervening against the cruelty that school cultures often practice toward those who don't fit in—an exclusion sometimes led by the popular, attractive, and athletic students who are the most rewarded. What we might call "geek profiling" seems to be a part of some of these tragedies. Some of the "geeks" are being picked on, and some of them are striking back grotesquely. In the aftermath of the school shootings, every kid who's a little odd or alienated should not be suspected of being a potential mass murderer. But troubled kids need to be helped. Both parents and teachers need to intervene in the destructive and dangerous cycle of rejection and revenge.

Hold guns responsible. It used to be that boys expressed their conflicts with fistfights on playgrounds. Now they use arsenals. There is no doubt that the easy availability of guns is part of the reason why so many kids are getting killed. Let me make a politically blasphemous statement: Because it promotes a culture of plentiful, available, and ever more lethal weapons and resists even the most moderate regulations on lethal firearms, the National Rifle Association should be held directly responsible for what happened in Littleton. Before Littleton, the state of Colorado was on the verge of lifting restrictions on carrying concealed weapons, which would have allowed Denver Broncos fans to bring their guns along with them to the game. The suggestion by several gun-lobby spokesmen that if more people in Columbine High School had had guns, lives might have been saved conjures up a vision of a society in which the good kids have regular shootouts with the bad kids in their school corridors. People who say really stupid things like that are responsible for the consequences in a gun-toting nation. Guns may not be the whole problem, but much stronger gun-control laws are surely part of the solution.

Hold the media responsible. Hollywood is clearly part of the problem, as are video and computer games that promote death and destruction and music that celebrates violence. Alienated young people are especially susceptible to the influence of powerful media and cultural forces. We let kids play with computer games that stalk and execute people in bloody detail, all the while listening on their headphones to pounding lyrics that scream rage and disrespect for human life, then go on-line to their favorite web sites with neo-Nazi propaganda or instructions on how to make pipe bombs. Why then are we so surprised when angry teenage shooters single out blacks and Christians for execution on Adolf Hitler's birthday? Because we don't believe that a diet of violence has consequences. Capitalism should be capable of having a conscience and working for the common good. And if the rock promoters, record companies, Hollywood producers, and computer-game companies don't rise to the challenge, there's always the weapon of organized, parent-enforced boycotts of the worst offenders.

We are a nation that likes to have wars without casualties (at least on our side), video games without reality checks, violent pop culture that's just fun, and the freedom to say anything we want, no matter how disrespectful or hateful to other people. We like to have the violence without the consequences. But violence does have consequences, and it's both terribly ironic and horribly painful that our children are the ones who are teaching us this lesson.

Jump into the Street

Peacemaking, as we have seen, has more to do with action than with theory. Jesus didn't say, "Blessed are the peace lovers." He said, "Blessed are the peacemakers." Peace must be *made*. That generally means stepping into the situations of conflict.

I remember a hot summer night in Washington, D.C., the kind for which the city is famous. I was on my way to a community meeting when I saw a crowd gathering at the side of the street. I looked to see what had attracted their attention and was startled to see a shirtless young man dancing down the center of the street in the middle of traffic. He seemed quite high on something, and when cars stopped for the traffic light, he banged on their hoods. The situation was dangerous: either he would be hurt or somebody else would, and he could easily cause a car accident. Everyone could tell the young man was on some kind of drug; he looked as if he could be on PCP, which really gets adrenaline pumping and greatly increases strength. He was a good-sized kid and was acting stark raving mad. Clearly, somebody had to go out into the street to pull him out of the traffic before he or someone else got hurt. He was black, and as the only white person on the scene, I wasn't the best candidate. But no one else was making any move. We all just stood and watched.

Finally I knew I had to try. I was almost his size, but as he was likely all doped up on PCP, I knew this was going to be a real struggle. But just as I stepped into the street, a young man on a motorcycle pulled up. "Hey, Jim," he said, "it looks like you could use some help." I recognized him immediately. "Anthony!" I replied. "What are you doing here?" Anthony was a difficult kid from the neighborhood whom we had tried to work with several years before, but in vain as far as we could tell. He was always fighting, stealing, and getting into trouble. He would steal apples out of our kitchen even though he knew he could have one just by asking. Stealing made him feel like a man, Anthony said. But I hadn't seen Anthony in a few years; he had just disappeared. Until now. Here he was—bigger, older, and offering to help me with a tough situation. "Boy, am I glad to see you!" I said. "Let's go," he answered.

It took all of our efforts to subdue the drug-hyped street dancer. All pumped up, he literally ripped my shirt off. But we finally got him to the curb, and immediately lots of other people moved in to help. Before long, the rescue squad showed up, and the young man was taken away for medical treatment. Anthony and I just sat on the curb, catching our breath and catching up with each other. I was amazed to learn that he was studying as an apprentice fireman for the city's fire department! "I guess all that stuff you guys kept telling me finally sunk in. I was glad to have a chance to help you today."

The experience confirmed some lessons about peacemaking that I've learned in my own neighborhood and around the world. First, it always starts with a personal decision to get involved. Second, it usually takes stepping out into the street, whether in front of your own house or someplace a long way from home. Third, it may entail some risk and always some apprehension. And lastly, after somebody starts the process, there are always more people ready to join in. These four observations have usually been my experience.

Violence is overcome only through such peacemaking. Even when violence seems to be all-consuming and in total control, a simple action is often able to break through to expose it and open up new possibilities for overcoming it. Sometimes those acts are symbolic, helping people to think about the violence in more spiritual and even theological ways. Sometimes the actions are very practical, such as taking back a park or a country from the rule of violence. But it always begins when someone decides to step forward and be a peacemaker.

CHAPTER THIRTEEN

Be a Contemplative

Do justice, love kindness, and walk humbly
with your God. (Micah 6:8)

I TOOK MY TWO-WEEK-OLD SON to hear Nelson Mandela speak in Harvard Yard. The regal eighty-year-old president of South Africa might have been the oldest person in the crowd of twenty-five thousand, while Luke Carroll Wallis, comfortably asleep in his stroller, might well have been the youngest. Joy and I thought their overlap in history would be a good beginning for our first child. I look forward to telling him about it someday.

Mandela was at Harvard to become only the third person in history to be given an honorary doctorate at a special convocation, the other two being George Washington and Winston Churchill. It was a perfect fall day, and a crowd weary of Washington scandals was eager to welcome and embrace a true moral leader. When Mandela's smiling face appeared and he waved to the gathered throng, you could feel the happiness and joy of the youthful audience as they cheered and waved back. Harvard's Henry Louis Gates welcomed the South African freedom fighter by exclaiming, "No one epitomizes commitment more to our generation than you." University President Neil Rudenstine said, "He has inspired the better angels of our nature."

The world's most respected and honored political leader told stories, made jokes (about himself mostly), graciously thanked everyone around him, and, characteristically, accepted the honor on behalf of his people. "We accept this great honor bestowed upon us today," he said. Also characteristically, he called his audience again to go forward in the next step on the road toward justice. "The greatest single challenge facing our globalized world," said Nelson Mandela, "is to combat and eradicate its disparities." As the planet's most revered practitioner of democracy, Mandela admonished:

While in all parts of the world, progress is being made in entrenching democratic forms of governance, we constantly need to remind ourselves that the freedoms which democracy brings will remain empty shells if they are not accompanied by real and tangible improvements in the material lives of the millions of ordinary citizens of those countries.

As a leader, Nelson Mandela is the epitome of discipline and preparation. We must take on an undisciplined society by calling for spiritual *discipline*, which is the key word here. I was a Boy Scout and still remember the motto "Be Prepared." It's a good motto for all who would like to change the world or their corner of it. Social movements do require spiritual preparation.

We need the kind of preparation today that enables us to develop a longer-term perspective, find an appropriate spiritual practice, stay focused, learn patience, and balance contemplation with action.

Be Prepared

Richard Rohr is both a good friend and a powerful spiritual teacher. Richard is a Franciscan priest who has recently been doing comparative studies of various initiation rites for young men in very diverse cultures, both ancient and contemporary. Initiation rites were characteristically used as an important means of spiritual preparation. Richard believes that our society has virtually lost the practice of initiating young people, especially young men, into mature adulthood, and that the social consequences are painfully evident.

He has found a remarkable similarity in the "lessons of life" that such rites attempt to teach across both cultures and time. Rohr summarizes these as the following:

1. Life is hard.

2. You're going to die.

3. You're not that important.

4. You're not in control.

5. Life is not just about you.

In a wide variety of cultures, these simple but common themes come through as the critical lessons young people need to assimilate if they ever hope to make the passage to mature adulthood. Now consider how utterly contrary those lessons are to what our modern culture teaches. In fact, one could argue that contemporary society literally turns these spiritual lessons on their head. If we were to compile the list of modern culture's assumptions, they might read:

1. Life can be easy.

2. You can stay young (or keep looking and feeling young) forever.

3. You are what's most important.

4. Above all else, you must stay in control.

5. Life is mostly about you and your fulfillment.

It's no wonder our young people are confused, not to mention all the rest of us. In a consumer culture that is both highly individualistic and extremely competitive, spiritual formation aimed at the common good isn't too popular. Ironically, however, when people in our society see someone exhibiting spiritual virtues, we are drawn to that person as by a magnet. That phenomenon speaks to our society's great hunger for spiritual meaning and social purpose, despite the opposing messages of popular culture and the marketplace. The ethos of modern advertising may control public discourse but it doesn't satisfy the human soul.

That's why we are so drawn to a Nelson Mandela. He doesn't represent the fast buck, quick fix, or immediate gratification. In Harvard Yard, I saw noisy students turn quiet and calm, straining to get just a glimpse of this old man. A faculty member later commented that his "pushy colleagues" who would normally fight for every square inch on the platform were awed by the magnitude of the man. Somehow he enables others to rise above it all, to transcend the pettiness, to transform the possibilities, to aspire to their better selves. For about two precious hours, Nelson Mandela had the whole Harvard community thinking about someone else and about how they too might help change the world.

I had seen this phenomenon before when I had the blessing to be present in a small meeting with Mandela and U.S. religious leaders shortly after his release from prison, and again at the extraordinary events of his inauguration as the first democratically elected president of South Africa. He has the power to transform people and situations, something we have not seen in a leader for some time.

But why? Is it because he won the Nobel Peace Prize, or the leadership of the African National Congress, or the South African presidency? I don't think so. I believe it is because of what happened to him during twenty-seven years in prison. It was there that Nelson Mandela had his spiritual formation, there that he prepared for a new nation, there that he began molding a people—black and white—to think in new ways.

There are many legends about Nelson Mandela on Robben Island, his prison home for most of those years. Many have called Robben Island Mandela University, because every day he was educating everyone around him to a vision of a new South Africa. The sweep of his influence was again demonstrated at his inauguration, when several of his former prison guards were given honored seats close to their former prisoner and teacher. Mandela got up every day to prepare himself, his colleagues, and his captors for a new day. His regimen was physically, emotionally, intellectually, and spiritually vigorous. He had no guarantee that he would ever live to see the new South Africa, or that he would ever get out of prison. But he knew that his task was to get ready. And by all reports, Mandela was utterly disciplined in that task. Separation from the increasingly shallow values of the outside Western world might have been a blessing for this political prisoner.

During Mandela's last visit to America before retiring from the South African presidency, many people recalled where they were on February 11, 1990, when Nelson Mandela walked out of prison in front of the eyes of the world—erect, strong, and astonishing. Some talked of how they woke up their children to witness the momentous event. He emerged with a spring in his step and a dignity on his face that belied his years of suffering. Henry Louis Gates testified in Harvard Yard that he always had a "Free Mandela" poster in his college dorm room and later hung it in his daughter's nursery. Gates said to the Harvard students, "Nelson Mandela didn't walk out of prison into freedom, but as one who had been free the whole time. Mandela has always been free." In his sermon the following Sunday, Peter Gomes, the dean of Harvard's Memorial Chapel, said of Mandela, "This is a man who knows who he is. His ideals are intact. He doesn't live with the illusions of his demons. He does not stagger at the uneven motions of the world."

That strength comes from spiritual preparation. There is an important distinction between power and moral authority that the modern world fails to understand. Power is the ability to control things; moral authority is the capacity to change things. Those in power really don't change anything. They just manage things as they are, because to gain power they have agreed to accept things as they are. On the contrary, those with moral authority can transform political realities, in part because they have chosen not to accept the current definitions of those realities. Power depends on coercion; moral authority utilizes inspiration.

Pharaoh had the power, but Moses had the authority. Pilate had the power, but Jesus had the authority. The medieval popes had the power, but Saint Francis had the authority. The British had the power, but Gandhi had the authority. The southern governors had the power, but Martin Luther King, Jr., had the authority. The rulers of apartheid in Pretoria had the power, but Nelson Mandela had the authority. In every case, those with the power are not even remembered now, except in relation to those who had the authority.

But authority doesn't come easily or without cost. It comes only through spiritual preparation and formation. Moses struggled with his calling in the wilderness. Jesus went out into the desert at the onset of his ministry to fast for forty days. Saint Francis led a life of poverty, chastity, and obedience. Martin Luther King, Jr., suffered death threats, thirty arrests and imprisonments, and an assassin's bullet. Nelson Mandela spent twenty-seven years in prison. All had to prepare, all got ready, and all paid the price.

The man who sustained his fellow prisoners now charms all of us. Everyone knows that Nelson Mandela led not by relying on opinion polls but rather by changing people's opinions. He is someone the world believes to have integrity and character. He also was smart enough not to believe his own press clippings. When you hear Mandela speak, genuine humility and humanity come through, traits we are unfamiliar with in most political leaders today. Mandela knows who he is. And that is not a perfect person, nor one without sin and flaws, nor someone who hasn't made mistakes.

It was amazing to see every political leader—even former segregationists like Senator Strom Thurmond—in Washington clamoring to get near to Mandela when he came to receive the Congressional Gold Medal on September 23, 1998. Integrity brings people together and crosses partisan political lines. And here is where leaders with moral authority always differ from their counterparts with political power only: They are not interested in revenge. As Harvard's Neil Rudenstine said, "He never sought to harm those who harmed him, or to punish his abusers. He looks forward to justice, not backward to revenge."

Mandela smiled at the crowd often during his speech at Harvard, and accused the students of coming just to "see how a man of eighty looks." Then he looked seriously at the crowd and said, "There is no easy walk to freedom, but it is the only walk worth taking." Mandela inspires me like no other modern political leader. But it is time for him to rest now. He spoke of that in his speech at the United Nations on September 21, 1998.

> I have reached that part of the long walk when the opportunity is granted, as it should be to all men and women, to retire to some rest and tranquillity in the village of my birth. As I sit in Qunu and grow as ancient as its hills, I will continue to entertain the hope that there has emerged a cadre of leaders in my own country and region, on my continent and in the world, which will not allow that any should be denied their freedom as we were; that any should be

turned into refugees as we were; that any should be condemned to
go hungry as we were; that any should be stripped of their human
dignity as we were.

Were all these hopes to translate into a realizable dream and not
a nightmare to torment the soul of the aged, then will I, indeed,
have peace and tranquillity.

Are we preparing the way for those kinds of leaders?

Be Consistent

Traveling across the country during the fall 1996 election campaign, I saw almost no yard signs or bumper stickers with the names
of the presidential candidates on them. Only 48 percent of
America's registered voters showed up on the first Tuesday of that
November, and of those who did, exit polls showed, the clear
majority had little enthusiasm for either choice. Even each candidate's most partisan supporters, when assessing their candidate's
strengths, would never have suggested that Clinton or Dole pos-
sessed the qualities of a great leader. They were only, once again,
our less than inspiring political choices.

But about ten days after the lackluster election, we witnessed a
dramatically different and rather amazing drama unfolding in
Chicago. After an eighteen-month battle with cancer, Cardinal
Joseph L. Bernardin died. The thousands upon thousands of people who lined up for days to say good-bye to the beloved Catholic
prelate came from far beyond the confines of his own church.
Prayers and services for the departed leader of the country's second-
largest Catholic diocese were offered by leaders from virtually every
religious tradition in the city, and the mourners included many who
claimed no religion at all. His brother bishops, meeting in
Washington, left his chair empty and halfheartedly carried on their
business without the man who was both the most influential bishop in the country and the one who had showed the most capacity
to bring them all together.

In the countless eulogies and obituaries that followed in succeeding days, the nation viewed the passing of a man who was

something very rare in both church and state today—a leader. In a world of winners and losers, powerful and powerless, it is worth reflecting on the qualities of leadership that Joseph Bernadin exemplified.

As the rest of the country was polarizing between Right and Left, and over issues from abortion to nuclear weapons, Bernardin identified the most important religious question at stake in all the debates: namely, the defense of life. He led the way by being the first to articulate the "consistent ethic of life" that has become so basic to Catholic social teaching. Life, he said, is a "seamless garment" that must be defended against many assaults, be they abortion, nuclear weapons, the death penalty, euthanasia, poverty, or racism. Breaking apart the predictable categories of Right and Left, Bernardin's consistent ethic showed a characteristic creativity and courage in challenging ideological shortsightedness across the political spectrum and offering the possibility of a more independent and prophetic spiritual politics.

As the acknowledged leader of the American Catholic bishops, Bernardin again and again demonstrated the capacity to bring people of divergent views together. He led the task force that produced the bishops' most significant and influential pastoral letter on nuclear weapons: "The Challenge of Peace." (The group included both Cardinal John O'Connor of New York and Bishop Thomas J. Gumbleton of Detroit, who represented the Church's opposing views on the question.) Similarly, when Rome and the American Church came into conflict, it was often Bernardin who was called upon to seek some reconciliation. He seemed able to genuinely listen to people, while gaining their trust as a man of principle. Bernardin was a voice of conciliation and conviction in a time when the two almost never go together.

At the end of his life, the cardinal again showed his open and reconciling spirit by seeking to bridge the growing gaps between increasingly divergent camps in the Catholic Church, especially between the Church's hierarchy and those frustrated by Rome's refusal to discuss disagreements. In the months before he died, Bernardin had just launched the Catholic Common Ground Project, a new effort to convene respectful and constructive dialogue on many of the pastoral issues dividing the church. Though it attracted considerable criticism from several of his fellow cardinals, the new initiative brought sighs of relief and hope from many (perhaps particularly Catholic women) who were feeling shut out of the Church. Bernardin seemed to accomplish successful dialogue because of both his commitment to Catholic tradition and his willingness to talk about it. He was neither a liberal nor a conservative Catholic, but one who believed that tradition could deepen and grow.

Perhaps his greatest moments of exemplary leadership came in response to two events at the end of his life. First, in 1993, when a young man accused Bernardin of earlier sexual abuse, he clearly denied the allegations but refused to counterattack his accuser. Despite having great power as the Catholic cardinal of Chicago, he refrained from using it in his own defense. Bernardin told his lawyers not to go after the young man for fear that it would discourage genuine victims of sexual abuse from coming forward. The troubled young man later admitted that he had lied, and Bernardin ministered to him as he died of AIDS in what he called a "powerful reconciliation." Barbara Blaine, a survivor of sexual abuse, a lawyer, and the head of the Survivors Network of those Abused by Priests, told the Chicago *Sun-Times*, "Our hearts go out to Cardinal Bernardin....We hope that other accused church leaders follow the cardinal's example of defending himself without attacking his accusers."

Second, when Cardinal Bernardin was diagnosed with incurable cancer, he called a press conference and actually asked the tearful reporters to pray for him as he would for them. He said that he thought his greatest contribution would be in the way he died. That proved to be true. He spent the last months of his life visiting with the dying in cancer wards and death-row cells and, apparently, witnessed to people around the country about the meaning of death. "As a person of faith, I see death as a friend." Joseph Cardinal Bernardin died at a time when we needed his kind of leadership. But in showing us how to both live and die with consistency and integrity, he will lead us for many years to come.

The Nature of Leadership

For more than a year, President Clinton argued that he should be judged on the basis of his policies, and that personal moral failures, while regrettable, were not really relevant to the job he is doing for the American people.

I often felt politically homeless during the Clinton scandal. Most Democrats and liberals ended up making excuses for Clinton and defending him. I wasn't comfortable with that. But the Republicans ended up looking like the Pharisees who were ready to stone the woman taken in adultery. And while I often agreed with the conservatives on how much Clinton was morally damaging the country, I was uncomfortable with their broader political agenda.

An old friend and I decided to write about the problem. He is a denominational church leader—Wes Granberg-Michaelson leads the Reformed Church in America—and was formerly chief of staff to U.S. Senator Mark Hatfield. We tried to reflect upon the lessons the country learned or failed to learn in the course of the nation's yearlong Washington-produced drama of sex and politics. And we asked what lasting wisdom about leadership would be left after the curtain was drawn and this morality play went off the air.

In an op-ed piece for the *Chicago Tribune*, Wes and I suggested that this sad chapter in American history could turn out to be a teachable moment on the nature of leadership, and that the country shouldn't miss this opportunity to reflect upon it. These are not Left or Right issues, and they have little to do with whether or not one supported Bill Clinton's political agenda.

First, effective public leadership cannot be severed from the trustworthiness of personal character. Ethics and integrity do matter, and not just superficially. Leaders need to be believed. They have to engender trust not only in their policies but also in their judgment. They must create a climate of faithfulness to shared commitments among colleagues and supporters. Thus leadership derives credibility from example, and not simply from pronouncements. In times of crisis, people follow courage rather than charm.

The final years of the Clinton presidency illustrate a successful leadership that skillfully segregated public policy from personal integrity. Morality in politics, especially for many Democrats, is defined only by the pragmatic effectiveness of policies. Conversely, many Republicans see morality exclusively in terms of personal behavior and are blind to the sins of social injustice. This will not work. And religious people should be the first to say so. A firewall between the personal and public dimensions of our lives is a secular fiction. And it is dangerous to both people and politics. Faith nurtures a healthy congruity between one's inner and outer lives. Its understanding of sin and its vision of wholeness weave together the social and the personal. Any discerning ethic of leadership does the same.

Second, a poll-driven presidency lacks a moral foundation and vision. Faced with perhaps the most important personal decision of his presidency, Clinton trusted his pollsters rather than his pastors. Some leaders have the moral and political authority to shape, and even change, public opinion. But for that, a moral compass is needed—a compass whose needle points toward where we, as a society, should be heading, rather than simply toward the next election. Politicians today try to govern by perpetual campaigns. As a result, the overriding principle is to satisfy 51 percent of the voters rather than to serve a compelling moral and political vision for our society.

Third, style is not more important than substance. Democrats, liberals, and progressives kept saying that Clinton was a good president even if he could be a better man. But Clinton was more style than substance. If a Republican president had done many of the things that Bill Clinton did in his domestic and foreign policies, there would have been a Democratic outcry, but with a Democrat in charge, hardly a peep was heard. Clinton maintained a liberal language and cultural style, and for most liberals that seemed to be enough. But is being comfortable in black churches and even appointing a record number of minorities and women to government posts enough to counterbalance cozying up to Wall Street and playing to suburban voters while virtually abandoning the underclass? The attacks upon him by right-wing conservatives somehow made liberals even more defensive of Clinton.

Fourth, sexual ethics are important. You don't have to be a prude or a puritan to be worried about a sexual ethic that is merely recreational instead of covenantal. That value-free sexual ethic has devastating consequences for a society, especially for the young, and most brutally for the poor. Clinton didn't create the nation's declining sexual ethics, but the Clinton scandal served to reveal them and help support them.

The question "What's more important, a leader's personal morality or his or her public policy?" may really be the wrong one. The more important issue may be the *connection* between the personal and the public. The idea that public leadership can be partitioned from personal integrity is, as most of us should know, a dangerous illusion. And the fact that several past political leaders have gotten away with doing so hardly establishes a reliable pattern of leadership for the future. Old styles of leadership are now passing, and new models are already in formation.

The information revolution has subverted the systems of hierarchical authority, transforming our institutions and the imperatives of leadership. The task of leaders today is to articulate vision, build trust, and create an open climate of integrity that facilitates decisions. Any leader who wants to be a leader in the twenty-first century needs to sustain values, nurture community, and clarify common mission. That is equally true for a pastor, a principal, a president, or a pope.

In the end, leaders lead by behavior and not just by skill. And in any institution, people yearn for leadership that is morally seamless. Yes, they want imaginative and effective policies. But they also desire leaders whose example walks their talk. A healthier blend of talent and character is needed to shape our next generation of leaders.

That coherence is quite different from the futile quest for leaders who we hope are perfect. Those of us who seek to embed our lives in religious faith know full well the tenacity of selfish, sinful behavior. The power, adulation, and pressure inherent in positions of leadership make leaders more likely to fall victim to their own vulnerabilities—whether it is pride, promiscuity, or political prostitution. But because of this reality, leaders in particular need to undertake the difficult task of self-examination. That's why leaders bear a particular responsibility to nurture their private souls and not just their public personas.

We all have flaws, as Jesus was quick to point out to those who would have stoned the adulterous woman. But we don't get past our flaws by denying them and trying to manage the public fallout. In his or her heart, every leader knows that this denial—in the words of Jesus—is the path to destruction.

Mature leaders are those who not only rely on their strengths but also learn how to deal consciously with their weaknesses. In some safe and secure place, they bring their brokenness into the light and turn toward inner coherence. Thus they guard themselves against the disintegration of their inward life that could finally result in outward paralysis. Dealing with flaws and weaknesses is important for anyone, but especially for those who have responsibility for others.

In the future, we need leaders with the ability to navigate the troubled waters of their inner lives as well as the turbulent seas of public discourse. If institutions and societies are ultimately shaped by both the personal and the public ethics of their leaders, the concept of "spiritual formation" should become increasingly important as a component of the education needed for leadership development. Ultimately, personal integrity is vital to public trust.

Leadership instills vision, values, trust, mission, and community. These rest upon the habits of the heart. Perhaps the main question to ask about leaders concerns the trustworthiness of their moral compass, upon which all of their judgments depend. Effective leadership is finally sustained not just by what people say but by who they are.

The Contemplative Life

Henri Nouwen was the author of dozens of books on spirituality. A native of Holland who lived and worked in North America, he was a friend and a frequent visitor to Sojourners. When he died in 1996, eulogies praised him as one of the most significant spiritual writers of the century. Nouwen understood that spirituality had social implications, and his writings are rich material for reflection.

To make that connection between the spiritual and the social wasn't always easy for a contemplative like Henri. We spent many hours talking together about his struggle to make justice and peace an essential part of his walk with Jesus. From Selma to Atlanta, from Nicaragua to Peru, from the Nevada nuclear test site to the Peace Pentecost demonstrations in Washington, D.C., he tried to connect the inner life with the outward journey. Henri was never at home with big marches and crowds or with the intensity of political activism. Yet he would often call to ask whether he could be part of an event or action, such as an all-night prayer vigil in the midst of great controversy over an issue like the Gulf War. He knew he had to stretch himself by taking his prayers to the streets because, in spite of his private personality, his spirituality sought to connect with those active efforts for justice and peace.

I have often wished that many activists would similarly stretch themselves by linking their actions to contemplation. The essential element of the quest for justice and peace for Nouwen was prayer. But finding time for prayer, and even for some quiet contemplation, is a constant challenge for an activist.

Henri also spoke about the "three disciplines" of the contemplative life. All three are essential to the life of an activist. Yet "disciplines" is indeed the right word, because the contemplative life does not come easily to any of us. Nouwen's disciplines of solitude, community, and ministry would deepen the life and work of anyone who wants to change a community.

> The first discipline is the discipline of solitude. It's only in solitude that we can get in touch with the Spirit of God in us. Solitude is an important discipline in a busy world. Solitude involves prayer, spiritual reading, and being alone with God.
>
> The second discipline is the discipline of community. Out of solitude we go into community. Community is not just a place where we do things together, but a place where together we recognize the presence of God.... Community, whether a parish, a family, or an intentional community, is where people live together and want to discover in each other the presence of God.

The third discipline is ministry, reaching out to others. It's important to reach out to others because we want to share from the abundance of our life, not because we have a need to be good helpers or because we have something to prove.

Nouwen knew the importance of a spiritual life of faith deeply rooted in an intimate communion with God. But he also knew the importance of an active commitment to healing the brokenness of the world. For example, Henri wrote on the question of Christ's judgment, "As long as there are strangers; hungry, naked, and sick people; prisoners, refugees, and slaves; people who are handicapped physically, mentally, or emotionally; people without work, a home, or a piece of land, there will be that haunting question from the throne of judgment: 'What have you done for the least of mine?'"

I remember one weekend Henri visited Sojourners. That particular weekend, Brazilian archbishop Dom Helder Câmara was also in town to speak to a large church convention in a downtown hotel. I've already mentioned the visit, but here is the bigger story. We got a call from Dom Helder's aides saying that he felt uncomfortable in the big, fancy hotel and wanted to spend the afternoon in a base community like Sojourners. We were thrilled, and I hurried across the invisible racial and class boundaries of D.C. to pick up the diminutive and passionate prelate of the people from Recife, Brazil.

The community quickly gathered, and the next several hours we spent together were memorable ones—highlighted by the dialogue between Henri Nouwen and Dom Helder Câmara. The Dutch priest from the first world was one of the most intense people I have ever met, and his questions of the archbishop from the third world were relentless. That afternoon, Henri seemed to sense that there were truths he would never find in the affluent first world, that it was among the despised and rejected of the third world that his search would have to continue. Later, he would leave the academic cocoons of Yale and Harvard to make his own pilgrimage into Latin America, and he wouldn't really find home until he entered into sharing a life with the mentally and physically handicapped of L'Arche Daybreak Community near Toronto, Canada.

The intensity of his spiritual search is what I will always most remember about Henri. He could spend hours with you—talking, walking, and very often anguishing about the deepest questions of life and faith. He was not a Christian who had it all figured out. On the contrary, Henri wrestled like Jacob with the God he so dearly loved. And that made him wrestle with all of us, too.

The shock of his sudden death from a heart attack on an airplane lingered for some time. But his legacy continues with those whose faith drives them both to retreat centers and to the streets. Plucked from us before his time, like another monastic named Thomas Merton, Henri Nouwen leaves us a rich legacy and a whole library of spiritual struggle. Through his endless stream of books, the countless students he touched, L'Arche residents who touched him, and the thousands and thousands of people who attended the regular and intimate Eucharists he insisted upon having wherever he was, Henri's spiritual intensity will live on. I can only give thanks for Henri Nouwen's life and witness, and be grateful that Henri is finally at rest in the arms of the loving God who always pursued him like the hound of heaven.

The Hope of Results

To be a contemplative means to find a motivation deeper than the hope of results. You have to be sustained by more important things. And anyone who gets involved in the struggle for social change may eventually confront the problem of burnout. It was that other monastic, Trappist monk Thomas Merton, who spoke so eloquently to this problem, common especially among social activists. He did so in "A Letter to a Young Activist," sent to a young man named Jim Forest. Jim is older now, yet still very much involved as a peace activist in Holland. I recall many late-night conversations with Jim, talking about the problem of burnout. We spoke of the faith that sometimes can help people persevere in the face of seemingly hopeless struggles. And how that faith must ultimately depend not on the hope of results, especially in the short term, but on something deeper. It is a paradox: to be successful you must finally give up the demand for success and do what you do from the deeper motivations of what you believe is right. And this isn't a merely religious issue; I've known nonreligious people who stick to their principles and causes long after many church types have given up and gone home. Ultimately, you must find a reason to continue that derives its satisfactions from the truth of the work itself. Then, when results do come, they can be welcomed as a surprising grace rather than as the necessary vindication for exhausting and despairing work.

We end here with the letter that Thomas Merton sent to Forest in 1966, during a period when he felt "pretty close to burn-out." Merton died in 1968, but this letter has been reprinted many times and in various languages over the past thirty years. It's a good thing to put up on your wall. It will help you to understand how to be a contemplative.

Dear Jim,

Do not depend on the hope of results. When you are doing the sort of work you have taken on, essentially an apostolic work, you may have to face the fact that your work will be apparently worthless and even achieve no result at all, if not perhaps results opposite to what you expect. As you get used to this idea, you start more and more to concentrate not on the results but on the value, the rightness, the truth of the work itself. And there too a great deal has to be gone through, as gradually you struggle less and less for an idea and more and more for specific people. The range tends to narrow down, but it gets much more real. In the end, it is the reality of personal relationships that saves everything.

You are fed up with words, and I don't blame you. I am nauseated by them sometimes. I am also, to tell the truth, nauseated by ideals and with causes. This sounds like heresy, but I think you will understand what I mean. It is so easy to get engrossed with ideas and slogans and myths that in the end one is left holding the bag, empty, with no trace of meaning left in it. And then the temptation is to yell louder than ever in order to make the meaning be there again by magic. Going through this kind of reaction helps you to guard against this. Your system is complaining of too much verbalizing, and it is right.

The big results are not in your hands or mine, but they suddenly happen, and we can share in them; but there is no point in building our lives on this personal satisfaction, which may be denied us and which after all is not that important.

The next step in the process is for you to see that your own thinking about what you are doing is crucially important. You are probably striving to build yourself an identity in your work, out of your work and your witness. You are using it, so to speak, to protect yourself against nothingness, annihilation. That is not the right use of your work. All the good that you will do will come not from you but from the fact that you have allowed yourself, in the obedience of faith, to be used by God's love. Think of this more, and gradually you will be free from the need to prove yourself, and you can be more open to the power that will work through you without your knowing it.

The great thing after all is to live, not to pour out your life in the service of a myth: and we turn the best things into myths. If you can get free from the domination of causes and just serve Christ's truth, you will be able to do more and will be less crushed by the inevitable disappointments. Because I see nothing whatever in sight but much disappointment, frustration and confusion....

The real hope, then, is not in something we think we can do but in God who is making something good out of it in some way we cannot see. If we can do His will, we will be helping in this process. But we will not necessarily know all about it beforehand...

Enough of this...it is at least a gesture....I will keep you in my prayers.

                                        All the best, in Christ,
                                        Tom

CHAPTER FOURTEEN

Keep It Human

For we have this treasure in earthen vessels.
(II Corinthians 4:7)

It started with a phone call from Jeffrey Katzenberg at the DreamWorks SKG film company. Katzenberg is the former Disney producer who did *Aladdin* and *The Lion King*. Now he was busily at work on a new animated blockbuster called *The Prince of Egypt*. It would be the first attempt since *The Ten Commandments* to bring the story of Moses to the big screen.

Hollywood hadn't made a Bible movie in many years, and the caller asked if I would fly out to Universal Studios to view the footage of the new film and offer my critique and feedback. This would be a new experience for me, and, since I needed to be on the West Coast in a few weeks anyway, I agreed to be a theological film critic.

After a short tour of the Universal lot, the DreamWorks team warmly received me. They told me that dozens and dozens of theologians and preachers were being brought to Hollywood to offer their opinions of *The Prince of Egypt*. So much for Tinseltown's demand for my unique perspective. In the next two hours, I learned a lot about animation. Did you know it takes one million individual drawings to make an eighty-eight-minute animated feature? The complexity and artistry of the project was impressive indeed, as was the emotional impact of the pieces of the film already completed. I suspected that this was going to be a big box-office success.

After the preview I sat down with Katzenberg to give him my reaction. I really had only one comment to make: Don't make Moses into a superhero. Keep it human, I pleaded. Katzenberg and I then talked about the conversation between Moses and God in the book of Exodus, when the great liberator receives his calling. This is one of the most extraordinary conversations ever reported. It's an argument, really, between God and Moses. God says that the cries and sufferings of the Israelites have reached his ears, and God tells Moses that he has been chosen to go to Pharaoh and instruct the Egyptian ruler, "Let my people go."

This is indeed a Hollywood moment, arguably the most dramatic divine call in human history. But Moses isn't exactly thrilled with the idea. "Who, me?" is the essence of his reply. He's just a simple goat herder, out in the desert, with family responsibilities and without great ambitions. Moses protests, "Who am I to go to Pharaoh?" Moses pleads and tries to persuade God to find somebody else. "Not me, Lord!" was, in a nutshell, the great liberator's response. The scene of Moses's great calling is a Hollywood director's dream. It's filled with high drama, but Moses's less than heroic response hardly makes this the material for a cinematic triumph.

Moses is a reluctant leader right from the beginning. His reticence toward God is something each of us can relate to. Moses gives a whole list of excuses about why he is not the best choice for this assignment. "They won't believe me," he complains; "they won't believe you sent me." So Moses receives God's promise to be with him in Egypt. But even after God performs a whole series of rather extraordinary miracles and then promises to repeat these wonders in front of Pharaoh, Moses still demurs.

My favorite excuse from Moses is his claim that he is not a good public speaker. "I am not eloquent," Moses says, suspecting this mission will require some persuasive public speeches. Some biblical scholars suspect Moses might have been a stutterer, terrified by public verbal confrontation. I like that one, having been a stutterer myself from an early age. Even today, every time I get up to speak there is always the question "Will I be able to do this?" But God gets angry with him: "Moses, who made your mouth?" And God tells Moses that his brother Aaron can go along to help. Throughout the whole discussion, Moses never really agrees to go to Egypt. God simply tells Moses that he is going.

As they say, the rest is history. A slave people are freed through the mighty acts of God. The Exodus story has been an inspiration for oppressed people ever since, and Moses's name is synonymous with the word "liberation." And the makers of *The Prince of Egypt* brought this powerful story to center stage in American popular culture.

But Moses is no Charlton Heston. He performed the role of Moses in Hollywood many years ago and nowadays is the media-genic head of the National Rifle Association. With Heston in the role, Moses was a larger-than-life hero. But, no, Moses was more like most of us. He didn't feel up to the job, he didn't feel self-confident, he didn't feel ready, and he sure didn't want to be a hero. "Please, God, send somebody else," he kept saying. Moses is not a superhero role model but an example of how extraordinary things can be accomplished through ordinary people—like us.

Most of the people I know who have made a difference are not superheroes either. They are really quite ordinary. They just felt a sense of call and commitment that enabled them to do important things. It's a commitment that anyone can make, and when you do, things begin to happen. The call may not always be as clear as the voice from the burning bush that Moses heard, but most of us have a pretty good idea about what we should do. Just listen to your heart, trust it, and act on what you believe. And remember to keep it human. That's what begins to change the world, or at least our little part of it.

The Personal Stuff

Let me explain what I mean by keeping it human. In the struggle for social change, it is very important to take care of one another—our families, our kids, and ourselves. The human dimension is so easy to lose and so crucial to maintain. It's so important to stay grounded, not get too grandiose or self-important, keep humble, and, above all, keep your sense of humor. Heavy tasks and important work often require a certain lightheartedness. And that arises from a place of freedom rather than compulsion, from giving up the illusions of control and trusting results to God. We have to learn how to enjoy the world while we try to change it. After all, changing our communities should not only be challenging; it should also be fun.

Social change is not easy; it's often very frustrating. And there are as many lessons in the setbacks, difficulties, and even failures, as there are in the successes. It's important to be as honest about the problems and the defeats as it is about the victories.

The hardest things are not always what you would expect. I've found that living in the inner city, traveling to dangerous war zones, and going to jail have not been the hardest things. Though they have often been the most exciting. Most difficult for me have been the personal failures and the breakdown of relationships.

While community creates a powerful resource for change, it also generates real tensions among people. I've learned those lessons firsthand, when our own Sojourners Community experienced a painful split in the early 1990s. We had always talked about growing up and old together, and we believed our relationships could sustain many challenges. But some of the young families didn't want to raise their children in the inner city (which was a reasonable concern), and those who stayed felt disappointed and even betrayed by those who left (which was also understandable). Differences in vision arose too, and personality conflicts ensued (or was it the other way around?). And the inevitable conflicts over leadership emerged. I had seen the same tensions in many other small communities and projects and had often been called in to be a mediator. Now it was happening in my own community, and I felt helpless to do anything about it.

I learned then that we can invest too much in community as well as too little. Our expectations can be too high and quite unrealistic. In a society of rampant individualism, there is a danger of overreacting and defining community in ways that are both too intense and too close. People need space, even in community, and that's especially true for families.

The breakups that occur closest to home are the ones that hurt the most. Sometimes the intensity of the vision and the pace of the work can wreak havoc in the marriages and families of activists. The rate of divorce, which is so tragically high in our contemporary society, is sometimes even higher among those who are trying to change the world. My own short-lived first marriage was one of those casualties. The pain and self-doubt that came from that personal failure was more difficult than all the disappointments and setbacks of years of social action.

An important lesson learned from communal and personal breakups is the crucial value of our relationships, especially with our spouses and children. The very best causes and visions can turn us into people far too driven by the desire for success and results. The temptations to overwork, the dangers of pride and self-importance, and the severe burdens of the cause can drive the joy from our lives. It is vital to maintain a balance between the cause and our own lives, and, in fact, I've noticed that both family and friendships seem to become increasingly important over the long haul. The good news is that our mistakes don't need to ruin our lives. Grace, new beginnings, and second chances are always possible, as I've discovered in my own life.

Always remember that when you're dealing with projects and campaigns, you're dealing with people. Just as the work for justice can inspire and call forth our best selves, our worst selves can also become very evident in the process. Competition, ego, pride, money, sex, and power have often foiled the most hopeful efforts for change. Some of the greatest tragedies I've ever witnessed have been the personal falls from influence and power of some social-movement leaders who had the greatest potential. I've been close enough to several of those tragedies to observe both the rise and the fall, and to see how it all happens. It teaches you the critical importance of personal integrity in the struggle for social change. Shortcuts in personal ethics will usually have long-term consequences.

Financial or sexual corruption is often involved in the great public falls, but the deeper moral issue is usually the corruption of power. Our society needs more leadership and less celebrity, more character and less charisma. Clear mechanisms for the accountability of leadership have proven to be key for the integrity of social movements and causes. The old adage "Practice what you preach" is still the best guide.

Don't Forget to Have Fun

At the end of Dorothy Day's life, everybody wanted to meet and talk with her. The steady flow of visitors to New York City's Mary House often tired her out. Some of the young volunteers working there at the Catholic Worker were most insistent. One day, several of them approached her, hoping to persuade her to join them in a big demonstration against nuclear weapons at the United Nations. Mass arrests were expected at the planned UN sit-in, and she guessed that the youthful activists were secretly wanting to tell their children one day that they had once been arrested with Dorothy Day. Dorothy, however, was quite unenthusiastic. "I've done that enough times already; you go ahead without me," she told them. "Oh, please, Dorothy," they replied. "It would be such a great experience!" After their repeated efforts to change her mind, Dorothy finally said, "Look, if I came along, here's what would happen. We would all be sitting in a circle, and the police would come. They would take all of you away and leave me for last because I'm so old. I'd be sitting there alone. Finally, the police would all be standing over me, shaking their heads, and asking, 'What are you doing here?' And I'd probably forget!"

Along with humor, music is essential to any successful movement for social change. If a movement doesn't produce good jokes and good songs, it probably isn't worth joining. Emma Goldman is renowned for her famous quip "If I can't dance, I won't join your revolution." Where would we be without Woody Guthrie, Pete Seeger, and all the minstrels of the civil rights movement? Singing together is probably one of the most bonding experiences people have. And those who were in the inner circle of the civil rights movement report the raucous atmosphere of jokes and pranks that kept Martin Luther King, Jr., and his closest associates sane during the most difficult, frightening, and violent of times.

I've often traveled with Ken Medema, truly one of the best singer-songwriters of our generation. And nobody is a better improviser. Blind from birth, Ken sees things the rest of us don't; at a moment's notice he can create a song in response to a sermon, a story, or just a word from his audiences. Ken often joins us for our big conferences and events in Washington, D.C. Ken Medema is the minstrel of our movement. Together, we do something called Let Justice Roll, which is a concert, rally, and revival all rolled into one. We've held them across the country, always sponsored by groups who are trying to make a difference in their community. Ken opens up with a medley of his music, I tell a story or do about five or ten minutes of preaching, and then it's back to Ken to do a song, literally from what I've just said. We just kick it back and forth, the whole audience gets engaged, and the evening takes off. It's always a wonderful experience, with the whole range of emotions over an hour and a half, and usually ending with the crowd clapping and dancing in the aisles. The purpose is to bring together the people of a city and to support the best local ministries in that community. We want to energize, nurture, and inspire.

Several times, Ken, his manager, Beverly Vander Molen, and I have taken our road show out for a couple weeks at a time, doing a different city almost every night. We always have a lot of fun, even though the vision we're singing and preaching about is a serious one. And sometimes funny things happen.

One night we had just finished a two-week tour with a Let Justice Roll concert in the Duke University chapel. Our good friend Will Willimon, dean of the chapel, had invited us to come, and we had an absolutely wonderful night. After it was over, we went with students to the campus grill for a late meal before returning to the chapel to pick up the musical equipment. It was late when the three of us entered the large and beautiful Gothic chapel. As we began to pack up, Ken started doing Gregorian chants, just to see what they would sound like in that cavernous place. Beverly had been threatening to sing "The Holy City" throughout the tour, and now began her rendition. The only musical performance of my life was singing a solo of "Maria," from *West Side Story*, at a high school spring concert many years ago. Ken and Beverly had often teased me to sing it for them and this seemed just the right moment. Try to imagine the strains of a Gregorian chant, "The Holy City," and "Maria" mingling in Duke's magnificent chapel! We had a great time together, all alone in a cathedral as midnight approached. Afterward, we gathered up the keyboards and miscellaneous equipment, and I started carrying the first load out to the van. When I opened the front door of the chapel, there was a very dazed student sitting on the front steps and gazing in my direction. "Was that you guys in the chapel?" he asked me. "Why, yes, it was," I replied. "Man," he said, "I thought it must have been some monks on speed!"

Another time, a group of us were trying to draw attention to a crucial decision regarding the licensing of a nuclear power plant at Seabrook, New Hampshire. A long campaign had been conducted at the New England plant by many in the region who were concerned about its safety. They asked some of us in Washington, D.C., to undertake a vigil at the Department of Energy in order to bring more public attention to the issue. We agreed and spent eight long hours on an unusually warm late-spring day in the nation's capital, marching up and down in front of the government building. But no matter what we did, we couldn't convince the Washington media to pay any attention to the story. Nobody cared. By the end of the day, we were not only frustrated but also hot and tired. Finally, we gave up and all headed down to Rock Creek Park, where we threw ourselves into the refreshing coolness of the creek. Cool and relaxed, we were all just splashing around when someone pointed up to the bridge right over our heads. There they were, a local TV camera crew taking our pictures. Having finally succeeded in attracting their attention, we waved triumphantly. That evening we howled as we watched ourselves in a television story about D.C.'s early hot spell and the first swim of the season by some area residents. We made the news, but not quite in the way we were expecting. All we could do was laugh at ourselves.

Laughing at ourselves and our carefully made plans can sometimes be very healthy, as is the use of a little satire once in a while. I remember a high-level delegation of American church leaders who went to Baghdad, hoping to prevent a war with Iraq. Most were heads of churches, and the leader of the official delegation was Edmond L. Browning, then the presiding bishop of the Episcopal Church. We went with the hope and expectation of speaking directly with Saddam Hussein to try and persuade him to avoid the confrontation with the United States. Maybe for the sake of peace he would make some concessions to American religious leaders that he would be unlikely to make to American government leaders. Ed is a good friend, and we worked together on what he, as head of our delegation, might say to Saddam when we met him for the first time.

We waited for days for a meeting with the Iraqi president, but slowly it became clear that he was not going to see us and was enjoying making us wait. It was nearing Christmas, so after several meetings with Iraqi religious leaders and other civic and governmental officials, we decided to go home. We were very disappointed at our lack of success, and especially to be going home empty-handed, with our country on the brink of war. The atmosphere was quiet and sullen at the airport as we waited in the special lounge to which we had been escorted by a contingent of Iraqi soldiers, who now were watching over us very carefully.

I spotted a picture of Saddam Hussein on the wall of the airport lounge; his photograph seemed to be on every wall we had seen throughout our visit to Iraq. Suddenly I had an idea and walked over to Ed to whisper it in his ear. "Why not give Saddam your speech right now!" I told him. "Tell him what you wanted to say and didn't get the chance to before. Now is your opportunity!" I said, smiling and nodding toward the picture on the airport wall. Browning got a twinkle in his eye and slowly got up to walk over to face the picture while Saddam's guards eyed him suspiciously.

Speaking with a strong and clear voice, our leader quickly got all our attention. He began to gesture dramatically and shake his finger at Saddam, looking directly into the eyes of the Iraqi dictator while telling him exactly what he really thought. Finally, Ed was giving the speech he had been preparing for all week. The beleaguered church leaders began to laugh for the first time during the trip while the military police glared in helpless anger. What were they going to do, shoot Ed for talking to a picture? It was a great moment of emotional release and effective satire at the same time. Soon we were all doubled over, and it was the only time all week when we felt we really had the upper hand in a situation that had been stacked against us from the beginning. We all went home with a smile on our faces.

At an annual spiritual retreat in Pennsylvania, about fifty committed social activists would admit (if they were honest) that the highlights of the weekend are the afternoon basketball games for aging former jocks, the evening excursions to the local country-western tavern, and the final night's party, where some of the world's worst jokes are told every year. The retreats are focused on important topics and issues, but what keeps bringing busy people back, year after year, is the time for genuine retreat and real relaxation with friends who share in the work for justice but know they need some time away from it too. Somehow, we are always more able to get back to our work after those three days in the mountains together.

Taking seriously the need for real social change is very important. But taking ourselves too seriously can be a real danger. Nothing is worse than people, including social activists, who take themselves too seriously and impose their glum state on everyone around them. It really does drive people away from involvement in social action when the people involved don't seem to be having any fun. We are all very human, frail, funny, sometimes confused, and often less sure of ourselves than we would like to admit. Humor helps us to admit that, and therefore keep our lives and work much more human.

Common Grace

Sometimes people working for change can become far too ideological, or even far too spiritual, about things. They just need to lighten up a little and find the grace abundant in this world, especially in the most common of experiences. I've mentioned some of my own encounters with such grace, often in the form of second chances. That's what happened for me when I met Joy Carroll, an Anglican priest from the inner city of South London. We met on a panel discussion in front of two thousand British young people attending an arts-and-music festival. Because of the breakup of my earlier marriage, I had given up on the kind of personal happiness that isn't dependent on the results of work or the successes of campaigns. Joy made me believe in it again.

After a two-year transatlantic romance, Joy Carroll and I were married on October 25, 1997, in Immanuel Church, Streatham, South London, where she had been serving as a priest. A wonderful service and lively reception complete with Indian food (our favorite) was followed by a great English working-class party, where we danced the night away. Highlights for my siblings, who had flown across the Atlantic for the big event, were my father being pulled onto the dance floor by an exuberant woman from Joy's church and, by the end of the evening, the sight of my parents dancing cheek to cheek. Cameras were quickly out to record the first time any of us ever saw my parents dance, as far as we could remember. Even for them, the occasion seemed to call for dancing.

Joy is the kind of person who's learned that having a great time is part of the Christian life. She'll often ask me, "What are we going to do for fun today?" I confess that I hadn't asked that question often before. Having been one of the first women ordained in the Church of England, who took a parish in one of London's toughest housing estates, served as the youngest member of the church's governing synod, and was called upon to be a frequent public and media spokesperson for women and other marginalized people, Joy knows the struggle for justice. But she also knows when to take a break or have a party.

One of the most fun things Joy did was to serve as the script consultant and role model for the highly successful British comedy series *The Vicar of Dibley*, a very humorous look at the trials and tribulations of a female country priest, starring famed English comic actress Dawn French. South London is a long way from the fictitious Dibley, and the television magazines made quite a story about "the real vicar of Dibley." The BBC followed with a television profile of Joy and her inner-city work entitled "Not the Vicar of Dibley." When we got married, Dawn and her husband, British comedian Lenny Henry, showed up for the wedding, which was dutifully covered by the British tabloids (THE REAL VICAR OF DIBLEY MARRIES!). That made for an interesting first day of our honeymoon beach holiday as we peered through our sunglasses at tourists reading the story of our wedding in *The Daily Mail*. The irony of it all had two seriously dedicated urban activists chuckling all day.

The surprise of meeting Joy Carroll, developing a fresh relationship in the midst of many responsibilities, and then settling into a new married life has taught me lessons I'd never really known before. They are about the grace of God, who gives second chances, the satisfactions that go deeper than the best of good work, and the personal happiness that changes one's perception of the most mundane realities of everyday life. As I said in my groom's speech (an English tradition), "I've found a wonderful woman of great substance and deep passion, and these days feel like the best days of my life." I'm learning that keeping substance and passion together is the key.

At 6:56 P.M., September 3, 1998, Luke Carroll Wallis came into the world. Seven pounds, seven ounces, and twenty inches long were the vital statistics. More vital was a healthy baby who entered the world without distress in a good natural labor. Sporting lots of dark hair and big blue eyes, Luke went straight to his mother's breast and to his happy parents' hearts. For both of us, he is a first child. And the first week of Luke's life was full of pure delights. Helping him learn to feed, watching him sleep, giving him his first bath, getting to know every part of his little body, interacting with those lovely blue eyes, taking him out for his first walk and enjoying people's smiles and attention, wondering about his future, smiling at each other a lot—those were the initial wonders for Joy and me. Our world was full of light.

I often reflected, throughout that first week, how universal these experiences are. Parents rich and poor, of all colors, and in every culture and nation have known these delights for millennia. Having a baby is the most common thing in the world. And yet each little part of welcoming this new life into your life seems unique and special to the parents and family involved. That's common grace. It is indeed a gift from God, and nothing makes us more aware of how precious God's gifts are than a newborn baby. Life itself seems more precious to us than it ever did before. Again, an almost universal experience for parents.

Perhaps that's why our hearts go out to them when we see other little babies threatened by famine, war, or extreme poverty. This is not supposed to happen to them. Everything in you wants to protect and nurture your child. I now can imagine what the parents of those greatly-at-risk children must feel when they are unable to protect them. As new parents, we didn't really know that in addition to loving each other, we could love someone else so much and so immediately. It's a powerful feeling and one, we suspect, that God has a great deal to do with.

I was a Fellow at Harvard at the time, and we had a lot of time together as a family—yet another blessing. On Luke's first-week birthday, we walked all around the beautiful campus of the Episcopal Divinity School, where we were living, on a perfect fall day. All the new students were having their orientation, just as we were having ours as new parents. We wandered into the empty chapel, and I realized it was Luke's first time in church. When I saw the pulpit, I couldn't resist climbing up there with Luke asleep in the baby carrier against my chest. I guess I just wanted him to get used to being in a pulpit—you know, just in case. I thought he seemed remarkably comfortable! Joy noted that he was asleep.

Holding him in the delivery room, I did pray, as many parents do, that Luke would be everything that God desires of him and created him to be. Offering your child to God is a way of offering yourself to God again, and it felt that way to me. For the religious and for those who are not, there is powerful spirituality in the birth of a child. Already we're learning a little about the unconditional love of God for us through the way we feel about our own child. Through one of the most universal human experiences, parent after parent is taught the lessons of love and life. And all this is grace.

Bound Together

My dear friend Yvonne Delk has a wonderful phrase, "binding covenant relationships." As an African-American woman and powerful preacher, she speaks movingly about those relationships that bind people together in covenants of friendship across all humanly conceived barriers and divisions. The phrase means sticking together no matter what, and going through together whatever comes along. Having people like that in your life is perhaps the best way to keep everything very human.

I'll never forget a very dramatic moment in the Rotunda of the U.S. Capitol, when fifty-five religious leaders stood reading Scripture, praying, and singing in response to the nation's changing welfare policy. "Woe to you legislators!" echoed the voices quoting Isaiah, Chapter 10. Standing in a circle, wearing full clerical garb, the clergy made a strong visual statement.

A group of eighth graders from a Virginia Catholic school happened to be in the Rotunda when the clergy arrived. They were there for a civics lesson and were getting an eyeful about the practice of democracy. The young people became very quiet, and ventured close to the clergy circle. At that moment, the Capitol police announced through a bullhorn that the ministers would be arrested if they didn't stop praying. They all stood their ground, and the authorities began to handcuff and lead the clerics away, one at a time. The students watched in silence, but when the last pastor had been taken away, they burst into applause for the ministers.

Both *The New York Times* and National Public Radio were on hand, and immediately approached the young students to get their response. "What did you learn today?" asked the reporters.

"Unity," said one young man. "That you should all come together if you want to fight something; you can't do it independently." Then a young woman said, "Today taught me about courage. Sometimes you just have to stand up for something." Another student agreed. "But when you do stand up," he said, "it's really good to have some other people with you!"

Courage can come from those binding covenant relationships that Yvonne talks about. It was evident that day in the jail cell. For more than twelve hours, before we were finally released with a court date, the religious leaders deepened their relationships. I sat for a while between Christian evangelist Tony Campolo and Jewish rabbi Michael Lerner as they discussed points of convergence and differences in their respective faiths. I watched black clergy talk about the experience of jail during the civil rights movement with white pastors who were experiencing it for the first time. There were no phones, no appointments, and no projects to finish. We just hung out in the jail cell together and got close. I've learned it is those kinds of relationships that will keep us human and carry us through whatever we have to face.

Speaking Up and Stepping Out

A big part of being human is sometimes being reluctant to speak up and step out. Moses isn't the only one who had that problem. Here is where we really do need one another.

I recall the night when I preached for the first time at the Ebenezer Baptist Church in Atlanta, Georgia, the home church of Martin Luther King, Jr. I was there for the first annual Peace and Justice Service on the anniversary of his birthday. But because that church had such a rich history, I was intimidated. When I thought about all the people who had preached from that august church's pulpit, it just got worse. As I began to preach, I could feel just how timid and nervous I was.

But after a few minutes, I began to get some unexpected help from down in the front row on the left side of the church. An old man began to respond to my preaching by calling back, "C'mon now, son, keep comin', preach it now, yes, well, keep goin', that's right, yessir, talk, sir, tell the truth, keep on now, that's right," and so on. I started to relax, to breathe deeply, and to remember the things I wanted to say, and began to really preach. The more I got going, the more he got going. "Now you're talkin', preach it, yes, well, oh mercy, amen!" That old man literally drew the sermon out of me. It's known as "call and response," and it's the accepted style of preaching and "listening" in the black church. When the preacher speaks, he or she gets a response from the congregation. "Can I get a witness?" says the preacher, and the church erupts. "Somebody say amen!" the preacher exclaims from the pulpit, and somebody always does.

A rhythm and cadence gets going between preacher and congregation, and the sermon gets better and better. I love to preach in black churches. Any good preacher will tell you that black churches bring out their very best. When you're finished, you don't feel as if you've just talked to passive listeners, you never have to wonder what people thought, and you won't have to guess whether they understood what you were saying. You and the congregation have been in dialogue; you have been in relationship. Often, the most vocal of the responders inhabits what gets called the Amen corner of a church. It's the corner of the church you can always look to for a hearty "Amen" when you need one.

Well, my Amen corner at Ebenezer served me well. When I finished, I felt exhausted but very satisfied that I had said what I wanted to say. I quickly came down from the pulpit and rushed over to the gentleman who had helped me so much and, really, made the sermon come to life. I thanked him profusely and told him that I couldn't have preached that sermon without him. "Oh, that's all right, young man," he said. "I've raised up many a preacher in my day!" At that moment, it all felt very human to me. Sometimes, we do need other people to help us to speak out.

Audiences may soon get tired of my doing this, but my son, Luke, is currently providing some of my best sermon illustrations and keeping my preaching very human indeed. My most important task at the moment is helping him learn how to walk. He's just nine months old, but he wants to go. He'll hang on to one of my fingers with each hand and just start stepping out. He's not really ready to walk yet, and, if I ever let go, he would fall right down. But that doesn't stop him. He literally prances around the house.

A baby doesn't think to form a committee to study the problem, assess his resources, and calculate exactly when his strength and balance will be sufficient to take the first step on his own. That's what most of us feel we have to do. Luke just steps out, even though he isn't ready. It's the only way he is going to learn how to walk. And that's what I find so wonderfully human about it all. Just stepping out is the key to learning how to do something. You're guaranteed not to get it right the first time, or even the first several times. You'll probably fall down a lot. But keep at it and eventually you'll be walking. Every time Luke succeeds in doing something new, like pulling himself up on a chair for the first time, he looks at us and grins from ear to ear. It's an absolute delight to watch. I wonder sometimes whether that's a little taste of what God must feel when watching us try to do something important for the first time. Take the lesson and just step out, and before long you'll be amazed at how far you've gone.

A Cloud of Witnesses

In my study, above the desk where I write, is a wall full of pictures. I've put up photos of many of the people who have inspired or nurtured me over the years. Most I never met, but a few I've had the privilege to know. Many of them are referred to in this book. There are Martin Luther King, Jr., and Malcolm X, who led the movement that shaped my view of the world. Mentors like William Stringfellow, Daniel Berrigan, and Dorothy Day are prominently featured. South African leaders Nelson Mandela, Desmond Tutu, and Steve Biko are all here, along with Beyers Naudé, the white church leader who was defrocked as a minister for opposing apartheid. There are people like Clarence Jordan, a white peanut farmer and Bible scholar who stuck his neck out to establish an interracial community and farm in rural Georgia in the 1950s. Some, like Gandhi, caused great changes to occur in the world, while others, like the monk Thomas Merton, caused people to think in entirely different ways. Some, such as archbishops Oscar Romero and Dom Helder Câmara, were established and comfortable church leaders until they spoke out for justice and found themselves under attack or even were killed. They include both the famous and the obscure: the renowned German pastor Dietrich Bonhoeffer, who stood up to Hitler and was hanged, and the little-known Austrian peasant Franz Jagerstatter, who refused to serve in the Third Reich's army and was summarily executed. There are powerful women like Sojourner Truth and Harriet Tubman, who challenged several kinds of injustices at the same time. Some were very learned, like theologian Karl Barth, and some had little formal education, like Mississippi sharecropper and civil rights leader Fannie Lou Hamer, who challenged the Democratic party to be more democratic. Some, like activist Jean Sindab and journalist Penny Lernoux, are dear departed friends or coworkers who, while not so famous, made a difference in the lives of many people.

The first time I read books by or about my heroes, I was hungry to learn about their ideas and their accomplishments. What I learned inspired and guided me. But now what I look for in the books and stories about their lives are the more human things. What were their weaknesses, as well as their strengths? How did they connect their personal lives with their public personae? In particular, how did they cope with failure, as well as success? I want to learn how they lived their lives, including their personal and family lives, not just how they shared their ideas or accomplished their work. I want to learn about their humanity. From my heroes, I want to learn two things now: not only what to live for but also how to live.

In the process of that learning, I've discovered how utterly human they all were—and are—even in the midst of their greatness. And that is the greatest comfort of all. Because if we are going to change the world, we've got to keep it human.

Think
Movement

CHAPTER FIFTEEN

Have a Dream

They shall all sit under their own vines and under their own fig trees, and no one shall make them afraid. (Micah 4:4)

MARTIN LUTHER KING, JR., gave his most famous speech at the Lincoln Memorial on August 28, 1963. "I have a dream" became his most frequently quoted line. His dream had to do with both a vision and an agenda. King called his vision the beloved community. And his agenda concerned civil rights, voting rights, and, later, economic justice and peace. The vision of the beloved community was the foundation for the agenda of the civil rights movement. It was and is both powerful and compelling. But visions don't mean much if they are not tied to concrete agendas and campaigns to advance them. Without the practical agendas of civil rights and voting rights, King would have remained only a visionary dreamer, not "a drum major for justice," the epitaph he chose for himself. Visions have to be expressed in practical agendas.

Throughout this book, we've used the biblical vision of justice, exemplified by both the Hebrew prophets and Jesus, that upholds the dignity of every person as a child of God. But how will that vision become practical? I love the vision of the biblical prophet Micah quoted above. It's a picture of justice and security—everyone beneath their own vine and fig tree, living in peace and unafraid; everybody having enough of economic life to sustain them, without being threatened by anybody else. It's a wonderful vision.

Are there priorities and campaigns that exemplify the vision today? I believe there are—some critical commitments that begin to implement that vision in the real world, or at least bring us closer to it. Taken together they form a real agenda for justice in our day. Each is a plank or platform of a modern movement for justice. I offer these priorities and campaigns as examples of practical agendas, but also to invite your own involvement in them. You can also learn things that could help guide your local actions. Ordinary people are joining these campaigns. And because of that, they are beginning to make a difference.

I want to suggest some critical priorities that might lead us to common ground. These are not the only priorities, but they are all essential ones, which I believe are possible to achieve. Part of the question is how to talk about controversial social and political issues in ways that could bring us together. From my experience then, here are some priorities, and ways of talking about them, that might take us forward.

Priorities

Children

I believe we could create a broad consensus about our collective responsibility to children, especially those most at risk. The facts alone are stark. In the wealthiest nation in the history of the world, 17 percent of all our children live in poverty. That jumps to 30 percent of all Hispanic children and 33 percent of black children. (In contrast, in Sweden and Belgium 2 percent of children live in poverty; in Germany, 6 percent; and in Britain, 9 percent.) These children did not choose the adverse circumstances that their society, economy, and many of their families have thrust upon them. "Putting children first" is becoming a rallying cry from many quarters. Most people really do care about kids. A serious discussion of a real safety net for children, as well as the opportunities each child deserves as a right of citizenship, could become a first order of public business if we commit to make it so, and that conversation could certainly transcend our political divisions. The religious community especially is moving in this direction because the first priority of a "biblical politics" is how the poor and vulnerable are treated, and the children we have simply left behind are a litmus test for any notion of a moral politics. Just as we succeeded in ending poverty for most of our older citizens through deliberate social policies, we could do the same for our youngest. Try this: Whenever a debate is going on in your community about a contentious social or political issue, just raise the question of what the impact of the decision will be on the kids. That won't provide easy answers but tends to focus the questions in the right way.

Diversity

The goal here is to view America's growing racial diversity more as a gift to be embraced than as a problem to be solved. That's a fundamental attitude that all of us can commit ourselves to. The old notions of a melting pot must give way to a healthy cultural pluralism supported by an underlying national unity. Racial justice and reconciliation must be taught to our children as nonnegotiable principles, and the best way to do that is for adults to act on those principles. Children learn what they see. We must also speak publicly about the root problem of white privilege, and show how it distorts and diminishes life for everybody—including white people. Overcoming our racial divisions is crucial as we begin the new century. Whether we are brought together or further divided must become a moral criterion for evaluating our political goals and processes. Despite evidences of growing racial polarization, we are also witnessing a deep desire for racial reconciliation in many quarters, including some unexpected places. The leadership being offered by a new generation of black and Hispanic urban leaders is winning respect across the political spectrum. If the young leaders of America's diverse minorities can forge a common interest in breaking down the walls of white privilege instead of fighting with one another, they will accomplish significant social victories, especially if they can form effective alliances with young whites who find the old racial privilege more a burden than a blessing.

Family

Family is becoming an issue that crosses political boundaries, as parents of all political stripes face a culture increasingly hostile to raising children. I recall an appeal made to me from the head of a very liberal communications company in Washington, D.C., to bring religious and political leaders together to confront the increasing output of greed, sex, and violence on television. This was a Washington political figure well-known for his left-wing causes, but his concerns sounded remarkably familiar to the alarms sounded by a leader of the religious right I had had lunch with the previous week. Both had children who were watching television, and that became these parents' common bond. Ironically, both were also concerned about the epidemic of corporate downsizing, which deprived wage earners of the living-wage job that is crucial in holding their families together. One would have framed his concerns in terms of social justice, the other of protecting family values, but their conclusions were much the same.

There is an opportunity here. Protecting and sustaining the bonds that nurture us as we raise our young could become a central priority for both cultural affirmation and public policy, and many across the political spectrum would support that. And we can learn that seeking to nurture a critical mass of healthy, self-sustaining two-parent families does not preclude protecting the rights of those who don't fit the traditional pattern; in fact, justice requires it. Let's talk about the importance of family values every chance we can, not as a code language for pitched battles between Left and Right, but rather as a commitment we all make to the kind of loving and caring families capable of raising our children and holding our society together.

Community

Coach your kid's soccer or baseball team, or just go to the games. The community building that goes on between parents and brothers and sisters along the sidelines is not just a game. Or get involved in your child's school, volunteer for a community organization, go to church. The erosion of systems of caring and nurturing goes well beyond the breakdown of family life. Reweaving the bonds of both family and community is essential to our collective well-being. I know we're all busy, but even busy people find the time to do the things that are their highest priorities. We all need to help re-create communal institutions and spaces for connecting, which are the antidote for the loneliness, spiritual malnutrition, and dangerous isolation that can result in the terrible tragedies we have seen in our schools. Families must connect to neighborhoods, which connect to communities, which connect to nations.

Our neighborhoods must not be mere outposts for the chain stores of the global economy, whose market values threaten to usurp more and more of the space of human life and outrun both community and self-government. We need countervailing institutions and networks both for personal nurture and for preserving space for nonmarket values like compassion, service, and community. Congregations, voluntary associations of all kinds, and a myriad of not-for-profit organizations have the capacity to value people and their relationships beyond the bottom line of the marketplace. But those organizations have no power without the involvement of an active citizenry. That's where you and I come in.

Citizenship

National politics has become a failing spectator sport, with campaigns reduced to advertising and citizens reduced to consumers. I don't think anybody likes that, even though many of us are quite cynical about politics. As we saw in chapter five, voter participation and citizen involvement in political decisions have fallen to alarming levels and must be restored. But how do we do that? Curbing the power of money over the political process is a necessary part of the solution. So is requiring the media to play a much more positive role in the honest, truthful, and fair airing of genuine public debate.

A new movement for democracy is growing across the country around the issues of money and politics, and many people are becoming involved. Still mostly beneath the media radar screen, grassroots efforts for campaign finance reform are having some real success in winning local referendums in several states. I've joined

the advisory board of a group called Public Campaign, which is
backing those local efforts, because I believe that the fight for
democracy is ultimately a moral issue and a spiritual imperative. We
should all support this hopeful movement; the concern about the
excessive influence of money in controlling political ideas and candidates is so basic to our future that it is gaining support across the
political spectrum. I helped in the launch of a grassroots campaign
in the Midwest called Dollars and Democracy, initiated by Catholics
and Quakers. Their effort is focused on creating a new public dialogue through thousands of local forums in Ohio and Illinois.
Rather than starting with new legislation in a Congress already
bought and sold by special interests, they are beginning with a new
democratic discussion at the local level. That's a good plan. If the
power of money over our political process could be substantially
reduced, through a variety of means, the possibility of other needed political reforms would dramatically increase. Raise the issue in
whatever public forums you can, and you'll be surprised at the positive response.

A final note on cynicism. If the broad public cynicism about politics is to be reversed, the process will require a renewed level
of civility and solution-based political problem solving on the part
of elected officials, but that will happen only if they are held
accountable by a motivated electorate. Politics today will be most
renewed by community-based citizen involvement around local
issues, which could ultimately transform the national debate. The
good news is that more and more people are busy organizing.
Despite the lack of attention from Washington, citizens are mobilizing in their own communities for a new kind of direct-action politics. Make sure you're a part of it. Out of all that grassroots community work, a new political agenda may be in the making. In time,
the national politicians may get the agenda. The antidote to cynicism is activism.

Ethics

Ideological confrontation has exhausted itself in polarized
extremes that fail to resolve deep moral debates. At the same time,

there is a new conversation about ethics and public life going on almost anywhere you turn these days. Perhaps more serious discussion of ethics may help us to transcend some of the ideological conflicts that have led to so many political dead ends. We have to learn to talk about issues in new ways. I believe that many people want to move beyond the old entrenched battle lines and talk about the spiritual values that should undergird our social and political life. Searching for some common ground must become more important than merely organizing against our opponents. All of us can do that, wherever we are. We will find it very challenging, but it is absolutely necessary if we are ever to resolve our endless conflicts around incendiary issues such as abortion, family values, and gay rights. Learning to talk more carefully about volatile issues is critically important. I believe we are beginning to see the outlines of such a common-ground politics.

For example, I've seen both pro-life and pro-choice people coming to the table to discuss ways they can work together to reduce dramatically the tragic number of 1.5 million abortions each year, instead of just carrying on an increasingly futile debate about a constitutional amendment that everyone knows will never pass anyway. Progress is made when people on both sides of the debate look for ways to reverse the alarming abortion rate, both by prevention (combating teenage pregnancy, reforming adoption laws, and providing needed alternatives to women) and by adopting reasonable restrictions to discourage but not criminalize abortions to avoid a climate that might well lead desperate women to back alleys. Similarly, the affirmation of family life need not be the occasion for scapegoating homosexuals or denying them their civil rights. In Colorado Springs, evangelical pro-family advocates at the Call to Renewal town meeting agreed that family breakdown is due more to heterosexual family dysfunction than to homosexuals. That breakthrough allowed participants to de-link genuine family concerns from questions regarding homosexuality and deal honestly with each on their own merits.

Dialogue occurs when people learn to engage in more civil exchanges about their mutual concerns. In the discussions described above, for example, people have discovered that the sacredness of life and the rights of women are not polar opposites after all. Bringing ethics into public debate should not entail imposing religion on policy decisions; rather, using the multiple religious and ethical traditions and resources of our national life could help us achieve deeper understandings of the issues at stake, and even yield some agreements and acceptable compromises.

Living-Wage Campaigns

In April 2001, a great moral drama unfolded at the world's most famous university. Harvard is the second-richest nonprofit organization in the world; the wealthiest is the Vatican. With a $19 billion endowment, Harvard is arguably the most influential university in the world, priding itself on offering intellectual and moral leadership to the global community. So why wasn't it paying its poorest workers a living family wage?

Nearly forty Harvard students and community supporters conducted a three-week peaceful sit-in to ask that question. They entered the University's Massachusetts Hall, which houses the offices of the president and provost, with the simple demand that all Harvard workers be paid a living wage of at least $10.25 an hour, with basic health benefits. A city living-wage ordinance passed by the Cambridge City Council determined the amount.

The Harvard Living Wage Campaign began in the winter of 1999 when I was living in Cambridge for the year, and I talked often with the students involved. They questioned why this powerful academic institution was unwilling to pay its security guards, janitors, and dining-room workers a wage sufficient to support their families. Yet the University continued to outsource jobs to private firms paying poverty-level wages. After several unsuccessful meetings with University administrators, the sit-in began.

As the sit-in went on, the support for their campaign grew to include national union leaders, politicians, Harvard alumni, families of the participating students, and similar living wage campaigns at other universities. Nearly three hundred Harvard faculty signed a full-page ad in the *Boston Globe* in support of the student campaign, saying: "We believe Harvard, as a global leader in higher education, has a responsibility to lead by example in promoting economic fairness and human dignity." I signed as an adjunct lecturer at the Kennedy School. Some of my students participated in the sit-in and called me on their cell phones from inside Massachusetts Hall.

Finally, three weeks later, the University agreed to create a new committee, including students and union representatives, to make recommendations on compensation policy, to begin new collective bargaining with the custodian's union, and to declare a moratorium on outsourcing jobs. With that agreement, the student sit-in peacefully ended with a significant victory.

Living wage campaigns are good examples of making a vision practical, and they are one of the fastest growing movements in the United States. Nearly fifty cities have passed living wage ordinances, and campaigns are currently being organized in more than seventy cities and twelve campuses. The movement has a simple assertion: people who work full-time should be able to support their families. The idea that people who work should earn a wage that allows them to support a family is not a radical one, at Harvard University or anywhere else. It is a fundamental moral issue.

In Los Angeles, a remarkable alliance between religious leaders, labor unions, and low-income workers produced a historic victory in 1997. The Los Angeles City Council unanimously voted a living-wage ordinance that required city contractors to pay employees $7.25 an hour if they provided health insurance or $8.50 if they didn't. It was the result of months of education and advocacy by community leaders and groups, including many local religious figures, who stood alongside low-wage workers and the unemployed to seek better wages and working conditions.

Attention was then turned to the city's world-class hotels, which charge premium prices but pay extremely low wages to the almost invisible workers who make everything convenient and comfortable for their guests. Here was a clear campaign for justice and fairness in the lap of luxury. Some downtown hotels signed new contracts, but the posh Westside hotels held out. Methodist pastor Rev. James Lawson brought a wide range of churches to the effort and provided significant leadership, just as he had as a young civil rights activist in Memphis as a protégé of Martin Luther King, Jr. The Jewish community also joined in and mobilized to challenge the hotel owners.

Perhaps the most dramatic moment came with a Holy Week silent procession in Beverly Hills, with Christian and Jewish religious leaders in their full clerical regalia alongside hotel workers in windbreakers and jeans. One reporter said, "Shoppers froze in their tracks as they witnessed the colorful block-long procession of religious figures and laborers led by three workers carrying baskets containing Easter lilies, bitter herbs, a cup of milk, matzoh, and a charoset mixture of ground fruits and nuts." Religious symbols were confronting economic injustice. On the sidewalk in front of one hotel, Rabbi Neil Comess-Daniels conducted a mini-seder marking the Jew's liberation from slavery in Egypt—an obvious challenge to the wage slavery of the modern tourism industry, where workers toil for as long as twenty years in the same hotel without receiving any health or retirement benefits. Rev. Dick Gillett, a retired Episcopal priest, called on the hotel owners to sign new contracts with their workers to "signal to all of Los Angeles that hardworking people deserve better than perpetual poverty." By mid-January, all fourteen hotels had signed an excellent contract that could serve as a model for hotels around the country. The new alliance between religion and labor is now turning to the plight of Los Angeles garment workers.

A living wage, simply put, is an hourly wage that allows a person working full-time to pay for the basic necessities of life—food, shelter, clothing, health care, transportation, child care, and so on. Our current federal minimum wage barely provides enough money for a single person to live above the poverty line, let alone a family with children. Living-wage campaigns assert that people who work full-time ought to be able to support their families. There is a political argument as well: the more a working family makes, the less that family turns to public subsidies such as food stamps, subsidized housing or child care, or other government assistance. In the midst of a political ethos emphasizing personal responsibility and leading to welfare reform, many campaigns argue that enabling working families to support themselves is a logical political platform.

Each living-wage initiative is specific to its location, goals, organizing capacity, and political climate, yet there are common elements. Living-wage campaigns focus on passing local ordinances that require private businesses that benefit from public funds (in any form, including grants, loans, subsidies, or tax breaks) to pay their employees a living wage. As ACORN, a grassroots economic-justice group, states: "The concept behind any living-wage campaign is simple: Our limited public dollars should not be subsidizing poverty-wage work. When subsidized employers are allowed to pay their workers less than a living wage, taxpayers end up footing a double bill: the initial subsidy and then the food stamps, emergency medical, housing and other social services low-wage workers may require to support themselves and their families even minimally. Public dollars should be leveraged for the public good—reserved for those private-sector employers who demonstrate a commitment to providing decent, family-supporting jobs in our local communities."

Another interesting side effect of these campaigns is the renewal of discourse about labor relations. Many campaigns have moved beyond negotiating about an hourly wage and now include such issues as greater accountability in hiring practices, incentives to hire economically disadvantaged employees, and obligation of the corporation to invest in the community. Living-wage campaigns are growing exponentially across the country.

Living-wage campaigns make the moral argument that people who work hard and full-time shouldn't be poor. But there are honest questions concerning the living wage, such as how it impacts small business owners or nonprofit organizations dealing with a city. Some ask whether business should pay the whole bill to move people out of poverty. Fair enough. But if we affirm the moral principle that someone who is working hard and full-time shouldn't be poor or unable to support a family, some alternative approaches must be found. One idea is the "living income." This would be a combination of the best wage that can be attained and targeted government supports, like an expanded Earned Income Tax Credit for low-income families (originally a Republican idea to help working families that now has broad bipartisan support). It would also include providing health care, child care, transportation, and food stamps where necessary; these are critical for bringing families out of poverty, as is a public commitment to affordable housing.

There are some basics, such as food, medicine, shelter, and education, that ought to be assured for the nation's poorest children. Guaranteeing them would finally provide a floor beneath which people shouldn't fall if they abide by certain responsibilities. Most Americans don't mind helping children and families that are working and trying to escape from poverty. It is hardly something for nothing. A new combination of a living wage and a living income might be just what is needed to assist a family's efforts to build a better life for their children. It's a proposal that could gain support across the political spectrum.

I've spent time with some of the student leaders of the Harvard living-wage campaign and visited with some of the leaders of the Los Angeles effort. I was impressed by the broad-based nature of both campaigns, bringing people together from across the political spectrum. The moral language the living-wage campaigners used also struck me. That moral appeal is part of the growing success of these efforts. Ordinary people sense that there are some fundamental issues of right and wrong here, that people ought to be able to support their families if they work hard. It's a movement in which the participation of a wide spectrum of people and organizations is making a real difference.

Sweatshop Initiatives

One average-size church in Brooklyn, New York, began a campaign that led the Gap clothing company to end its sweatshop activity in El Salvador. Momentum for this movement began when Christian parents looked at labels on the clothes their children were wearing and realized that they were participating in the exploitation of children's labor in other parts of the world. People of Faith Network came into being in 1994, as the Lafayette Avenue Presbyterian Church in Brooklyn became aware of the growing economic injustices of the wage gap, stagnant worker wages, and the epidemic growth of sweatshops. Under the leadership of Rev. David Dyson, the congregation drew on their New York connections to create a national network of clergy and lay people who would mobilize campaigns for political and economic justice. As a result of their efforts, People of Faith was instrumental in obtaining a strict code of conduct for the Gap, including the rehiring of workers fired because of union activity and the formation of an independent team of human rights monitors in the plants. People of Faith also had success stopping sweatshop production of a line of clothing endorsed by television personality Kathie Lee Gifford. Now they're working on campaigns advocating for the workers in sweatshops for both Wal-Mart and Disney products.

The U.S. General Accounting Office's working definition of a "sweatshop" is "an employer that violates more than one federal or state labor, industrial homework, occupational safety and health, workers' compensation, or industry registration law." What this definition means in reality is exploitative wages, harsh and unsafe working conditions, long hours, arbitrary discipline, and even harassment.

While not all garment workers are employed by sweatshops, the Department of Labor estimates that more than half of the United States's twenty-two thousand sewing shops violate minimum-wage and overtime laws. Furthermore, over 75 percent violate safety and health laws, posing a "substantial probability of death or serious physical harm," according to the department. Also, most workers are immigrants, particularly women, who fear being fired or even deported if they challenge the illegal conditions or abuse. "When we told the truth about our subminimum wages to a monitor, we were fired," said Samuel Guerra, a garment worker for fifteen years in Los Angeles, who reported to the advocacy group Sweatshop Watch. Guerra's wife and daughter, who worked in the same factory, were fired as well. Recently in Los Angeles, I learned that there are at least forty-five hundred sweatshops now operating in that city alone. I couldn't help remembering that exploitative labor conditions motivated faith-based movements for reform more than a century ago. Could that happen again today?

People of Faith Network's mission statement reads: "People of Faith Network is a national, multi-faith coalition. We unite local congregations, clergy, and activists to fight growing inequality and mean-spiritedness, which are linked to changes wrought by economic globalization. We seek to win concrete advances through targeted campaigns and, in the process, to reinvigorate our religious communities." The link between taking action for justice and revitalizing religious communities is crucial. As in the living-wage campaigns in Los Angeles and around the country, religious symbols and communities are being deployed against economic injustice. Why are religious congregations targeting sweatshops?

The domestic sweatshop problem came into the public eye in 1995 with the discovery of the El Monte, California, sweatshop. At El Monte, seventy-two Thai immigrants worked eighteen-hour days at $1.60 an hour; they were kept behind barbed wire as they sewed for many major retailers and manufacturers, with no access to legal help. Former secretary of labor Robert Reich has described the El Monte situation as "slave-like." Reich stated, "Today, sweatshops are an ugly stain on American fashion, and it is up to all of us to remove it." However, the structure of the garment industry makes the creation and maintenance of sweatshops all too easy. Large-scale retailers set the prices for the clothes they sell. As a result, the manufacturers—the next group down on the corporate ladder—must produce clothes well below that price to make a profit. The lowest tiers—sweatshops—are thus squeezed even more tightly to produce high volumes of clothes for a very low cost. Whenever retailers choose to lower prices, the sweatshop workers feel the brunt of the change most severely. Rojana Chuenchujit, a former El Monte sweatshop worker, said, "I once asked my contractor employer why we got paid so little. She said it was because she did not receive much money from the manufacturers. So that was the reason I would not get paid minimum wage."

Furthermore, the garment industry extends beyond the borders of the U.S. into areas where labor is viewed as even cheaper. For example, Sweatshop Watch documents that workers in Vietnam average twelve cents an hour, while those in Honduras make about sixty cents. Co-op America reports on the gap between sweatshop wages and corporate profits: "At the Chentex Factory in the Free Trade Zone in Nicaragua, a young woman earns 11 cents to sew a pair of Arizona jeans that sell at J. C. Penney for $14.99. Meanwhile, J. C. Penney earned $566 million in profits, almost equal to Nicaragua's annual national budget." The sweatshop advocacy group explains, "Sweatshops can be viewed as a product of the global economy. Fueled by an abundant supply of labor in the global market, capital mobility, and free trade, garment industry giants move from country to country, seeking the lowest labor costs and the highest profit, exploiting workers the world over."

Many different groups are contributing to the anti-sweatshop campaigns at both the national and international level. These groups share a few major goals. Of primary importance among these is a living wage, defined as enough to provide basic living conditions for a family by the standards of the country or area. Another anti-sweatshop campaign goal is better working conditions since many sweatshops pose substantial danger to health and even life, with dangerous equipment, unsanitary working conditions, and exposure to toxic chemicals. A third important aspect of anti-sweatshops campaigns is the right to organize. Both in this country and around the world, garment workers have been denied the right to collective bargaining, often facing sanctions or even being fired if they challenged management. This is a major reason why many unions are joining in the campaigns against sweatshops. These labor unions often work in conjunction with groups such as the National Interfaith Committee for Worker Justice, led by Kim Bobo, which links churches and labor unions and produces worship and educational materials to help congregations to get involved.

An additional goal is corporate accountability. Many large-scale retail organizations hire managers to serve as middlemen between the big-name stores and the sweatshops; this distancing allows corporations to continue exploitative practices without gaining a bad reputation. One religious organization involved in pushing for accountability is the Interfaith Center for Corporate Responsibility, a faith-based coalition of 275 Protestant, Catholic, and Jewish institutional investors who raise social issues with the corporations in which they invest; ICCR has a combined portfolio of $50 billion. Through a variety of methods, including the use of proxy votes at corporate board meetings, they seek to raise the ethical issues that otherwise might not be on the table.

Another means for holding corporations accountable is through establishing codes of conduct. Students at the University of California waged one of the most successful campaigns for a code of conduct. A resolution was passed in 1998 that requires the university to demand that any corporation producing items with the UC trademark adhere to the following guidelines: a living wage and benefits, a forty-eight-hour workweek, overtime pay, nondiscrimination in employment, no child labor or forced labor practices, no harassment or abuse, and the freedom to organize. With ten campuses and hundreds of thousands of students, the UC's campaign was a significant step for the anti-sweatshop movement's push toward corporate accountability. The UC campaign is just one part of a nationwide student movement geared toward worker justice for those who make university clothing and products, with similar campaigns on many campuses across the country.

Today, thirteen-year-old kids are deciding to start their own campaigns against sweatshops. They say that kids in the third world don't get to play because they're making the jeans and basketball shoes of first world kids. They don't think that's right, and they're taking action. If they can see the issue so clearly, so should we.

Jubilee 2000

One of the most exciting campaigns moving across the globe today is called Jubilee 2000. This call to cancel the unpayable debt that is crushing the world's poorest countries is exciting the imagination of people everywhere. Led by the religious community, Jubilee 2000 is drawing very diverse people together to make a moral demand on the leaders of the global economy. Again, religious language and symbols are being employed to attack economic injustice.

Global economic inequality stands today as an increasingly desperate problem for most of the world's people. A major factor in this inequality is poor countries' indebtedness to wealthier countries, which has caused entire nations to declare bankruptcy as the drain on their resources accelerates. A result of this international debt is rapidly degenerating social conditions for the poorest of the poor, as education, health care, and the environment continue to deteriorate.

In 1996, the situation's desperateness was finally recognized by donor nations, who responded by creating the Heavily Indebted Poor Countries (HIPC) initiative, which aimed to achieve "debt sustainability" for the poorest countries. However, religious people worldwide are protesting that debt sustainability is not adequate; they claim that debt cancellation, not management, is the moral imperative. The result is an international campaign known as Jubilee 2000.

This movement draws its inspiration from the book of Leviticus in the Hebrew Scriptures, which calls for a Year of Jubilee every fifty years. In the Jubilee Year, social inequalities are rectified: slaves are freed, land is returned to its original owners, and debts are canceled. The campaign is now organized in sixty countries, and petitions for debt cancellation are being collected in over one hundred nations. Numerous international figures—from Pope John Paul II to U2 lead singer, Bono—support the campaign.

While the international economic crisis has a complex history, it is indisputable that there is a strong correlation between a citizen's poverty and his or her nation's level of indebtedness. Jubilee 2000 has marked fifty-two countries as in desperate need of having their external debt canceled because of its detrimental effects on their citizens. In 1996, there were 984 million people in these countries; each man, woman, and child's average share of the foreign debt was $377 and their annual income was $425! In thirty-one countries, the per capita share of debt was larger than the per capita annual income.

Debt plays a major role in what support and opportunities a national community is able to provide for its citizens. For example,

Jubilee 2000's Jo Marie Griesgraber reports that in 1996 the Ugandan government spent three dollars per person on health care, while it spent seventeen dollars per person on repaying its foreign debt. When one multiplies these examples by the level of debt over-all—over $2 trillion, of which $250 billion is owed by the poorest countries—the ramifications for quality of life, and even survival, are overwhelming. Returning to the Ugandan example, Griesgraber writes, "One in five Ugandan children will not reach their fifth birthday as a result of diseases that could be prevented through investment in primary health care." It is hard to argue that situations like Uganda's have not reached crisis level.

Using the slogan "Break the Chains of Debt," organizers around the world have come up with a variety of creative applications of that symbolism. The formation of human chains has become an international symbol. In May 1998, during the annual summit of the G8 heads of state in Birmingham, England, seventy thousand people formed a human chain around the City Center meeting location.

Bishop John Davies, one of the participants, reported: "I got caught up with a group of about sixteen Bishops.…we walked around about half the chain ending up at St. Philip's Cathedral.… This procession was an extraordinary experience. As we walked we were greeted all along with deafening cheering, whistles, drums, rattles, as if we were a winning football team.…At Birmingham, thousands of people had caught a straight simple enthusiasm for a straight simple idea: whatever the complications and difficulties, it is intolerable to allow the present arrangements of unpayable debt to continue."

At the height of the event, eight schoolchildren walked around the chain, each carrying a box of petitions and representing a G8 country. They were accompanied by a town crier and a host of bishops, and were greeted with huge cheers from everyone spread out along the chain. They delivered the petitions (a total of 1.5 million signatures) to a summit representative.

Some ask who will pay for the canceled debt. From a moral point of view, the question is compelling indeed. Consider these facts:

The people in the rich countries who made these loans are not poor. The people in the developing countries who received and mostly benefited from those loans are not poor either. But the people who are suffering the most from the burden of the debt are poor. The biblical wisdom, recognizing that such disparities and injustices will occur, calls for periodic debt relief to begin to level the playing field at least a little.

At this stage in the international debt crisis, Jubilee 2000 is emerging as a growing moral force in the debate. In the United States, the Jubilee 2000 USA campaign was founded in June 1997. While it largely draws from religious organizations, it is not limited to them. Over one hundred major organizations and thousands of individuals have endorsed Jubilee 2000 in the United States. The platform of Jubilee 2000 USA calls for:

- Definitive cancellation of the crushing international debt in situations where countries burdened with high levels of human need and environmental distress are unable to meet the basic needs of their people or achieve a level of sustainable development that ensures a decent quality of life

- Definitive debt cancellation that benefits ordinary people and facilitates their participation in the process of determining the scope, timing, and conditions of debt relief, as well as the future direction and priorities of their national and local economies

- Definitive debt cancellation that is not conditioned on policy reforms that perpetuate or deepen poverty or environmental degradation

- Acknowledgment of responsibility by both lenders and borrowers, and action to recover resources that were diverted to corrupt regimes, institutions, and individuals

- Establishment of a transparent and participatory process to develop mechanisms to monitor international monetary flows and prevent recurring destructive cycles of indebtedness.

The campaign's efforts include education, building consensus, organizing grassroots networks, and conducting an advocacy campaign. It held its first national conference in 1998 in Washington, D.C., to further develop an education and organizing strategy. People attended the conference from twenty-six states and several other countries. It concluded with the formation of a human chain around the headquarters of the International Monetary Fund.

During the G8 summit in 1999, over one million people around the world participated in a variety of activities, culminating in human chains in major world capitals. Hundreds of thousands of people circled the meeting place in Cologne, Germany, and a petition with over two million signatures was handed to the leaders gathered there.

At the Cologne summit, the heads of the creditor nations reached agreement on a plan to triple the debt relief available for the world's poorest nations. The Cologne Debt Initiative provided a significant reduction of debts owed to international creditor agencies by some countries. While Jubilee 2000 USA continued to insist on definitive cancellation of crushing debt, without harmful conditions, the Campaign strongly believed that full financing of the Cologne Initiative could deliver substantial debt relief for some countries that are desperately in need, as an initial step forward.

Yet financing for full US participation in the Cologne Debt Initiative for fiscal year 2000 faced a major struggle in Congress. The Senate Appropriations Committee initially approved a foreign operations appropriations bill that included only $75 million for debt relief, although $435 had been requested in order to fulfill the U.S. government's commitment. A grassroots Jubilee 2000 campaign swung into action.

Letters and phone calls poured into Congress. On April 9, 2000, a "Cancel the Debt" rally was held in Washington, D.C., culminating with thousands of people forming a human chain around the U.S. Capitol. During the summer, the diversity of the debt relief coalition was on display at a White House meeting as televangelist Pat Robertson and U2 lead singer, Bono, appeared at a press briefing with President Clinton to urge passage of the appropriation. In the fall, the Congressional leadership finally agreed to fund the full request, and it was signed into law at a White House ceremony attended by many Jubilee 2000 representatives.

Rep. Sonny Callahan (R-AL), ranking member of the House committee that controls the foreign aid budget, was quoted in *The New York Times*: "The debt relief issue is now a speeding train. We've got the pope and every missionary in the world involved in this thing, and they persuaded just about everyone here that this is the noble thing to do."

The *Times* reporter noted that the Congressional agreement was "a sign that street protests and parish activism about the problems of globalization have had an impact on Congress." And President Clinton proclaimed, "It's not often we have a chance to do something that economists tell us is a financial imperative and religious leaders say is a moral imperative."

Following a meeting with Bono, even archconservative Sen. Jesse Helms got on board the train. In a *New York Times* interview, Bono said: "When I met with Sen. Jesse Helms, he wept. I talked to him about the biblical origin of the idea of Jubilee Year, the idea that every 49 years, you were supposed to release people from their debt and slaves were supposed to be set free. It's very punk rock for God, but I think it's in Leviticus. He was genuinely moved by the story of the continent of Africa, and he said to me, 'America needs to do more.' I think he felt it as a burden on a spiritual level."

It was, as the *Times* story concluded, "a victory for a coalition of rock stars, religious figures, and charity groups that have made debt forgiveness a moral touchstone for wealthy nations." And it's yet another example of how a movement of concerned and active people, grounded in moral and religious beliefs, can change the wind to accomplish what only a few short years ago seemed impossible.

The Jubilee Network continues to call for the definitive cancellation of international debt for countries burdened with high levels of human need and environmental distress, in ways that benefit ordinary people and include their participation, and without conditions that perpetuate or deepen poverty. And the growing participation of people around the world is giving a strong momentum to that moral imperative.

Closing the Gap

During the 1998–99 academic year at Harvard, I did regular forums titled "Inequality As a Religious Issue." Chuck Collins and other staff members of a Boston-based group called United for a Fair Economy were frequent participants in the forums. Their mission statement defines their organization as part of a broad social movement of people concerned that the concentration of wealth is hurting our nation. Its goal is to revitalize America through a more fair distribution of wealth. Formed in 1994, UFE brings diverse community forces together to address the increasingly dramatic gap between rich and poor.

In chapter five on the three poverties, we stated that the problem of poverty was, at root, a problem with the way wealth is distributed. That's what all the biblical prophets say. So as we work on campaigns to raise the floor for people who are poor—through living-wage campaigns, sweatshop initiatives, and canceling unpayable debt—we must also examine how we might lower the ceiling of this global economy a little.

The economic statistics cited above have cultural, political, and even spiritual ramifications. For instance, economic security for most Americans is decreasing; the tax burden has been shifted from huge corporations onto low- and middle-income people; and community institutions such as schools, libraries, parks, and streets are suffering because of government's "lack of money."

But the gap between rich and poor is not an irrevocable consequence of our economic system. It can be addressed through community action, effective public policy, and different financial choices across the economic spectrum. UFE explains, "This rapid shift and concentration of wealth occurred because government rules were changed to help the richest 5 percent get richer, while the rest lost and suffered. Tax rules were changed to further benefit the owners of 'assets' (lands, rental property, stocks, bonds, etc.) at the expense of everyday wage earners. As a result, wealth has 'flowed up' to a handful of people who need it the least [instead of 'trickled down' to those who need it most]. While corporate profits have soared to new heights, their gains have been at the expense of both union and non-union workers." Therefore UFE is advocating a change in rules through its growing Wage Gap Campaign.

The Wage Gap Campaign draws attention to the growing income inequality through a variety of means, including educational workshops, tools for organizing and creative action, conducting research, and publishing excellent reports. While these activities are open to participation by people from across the economic spectrum, another arm of the Wage Gap Campaign is a unique effort called the Responsible Wealth movement.

Responsible Wealth members identify themselves as "a group of business leaders and wealthy individuals among the top 5 percent of income earners and asset holders in the US who are concerned about the rise in power of large corporations and the growing gap between the rich and everyone else....As beneficiaries of an economic system that is heavily tilted in our favor, we feel a responsibility to join with others in examining and changing the corporate and government policies that are widening the economic gap."

Responsible Wealth works in two major capacities: by introducing shareholder resolutions addressing the wage gap into corporations in which they are investors, and by taking the "Tax Pledge" to refuse to take advantage of further tax breaks for the wealthy which would otherwise benefit them. Through education and speaking out from a position of wealth, Responsible Wealth hopes to "help create an economy where the rising tide of prosperity lifts all boats, not just those of the wealthiest among us." My friend Roger Rath, a former board member of Sojourners, is a member of Responsible Wealth. He called me one day to report that he was going to present a stockholder resolution at the Citibank corporate board meeting that would call for a reduction in excessive executive compensation. Roger is a successful investment counselor and is hardly anti-business. But he is also a Christian, has a heart for the poor, and believes our economic system has just gone "crazy."

Both Responsible Wealth and the Wage Gap Campaign support measures that would work to close the wage gap from both the highest-paid and the lowest-paid ends—such as legislation that would deny employers the right to deduct excessive compensation from the corporation's taxes. That's right, those huge CEO salaries can currently be deducted from corporation tax payments as business expenses! The result of changing policies that permit excessive executive pay could be higher worker morale, increased revenues for government, and furthered economic equality.

Religious groups are a major part of the Wage Gap Campaign, and the unique capabilities of congregations, denominations, and faith-based organizations were highlighted at UFE's 1999 conference, "Putting Your Values into Action: A Religious Response to Growing Inequality." As one speaker put it at the conference, "The concentration of wealth is not a natural disaster like a hurricane. It is a problem that people created and people can change....We all need to work together to create such a society. And we all will reap the reward."

Each of these four concrete campaigns—living wage, sweatshop initiatives, Jubilee 2000, and Closing the Gap—is furthering the biblical vision of economic justice. Each involves many ordinary people. And each is making a difference. Check them out. And look for ways that you can join in. But I use them here only as four examples of practical efforts toward implementing our dreams of justice. There are many other ways to help make those dreams into realities. The key is to get involved.

Call to Renewal

Call to Renewal supports all the above efforts and the myriad projects now under way to make social and economic justice more possible. Many of those are faith based. I've discussed Call to Renewal at several points in this book and told the story of how the crisis facing poor people in this nation is bringing the churches back together again.

Simply put, Call to Renewal seeks to unite churches and faith-based organizations in a biblical commitment to overcome poverty and the problems that fuel it. We want to bring people together for spiritual renewal, social responsibility, and moral politics. We help create new networks of cooperation among churches and faith-based organizations at the national and local levels. We

build partnerships with other faith traditions, nonprofit organizations, business, labor, and government officials. We are forging a
unified faith-based and nonpartisan voice on the most critical public issues that affect people who are poor, and, indeed, that might
shape a more fair and just society for us all.

As church leaders and organizers have come together, four priorities have emerged:

- Overcoming poverty. We must expand economic opportunity and secure economic justice. Both personal and societal
  responsibilities are necessary to break the grip of poverty
  over people's lives.
- Dismantling racism and white privilege in our society. We
  must commit ourselves to racial justice and reconciliation in
  our personal lives, our congregations, our neighborhoods,
  and in the very structures of our society.
- Rebuilding the bonds of healthy families and supportive
  communities. These hold our society together and, especially, nurture and raise our children.
- Reasserting the fundamental dignity of each human life. We
  must commit ourselves to treating every person with the
  full rights of citizenship and full respect, as being created in
  the image of God.

The opportunity is real and present. Our nation is experiencing
unprecedented economic growth and prosperity, but this economic boom is not being adequately shared—in fact, the income gap
between rich and poor continues to grow. The biblical mandate to
overcome poverty is clear: the Bible says the ultimate test of a society's integrity in God's eyes is how it treats those who are poor and
marginalized. The time has come to answer this moral dilemma
with a spiritual charge. Looking both to the biblical imperatives and
the societal situation, to avoid danger faith communities must seize
the opportunity to step forward and declare, "If not now, when?"

Call to Renewal is not a new organization; it is a federation with
which individuals, local churches, faith-based organizations, and
national bodies are invited to affiliate. Our intention is not to
replace or undermine any existing efforts or institutions but rather

to connect and strengthen them, then expand their influence by magnifying their collective voice. Our structure is federated, but our spirituality will be covenantal. We will be bound together in our diversity by a spiritual covenant to act by faith in overcoming poverty. That covenant reads as follows:

> The persistence of widespread poverty in our midst is morally unacceptable. Just as some of our religious forebears decided to no longer accept slavery or segregation, we decide to no longer accept poverty. In the biblical tradition, we covenant together in a Call to Renewal. By entering into this Covenant, we commit ourselves to:
>
> 1. PRIORITIZE people who are poor—both in our personal, family, and vocational lives and in our congregational and organizational practices—through prayer and dedication of our time and resources.
> 2. DECIDE our own financial choices in ways that promote economic opportunity and justice for those in poverty.
> 3. EVALUATE all public policies and political candidates by how they affect people who are poor.
> 4. CHALLENGE racism, dismantle the structures of racial injustice and white privilege still present, and seek reconciliation among all groups in our society.
> 5. NURTURE the bonds of family and community and protect the dignity of each person.
> 6. ORGANIZE across barriers of race, denomination, and social boundaries in common commitment and action to overcome poverty in our own communities, our nation, and our world.

The "Covenant to Overcome Poverty" was publicly announced on the East steps of the U.S. Capitol on February 16, 2000, by leaders of the nation's churches and church-based organizations, who then committed themselves to a ten-year campaign to implement it. As *The New York Times* wrote, "Concerned that poverty persists in America despite a prolonged period of national prosperity, a broad group of Christian leaders gathered in Washington yesterday to call for an effort by churches, businesses, labor and government to help poor people."

The statements from every sector of the church were concise, clear, and compelling. John Carr of the U.S. Catholic Conference said, "Today, the Christian churches come together across denominational and ideological lines to insist we will measure this (election) campaign by how it treats the least of these." Rich Cizik of the National Association of Evangelicals added: "There is no way that we can say we are committed to the authoritative Word of God, inspired Scriptures, unless we are committed, I believe, to the cause of the poor."

The new general secretary of the National Council of Churches, Bob Edgar, concurred by saying, "It's not too late for people of faith from all traditions—liberal, conservative, and moderate—to covenant together to make sure that within the next few years no child in America has to live in poverty." And Rev. Wallace Charles Smith spoke for the Progressive National Baptist Convention and testified to the God the black church knows who is "inside the furnace with the poor, the oppressed, and the afflicted."

Mark Publow of World Vision, Bread for the World's David Beckmann, and Sharon Daly of Catholic Charities USA added their words of support.

Nearly seventy religious leaders have now signed the Covenant, and are working together on the campaign. The campaign declares that while we do not have a detailed blueprint for overcoming poverty, we can set forth practical goals that a good society should achieve. These goals are:
  ♦ a living family income for all who responsibly work
  ♦ full participation by people of all races
  ♦ affordable, quality health care for all, regardless of income
  ♦ schools that work for all our children
  ♦ safe, affordable housing
  ♦ safe and secure neighborhoods
  ♦ family-friendly policies and programs in every sector of society

We are committed to each of these goals as a moral priority, and are now working for the concrete policies that can accomplish them.

Already, Call to Renewal has convened the broadest faith-based national roundtables in years around the issue of poverty, and there is Call to Renewal activity in more than fifty cities and local communities, where many are forming local roundtables. If the vision, goals, and covenant of Call to Renewal strike a chord within you, we would invite your involvement with us. Information at the end of the book will supply the details you need to become involved.

Call to Renewal will stay focused on overcoming poverty and the problems that fuel it, rather than be drawn into debates over theology, doctrine, tradition, or other contentious social issues—important issues but not our focus. Our focus and our unity will be on the biblical imperative to overcome poverty. Call to Renewal is a *network* and a *voice* hoping to spark a *movement*—the final subject of this book, to which we will now turn.

CHAPTER SIXTEEN

Change the Wind

Therefore, since we are surrounded by so great a cloud of witnesses, let us also lay aside every weight and the sin that clings so closely, and let us run with perseverance the race that is set before us. (Hebrews 12:1)

In Washington, D.C., most of our elected officials suffer a common affliction. I call it the "wet-finger politician syndrome." You get it by constantly licking your finger and putting it up in the air to see which way the wind is blowing.

Many people, both inside and outside the Capital City, have a similar bad habit when it comes to politics. They have become convinced that you can change things by merely replacing one wet-finger politician with another. Millions of dollars are spent in this pursuit, but nothing much changes.

There is another approach—a better strategy used effectively by the most successful social movements throughout history. It's called *changing the wind*. When you change the wind the politicians will quickly sense it and, remarkably, change their direction too. Moral leaders like Martin Luther King, Jr., and Mahatma Gandhi understood this. To accomplish their bold agendas, they knew their movements would have to change the way people think. The very spiritual climate of the nation would have to be altered. Change the wind, and the necessary political reforms will follow.

For example, the U.S. Congress passed the historic Civil Rights Act in July of 1964. Six months later, after his return from the Nobel Peace Prize ceremonies in Oslo, Norway, Dr. Martin Luther King, Jr., went to see Lyndon Johnson. The civil rights leader told the president that the country now needed a voting rights act. He pressed hard for federal action.

But the consummate politician from Texas told the nation's moral leader that a new voting rights law was impossible. Johnson claimed that he had just cashed in all his political chips with the Southern senators to get the Civil Rights Act through Congress and he had no political capital left. But Martin Luther King, Jr., persisted; without the right to vote in the South, blacks could not change their own communities. Lyndon Johnson was the master of political realism. The president said he was sorry, but insisted that it would be five or ten years before it would be possible to achieve voting rights. But King said the nation couldn't wait that long.

Not one to just complain or give up, King began to organize. He chose a sleepy little town of which the world had never heard— Selma, Alabama. A new campaign would be focused there, one that would draw the nation's attention to the moral imperative of gaining the right to vote for America's black citizens. The campaign made Selma internationally famous, and the marches there became a watershed event, just as the Birmingham demonstrations had been before the civil rights law was passed. On March 7, 1965, the "bloody Sunday" march took civil rights workers across the Edmund Pettus Bridge to confront Sheriff Jim Clark's brutal troopers. On that day, many marchers were badly beaten, including a young man from Atlanta named John Lewis, now a highly respected congressman from Georgia. The very public confrontation galvanized the nation, and on March 15, President Lyndon Johnson appeared before a joint session of Congress to submit the Voting Rights Act.

On March 21, the famed Selma-to-Montgomery march took place with the whole nation watching. The nation's religious community mobilized as never before. Hundreds of ministers, white and black, from many denominations across the country, joined civil rights workers and the courageous people of Alabama to make the historic trek. Jewish rabbi Abraham Joshua Heschel marched shoulder to shoulder with Baptist minister Martin Luther King, Jr. The dramatic scene flashed across the nation's consciousness, and the whole world was moved by the moral struggle for political freedom in the American South.

Within five months, Congress passed the historic Voting Rights Act. What was said to be impossible suddenly became possible. On August 6, President Johnson, with Dr. Martin Luther King, Jr., attending the ceremony in the U.S. Capitol Rotunda, signed the act into law. Selma had altered the calculation of what was politically realistic. King had changed the wind.

The whole history of the civil rights movement demonstrated the power of the "outside/inside" strategy that can be most effective in seeking social change. King and others pounded on the doors of power with the persistence of the poor woman in the Gospel story of the widow and the judge. He didn't want to be bothered with her, but she kept knocking on his door until he finally had to open it and pay attention to her honest demands. This time, it was the grassroots movement that attracted the national attention that finally opened the doors of change. Those who want to change the world have to change the way the wind is blowing on the issues they care most about. Don't settle for surface political goals; go for real change, aim at changing the way people think and feel, and the political changes will follow. The stories of successful social movements all prove that.

A New Movement?

I believe we are on the verge of a spiritually based movement for social change. I'm using that word "movement" deliberately, even daringly. For too long we've been afraid to speak of a movement, ever since the death of Martin Luther King, Jr.

The movement question came up in a conversation I was having with about fifty Denver civic leaders about the relationship between faith and public life. The woman who posed it was a veteran of many social and political campaigns. "I remember my early days and the feeling of being part of a movement," she said. "But we lost that and seem to have gotten very scattered. I'm wondering if the time has come to refocus our energies, to come together around something. Is that possible?" Her question was deep and heartfelt. The nodding heads from around the room suggested that it was everyone's question, not only people of her generation but young people eager to commit their lives to something that would make a difference.

I answered with my Memphis story. In the fall of 1996, I was on a whirlwind speaking tour that took me to almost every part of the country. We held sixty-five town meetings and public events in thirty-four cities in just seven weeks. It was an organizing tour to unite the churches and local communities around the challenging process of welfare reform and the deeper agenda of overcoming poverty. After our opening conference in Washington, D.C., attracted front-page coverage in *The New York Times*, the tour moved into high gear.

Near the very end, we arrived in Memphis, tired but buoyed up by the enthusiastic response we had received along the way. Since so much of my personal history is bound up with the civil rights movement, I was especially looking forward to visiting the National Civil Rights Museum, located in what was formerly the Lorraine Motel, the place where Dr. King was assassinated. I knew I would be fascinated by the museum, and I was. But it was the very end of the museum tour that I found so startling.

The museum's story of the freedom movement ends in the exact space where Dr. King was shot. It's a small glass-enclosed cubicle with two preserved motel rooms on either side: 306 and 307, the rooms where Martin Luther King, Jr., and his colleagues normally stayed. Peering through the glass into Room 306, the last place King would ever sleep, I could see the room just as it had been on that fateful day: the unmade bed, the half-eaten lunch, the open suitcases on the floor. Looking straight ahead, my eyes focused on the balcony, the balcony, where Dr. King was standing when struck by an assassin's bullet. I slowly approached the edge of the glass, now almost standing on the balcony myself and looking over into the parking lot where King's young lieutenants—Jesse Jackson, Andrew Young, and others—had stood bantering and laughing with their leader. They were all waiting for Rev. Ralph Abernathy, King's longtime friend and coworker, who was still in the room knotting his tie, so they could all go to dinner at the home of a local clergyman.

All along the inside wall of the glass cubicle is a detailed chronology of the last days and hours of Martin Luther King, Jr. I already knew the story pretty well, but there was much more detail here than I had ever read before. I started at the beginning and carefully read every word, slowly making my way around the little room, pausing every few steps to look again into the two rooms or over the balcony. I remembered how Dr. King had called down to Ben Branch, standing in the parking lot below, "Ben, would you play 'Precious Lord' for me at the meeting tonight?" The piano player responded, "Dr. King, you know I always play 'Precious Lord' for you!" King replied, "I know, Ben, but could you play it especially pretty for me tonight?" Branch responded, "You know I will, Doctor, you know I will." Now, in that tiny room at the end of the civil rights museum tour, "Precious Lord" was playing...over and over again.

Precious Lord, take my hand.
Lead me on, let me stand.

The experience was overwhelming. For myself and many others, what happened that day on the balcony became a pivotal moment in our lives. Though I had never been to the Lorraine Motel before, I had visited there many times in my mind and heart. Now I was really there, seeing how it actually was, reading the account of every step and event, listening to the repeated strains of the old gospel hymn.

It was near the end of the inscribed chronicle on the wall that I found something that almost made my heart stand still. In the account of King's last moments, I discovered an exchange of words and emotions I had never read or heard before. After he was shot, the museum's solemn narrative reported, Andrew Young and Ralph Abernathy reached King at about the same time and were both cradling him in their arms as he was dying. Andy Young wailed, "It's over, it's all over!" But Abernathy rebuked him. "Don't say that. It's not over; it will never be over."

I couldn't contain my emotions any longer and felt the tears welling up inside. But a question welled up along with the tears: Who turned out to be right: Young or Abernathy? I sorrowfully concluded that Andrew Young's lament had proven true. As far as the movement was concerned, it was over with the death of Martin Luther King, Jr.

Of course, many powerful things have been done since that sorrowful spring day in 1968. Organizations, projects, campaigns, and coalitions have accomplished momentous and truly wonderful deeds. Our own work at Sojourners Community and *Sojourners* magazine was inspired in part by the civil rights movement. But I realized in Memphis that we haven't really dared to speak about movement since then. We've talked more about various rights than about our responsibilities to really change society. Many people have organized around a myriad of individual issues, but we haven't committed ourselves to building a movement for fundamental social change since the day King was killed.

King was in Memphis on behalf of garbage workers. He was in the midst of constructing a "poor people's campaign" to address the massive poverty still persistent in the richest nation on earth when he was cut down. Like the prophet he was, King had moved beyond civil rights and was confronting the endemic economic injustice in the land. There was great potential for such a movement, based on the success of the freedom struggle and the new coalitions it had brought into being. But it never happened. The dreamer died, and the poor people's campaign he wanted to begin never got off the ground. When other civil rights leaders tried to bring the campaign to Washington many months later, they were confronted by torrential rains and public indifference. They pitched their tents outside the corridors of power, but the vision of a new poor people's movement just sank in the mud of a Washington monsoon. More than thirty years later, we have never been able to recapture it.

Standing there on the balcony of the Lorraine Motel, I asked myself if the time was right again. After experiencing the public response in thirty-four very different American cities, I was beginning to feel that it might be. I was feeling the coming together, the new energy, the crossing of boundaries, the feelings of connection between people and places. And after all, the biblical tradition testifies that in the end, Rev. Ralph Abernathy will be proven right: "It's not over; it will never be over."

When I finished telling the story, the woman who asked the question nodded her head, and I could see the tears welling up in her eyes too. After the session was over she came up to quietly shake my hand and tell me that the morning was probably going to change her life more than anything in many years.

That's the question. Is there anything worth changing our lives for? That's what a social movement is all about—when enough people decide that there is. As I travel the country today, I hear people asking those questions again. The answers to the questions will have a lot to do with our future.

Perhaps the most powerful thing about a movement is that anybody can be a part of it. It's not just for leaders and certainly not only for politicians, pundits, and the politically correct. I put the stress on ordinary people because they are who finally make a difference in real social movements. People come as they are, participate as they can and at any level they are able. Some people in the civil rights movement gave their lives, others risked what they could, many marched, more supported them in other ways, even more spoke out in their own places where they had some voice, and more still decided to act and vote in different ways. That's what a movement is, and many people can be part of it, including you.

Think Movement

Thinking movement is the first step: not creating a movement (nobody can really do that) but laying the groundwork for one. Vincent Harding was a leader in the Southern Freedom Movement and a close associate of Martin Luther King, Jr. Now a professor at the Illiff School of Theology in Denver, Colorado, he is an eminent historian of the freedom movement. Harding's book, *There Is a River*, on the long history of the black freedom struggle, is a classic. Vincent has also been a wise mentor and elder to me over many years now. When I get impatient with the pace of change, he will say to me, "You can't start a movement, but you can get ready for one!" My old friend is not hesitant to remind me of the need for such preparation, and that wisdom has often carried me.

On December 1, 1955, Rosa Parks refused to give up her seat on a bus in Montgomery, Alabama, but not just because she was tired. She had been on retreats with other activists, at places like the Highlander Center in the hills of Tennessee, training and preparing with a network of young African Americans throughout the South who sensed that history was about to change. They didn't know where, when, or how the moment of opportunity would arise, but they wanted to be ready. They felt their times were pregnant with possibilities. Without the preparation from a network of those committed activists and the spiritual base of the black church, there never would have been a civil rights movement. A whole generation of black people in the South were preparing for a movement long before Rosa Parks decided not to give up her seat on the bus. They were motivated by a set of core values—values that would shape a new politics and shake a nation. And the moral appeal of that movement was the ultimate reason why the politics of the civil rights movement succeeded.

I've seen the wind change because of other movements in which I've been involved. In the 1960s, college students changed the way America thought about the war in Vietnam. In the 1970s, determined activists changed the way the whole country thought about the environment and women's rights. In the 1980s, churches made a moral issue of nuclear weapons, U.S. policies in Central America, and the nation's abortion rate. And in the 1990s, a handful of organizers led a campaign that caused the United States government to reverse its position and support economic sanctions against South Africa's white regime, an action that became the final straw that broke the back of apartheid. An even smaller group of late-1990s campaigners worked the Internet to turn almost the entire international community against land mines, and won a Nobel Peace Prize for their efforts. In each case, a moral argument changed the wind. Historically, social movements seem to have several characteristics in common.

First, social movements are not just about self-interest, but are about right and wrong. They raise moral issues, not just political ones. Movements involve people by appealing to their best selves, their best visions, and their best hopes for their children. They ask what is the right thing to do, the moral thing to do, the Christian thing to do, and so on. For example, the growing social inequality in America and the world doesn't just pose economic challenges but raises fundamental issues of justice, a religious concern. A social movement to address those issues should make the moral questions clear. Recovering the transcendent character of moral values in a rights-based culture is key to the success of any social movement. Don't be afraid to raise the moral issues at the root of the questions you want to address and the things you want to change. It's the best way to mobilize people around a social movement.

Second, minorities, not majorities, always begin movements. Historically, it has usually been committed minorities, acting on moral concerns, that bring issues to public consciousness. Minorities catalyze the situation, establish new agendas, and succeed, finally, when majorities choose not to oppose them. If they win the majority's agreement, it's usually owing to the moral force as well as the political logic of their argument. Majorities seldom become involved, but they eventually agree to the proposed changes, or at least decide not to resist them. It is minorities that change the terms of public debate; majorities just watch the discussion. The late anthropologist Margaret Mead said it well: "Don't think that small groups of people can't change the world; they're the only ones who ever have." That means you don't have to convince the majority in your church, neighborhood, or nation before you begin to act. All you need is a committed and motivated minority in order to begin.

Third, action changes the terms of the public debate. Discussion is usually not enough. It takes action to get people's attention. From the biblical prophets to the great social movements we've discussed to the many examples I've cited of what people are doing today in their local communities, it's taking action that *creates* a new dialogue. After a public action has been taken and people have seen it, the discussion about the issues at stake becomes a public one. Until that point, there might have been many private conversations, but nothing had brought the issue out into the open. Action has the power to do that. It often takes action on the part of some individual or group (much better if it's a group) to make a community or a society deal with something they haven't dealt with before. So don't just sit around talking forever about your concerns. Find a way to take action, the more creative and courageous the better.

Fourth, movements make the connection between the personal and the social. In building social movements, it's not that self-interest is unimportant but rather that it gets redefined. Perhaps the most important question a movement can ask is who the "we" is. I do a sermon entitled "How Big Is Your We?" I ask the audience to consider how wide their circle is, who's part of the family, who's in and who's out, and who is it that we're fighting for? It's a critical question. The best movements are those that enable people to connect their own self-interest to the interests of others. We are most satisfied when we feel part of something larger than ourselves. In a movement, self-interest becomes engaged in a larger common interest, and personal agendas become shaped by the common good. In your own situation, ask how you can connect people's personal interests to the problems at stake in the community. Find ways for the interests of the community to intersect with the personal and family concerns in people's hearts. You'll give people a larger purpose and find it creates both satisfaction and fulfillment.

Fifth, movements develop inclusive agendas. For example, social inequality and the pressures of a global economy don't impact poor people only. There is enormous pain in our middle-class neighborhoods and churches, where people are trying to hold their jobs and their families together, not to mention find time for significant involvement in wider community activities. We know that many single parents are not making it, but many two-parent families are also struggling just to keep up. Economics, family, and community are not coming together for millions of people in America today. A good society would want to support all three and keep them in balance. But we've lost our balance. Many people are hurting, and they're not all poor, and taking seriously the depth of that social and economic pain is crucial to building a movement for economic justice. Calls to help the poor may sound like just another demand for time and money from people who feel they have less and less of both. People who feel squeezed normally don't feel generous. But if the call can be framed in the context of the common good, asking what we all need and putting forward a vision of economics, family, and community that might work better for *everyone*, including the poor, it will come across much more effectively. Ask yourself what some of the issues are that will bring in many people. How can we connect the needs of the poor with the needs and well-being of the wider community?

Sixth, movements are visionary. The role of a movement, especially one that is spiritually or religiously based, should be to offer a vision for what society should be or do. What kind of country do we want to be, and what should America mean to the rest of the world? Those are the kinds of questions a movement asks. Such questions also help people understand themselves as a democratic people, not just as cogs in a world of economic determinism. We are asked to set aside the relentless demands of technology and the global economy for a moment, and to consider the larger questions of what we want as a nation and what quality and style of life we are trying to achieve. Those seeking a new vision talk about covenants, they make compacts, they pledge commitments. Movements speak a moral language that calls us back to the things we value most, which helps us remember that there are things we regard as more important than the pressures of our daily lives. Social change movements don't seek volunteers just to make the present more tolerable; they recruit members who together take a stance for a better future. Movements talk past the present and imagine a new future. The only way you can do that is to assert moral agency and responsibility in the midst of assumptions and structures that militate against both. Moral claims are made on social conditions, and that becomes a matter of faith. While both secular therapists and religious pietists encourage their clients and converts to seek private solutions to social problems, movements invite people to find public solutions as well. So don't just spend your time volunteering and filling up your life with social service; instead join with others around a real vision for changing something important.

Seventh, movements are prophetic. Religious communities and people of faith have played a key role in starting and sustaining social movements, as we have noted throughout this book. Abolition of slavery, civil rights, women's suffrage, child protection, labor laws, peace, and human rights were all movements that relied heavily on the participation of communities motivated by spiritual values. There are good reasons for that. Religious communities have the capacity to create movements precisely because of their belief systems. None of the above causes were ready to become part of the governing politics of their times when they first became social movements. In other words, movement politics never start with electoral politics. Rather, they begin to raise a public voice that, over time, politicians will be unable to ignore. Many social movements begin by asserting a moral claim or vision as an article of faith. Economic justice, for example, is a tenet of biblical faith just as are many other religious doctrines. It remains a tenet of faith whether or not the economic boom pays any attention to it, or whether or not it is possible today to immediately create an economy that is more just and fair. If the Bible says that economic injustice should be corrected and massive inequalities require periodic redistribution of wealth, that's enough to undergird and motivate a spiritual movement.

The civil rights movement didn't begin in Selma. Black churches were protesting lynchings at the turn of the century, developing leadership, protecting the community in numerous ways, supporting the legal battles of the NAACP, and much more. It wasn't a surprise when many black churches became the institutional support bases for the civil rights movement. It is the job of faith communities to put issues on the public agenda long before they can be achieved. But putting them on the agenda is the beginning of the long process that leads to eventual victory. So don't be intimidated by somebody else's political realism. Be willing to make a bold faith statement and put something on the agenda as the first step toward making it happen.

Ask yourself how the attributes of the social movements described above apply to your own personal involvements or the organizations you work with. Are you just thinking about volunteering or are you thinking movement? Are they just thinking about service, or are they thinking about a movement for social change?

What If?

Today, the moral case is growing for dealing with the unfinished agenda of overcoming poverty in the wealthiest country in the world and addressing the tremendous gulf between the so-called developed and developing worlds. In particular, the fate of millions of children, whom we have talked about throughout this book, is becoming a common focus.

As we have seen, a new unity in the religious community concerning poverty promises to provide the leadership that we have lacked. In many quarters, the commitment to connect economics to moral concerns is growing. But this would probably not become a movement if it were focused only on the poor. Because the issues of economic fairness touch the lives of so many people today, and because the moral questions at stake have to do with the well-being of our very souls, many different kinds of people are becoming involved.

Many Americans are feeling the need for a spiritual renewal of democracy itself, whose soul is also in crisis, as evidenced by the dramatic decline of voter participation in U.S. elections. If democracy is to be renewed in our time, if the poor are to be included in the mainstream of our society and treated more fairly around the world, and if the middle class is to find a purpose deeper than shopping, we will need to change the wind and alter our moral framework. Only a more spiritual language can renew our society and accomplish these things. We need to make the spiritual connections between the great issues of our time, while linking real solutions to the best moral values of both our religious and our political traditions. Only then will the wind begin to change.

In the 1960s, the country finally agreed that black people in America should be equal citizens under the law. When Dr. Martin Luther King, Jr., was assassinated in 1968, the agenda of establishing basic civil rights for all Americans, regardless of race, had been substantially accomplished. But the new mission to which he had turned his attention—to confront the massive poverty of American society—had hardly begun. That agenda remains unfinished.

For too long, efforts to relieve poverty in America have often been halfhearted and ill conceived. The great ideological debate between liberals and conservatives over social entitlement versus personal responsibility has left us incapable of acting. The practical result of that tired debate has produced a societal schizophrenia gravitating between substandard maintenance or neglectful abandonment of the lives of America's most vulnerable families, predominantly women and children.

Now the nation must decide whether its poorest, youngest, and most vulnerable citizens are part of the nation and the economy. That will require a change in the wind, but it's something we can do. And it's something you can help to accomplish. Don't be daunted by the task; it's only by joining together that we will change the wind. In the words of the biblical writer of the Book of Hebrews, we are invited to "lay aside every weight...and run the race that is set before us."

The task of overcoming poverty is a spiritual one. The call is to renewal—in our personal and family lives, in our congregations, in our neighborhoods and cities, and in our nation. For all of us, it is a matter of civic responsibility to make sure our poorest citizens are not left behind. For biblical people it is a matter of obedience to the admonition of the prophet Micah to "do justice, love kindness, and walk humbly with your God." For Christians, it is a matter of discipleship to Jesus Christ, who reminds us "as you have done it to the least of these, you have done it to me."

What if poor people finally got our attention? What if we started also paying attention to what the Bible says about wealth and poverty? What if we decided to include the bottom 25 percent of Americans and their fifteen million children in our society? What if we stopped arguing about the many reasons why people are poor and instead began focusing our collective energies on really overcoming poverty? What if we called off the old debates about welfare (since the government is all but ending it anyway) and instead pulled together to assist poor families in making the difficult passage from welfare and poverty to work, dignity, and community? What if we started moving beyond just providing services for poor people to actually helping them move out of poverty? What if we stopped talking about "the poor" and instead started including everybody in "the community"?

What if we stopped making the false choices that have impoverished our political debate and failed to resolve the vexing issues of poverty? And what if we replaced false choices with critical connections between good values and good jobs, between personal responsibility and social justice, between rebuilding families and rebuilding neighborhoods, between good parenting and livable family wages, between individual moral choices and governmental responsibility?

What if poor people brought the churches back together again? What if that new unity in the religious community could lead the way for the rest of the society by making an irresistible moral argument for including those at the bottom in the mainstream? What if we stopped arguing about government solutions and private charity and instead formed new partnerships between government, business, labor, churches, and other nonprofit organizations in each of our local communities, based on the principle of all people doing their fair share and doing what they do best?

What if we accepted the reality that both conservatives and liberals have useful insights about the complex causes of poverty, but that real solutions will challenge them both? What if people across the political spectrum could jointly get on with the task of improving the quality of life for our poorest, youngest, and most vulnerable citizens? What if we replaced the dysfunctional categories of Left and Right, liberal and conservative, with two new questions: What's right and what works? What if we declared that the cold war over poverty is finished?

A Statement of Faith

The good news is that it's beginning to happen. When I went to Harvard for the academic year of 1998–99, I didn't know what to expect. I would be a Fellow at the new Center for the Study of Values in Public Life based at the Harvard Divinity School. My responsibilities were simply to research, write, and lecture. But when the opening lecture on faith and politics drew several hundred students and faculty, I suspected I was not going to have a quiet year. Regular forums on faith and politics followed every two weeks, focusing on such topics as "The Churches and Welfare Reform," "The Bible and the Poor," "The Big Gap," "Faith-Based Organizations in American Public Life," and "A Movement for Economic Justice." Our gatherings attracted literally hundreds of students from the Divinity School, the Kennedy School of Government, the Law School, and even the Harvard Business School, and included many Harvard undergraduates, students from other schools in Boston, and leaders from the local community. We established a large core group for the regular forums and had many visitors each time as well. A sense of continuity and community developed, with a great feeling of progress made on the content of the discussions. Several faculty members and Fellows from the Divinity School and the Kennedy School joined us and enriched our deliberations. The emphasis was on faith and action, and the response was almost overwhelming. We had clearly struck a chord.

Throughout the year, the conversation about faith and politics continued to pick up steam. We focused in particular on the emerging role of faith-based organizations in critical areas of social policy, from welfare reform to the deeper agenda of overcoming poverty. I was amazed at how that topic was being energetically discussed around the university. And I discovered that a new acronym had been created for faith-based organizations—FBOs! In our forums, we began to look at economic inequality as a religious issue and how it might be put on the churches' agendas and brought into the political debate. What was most heartening was the number and diversity of people—students, faculty, and community leaders—who joined in the discussion.

The forums at the Divinity School's Andover Hall quickly branched out, with invitations from the John F. Kennedy School of Government to do suppers, forums, and brown-bag lunches on various topics concerning religion and public life and the social role of faith communities, a new topic for a school of government. Other university departments and centers became involved, I was invited to speak to countless classes, and several campus student groups wanted similar discussions. Everywhere I went to talk about faith and action, I encountered packed rooms.

Especially stimulating was the broad range of meetings and conversations I had with members of the Harvard faculty. In several regular gatherings for discussions of social policy and politics, the subject of religion and politics came up again and again. My friend Richard Parker and I hosted several potluck discussions of faith and politics for Harvard faculty and staff members, which proved to be very fruitful as well as a lot of fun. His history course, "Religion, Politics, and Public Policy," the first ever at the Kennedy School of Government, drew almost one hundred students the first day of class. When I suggested he had a revival going on over there, he told me that was impossible. "I am an Episcopalian," he said.

Best of all were the countless personal conversations with students at Harvard. It's a real privilege to be part of a young person's discernment about his or her future. Several of my students were deciding to act on their faith by going into various public ministries in medicine, journalism, community organizing, and political advocacy. Others were involved in a living-wage campaign at Harvard in support of campus workers. The friendships formed with many of those young people will, I suspect, continue for many years. As I approached the end of my year at Harvard, the interest in the work that we were doing around faith and politics was still just building. Something was certainly happening, and, even at Harvard, it began to feel a little like a movement.

In the middle of my time in Cambridge, I returned to Washington for the Call to Renewal's National Summit. The night that Riverside Church's Rev. James Forbes and I preached together, along with the music of Ken Medema, on the topic "Meeting and Movement" was especially memorable. Jim announced that there were meetings and there were movements, and some meetings led to movements. He then traced meetings in the Bible that led to movements. "Is this just a meeting," Forbes asked, "or is this a movement?" I preached about changing the wind and told the story of Memphis. "Is it time to dare to speak the language of movement again?" I asked. The response was electric that night. And for the rest of the conference, the place was abuzz with the question.

I traveled to many other places during that first Harvard year and have been on the road ever since I came back home to Washington, D.C., including now regular weekly trips back up to Cambridge to teach a course at the Kennedy School, "Faith, Politics, and Society." Everywhere I find the same question: Is a movement coming? I find myself repeating Vincent Harding's adage often: "You can't start a movement, but you can prepare for one!" I ask almost every audience I speak to, "Are you getting ready?" That's something each and every one of us can do. There are signs of movement everywhere now. The living-wage campaigns, sweatshop initiatives, Jubilee 2000 campaign to cancel third world debt, and the responsible wealth movement to close the economic gap are but a few of them. Many local efforts are trying to make welfare-to-work a reality for poor families and to engage whole communities in the deeper agenda of overcoming poverty.

I've said that movements are built on statements of faith. So I'm going to end this book by making one. *I believe we are on the verge of a new movement for economic justice, led in large part by communities of faith.* To make such a prediction today is certainly a faith statement. But remember, that's how movements begin. And your involvement just might make the critical difference.

Allow me to conclude with a new-father story. When Joy was pregnant, she told me one night in bed that according to all the books, the child in her womb could hear us talking right then. I

Notes

INTRODUCTION The Difference That Faith Makes

page

1   Biblical definition of "faith" from Hebrews 11:1.

4   For a history of eighteenth- and nineteenth-century evangelical social involvement, see Donald Dayton, *Discovering an Evangelical Heritage* (New York: Harper and Row, 1976). For the history of the U.S. civil rights movement, see Taylor Branch, *Parting the Waters* (New York: Simon and Schuster, 1988) and *Pillar of Fire* (New York: Simon and Schuster, 1998); and David Garrow, *Bearing the Cross* (New York: William Morrow, 1986).

5   For the story of the South African struggle against apartheid, see Nelson Mandela, *Long Walk to Freedom* (New York: Doubleday, 1994) and Desmond Tutu, *The Rainbow People of Hope* (New York: Doubleday, 1994).

9   For a comprehensive compilation of organizations, publications, and descriptions of programs involving the faith community, see the Welfare Information Center at www.welfareinfo.org/faithbase.htm. See also "Research Report on Faith-Based Organizations and Social Provision," by the Center for the Study of Values in Public Life, Harvard Divinity School, September 1998.

10   The *Time* cover "Is God Dead?" appeared on April 8, 1966. The other covers were: "Can We Still Believe in Miracles?," April 10, 1995; "The Search for Jesus," April 8, 1996; "Faith and Healing," June 24, 1996; "And God Said: The Genesis Revival," October 28, 1996; "Jesus Online: Finding God on the Web," December 16, 1996; and "Does Heaven Exist?" March 24, 1997. See www.time.com.

11   The *Newsweek* cover story "God and Gangs," was on June 1, 1998. *The New Yorker* story "In God They Trust," was published in the June 16, 1997, issue.

CHAPTER ONE Trust Your Questions

20   William E. Pannell, *My Friend, the Enemy* (Waco: Word Books, 1968).

21   *Report of the National Advisory Commission on Civil Disorders* (Kerner Report) (New York: Bantam Books, 1968).

21   Malcolm X, with Alex Haley, *The Autobiography of Malcolm X* (New York: Grove Press, 1965).

24   Martin Luther King quote from a speech titled "Why I Oppose the War," April 16, 1967.

32   Quote from Rich Cizik of the National Association of Evangelicals, in "Christian Groups Seek Unity in Fight Against Poverty" by Carlye Murphy, *The Washington Post*, October 18, 1997.

CHAPTER TWO Get out of the House More Often

36   Estimates that 5 million people, including 2.5 million children, die from unsafe drinking water and sanitation, from World Health Organization, www.who.org.

37–39 John Fife story from "Conspiracy of Compassion," *Sojourners*, March 1985.

40   Story of Olga from Joe Nangle, "The Nature of God," *Sojourners*, July/August 1998.

41–42 Dale S. Recinella, "What's in a Name?"

43   Jesuit Volunteer Corps, 18th and Thompson Streets, Philadelphia, PA 19151.

44   Mission Year, P.O. Box 12589, Philadelphia, PA 19151.

CHAPTER THREE Use Your Gift

54 Cost figures for Christ House and D.C. Hospital system from Christ House, 1717 Columbia Rd., NW, Washington, DC, 20009.

57 Habitat housing figures from www.habitat.org.

60 Sojourners Neighborhood Center mural, in *The Washington Post*, August 2, 1990.

61 The Jobs Partnership, P.O. Box 31768, Raleigh, NC 31768.

The Samaritan Project, 513 East Eighth Street, Holland, MI 49423.

Riverside Church, 490 Riverside Drive, New York, NY 10027.

62 Windsor Village St. Johns UMC, 6000 Heatherbrook Drive, Houston, TX 77085. See also Kirbyjon Caldwell, *The Gospel of Good Success* (New York: Simon and Schuster, 1999).

62 Hillel quote from *Pirke Aboth* (Sayings of the Fathers), I.14.

63–64 Marshall Ganz story on David and Goliath from a talk given at a labor retreat, May 24, 1999.

64–66 For the Sing Sing story, see Hans Hallundbaek, "Stone Upon Stone," *Sojourners*, March/April 1999.

CHAPTER FOUR Do the Work and You'll Find the Spirit

69 Robert Putnam, "Bowling Alone," *Journal of Democracy* 6:1, January 1995.

72 Sojourners Neighborhood Center, 1323 Girard Street, NW, Washington, DC 20009.

CHAPTER FIVE Recognize the Three Faces of Poverty

78 "The New American Consensus," Nicholas Lemann, *The New York Times Magazine*, November 1, 1998.

Michael Harrington, *The Other America* (New York: Macmillan, 1962).

80 Peter Wehner, "Woe to You Who Are Rich," *The Washington Post*, January 12, 1997.

80–81 Rep. Tony Hall from Call to Renewal videotape of Capitol Preach-in, June 1, 1998.

83 Poverty figures from "Poverty in the United States 1999," U.S. Census Bureau, September 2000.

Unemployment rates during recessions between 1970 and 1985 Robert B. Hill, "The Black Middle Class," *The State of Black America 1986* (New York: National Urban League, 1986).

84 Critical mass of poor children with a cost to society of $8 to $10 trillion, see John DiIulio, "How to Defuse the Youth Crime Bomb," The *Weekly Standard*, March 10, 1997.

85 On distribution of benefits from stock market, see United for a Fair Economy, *Shifting Fortunes* (Boston: UFE, 1999), pp. 12–13.

After-tax income from "Pathbreaking CBO Study Shows Dramatic Increases in Income Disparities in 1980s and 1990s," *Center on Budget and Policy Priorities*, May 31, 2001.

85 Salary gap of 531 to 1 between CEO and average worker, see Jennifer Gill, "We're Back to Serfs and Royalty," *Business Week*, April 9, 2001.

On distribution of wealth, see *Shifting Fortunes*, p. 6 (from Edward Wolff, "Recent Trends in Wealth Ownership," December 1998.

86 United Nations Human Development Report, "Human Development Report 1998," www.undp.org/hdro/98.htm.

86 United Nations Development Programme, "Human Development Report 1997." Press release "Extreme Poverty Could Be Banished from Globe by Early

Next Century, According to Latest Human Develop-ment Report," UNDP, June 12, 1997, www.undp.org/news/HDR97/prl-eng.htm.

87   Michael Eisner ($97,000 per hour) and Disney worker in Haiti (28 cents per hour) from National Labor Committee/People of Faith Network Disney Campaign, 1997.

Michael Jordan making more from Nike than all Asian workers combined, from Richard Barnet, *The Global War Against the Poor* (Washington, D.C.: Servant Leadership Press).

89   Regina Herzlinger, *Market-Driven Health Care: Who Wins, Who Loses in the Transformation of America's Largest Service Industry* (Reading, Mass.: Perseus Press, 1997).

90   Gandhi's Seven Deadly Sins from Arun Gandhi of the M. K. Gandhi Institute for the Study of Nonviolence: "The seven deadly sins...were part of my lessons when I lived with Grandfather in 1945–46 as a boy of 12. He made me, and other children in the ashram, memorize them. . . . I don't know if there is any source you can attribute this list to."

93   John DiIulio manuscript, "Moral Poverty, Churches, and the Inner City."

95   "Tamraz Defends Political Gifts for Clinton Access," by Edward Walsh, *The Washington Post*, September 19, 1997.

95–96 Examples of the tobacco industry, clean-air standards, and quote from a speech by Bill Moyers, "The Soul of Democracy," delivered December 3, 1997 in San Francisco, see "Hostile Takeover," *Sojourners*, July/August 1998.

Corporations paying 31 percent of federal taxes in the 1950s and 15 percent now, from *The Growing Divide* (Boston: United for a Fair Economy, 1999).

Eighty percent of campaign funding from business contributors, Center for Responsive Politics.

97   Voter participation statistics from Sidney Verba, Kay Lehman Scholzman, and Henry E. Brady, "The Big Tilt: Participatory Inequality in America," *The American Prospect*, May–June 1997.

2000 presidential election turnout from "Presidential Voter Election Turnout," Committee for the Study of the American Electorate, 2000, www.fairvote.org/turnout/preturn.htm

CHAPTER SIX Listen to Those Closest to the Problem

101   Rev. Eugene Rivers and Ten Point Coalition, Anthony A. Parker, "Salvation in the Streets," *Sojourners*, May 1993. See also Eugene F. Rivers, "Take Your Inheri-tance: The Challenge Before the Churches," *Sojourners*, February–March, 1994.

102   Rev. Jeff Brown quote from personal conversation with the author.

103–04 Boston crime statistics from Boston Police Department and Partners, *The Boston Strategy to Prevent Youth Violence,* Boston Police Department, 1997. Cited in Jenny Drake Berrien, *The Boston Miracle*, Harvard and Radcliffe Colleges, 1997.

104   Rev. Ray Hammond quote from personal conversation with the author.

Rev. Jeff Brown quote from statement at Call to Renewal press conference, National Press Club, Washington, D.C., December 16, 1997.

105   Barrios Unidos, 1817 Soquel Ave., Santa Cruz, CA 95062.

107–11 On Bethel New Life and Mary Nelson, see Kevin Clarke, "Leaven in the Loaf," *Sojourners*, November-December 1998. Additional information from Mary Nelson.

110   On asset-based community development: Asset Based Community Development Institute, 2040 Sheridan Rd., Evanston, IL 60208.

111-12 Isaiah 65:21–23 and Micah 4:4.

114   Tom Jones quote from personal letter, January 4, 1999.

116   On the Springfield, Ohio, conference, see *Springfield News-Sun*: "Ministers Get a Dose of Reality," November 19, 1998; "Youths Have a Spirited Summit," November 20, 1998; "Speaker Delivers a Message of Hope," November 21, 1998. On Springfield, Ohio, doctor partnering with churches to found a new pediatric health care clinic, see "Church Puts Its Faith into Action with Health Clinic," *Springfield News-Sun*, February 22, 1998.

CHAPTER SEVEN Get to the Heart of the Matter

121   *Entertaining Angels: The Dorothy Day Story*, directed by Michael Ray Rhodes, produced by Ellwood E. Kieser, OSP; Paulist Pictures, 1996.

123   See Bill Wylie-Kellermann, *A Keeper of the Word: Selected Writings of William Stringfellow* (Grand Rapids, Mich.: William B. Eerdmans, 1994).

        Quote beginning "One gift a church may bring..." from "The Power of Alliance," *Sojourners*, September/October 1998.

123–24 "The Market and the Common Good": Portions of this section appeared on MSNBC Online, "Happy Holidays—You're Fired," by Jim Wallis, December 16, 1998.

125     $1.2 billion in salaries offered to top forty free-agent baseball players in fall of 1998 compiled from information on www.fastball.com.

127–28 Conference at National Press Club, June 5, 1998, sponsored by the James MacGregor Burns Academy of Leadership.

128   Letter from security guard, James Sullivan, "The Realities of Guarding Harvard," *Harvard Crimson*, March 23, 1999.

133   Promise Keepers, P.O. Box 103001, Denver, CO 80250.

135   Each church would have to add $250,000, from *The Wall Street Journal*, November 7, 1995.

CHAPTER EIGHT Throw Away Old Labels—It's Values That Count

145   Secretary Andrew Cuomo, "Remarks to National Summit on Churches and Welfare Reform," February 2, 1999, www.hud.gov/spchchur.html.

146   Urban Institute prediction of a million more children in poverty, from Sandra Zedlewski et al., "Potential Effects of Congressional Welfare Reform Legislation on Family Incomes," Urban Institute, July 26, 1996.

148   "Be sure your sin will find you out," Numbers 32:23.

149   On reductions in caseloads as not the only measure of success, see "Governors Reflect on Welfare Reform's Second Year," National Association of Governors, July 28, 1998.

        Mary Jo Bane quote from presentation at Call to Renewal National Summit on the Churches and Welfare Reform, February 1, 1999.

149-50 Fifty percent of former welfare recipients finding jobs, see "Tracking Recipients After They Leave Welfare: Summaries of State Follow-up Studies," National Association of Governors, National Association of State Legislators, and American Public Welfare Association, July 1998.

        On work at longer hours and lower wages, typically $8000–$10,800 annually, see Sharon Parrott, "Welfare Recipients Who Find Jobs: What Do We Know About Their Employment and Earnings?" Center on Budget and Policy Priorities, November 16, 1998.

        Those going to missions for shelter having lost government benefits in the last year, see "The Changing Face of America's Homeless: IUGM Issues Tenth Annual Survey," International Union of Gospel Missions, November 23, 1998.

        Children accounting for 38 percent of the homeless population, problem of low-paying jobs, and negative impact of welfare reform, from "A Status Report on Hunger and Homelessness in America's Cities: U.S. Conference of Mayors, January 5, 1999.

Wisconsin survey from "A Welfare Plan Justifies Hopes and Some Fears," Jason DeParle, *The New York Times*, January 15, 1999.

150   Investigative series in *Time*, Donald L. Bartlett and James B. Steele, "Corporate Welfare," November 9, 16, and 23, 1998.

152   On the National Summit on the Churches and Welfare Reform, see Ryan Rockwood, "Church Leaders Lay Out Campaign Against Poverty," Religion News Service, in Minneapolis *Star Tribune*, February 13, 1999; "Pastors decry plight of poor after welfare," Associated Press, February 4, 1999; "The Working Poor," editorial in *St. Louis Post-Dispatch*, February 6, 1999; and "Religious Groups Unite for Stronger Voice in Welfare Debate," Diego Ribadeneira, *Boston Globe*, February 13, 1999.

153–54 Meeting in Lancaster, Pa., on October 5, 1997.

154–56 For a representative sample of clips on the 1996 tour, see Cindy Kranz, "Christian Network Talks Non-partisan Politics," *The Cincinnati Enquirer*, September 12, 1996; Diego Ribadeneira, "New Christian Group Pushes Agenda of Helping the Poor," *The Boston Globe*, September 19, 1996; Clark Morphew, "Editor Seeks Renewed Compassion Toward Poor," *Saint Paul Pioneer-Press*, September 28, 1996; Sandi Dolbee, "Spreading a Gospel of Social Justice," *The San Diego Union-Tribune*, October 18, 1996; April Witt, "Politics and the Pew," *The Miami Herald*, October 23, 1996; Lee Romney, "O.C. Christians Left and Center Join 'Renewal,'" *Los Angeles Times*, November 17, 1996.

CHAPTER NINE   Find New Allies and Search for Common Ground

161–65 On the "Christian Roundtable on the Churches and Welfare Reform," see David E. Anderson, "60 Leaders Meet to Join Forces to Help the Poor," Religion News Service in *Los Angeles Times*, May 3, 1997.

162   Quote from Wes Granberg-Michaelson and "humble" atmosphere from Richard A. Kauffman, "Leaders Pursue Unity in Fighting Poverty," *Christianity Today*, June 16, 1997.

171   Luis E. Lugo, "Equal Partners: The Welfare Responsibility of Governments and Churches," (Washington, D.C.: Center for Public Justice, 1998).

171   The Catechism of the Catholic Church (Washington, D.C.: United States Catholic Conference, 1994).

175–76 Dani Barrett story from the Jobs Partnership.

CHAPTER TEN   Eyes on the Prize

178   U.S. Conference of Mayors, "Hunger and Homelessness in America's Cities, 2000," December 2000.

179   "More People Receive Emergency Food in Spite of Strong Economy," Catholic Charities USA, December 19, 2000.

180–81 Vice President Gore speech, see *The New York Times*, May 25, 1999, and *The Washington Post*, May 25, 1999.

181   Gov. George W. Bush, "The Duty of Hope," speech given July 22, 1999. Available at www.georgewbush.com.

184   John Dilulio, "Compassion in Truth and Action," speech to NAE, March 7, 2001. See www.whitehouse.gov/news/releases/2001/03/20010307-11.html

185   75% support from "Faith-Based Funding: Broad Support, Profound Questions," Pew Forum on Religion and Public Life with the Pew Research Center for the People and the Press, April 10, 2001.

186   What is popularly known as "charitable choice" is section 104 of the "Personal Responsibility and Work Opportunity Reconciliation Act of 1996." It provides

that if state governments engage nonprofit organizations in providing social services, through grants or vouchers, houses of worship and faith-based organizations must be permitted to participate in the process. For a compilation of articles pro and con, see Derek Davis and Barry Hankins, eds., Welfare Reform and Faith-Based Organizations (Waco: J. M. Dawson Institute of Church-State Studies, Baylor University, 1999).

189   Prime Minister Tony Blair speech, March 29, 2001, www.christiansocialist.org. uk/csmnet/blair29_3.doc.

192   Martin Luther King, "conscience of the state," The Strength to Love (1963), in A Testament of Hope, ed. James M. Washington (New York: Harper & Row, 1986), p. 501.

194   Elizabeth Baker, "Senate Delays Legislation on Aid to Church Charities," The New York Times, May 24, 2001.

195   Mary Leonard and Sue Kirchhoff, "Religious leaders ____ aid to poor," Boston Globe, May 26, 2001.

CHAPTER ELEVEN Tap the Power of Faith Communities

197–99 Garry Wills quotes from Under God: Religion and American Politics (New York: Simon and Schuster/Touchstone, 1990), pp. 16 and 25.

197–98 Polling on American religiosity from various Gallup polls, 1997–1999.

The Gallup figures clearly demonstrate the importance of religion to most Americans. However, "religious participation" is a difficult subject to measure, and some researchers claim that Gallup's numbers are too high. For example, one study states that church attendance could be as low as half of what the Gallup polls reveal, and that people give overly inflated information about their church attendance because it is a "socially desirable" activity. Other researchers assert that secularization—the idea that "modern material values are replacing the traditional spiritual outlook on life"—has increased, leading to a noticeable decrease in church membership.

Both these claims refuting the Gallup polls, however, are themselves subject to criticism. For instance, Michael Hout and Andrew Greeley comment, "We doubt that people exaggerate so much that reported attendance is actually twice as high as their actual attendance" ("What Church Official's Reports Don't Show: Another Look at Church Attendance Data," American Sociological Review, February 1998). Similarly, regarding the secularization claim, Hout and Greeley wrote, "We could find no evidence for religious secularization as measured by attendance at religious services in the United States over the past half century" ("The Center Doesn't Hold: Church Attendance in the United States, 1940–1984," American Sociological Review, June 1987).

Putting these data together, we can see that while there is some debate about the exact figures, the fact remains that Americans are a highly church-going population, and that religious participation is not fading as dramatically as critics would claim. Even a tendency to overestimate church attendance, for example, reinforces the point of the high degree of religiosity in America.

200   David Schribman, "One Nation Under God: How the Religious Right Changed the American Conversation," The Boston Globe Magazine, January 10, 1999.

200   View that churches should spend more time helping the poor, "God and Society in North America: A Survey of Religion, Politics, and Social Involvement in Canada and the United States," The Angus Reid Group.

200   IAF, 1106 Clayton, Suite 120W, Austin, TX 78723
        Gamaliel Foundation, 203 North Wabash Ave., Chicago, IL 60601
        DART, P.O. Box 370791, Miami, FL 33137
        PICO, 171 Santa Rosa Ave, Oakland, CA 94610

201 Ninety percent of churches have a social ministry, John McCarthy and Jim Castelli, "Religion-Sponsored Social Service Providers: The Not-So-Independent Sector," The Aspen Institute.

201 Joe Klein, "In God They Trust," *The New Yorker*, June 16, 1997.

Naomi Wolf, "Onward Christian Hippies," *George*, December 1997.

202–03 Number of Muslims, Buddhists, Hindus from David Barrett, *World Christian Encyclopedia* (Oxford University Press: 2001)

Ron Thiemann on "pilgrim discipleship" from a discussion as Harvard Divinity School.

On Jewish Renewal, see Michael Lerner, *Jewish Renewal: A Path to Healing and Transformation* (New York: G. P. Putnam's Sons, 1994) and Arthur Waskow, *Godwrestling Round 2: Ancient Wisdom, Future Paths* (Woodstock, Vt.: Jewish Lights Publishing, 1996).

203–04 For the William Wilberforce story, see Christopher D. Hancock, "The 'Shrimp' Who Stopped Slavery, *Christian History* 16, no. 1, 1997.

219 Eugene Rivers quote from Call to Renewal National Summit, February 1999.

221 Marshall Ganz quote from personal correspondence with author.

CHAPTER TWELVE Be a Peacemaker

226 Conflict-resolution statistics from Institute for Conflict Analysis and Resolution, George Mason University, www.gmu.edu/departments/ICAR/ICAR_field.html.

226–27 For Families Against Violence Advocacy Network, see Jim McGinnis, Ken and Gretchen Lovingood, and Jim Vogt, *Families Creating a Circle of Peace* (St. Louis: Institute for Peace and Justice, 1996). Families Against Violence Advocacy Network, 4144 Lindell Blvd., #408, St. Louis, MO 63108.

229 John Hume is leader of the Catholic Social Democratic and Labor Party, David Trimble of the Protestant Ulster Unionist Party; see Doug Mellgren, "Leaders in Northern Ireland Win Nobel Peace Prize," Associated Press, October 16, 1998.

230–31 Quote from Marion Stamps and Jerry McAfee are from Jim Wallis, "A Time to Heal, a Time to Build," *Sojourners*, August 1993.

233–34 Billy Graham quotes are from "A Change of Heart," *Sojourners*, August 1979.

234–35 Gen. Lee Butler, interviewed by David Cortright, "Unexpected Calling," *Sojourners*, January–February, 1999.

Portions of this section appeared on MSNBC Online as *A Better Way to Fight Terrorism*, August 24, 1998; *Topple a Tyrant, Protect the Innocent*, November 14, 1998; and *What Good Do Missiles Do?* January 26, 1999.

239–42 Glen Stassen, ed., *Just Peacemaking: Ten Practices for Abolishing War* (Cleveland, Ohio: Pilgrim Press, 1998).

243 Jonesboro parent quote from *Nightline*, April 22, 1999.

CHAPTER THIRTEEN Be a Contemplative

248, 252 Henry Louis Gates, Neil Rudenstine, and Peter Gomes quotes from speeches at Harvard University.

249 Nelson Mandela quote from speech at Harvard University.

250 Richard Rohr "lessons of life" from "Boys to Men: Rediscovering Rites of Passage for Our Time," *Sojourners*, May/June 1998.

253–54 On Nelson Mandela being awarded the Congressional Gold Medal, see Francis X. Clines, "The Great Conciliator at the Capital," *The New York Times*, September 24, 1998.

Mandela quote from speech to UN General Assembly, September 21, 1998.

254   See Joseph Cardinal Bernardin, *The Gift of Peace* (Chicago: Loyola Press, 1997).

255   *The Challenge of Peace: God's Promise and Our Response* (Washington, D.C.: United States Catholic Conference, 1983).

256   Barbara Blaine quote from *Chicago Sun-Times*, cited in Tim Unsworth, "In Chicago, Catholics React with Relief," *National Catholic Reporter*, March 11, 1994.

257   For op-ed piece, see Jim Wallis and Wes Granberg-Michaelson, "The Nature of Leadership and Personal Vulnerabilities," *Chicago Tribune*, February 25, 1998.

261–62 Henri Nouwen quotes are from *The Road to Peace*, ed. John Dear (Mary-knoll, N.Y.: Orbis Books, 1998). The "three disciplines," from an interview first published in Alive magazine, November/December 1994. Central America from "Christ of the Americas."

264–65 "Letter to a Young Activist," Thomas Merton, in *The Hidden Ground of Love* (New York: Farrar, Straus and Giroux, 1985).

CHAPTER FOURTEEN Keep It Human

267–68 The calling of Moses and his dialogue with God is from Exodus 3–4.

277   Wedding story from *The Daily Mail*, October 27, 1997.

279   Capitol Rotunda story from Francis X. Clines, "Christians Against Welfare Cuts Are Arrested in Capitol, *The New York Times*, December 8, 1995; and Lynn Neary, "All Things Considered," National Public Radio, December 7, 1995.

CHAPTER FIFTEEN Have a Dream

287   U.S. children in poverty figures from "Poverty in the United States 1999," U.S. Census Bureau, September 2000.

      Child poverty statistics from Cornel West at "The Future of American Progressivism," a forum at Harvard, fall 1998.

289   On families, see Cornel West and Sylvia Ann Hewlett, *The War Against Parents: What We Can Do for America's Beleaguered Moms and Dads* (Boston: Houghton Mifflin, 1998).

291   Public Campaign, 1320 19th Street, NW, Suite M-1, Washington, DC 20036. Dollars and Democracy, c/o AFSC, 512 West Exchange Street, Akron, OH 44302.

294–95 Story of Los Angeles living-wage campaign from Pat McDonnell Twair, "In the Lap of Luxury," *Sojourners*, September–October 1998.

296   ACORN quote from "An Introduction to Living Wage," at www.livingwage-campaign.org.

297   People of Faith Network information from People of Faith Network, 85 South Oxford Street, Brooklyn, NY 11217. See also Nile Harper, *Urban Churches, Vital Signs: Beyond Charity Toward Justice* (Grand Rapids, Mich.: Eerdmans, 1999), pp. 45–46.

298   GAO definition from www.sweatshopwatch.org/swatch/industry.

298   Department of Labor quote/estimate from *Los Angeles Times*, 1996, and article in *San Jose Mercury News*, June 1, 1999.

298   Samuel Guerra quote from www.sweatshopwatch.org/swatch/industry/cal/assembly.html.

299   People of Faith Network's mission from People of Faith, www.cloud9.net/~pofn.

299   El Monte scandal and Robert Reich quote from www.dol.gov/dol/opa/public/nosweat/ltr.htm.

299   Sweatshop Watch information from "What is a Sweatshop?" www.sweatshopwatch.org.

300   Co-op America quote from www.sweatshops.org.

300 National Interfaith Committee for Worker Justice, 1020 West Bryn Mawr, Chicago, IL 60660.

300 Interfaith Center for Corporate Responsibility, 475 Riverside Drive, New York, NY 10115.

301 University of California "code of conduct" campaign from University Coalition Against Sweatshops, www.sweatshopwatch.org/swatch/codes/ucas.

302 Fifty-two countries and debt statistics from www.oneworld.org/jubilee/jubilee2000/main.html.

303 Jo Marie Griesgraber quote from "Forgive Us Our Debts: The Third World's Financial Crisis," *Christian Century*, January 22, 1997.

303 Birmingham story and Bishop John Davies quote from www.oneworld.org/jubilee/jubilee2000/main.html.

304 Jubilee 2000 U.S. platform from www.jubilee2000usa.org/usa/platform.html.

306 "Speeding train" from Joseph Kahn, "Congressional Leadership Agrees to Debt Relief for Poor Nations," *New York Times*, October 18, 2000.

306 Interview with Bono from Susan Dominus, "The Way We Live Now: Questions for Bono," *New York Times Magazine*, October 8, 2000.

307 Information on United for a Fair Economy from www.stw.org/html/who_we_are.html.

308 On Wage Gap Campaign, see www.stw.org/html/wage_gap_campaign.html.

309 On Responsible Wealth, see www.stw.org/html/responsible_wealth.html.

309 Conference quote from www.stw.org/html.events.html.

310 Call to Renewal mission and four priorities from Call to Renewal Mission Statement.

311 Call to Renewal covenant from Call to Renewal.

311 Covenant signing see Gustav Niebuhr, "Christians Ask Renewed Attack on Poverty," *New York Times*, February 17, 2000.

CHAPTER SIXTEEN Change the Wind

315–16 For the story of Martin Luther King, Lyndon Johnson, Selma, and the Voting Rights Act, see Stephen Oates, *Let the Trumpet Sound*, (New York: Harper and Row, 1982), pp. 322–64, 370; and Garrow, *Bearing the Cross*, pp. 368–412.

316 "Colorado Conversations on Renewal," sponsored by the Colorado Civic League, July 31–August 1, 1998. See *Denver Post*, August 1, 1998.

317 *The New York Times* front-page story on the Call to Renewal conference was "A Religious Tilt Toward the Left," by Francis X. Clines, September 16, 1996.

317–18 The National Civil Rights Museum, which opened in 1991, is in what was formerly the Lorraine Motel. See www.civilrightsmuseum.org, which features an "interactive tour" of the museum, ending in rooms 306–307. For the Young/Abernathy story, see also Oates, *Let the Trumpet Sound*, pp. 488–90.

318 "Precious Lord" was written by the famed gospel singer/com-poser Thomas A. Dorsey in 1932 following the death of his wife and baby. It was a favorite song of Dr. Martin Luther King, Jr., and gained even greater recognition after Mahalia Jackson sang it at Dr. King's funeral. See "The Precious Legacy of Thomas Dorsey," by Bernice Johnson Reagon, *The Washington Post*, January 31, 1993.

320 Vincent Harding, *There Is a River* (New York: Harcourt Brace Jovanovich, 1981).

327 "lay aside every weight," Hebrews 12:1.

"do justice," Micah 6:8.

"you have done it to me," Matthew 25:40.

For Further Reading

The following is a selected list of books for further reading. It is not meant to be exhaustive.

Bakke, Raymond. A Theology as Big as the City (Downers Grove, Ill.: Intervarsity Press, 1997).

Bane, Mary Jo, and David T. Ellwood. Welfare Realities: From Rhetoric to Reform (Cambridge, Mass.: Harvard University Press, 1994).

Bernardin, Joseph Louis. Joseph Cardinal Bernardin: A Moral Vision for America. Ed. John P. Langan (Washington, D.C.: Georgetown University Press, 1998).

Blank, Rebecca. It Takes a Nation (Princeton: Princeton University Press, 1997).

Branch, Taylor. Parting the Waters: America During the King Years, 1954–63 (New York: Simon and Schuster, 1988).

————. Pillar of Fire: America During the King Years, 1963–65 (New York: Simon and Schuster, 1998).

Brown, Dorothy, and Elizabeth McKeown. The Poor Belong to Us: Catholic Charities and American Welfare (Cambridge, Mass.: Harvard University Press, 1997).

Carlson, Deana. The Welfare of My Neighbor: Our Churches and Welfare Reform (Washington, D.C.: Family Research Council, 1999).

Carlson-Thies, Stanley W., and James W. Skillen, eds. Welfare in America: Christian Perspectives on a Policy in Crisis (Grand Rapids, Mich.: William B. Eerdmans, 1996).

Carter, Stephen L. The Culture of Disbelief: How American Law and Politics Trivialize Religious Devotion (New York: Basic Books, 1993).

————. Integrity (New York: Basic Books, 1996).

Castillo, Richard and Richard A. Garcia. Cesar Chavez: A Triumph of Spirit (Norman, Okla.: University of Oklahoma Press, 1995).

Collins, Chuck, et al., Shifting Fortunes: The Perils of the Growing American Wealth Gap (Boston: United for a Fair Economy, 1999).

Daly, Herman, and John B. Cobb, Jr. For the Common Good (Boston: Beacon Press, 1989).

Danziger, Sheldon H., and Peter Gottschalk. America Unequal (Cambridge, Mass.: Harvard University Press, 1995).

Davis, Derek, and Barry Hankins, eds. Welfare Reform and Faith-Based Organizations (Waco: J. M. Dawson Institute of Church-State Studies, Baylor University, 1999).

Dayton, Donald. Discovering an Evangelical Heritage (New York: Harper and Row, 1976).

Dionne, E. J., Jr., and John J. DiIulio, Jr. "What's God Got to Do with the American Experiment?" (Washington, DC: Brookings Institution Press, 2000).

Dorr, Donal. Option for the Poor: A Hundred Years of Catholic Social Teaching (Maryknoll, N.Y.: Orbis Books, 1992).

Ellsberg, Robert, ed. By Little and by Little: The Selected Writings of Dorothy Day (New York: Alfred A. Knopf, 1983).

Ellwood, David T. Poor Support: Poverty in the American Family (New York: Basic Books, 1988).

Frank, Robert H. Luxury Fever (New York: Free Press, 1999).

Franklin, Robert M. Another Day's Journey: Black Churches Confronting the American Crisis (Minneapolis: Fortress Press, 1997).

Freedman, Samuel G. Upon This Rock (New York: HarperCollins, 1994).

Galbraith, James. Created Unequal: The Crisis in American Pay (New York: Free Press, 1998).

————. The Good Society: The Humane Agenda (New York: Houghton Mifflin, 1996).

Gans, Herbert. The War Against the Poor: The Underclass and Anti-poverty Policy (New York: Basic Books, 1995).

Garrow, David. Bearing the Cross (New York: William Morrow, 1986).

Greider, William. One World, Ready or Not: The Manic Logic of Global Capitalism (New York: Simon and Schuster, 1997).

————. Who Will Tell the People: The Betrayal of American Democracy (New York: Simon and Schuster, 1992).

Harding, Vincent. There Is a River (New York: Harcourt Brace Jovanovich, 1981).

Harper, Nile. Urban Churches, Vital Signs: Beyond Charity Toward Justice (Grand Rapids, Mich.: William B. Eerdmans, 1999).

Harris, Margaret. Organizing God's Work: Challenges for Churches and Synagogues (New York: St. Martin's Press, 1998).

Hutton, Will. The State We're In (London: Vintage, 1996).

Jencks, Christopher. Rethinking Social Policy: Race, Poverty, and the Underclass (New York: HarperCollins, 1992).

Jencks, Christopher, and Paul E. Peterson, eds. The Urban Underclass (Washington, D.C.: Brookings Institution Press, 1991).

Katz, Michael. The Undeserving Poor: From the War on Poverty to the War on Welfare (New York: Pantheon, 1989).

Korten, David. When Corporations Rule the World (San Francisco: Berrett-Koehler, 1995).

Kuttner, Robert. Everything for Sale: The Virtues and Limits of Markets (New York: Alfred A. Knopf, 1997).

Lerner, Michael. The Politics of Meaning (Reading, Mass.: Addison-Wesley, 1996).

Loury, Glenn C., James Skillen, and Daniel R. Coats. Mending Fences: Renewing Justice Between Government and Civil Society. Kuyper Lecture Series (Grand Rapids, Mich.: Baker Book House, 1998).

Lupton, Robert D. Theirs Is the Kingdom: Celebrating the Gospel in Urban America (San Francisco: Harper, 1989).

Mandela, Nelson. Long Walk to Freedom (New York: Doubleday, 1994).

Massaro, Thomas. Catholic Social Teaching and United States Welfare Reform (Collegeville, Minn.: Liturgical Press, 1998).

Myers, Ched. Say to This Mountain: Mark's Story of Discipleship. Ed. Karen Lattea (Maryknoll, N.Y.: Orbis Books, 1996).

————. Who Will Roll Away the Stone? Discipleship Queries for First World Christians (Maryknoll, N.Y.: Orbis Books, 1994).

National Conference of Catholic Bishops. Economic Justice for All: Pastoral Letter on Catholic Social Teaching and the U.S. Economy (Washington, D.C.: National Conference of Catholic Bishops, 1986).

Neuhaus, Richard John. Doing Well and Doing Good: The Challenge to the Christian Capitalist (New York: Doubleday, 1992).

Nouwen, Henri J. M. The Road to Peace. Ed. John Dear (Maryknoll, N.Y.: Orbis Books, 1998).

Oates, Stephen. Let the Trumpet Sound (New York: Harper and Row, 1982).

Perkins, John, ed. Beyond Charity: The Call to Christian Community Development (Grand Rapids, Mich.: Baker Book House, 1993).

————. Restoring At-Risk Communities: Doing It Together and Doing It Right (Grand Rapids, Mich.: Baker Book House, 1996).

Phillips, Kevin. Arrogant Capital (New York: Little Brown, 1994).

————. The Politics of Rich and Poor (New York: Random House, 1990).

Piven, Frances Fox, and Richard Cloward. Regulating the Poor: The Functions of Public Welfare. Updated ed. (New York: Vintage Books, 1993).

Pollin, Robert, and Stephanie Luce. The Living Wage: Building a Fair Economy (New York: New Press, 1998).

Reich, Robert B. Locked in the Cabinet (New York: Alfred A. Knopf, 1997).

Rifkin, Jeremy. The End of Work: The Decline of the Global Labor Force and the Dawn of the Post-Market Era (New York: G. P. Putnam's Sons, 1995).

Schor, Juliet. The Overspent American: Upscaling, Downshifting, and the New Consumer (New York: Basic Books, 1998).

———. The Overworked American (New York: Basic Books, 1993).

Schorr, Lisbeth B., and William Julius Wilson. Common Purpose: Strengthening Families and Neighborhoods to Rebuild America (New York: Doubleday, 1998).

Schwartz, John E. and Thomas J. Volgy. The Forgotten Americans: Thirty Million Working Poor in the Land of Opportunity (New York: W. W. Norton, 1992).

Shafer, Todd, and Jeff Faux. Reclaiming Prosperity (Armonk, N.Y.: M. E. Sharpe, 1996).

Sherman, Amy L. Restorers of Hope: Reaching the Poor in Your Community with Church-Based Ministries That Work (Wheaton, Ill.: Crossway Books, 1997).

Sider, Ronald J. Just Generosity (Grand Rapids, Mich.: Baker Book House, 1999).

———. Rich Christians in an Age of Hunger: Moving from Affluence to Generosity (Waco: Word Books, 1997).

Slessarev, Helene. The Betrayal of the Urban Poor (Philadelphia: Temple University Press, 1997).

Thiemann, Ronald F. Religion in Public Life: A Dilemma for Democracy (Washington, D.C.: Georgetown University Press, 1996).

Thomas, Cal and Ed Dobson. Blinded by Might (Grand Rapids, Mich.: Zondervan, 1999).

Thurow, Lester C. The Future of Capitalism (New York: William Morrow, 1996).

Tutu, Desmond. The Rainbow People of Hope (New York: Doubleday, 1994).

Wallis, Jim. The Soul of Politics: A Practical and Prophetic Vision for Change (New York: New Press, 1994).

———. Who Speaks for God? An Alternative to the Religious Right—A New Politics of Compassion, Community, and Civility (New York: Delacorte Press, 1996).

Washington, James, ed. A Testament of Hope: The Essential Writings of Martin Luther King, Jr. (San Francisco: Harper and Row, 1986).

West, Cornel. Race Matters (Boston: Beacon Press, 1993).

———. Restoring Hope: Conversations on the Future of Black America (Boston: Beacon Press, 1997).

West, Cornel, and Sylvia Ann Hewlett. The War Against Parents: What We Can Do for America's Beleaguered Moms and Dads (Boston: Houghton Mifflin, 1998).

Wills, Gary. Under God: Religion and American Politics (New York: Simon and Schuster/Touchstone, 1990).

Wilson, William Julius. The Bridge over the Racial Divide: Rising Inequality and Coalition Politics (Berkeley and Los Angeles: University of California Press, 1999).

———. The Truly Disadvantaged: The Inner City, the Underclass, and Public Policy (Chicago: University of Chicago Press, 1987).

———. When Work Disappears: The World of the New Urban Poor (New York: Alfred A. Knopf, 1996).

Wolman, William, and Anne Colamosca. The Judas Economy: The Triumph of Capital and the Betrayal of Work (Reading, Mass.: Addison-Wesley, 1997).

Woodson, Robert L., Sr. The Triumphs of Joseph: How Today's Community Healers Are Reviving Our Streets and Neighborhoods (New York: Free Press, 1998).

Wuthnow, Robert. Faith and Philanthropy in America (San Francisco: Jossey-Bass, 1990).

———. The Restructuring of American Religion: Society and Faith Since the 1950s (Princeton University Press, 1988).

———. Reviving Our Streets and Neighborhoods (New York: Free Press, 1998).

Wylie-Kellermann, Bill. A Keeper of the Word: Selected Writings of William Stringfellow (Grand Rapids, Mich.: William B. Eerdmans, 1994).

Getting Involved

Now that you've read this book, I encourage you to become involved in your community. Here are some organizations that are active around the country and can provide information on how you can become involved. They cover the political spectrum, and many of them address multiple issues, but all have programs dealing with poverty and the role of faith-based organizations.

Sojourners
2401 15th Street, NW
Washington, DC 20009
(202) 328-8842
(800) 714-7474
www.sojourners.com

Sojourners is a Christian ministry whose mission is to proclaim and practice the biblical call to integrate spiritual renewal and social justice, and promotes a vision for faith in public life by publishing *Sojourners* magazine, nurturing community, and preaching, teaching, organizing, and public witnessing.

Sojo.net is a media network sponsored by Sojourners. It offers a weekly e-mail netletter featuring commentary by Jim Wallis on late-breaking news and events, as well as ideas and inspiration to help put your values into action. To subscribe, visit the website or send an e-mail to subscribe@sojo.net.

Call to Renewal
2401 15th Street, NW
Washington, DC 20009
(202) 328-8745
(800) 714-7474
www.calltorenewal.com

Call to Renewal is a national federation of churches, faith-based organizations, and individuals working to overcome poverty. It sponsors an annual national summit, organizes local roundtables around the country, and brings organizations together through information and organizing. For information on

faith-based organizations in your community, the Call to Renewal website features a listing of the best projects and programs cited in this book as well as many others around the country.

It also cosponsors Churches at Work, a project of World Vision. Churches at Work is a website with a searchable database of hundreds of local churches and Christian faith-based organizations throughout the United States that are working to meet human needs in their communities. (*www.churchesatwork.org*)

Asset Based Community Development Institute: provides resources and tools for communities and governments involved in capacity-based development initiatives.
(847) 491-8711
www.nwu.edu/ipr/abcd.html

Bread for the World: a nationwide Christian citizens' movement seeking justice for the world's hungry people by lobbying our nation's decision makers.
(301) 608-2400, *www.bread.org*

Catholic Charities USA: works to reduce poverty, support families, and empower communities by providing for people in need and advocating for justice.
(703) 549-1390
www.catholiccharitiesusa.org

Children's Defense Fund: works through education and advocacy to ensure every child a healthy, fair, safe, and moral start in life for successful passage to adulthood.
(202) 628-8787, *www.childrensdefense.org*

Christian Community Development Association: a nationwide network of grassroots, community-based organizations working to provide social and spiritual service to those in poverty.

(773) 762-0994, *www.ccda.org*

Council of Leadership Foundations: a nationwide network of urban organizations acting as catalysts to mobilize all segments of society to meet the needs of people.

(412) 281-3752, *www.ontv.com/pghlead/council.html*

Direct Action and Research Training Center (DART): a national network of community-organizing efforts, many of which are congregation based.

(305) 576-8020, *www.fiu.edu/~dart*

Evangelicals for Social Action: promotes a lifestyle marked by service to poor and powerless people, reverence for life, care for creation, and witness to Jesus Christ.

(610) 645-9390, *www.esa-online.org*

Families Against Violence Advocacy Network: a broad-based network of organizations, families, and individuals committed to promoting alternatives to violence.

(314) 533-4445
www.members.aol.com/ppjn

Family Research Council: works to support efforts that look to locally funded social services, including churches and faith-based organizations, to help the poor.

(800) 225-4008, *www.frc.org*

Gamaliel Foundation: a national network of community-organizing efforts, many of which are congregation based.

(312) 357-2639, *www.gamaliel.org*

Habitat for Humanity: brings families and communities in need together with volunteers and resources to build decent, affordable housing through a national network of affiliates.

(912) 924-6935, *www.habitat.org*

Industrial Areas Foundation: a national network of community-organizing efforts, many of which are congregation based.

(512) 459-6551

Interfaith Center for Corporate Responsibility: works through education, organizing, and stockholder resolutions to promote more socially responsible actions by corporations.

(212) 870-2295

International Urban Associates: seeks to empower God's people in the largest cities of the world by generating vision, partnerships, motivations, and resources.

(312) 275-9260
www.cl.ais.net/iua1/index.html

Jesuit Volunteer Corps: a Catholic lay-volunteer program whose individuals work in grassroots organizations across the country to provide services to low-income people.

(202) 687-1132, *www.jesuitvolunteers.org*

Jobs Partnership: works with churches to train and mentor under- or unemployed persons seeking work and then matches them with businesses seeking employees.

(919) 571-8614, *www.tjp.org*

Jubilee 2000 USA: works as part of an international campaign to educate and advocate for debt cancellation for the world's poorest countries.

(202) 783-3566, *www.j2000usa.org*

Lutheran Volunteer Corps: provides one-year service terms in urban social-justice organizations and promotes simplicity and community living as part of that commitment.

(202) 387-3222, *www.lvchome.org*

Mennonite Central Committee: a relief, service, development, and peace agency working in fifty-eight countries among people suffering from poverty, conflict, and natural disaster.

(717) 859-1151, *www.mcc.org*

Mission Year: offers Christian young adults a one-year term of living and serving in a poor inner-city neighborhood alongside a solid local church.

(610) 645-0800, *www.missionyear.org*

National Center for Neighborhood Enterprise: works to empower neighborhoods to reduce crime and violence, restore families, and revitalize low-income communities.
(202) 518-6500, *www.ncne.com*

National Coalition of Barrios Unidos: works to prevent youth violence in urban neighborhoods and promotes gang truces, community development, and employment opportunities.
(831) 457-8208, *www.barriosunidos.com*

National Conference of Catholic Bishops/United States Catholic Conference, Department of Social Development and World Peace: the national public-policy agency of the U.S. Catholic bishops.
(202) 541-3000
www.nccbuscc.org/sdwp/index.htm

National Congress of Community Economic Development, Faith-Based Initiative: works to promote and facilitate faith-based community economic development.
(202) 289-9020, *www.ncced.org*

National Interfaith Committee for Worker Justice: works to educate and organize the faith community in the United States on issues and campaigns to benefit workers.
(773) 728-8400, *www.igc.org/nicwj*

National Living Wage Resource Center (ACORN): provides a clearinghouse of information and resources on living-wage campaigns around the country.
(202) 547-2500
www.livingwagecampaign.org

National Ten-Point Leadership Foundation: provides African-American churches with vision, programmatic structure, and resources to save at-risk inner-city youth.
(617) 282-6704
www.yesamerica.org/ntlf.html

NETWORK: a national Catholic social-justice lobby that educates and organizes to influence the formation of federal legislation to promote economic and social justice.
(202) 547-5556, *www.igc.org/network*

Network 9:35: a collaborative fellowship working to nurture and strengthen congregations, pastors, and leaders who are committed to holistic ministry.
(610) 645-9399, *www.esa-online.org*

Pacific Institute for Community Organization (PICO): a national network of community-organizing efforts, many of which are congregation based.
(510) 655-2801

Prison Fellowship: works to provide a biblical and comprehensive assault on crime through in-prison programs, programs with children of prisoners, and victims of crime.
(703) 478-0100, *www.pfm.org*

Public Campaign: a nonpartisan organization dedicated to reform that aims to dramatically reduce the role of special-interest money in America's elections.
(202) 293-0222, *www.publiccampaign.org*

Salvation Army: affiliates across the country provide a wide range of social, medical, educational, and other community services.
(703) 684-5500, *www.salvationarmy.org*

United for a Fair Economy: works to educate and organize on the dangers of the growing income, wage, and wealth inequality in the United States.
(617) 423-2148, *www.stw.org*

World Vision: an international partnership of Christians seeking to follow Jesus Christ through working in relief and development programs with the poor and oppressed.
(253) 815-1000, *www.worldvision.org*

Index

About the Author

Jim Wallis is a commentator on ethics and public life and a spokesperson for faith-based initiatives to overcome poverty. He is the editor of *Sojourners* magazine, covering faith, politics and culture for thirty years. He is also the convener of Call to Renewal, a national federation of churches, denominations and faith based organizations working to overcome poverty and revitalize American politics. A frequent speaker, he travels to more than 200 events a year to preach, teach and organize. He is a prolific writer whose columns appear in *The New York Times, Washington Post, Los Angeles Times*, MSNBC, and Beliefnet. His previous books include *Who Speaks for God?, The Soul of Politics,* and *The Call to Conversion.* He also regularly offers commentary and analysis for radio and television. He spent a year as a Fellow at the Center for the Study of Values in Public Life at Harvard Divinity School, and teaches at Harvard University's John F. Kennedy School of Government on "Faith, Politics and Society." Jim lives in Washington DC with his wife Joy and their son, Luke.

About the Press

"the language of the wise brings healing."
—Proverbs 12:18b

At PageMill Press, we publish books that explore and celebrate the Christian life. Our titles cover a wide range of topics including spiritual memoir, devotional and contemplative life, peace and justice issues, faith-based community work, spiritual disciplines, reference works, family and parenting, spirituality, and fiction.

We believe that publishing involves a partnership between author, publisher, the bookseller, and the reader. Our commitment as a publisher to this partnership is to produce wise and accessible books for thoughtful seekers across the full spectrum of the Christian tradition.

The Press seeks to honor the writer's craft by nurturing the felicitous use of language and the creative expression of ideas. We regard highly the collaboration of publisher, editor, and author, and the creative expression of ideas with the knowledge and wisdom that results.

For a catalogue of publications of PageMill Press, for editorial submissions, or for queries to the author, please direct correspondence to:

PageMill Press
2716 Ninth Street
Berkeley, CA 94710
Ph: 510-848-3600; Fax: 510-848-1326

More Titles from PageMill Press

THINKING WITH THE HEART: A MONK (AND PARENT) EXPLORES HIS
CHRISTIAN HERITAGE
A beautifully written exploration of the author's Christian legacy and a
spiritual will and testament for all seekers.
Tolbert McCarroll
$13.95 ISBN 1-879290-21-9

EVERYONE WANTS TO GO TO HEAVEN BUT...WIT, FAITH, AND A LIGHT
LUNCH
An ABC of terms that helps the reader turn Christianity upside down and
inside out and in the process actually helps us find new ways to look at faith.
C. McNair Wilson / Foreword by Ken Davis
$14.95 ISBN 1-879290-16-2

MISSING PEACE: A MODERN PARABLE ON RECOVERING YOUR SOUL IN A
MATERIAL WORLD
Through her correspondence with the fascinating and mysterious Brother
Theodore, skeptic lawyer Joan gains a new perspective on success and comes
to know that real fulfillment can only come through Christ.
Glandion Carney
$13.95 ISBN 1-879290-18-9

FINDING FAITH: LIFE-CHANGING ENCOUNTERS WITH CHRIST
The author tells the stories of people who in ways both expected and unex-
pected have come to faith and are willing to talk about their doubts and joys.
Sharon Gallagher
$13.95 ISBN 1-879290-17-0

REAWAKENING TO LIFE: RENEWAL AFTER A HUSBAND'S DEATH
Remarkable stories of how ordinary women make the transition from widow-
hood to seeing themselves as new people.
Mary Ellen Berry
$13.95 ISBN 1-879290-24-3

THE BOY WHO CRIED ABBA: A PARABLE OF TRUST AND ACCEPTANCE
A heartwarming parable about a young boy who is orphaned and disabled
but who finds unconditional love.
Brennan Manning
$13.95 ISBN 1-879290-19-7

Books are available at fine retailers nationwide.

Prices subject to change without notice.